CHRIS LANE

PANTO SCRIPTS

CHRIS LANE: PANTO SCRIPTS

These scripts have been performed all on every continent except Antarctica. Many of them have won awards, all have received excellent critical reviews and, more important, they are a great success with actors and audiences. Though sometimes performed by professionals they are specially crafted to be produced, directed and performed by enthusiastic amateurs – and still be funny!
Included here is a selection of full-length scripts. Shorter or easier versions, not included here, are available for use in offices, schools, small village halls, etc. Just contact me via my website: www.pantoscripts.me.uk
For vital tips and advice on finding a successful panto script that will fit your resources you really should first read **'How to Write or Choose the Perfect Panto Script'**: <u>CLICK HERE</u>.
There is more information about hiring, costs and such at the end <u>CLICK HERE</u>
For the moment just click on the title you want to read – and enjoy! But remember that you can't perform any of these in public without asking me first!!
Cheers
Chris Lane

And if you like this sense of humour you could try my bestselling comedy novels and How To books available at <u>AMAZON BOOKS</u>

AM DRAM 'HOW TO' BOOKS
HOW TO RUN A DRAMA GROUP.
HOW TO CREATE AN AMATEUR SHOW.
JUNIOR DRAMA GROUPS: HOW TO RUN THEM AND SURVIVE.
HOW TO CHOOSE OR WRITE THE PERFECT PANTO SCRIPT.
HOW TO PUBLISH YOUR E BOOK

COMEDY NOVELS
ALL TOP-TEN BESTSELLING COMEDY
E-BOOKS (some No 1 best-sellers)
THE CHARD SERIES: six novels of grusome murders and stupididty:
BLOODWRATH, MAKEOVER OF BLOOD, KILLED TO DEATH
SPLAT!, TROLLEY OF DOOM and in NZ: SKY TOWER.

THE 'FAIRY THE BLACKSMITH' SAGA
FAIRY & THE SHYTE WEASELS
AVALON
AT THE END OF THE WORLD
ARTHUR & MERLIN: The Idiot Years

MORE INFORMATION

These scripts are published here for three reasons:

First, as they are formally published, they have even stronger legal protection so if any original part of the script is 'nicked' it is easier to prove! If you are simply here to get ideas for your own writing I strongly recommend that you get back onto Amazon and download my book 'HOW TO WRITE OR CHOOSE THE PERFECT PANTO SCRIPT'. This will make your life a lot easier, and much more legal.

Secondly, many people just like reading scripts; if you are one of these fine people then I hope you enjoy this selection

Third, and this is why you are probably here, is because you have been given the terrible chore of choosing a script that is best for your club or business or charity or family to perform. Splendid.

But, before you start selecting a script, BE WARNED: there are hundreds of very weak scripts out there. For example: several stinkers think that Abanazer's name is 'have a banana' every time he comes on the stage and, worse, believe this alone is enough humour to fill a whole show (it isn't).

I really recommend you read my book 'HOW TO WRITE OR CHOOSE THE PERFECT PANTO SCRIPT', noting that its title includes the words 'choose a script'. Until you read that book you will not even be aware of the problems ahead of you!

Unbelievably many scripts, even ones from well-known organisations and publishers, were written over 30 years ago and never, ever updated (honest - look out for things like 'Dixon of Dock Green' or quotes from 'Ello Ello'.) By all means just choose any old script, but don't be upset when your audiences start to go down! My scripts have been written and rewritten and the versions here were all updated in 2018.

If you do want to produce one of these scripts e-mail via my website:
www.pantoscripts.me.uk
Most people who get in touch just want to ask how much it costs: as a guide I normally charge just £20 for each performance.
There is no charge for anything else, including amateur film/photo rights, copying scripts, rewrites, etc. In comparison I have been told by some clubs that they have paid well over £1,000 for use of a 'professional' script.
However, charities that have used my scripts in the past, such as 'Help The Heroes' or 'Crisis at Christmas' get to use them for nothing, while professional organisations such as Hotels and well-known oil companies, supermarkets and major computer manufacturers have paid a little more.

Why are my scripts so cheap? Well, 'Pantoscripts' is just me, not an office full of staff to pay and no commission to any middle-man. And I sell loads; they're performed all over the world every year. And it's just a hobby, I like to know the scripts are being used and getting such good reviews and feedback (some reviews are on my website if you want to check). And as you may have noticed I mostly write comedy novels (search Chris Lane on Amazon books) and movies.
And yes, I do write to commission (i.e. if you want something specific), often for free, and I do write other things besides pantos. If you want short comedy plays for any age or children's musicals then do get in touch.

If you have any questions or thoughts please contact me at: **www.pantoscripts.me.uk**
Cheers – Chris Lane
*

OTHER BOOKS BY CHRIS LANE
All books available from AMAZON
tinyurl.com/Chris-Lane-books

AM DRAM 'HOW TO' BOOKS

- **HOW TO RUN A DRAMA GROUP**

- **CREATE AN AMATEUR SHOW**

- **JUNIOR DRAMA GROUPS: HOW TO RUN THEM *AND SURVIVE***

- **THE PERFECT PANTO SCRIPT**

COMEDY NOVELS
ALL TOP-TEN BESTSELLING COMEDY
E-BOOKS (some No 1 best-sellers)
BLOODWRATH
MAKEOVER OF BLOOD
KILLED TO DEATH
SPLAT!
TROLLEY OF DOOM
SKY TOWER

THE 'FAIRY THE BLACKSMITH' SAGA
FAIRY & THE SHYTE WEASELS
AVALON
AT THE END OF THE WORLD
ARTHUR & MERLIN: The Idiot Years

CHILDREN'S BOOKS
THE DAFF WAR
THE SWIPERS

LIST OF TITLES

Click to select

1. <u>CINDERELLA</u>
2. <u>ROBIN HOOD</u>
3. <u>DICK WHITTINGTON</u>
4. <u>SLEEPING BEAUTY</u>
5. <u>RED RIDING HOOD & THE 3 PIGS</u>
6. <u>THREE MEN IN A TUB</u>
7. <u>JACK AND THE BEANSTALK</u>
8. <u>HANSEL AND GRETEL</u>
9. <u>SNOW WHITE & 7 DWARVES</u>

CONTACT INFORMATION
and PERFORMANCE RIGHTS here:

<u>PANTOSCRIPTS.ME.UK</u>

CINDERELLA

© Chris Lane 2018

First produced: Axminster Drama Club January 2009

ACT ONE

SCENE ONE: The ROSE GARDEN

A beautiful garden entirely pale pastel colours & cream (no primary colours). Stage Right is the side of a manor house with posh door up two steps. Stage Left is an ornate tall white metal double gate between tall white pillars. A tall wall covered in climbing flowers runs across the back of the stage, tree tops can be seen beyond. The garden is full of pastel rose bushes. Ella is sitting on a bench with **a book & small blackboard: '10 things for a perfect boyfriend'**. Village children sit at her feet. Servants & gardeners are busy in the background. All characters are in pastel colours, cream or white.

SONG: ELLA & CHILDREN & CHORUS: staff & gardeners: "Doe a deer"

ELLA: Quick – back to your books! Someone's coming! (They pretend to study)

Chorus exit gradually during the following lines. Remove blackboard.

BUTTONS: (enters through door with loo brush) Hmmm. Ella, you look very guilty. You all look very guilty. (Is only teasing them) (To children) Have you been working hard? (Nodding.) Or has Ella been telling you her romantic twaddle again?

ELLA: Me, Buttons? Romantic twaddle? Not at all. Why - you can ask the children.

BUTTONS: (pretends to be suspicious) I just might. Name of Boy 1. Tell me – what have you been learning?

BOY 1: (Not pleased) Hnn. Romantic twaddle!

GIRL 1: (Grins widely. Pause) It was lovely. (All girls agree)

BUTTONS: Laughs. If your father finds out …

ELLA: (joking) And who's going to tell him?

Boy 1 puts hand up but they over-rule him.

BUTTONS: Ha! Well I'm not saying anything! But don't forget: he's due back today, so he might catch you himself! (Turns to leave into house)

ELLA: Buttons?

BUTTONS: Mmm?

ELLA: Don't rush around. Sit in the garden a while.

BOY 1: Yes: we're going to do some hard sums!

BUTTONS: Er. That sounds lovely. But, you do the sums for me! Sadly, got to unblock the toilet again! (Waves loo brush)

BOY 1: Ooh! Can I help you will that?

BUTTONS: No, name, not after the last time. Remember? If I hadn't caught your ankles you'd have been gone! (Ruffles hair with loo brush) I know you blame yourself for blocking it, but…

BOY 1: Not my fault; my mums a vegetarian.

BUTTONS: Ah, right: (confused) I'm a Capricorn myself. Be good! (Exits)

ELLA: Poor Buttons. I'd better give him a hand. (Gets up. To kids) The place must look its best: have you heard the news - father is bringing home his new wife today.

CHILD 2: A new mother for you!

BOY 1: What's she like? Do you think she enjoys doing long division?

ELLA: I expect so!

CHILD 4: Tell us about her!

CHILD 5: Does she give children sweets?

ELLA: Slow down! (Stops on steps) I can't tell you <u>anything</u> about her – except father met her in Paris; she's a widow; and she has two children already.

GIRL 1: Children? I hope they're not smelly boys?! Eurgh! (Other girls groan)

BOY 1: Typical sexist remark. Tut! Just what I'd expect from a girl.

ELLA: I don't know any more than that! Now, back home with you. Same time tomorrow! And read those books!

Children exit through the gates saying: Bye! We will! Goodbye! They close the gates.

ELLA: Right – I must give Buttons a hand. He works really hard – I don't know what we'd do without him.

There is a commotion outside the gate.

ELLA: Now what?

COWSLIP: (offstage)(common voice) More faster like! Run!

PEASBLOSSOM: (posh voice) I <u>am</u> running!

NUTMEG: (Breathless) Is there a reason for running?

COWSLIP: Yeah – it is stayin' alive! Quick! In here!

They appear outside the gates. They are not all obviously fairies, but all have wings.

PEASBLOSSOM: Hurry – open the gates!

COWSLIP: I is hurryin' – they is locked!

NUTMEG: (Enthusiastic but dopey) Do you want me to bang my head on them - like the other ones?

COWSLIP: Yeah – go on then. But you is not to get blood all over us this time! Right?

NUTMEG: No blood. Right. (Takes a few steps back)

ELLA: It's not locked!

COWSLIP: What?

ELLA: I said – the gates – they're not locked.

COWSLIP: Not locked?

ELLA: No. You just have to push them.

COWSLIP: Yeah, right – I is knowin' that. Quick – everyone in. (they enter)

NUTMEG: Do you still want me to bang my head on the gates?

COWSLIP: Perhaps later on – if we gets bored. (They close gates quickly & hold them shut)

PEASBLOSSOM: I don't think these gates will keep out – you know who-ee.

COWSLIP: Oh crikey! (To Ella) Is you having somewhere for us to hide? (Ella shakes head) Or for defence!! Like maybe a great big cannon? (Ella shakes head) <u>Any</u> weapons? A spear!

PEASBLOSSOM: Sword?

COWSLIP: Dagger?

PEASBLOSSOM: Pointed stick?

COWSLIP: Sharp pencil?

PEASBLOSSOM: Drawing pin?

NUTMEG: (Slowly) How about a sausage roll that is past its sell-by date? (Others look in disbelief)

COWSLIP: Anything at all to defend ourselves with?!

ELLA: No. Not really. Why?

PEASBLOSSOM: Too long to explain. Just let me put it this way: we are in mortal peril! Running for 20 miles. Horrible death approaching. And (looks around) rather desperate for the loo actually.

COWSLIP: Too late! Look! (Points at wall behind them)

Lights dim. Ominous music. Above wall can be seen the top of the hairy head and horns of some huge shuffling creature. Grunting noises. It moves toward the gate &

out of sight.

FAIRIES: Aargh! (Try to hide behind each other)

ELLA: What <u>is</u> the matter?

COWSLIP: (panicking) It seems – apparently - we is upsetin' someone. So they is comin' to kill us in a slow and terrible manner.

Gates slowly open with a horror creak. Lights dim. Rumble of distant thunder.

FAIRIES: Aargh! (All try to hide behind Cinderella. Menacing music.)

RED RIDING HOOD: (enters through gates. She carries basket but her hood is not red but purple) Ha! At last! You are mine! Prepare - **to die**!

NUTMEG: No, not to-die; how about to-morrow!

COWSLIP: Hang about. Here. Is this it? Is this who we is runnin' from? (Circles her)

PEASBLOSSOM: nods frantically, still hiding.

COWSLIP: Then who was dat wot we just saw behind that wall?!

ELLA: Oh, him. He lives there. He's in a different panto.

Theme: Beauty and the Beast (Tale as old as time).

COWSLIP: (to music) Oy! Listen up: 'a different panto'! (Glares until it stops.) I as 'ad trouble wiv you before! (Gives the evils.) (Sound fx – raspberry) (Waves fist)

RED RIDING HOOD: So – I say again – prepare to die!

ELLA: I know you; you're Little Red, Little Red ... oh dear! Quite little - but not very 'red'.

RED RIDING HOOD: Exactly: no longer Little **Red** Riding Hood – not since these idiots tried to help, by washing it!

COWSLIP: It is not entirely our fault. Some of da washing got – sort of - mixed up.

PEASBLOSSOM: That's right. Your super little red cape, yah? Well, rather funny actually; it went into the wash with Cowslip's navy blue knickers!

RED RIDING HOOD: I know! She can have them back! (Reaches into cloak)

COWSLIP: No! Er ... not now! ... No – don't …. Aah!!

RED RIDING HOOD: (pulls out <u>very large</u> blue drawers) Here.

COWSLIP: (embarrassedly goes and gets them, RRH hangs on and they stretch to large size) They stretched in the machine! (Mutter from Buttons to Peasblossom) What did he/she say? What?!

PEASBLOSSOM: He/She said you must have washed your bottom in the same machine! I say – that is rather witty.

COWSLIP: I'll give him/her witty. (A fight is prevented.)

ELLA: I must say it does seem a bit much to kill someone, just because they made a mistake with the washing.

RED RIDING HOOD: Tell her. (Fairies look guilty) Go on – tell her what <u>else</u> you did.

COWSLIP: Not entirely our fault. We wus confused.

RED RIDING HOOD: Tell her about the wolf.

NUTMEG: (Alarmed) Which wolf?

COWSLIP: No wolf. There never wus no wolf!

PEASBLOSSOM: No. We didn't meet **any** wolf in the forest. Not jolly likely; not us!

NUTMEG: (thinks) Was that the wolf who asked us the way to Granny's house?

COWSLIP: No – dat never happened.

NUTMEG: And you told him there was a **shortcut** to Granny's house.

COWSLIP: Dat never happened neither.

NUTMEG: And you asked him why he was going to Granny's house.

COWSLIP: Never happened!

NUTMEG: And he said – you'll like this – he had a really gruff voice (does the voices) "I am going to granny's house and she will say '**My what big ears you have**' and I will say 'All the better to hear you with' and then she will say '**My what big eyes you have**' and I'll say 'All the better to see you with' and then .. then – this is the funny bit – then she'll say '**My what big teeth you have**' and I'll say – wait for it – 'All the better to eat you with!' and then I will swallow her whole!

COWSLIP: Never happened. Peasblossom; tell them: all that NEVER, EVER happened!

PEASBLOSSOM: No – indeed not. None of that ever happened. But Nutmeg **did** get the voice just right though! Just like the wolf! (Gets hit)

ELLA: My word. That's not good. But my understanding is, what normally happens in these cases, is that a passing woodman comes by, with his axe, opens up the wolf and lets the Granny out, still all in one piece.

PEASBLOSSOM: (guilty shuffling) Normally …. Yes.

COWSLIP: Not **entirely** our fault.

ELLA: (suspicious) What did you do?

NUTMEG: I remember now! You said to the wolf: 'That is not nice – swallowing an old lady whole'!

COWSLIP: Yes! YES! THAT happened. "Not nice – swallowing an old lady whole"! I did indeed say that! (Looks smug) Yes indeed.

NUTMEG: (Happy to be right for once.) So you gave him a food-mincer!

RED RIDING HOOD: Ha! Prepare to die!

BUTTONS: (enters hurriedly from door.) What's going on? Who's going to die?

NUTMEG: (Hand up & smiles) We are.

RED RIDING HOOD: Yes! These useless fairies are about to die!

BUTTONS: (Looks at RRH) How?

RED RIDING HOOD: What?

BUTTONS: How are they going to die? (Checks her basket) You don't seem to have any weapons. Do you do magic?

RED RIDING HOOD: Well … no.

BUTTONS: So?

RED RIDING HOOD: Don't know really.

BUTTONS: You haven't really thought it through properly. (Kindly) Tell you what. Why don't you go and make a proper plan! Perhaps get a really big weapon?

RED RIDING HOOD: A really big weapon?

NUTMEG: Like a cannon! (Others hit him)

RED RIDING HOOD: Right. OK then. (Turns to leave) I'll be back! (Exits)

COWSLIP: Yeah, whatever. Well done matey; nice one.

BUTTONS: You're very welcome.

ELLA: Right then, glad we could help; was there anything else…?

COWSLIP: Hang about. Hang – a - bout. Show us today's diary. Who was it we had to find?

PEASBLOSSOM: Here. (Shows diary/phone)

COWSLIP: OK. No mistakes this time. Proper check before we does anyfink.

PEASBLOSSOM: You see, we - are Fairy God-mothers.

COWSLIP: Nutmeg. Peasblossom. And Cowslip.

PEASBLOSSOM: Only a temporary position. Until we can find something better. Perhaps (something topical)

COWSLIP: And we 'as bin sent to help a young lady – (excited) a young lady very much fitting your description. What's your name?

ELLA: My name is Ella. Short for Eleanor. My father is Lord Table.

COWSLIP: (reads) Bum. Sorry not you. Right address: Rosebud Lane, but wrong name. We want a Sindy-Something.

BUTTONS: Oh! Do you perhaps think it's the girl next door? I don't suppose that 'Beauty' is her real name, do you?

Music plays Beauty & Beast again.

COWSLIP: (To orchestra) Oy! Different panto! What is your problem? (As Cowslip walks away music plays snippet of 'fat bottomed girls'.) Hold me back!

ELLA: Oh my! Well; it could be the girl next-door you're looking for. But I think she's gone home, to see her father.

COWSLIP: Next door? Sorted. Come, fellow fairy-godmothers. We is away!

PEASBLOSSOM: Very lovely to meet you.

NUTMEG: (To Ella) Did you use to be in the All Blacks?

COWSLIP: (Hits Nutmeg) Idiot! Come on! (They exit)

ELLA: (As she EXITS into house) What unusual people.

BUTTONS: Yes indeed. I hope they find this 'Sindy' they're looking for. (EXITS)

PEASBLOSSOM: (voices from behind wall; tops of heads showing) Shall we ring the bell?

COWSLIP: Just go on in, girl! Hello! Anyone home? Hello – er - what's her name?

PEASBLOSSOM: Sindy … Rella. (Louder) Sindy Rella?! Helloo?! Fairies here with good news!!

NUTMEG: Look! Someone's coming! (Beast's head appears again)

COWSLIP: Oh blimey. Hello – kind sir – does Sindy Rella live here? We are her fairy god… aaargh! (Much snarling, panic and yelling)

PEASBLOSSOM: Aaaaoooaaahh!

NUTMEG: No – don't bite that! Aarrr! He's bitten it!!

COWSLIP: Shut up – you 'as got anover one!

PEASBLOSSOM: Arrgh – I really need the loo! oOoOOooOoooooh!!!

COWSLIP: RUN!!! (Growling & shrieking. Bits of clothing, hair etc fly in air.)

(They EXIT. Mrs McChucker – security / body guard with ear-piece appears at the gate, looks around furtively)

MRS McCHUCKER: (presses earpiece and speaks into wrist) Area secure: (looks around) Perimeter secure. (Louder, through gate) Bring in PAPOP! (pay-pop)

HERALD: (Very posh) What a dreadful noise; I said we should have started in (Posh place). Are you sure it's safe? Sounded dreadful!

MRS McCHUCKER: Positive to the safety request. No obvious danger to PAPOP. Bring them in.

HERALD: Do you have to call them that silly name?

MRS McCHUCKER: Security code: PAPOP. Prince and Princess of Pimplevania.

HERALD: Good grief. (Checks list) In here, your Highnesses. Number One, Rosebud Lane.

PRINCESS: (Enter Prince, Princess: smart but **not** in royal gear) What a lovely garden! Who lives here?

HERALD: (Reads from clipboard) One gentleman – Lord Table; a widower. Aha! And one daughter name of - Eleanor.

PRINCE: Are you sure we have to sell tickets like this? I don't think a Prince and a Princess should really – you know – be doing this! Can't we just put an ad in the (name of paper): "Grand Ball at palace: all welcome"?

HERALD: Not really, you see, your highness – how can I put it ….?

MRS McCHUCKER: Security! Don't want just anyone turning up. They have to be – 'vetted'.

HERALD: Really?! Seems a bit drastic. Mind you, had it done to my dog. Don't think it minded much. Wouldn't like it m'self though.

MRS McCHUCKER: Not that sort of vetted!

PRINCESS: The reason you have to do this yourself is "Only <u>beautiful</u> girls wanted!" Remember you said that?

PRINCE: Maybe.

PRINCESS: And you are loving it! Admit it! Go on – how many really stunning girls have you invited so far?!

PRINCE: No idea. Not really noticed. (Princess gives him that look) OK: 37 and two 'not bads'. (Another look) And one a bit rough – but she can play the ukulele!

PRINCESS: Exactly. So stop complaining. (To Herald) Harold, you can go back to the palace now, if you like, this is the last one. Mrs McChucker will look after us. (they look at Mrs. M who is searching oddly) Give me a handful of tickets and we'll see you later.

HERALD: Very well, your highness. (Notices aud.) Ah – can I sing my song now? (Starts song)

PRINCE: Ah … not really the best time now, Harold.

PRINCESS: Definitely later though.

HERALD: Oh. (Looks sad) Alright then. (Bows and exits sadly)

Buttons appears, followed by Ella.

BUTTONS: Good morning. Can I help?

PRINCESS: Hello.

PRINCE: Hello. (To Ella, bit shy) Hello.

ELLA: (shyly) Hello. How can we help?

PRINCE: (bit awkward) Er….

PRINCESS: Good grief. My brother and I are here raising money for charity. We are selling tickets for a Grand Ball to be held at the Royal Palace tonight. (Goes toward Buttons) Not just girls – hunky-looking chaps invited too!

BUTTONS: Crumbs. gulp

PRINCE: It will be a really splendid ball. (To Ella) I do hope you can come. (Nudge from Princess) That is – I hope you <u>both</u> can come.

BUTTONS: At the Palace? They don't have parties up there. The king is too old for that sort of thing.

PRINCE: That's true, our – er – (gestures from Princess to be secretive) - the King! The king is a little past party age but – well, he's away at the moment so I – that is, the Prince, is back from his travels now, and wants everyone to enjoy the palace!

ELLA: The Prince? What's he like? I would so like to meet a prince.

BUTTONS: (who guesses the truth) I hear the Prince is really, really - **ugly**.

MRS McCHUCKER: appears from behind hedge and laughs: Ha!

ELLA: Oh my! Is this true?

PRINCESS: It certainly is. As ugly as can be. (The Prince nudges her) That's why he has to sell charity tickets. Nobody would dance with him if it wasn't for a good cause!

ELLA: I don't believe it. By law all princes have to be handsome!

PRINCE: Well spoken. And if it isn't a law then it should be!

BUTTONS: Perhaps you would like a cold drink? Cup of tea? Cake? I'll fetch you some if...

PRINCE: Not for me, very kind but...

PRINCESS: I could manage something!

BUTTONS: A pleasure – I'll just …

PRINCESS: I'll come and help.

BUTTONS: There's no need, I can...

PRINCESS: Come on – it's just an excuse to have a nose round inside.

BUTTONS: OK then. Follow me. (They start to go in)

MRS McCHUCKER: Hold on! Security clearance needed!

PRINCESS: (sighs) This is Mrs McChucker; our ... er ...

MRS McCHUCKER: 'Friend of the family'. How-do-you do. Marjorie McChucker. Personal Security, self-defence instructor and expert in camouflage.

ELLA: Camouflage?

MRS McCHUCKER: (smug grin) Watch. (Hides very badly in corner) There. Be honest! You can't see me can you!

ELLA: Er – no. Quite amazing!

MRS McCHUCKER: Just a natural talent I have. Before you go in can I just ... (she lifts Button's arms and frisks him) All clear. Now – the interior check!

Buttons panics and guards his rear but Mrs. M ignores him and does a spy entry into building then summons them. Buttons & Princess follow. Awkward silence.

ELLA: So; do you live around here?

PRINCE: Er – sort of. But enough about me! Tell me about yourself. (Awkward silence) Do you play golf?

DUET: Getting to know you?

They sit down. Mrs M, Buttons & Princess reappear.

PRINCESS: Thanks for the drink. We'd better be going; we have to get ready for the ball! (To Prince) It's a lovely house! You ready? (Gets Prince's attention) Hello? Shall we go - um -, Fred? (He is looking at Ella) Fred!

PRINCE: Fred?! Yes. Fred. Yes – right.

PRINCESS: We will leave you these tickets. Will three be enough?

ELLA: Why, yes - but we haven't paid.

PRINCE: You have paid with your kindness.

MRS McCHUCKER: (secretly to aud) Not too sure about this place; I mean – all that screaming when we arrived. I need to come back – under cover!! (Exits stealthily)

PRINCE: Until the ball. Bowing and curtseys. They exit.

BUTTONS: Today is getting more and more interesting! Just think – when I got up I thought the highlight of the day would be unblocking the toilet, and now...!

ELLA: I don't mind visitors who look like that.

BUTTONS: No – not at all! Wonder who'll be next through the gaa...aah!!(Goes to shut gate but as he turns he is suddenly faced with a woman all in black except a flash of crimson) (Crack of thunder)

MOTHER: Step aside! We have travelled a long way and we expect a better welcome than that!

BUTTONS: (Looks behind her for others) We?

MOTHER: What?

BUTTONS: You said 'we'.

MOTHER: (impatient) Yes – we!

BUTTONS: (confused, looking past her) We?

MOTHER: We! WE!

BUTTONS: Oh! Right! Upstairs. Little room on the left. Make sure you wash your hands!

MOTHER: What! I have never ...!

ELLA: (quickly) Madam – I don't – I mean: who <u>are</u> you?

MOTHER: Me? <u>I</u> am the one who asks the questions, not you. You! Your name?

BUTTONS: Me? Buttons. I work here.

MOTHER: Hmm. We shall see about that. And you? Do you work here also?

ELLA: Me? No? I …

MOTHER: I thought not. (Sneers) I know who you are. You are the daughter – 'Ella'. What a common name. Never mind – I shall change that to something more 'appropriate'. (Circles) But your father said that you were a beauty! Ha! Not where we come from. If you want to see beauty – take a look at my daughters: Whinge and Gripe! Girls! In here! (Two tasteless chavs enter sluggishly and look about rudely. Probably Dame roles)

GRIPE: Yuk – this place is so – you know - minging.

ELLA: Hello; welcome to …

WHINGE: Like – whatever!

GRIPE: What is she, you know, wearing? (They circle Ella sniggering)

WHINGE: Like, such a dork.

BUTTONS: Ladies! (Steps up to sisters and bows) Enchanted.

MOTHER: Ah – nicely spoken!

BUTTONS: Yes. You look as if you have been enchanted. (To aud) Turned into toads!

MOTHER: What? What was that?

BUTTONS: I said – let's help you with your loads. (Gets bags & puts on ground by gate)

ELLA: You are a friend of my father?

MOTHER: Friend? Friend?! My dear girl…………. I, am his **wife**!

ELLA: So you must be…

MOTHER: Yes. Your new mother. And these are your new sisters: Whinge and Gripe.

ELLA: (Curtseys) Lovely to meet you. Will you be using the title?

MOTHER: Of course – your father and I will be referred to as 'Lord and Lady'. Why ever not?

ELLA: Well, my mother never used the title. She said it caused amusement.

MOTHER: Then she was a fool. I can see nothing amusing in being called Lady Table. You – Bottom!

BUTTONS: Buttons!

MOTHER: Whatever. Show me to my room.

ELLA: (At gate, looking out) And is Father close behind?

MOTHER: Who? Oh, him. He's still back in Paris trying to sort out dreary business affairs. Now, let's have a look inside. (To Buttons) You. Butt-wipe!

BUTTONS: Buttons!

MOTHER: Whatever. (Waves arm vaguely) Get the bags inside!

BUTTONS: Right. (To the sisters) Oy – you two. Inside! (Grabs arms and rushes at house)

MOTHER: Not them! The suitcases! (Buttons returns them to starting place) (Up close to him and nasty) Take care – I am not always this nice. (Mother exits into house and Buttons follows with cases, hitting sisters on bums)

There is critical circling as the sisters eye Ella up.

GRIPE: (about Ella) It is so – you know – totally ugly.

WHINGE: Totally. Mingerrrr. They should not, like, allow something looking like this out in daylight.

GRIPE: No. Children might, you know, see it and have, you know, nightmares!

WHINGE: And, like, look at that face. No idea how to do make-up, proper like. (Models own over-made-up face)

GRIPE: None at all. Can hardly, you know, even see it. Totally feeble.

WHINGE: And, like, look at her figure. Totally nothing!

GRIPE: No wonder she is, you know, still single. No man wants to, you know, marry that.

WHINGE: They way like a bit of meat. (Slaps a belly if appropriate)

GRIPE: (Looks up at house) What a dump. Totally, you know, minging.

ELLA: It is a very nice house. It has lovely views of...

WHINGE: Like whatever. Come on, we'll chill in the dining room. Just looking at that 'bone' makes me, like, want more food. (They exit; jostling to go first)

Village children reappear.

CHILD _: Have they gone?

ELLA: Who?

CHILD _: (mimics) 'Like, whatever – you know'. (All giggle)

ELLA: They're inside. Why?

CHILD _: We were sent to follow them; see where they went!

CHILD _: They tried to steal things from every stall in the market!

BOY 1: I estimate the value of stolen goods was a least two gold coins! Plus tax!

Servants appear from house carrying bundles.

ELLA: What's happening? Where are you all going?

SERVANT 1: We've been told to get out.

SERVANT 2: And with no wages!

ELLA: But where will you go?

SERVANT 3: We'll manage. We've got family in the village.

SERVANT 4: Poor, Ella. Without us here, who's going to do all the cooking and the cleaning?

ELLA: Well, I don't really …

MOTHER: (appears at top of steps with sisters behind her, eating) Cooking? Cleaning? Why, my dear girl, who do you think? (Walks close) YOU will!

ELLA: But...

MOTHER: But?! Are you – refusing to help about the house? I have more than enough to do – I have 'duties'. It's not easy - being a **Lady**!

WHINGE: I dunno about that.

GRIPE: Not that hard really. Bit of lippie; some padding…

MOTHER: Surely you don't expect ME to do all the work?! (Ella shakes head) I should think not. Good. First you can clean that grubby little room at the top of the tower.

ELLA: My room? But…

WHINGE: Like – it is so totally OUR room now. Remove your junk, like, at once.

GRIPE: Or we will, you know, remove it for you.

WHINGE: Like, through the window.

GRIPE: Yeah! And it is, you know, totally minging. You clean it.

ELLA: But...

MOTHER: Again – another 'but'.

ELLA: But where will I sleep?

MOTHER: You, Ella? (Leans close) Do I look as if I care? (Turns to leave then has idea) You can sleep in the kitchen! You can curl up on the floor in the ashes and cinders! Cinders! I say! I have it! I have your new name! Everyone! She is to be called – **CINDER-**ELLA!

WHINGE: CINDERELLA! Perfect!

GRIPE: Just right.

SONG: Disney's CINDERELLA "Work Song" amended lyrics: sisters & mother plus Buttons & chorus

MOTHER: (to children & servants) Now get out of here before I set the dogs on you! (Some start to leave) (To Buttons who has reappeared carrying cases/trunk) No – not you, Buttocks!

BUTTONS: Buttons!

MOTHER: Whatever. I need someone who at least looks clean to wait on me. You can stay. At half the money. (Snarl) What are you peasants waiting for?! (All servants EXIT) Now – you. (To Cinders) Get out of those clothes into something more suitable and get to work! Hurry up ... **CINDER**-ELLA! (They EXIT laughing)

BUTTONS: They can't do this! You can't just let them...

CINDERELLA: We have to do what she says. She ...

MRS McCHUCKER enters badly disguised under a white sheet to match wall, holding two plastic roses. Stands in flower bed. They see her.

BUTTONS: Er – is that you, Mrs Muck-Chucker?

MRS McCHUCKER: Er ... might be. (Reluctantly steps forward and goes to leave) (Pokes head out) And it's McChucker – not MUCK Chucker! (Exits)

CINDERELLA: Rather odd. Anyway, this new woman runs the house now – at least until Father returns. We just have to stay cheerful.

BUTTONS: If you say so – but I'm still going to call you Ella – not 'CINDER-Ella!

Cinders looks sad. They both trail into the house. Fairies' faces appear over the back wall.

COWSLIP: Is you hearing that? I says – is you hearing that?!

NUTMEG: Yeah, sorry. Brussels sprouts last night. Always make me f...

COWSLIP: No, not that! Her name!

PEASBLOSSOM: Cinderella! Not a very nice name.

COWSLIP: No, but **look - in - your - planner**! Look at the name!

PEASBLOSSOM: Cinderella! Oh yah! What a coincidence!

COWSLIP: It is not a co-inki-dinky-dingle! It's her! She is da one we 'as come to help!

Top of Beast's head appears again next to Nutmeg but only Nutmeg notices.

NUTMEG: Cowslip!

COWSLIP: Not now – I is plannin'.

NUTMEG: But .... Cowslip!

PEASBLOSSOM: Shhh!

NUTMEG: But ...

COWSLIP: What is it?

NUTMEG: Is speechless and can only nod at monster. Others do double take then shriek. They disappear rapidly. Repeat of shrieking, tufts of hair flying, roaring etc. **BLACKOUT**

SCENE 2: THE SISTER'S ROOM (formerly Ella's)

Chair, large wooden box with double flaps on top with half circles cut out for head to poke through; trick door at rear in solid wall (hinged both sides: double frame) Dressing table. Sisters close door.

WHINGE: Now, like, what?

GRIPE: Live the life of, you know, luxury. Waited on, you know, foot and mouth.

WHINGE: Yeah, (unsure) or somefin'. Sweet as! (Bounce knuckles)

BUTTONS comes in door at rear and tries to go back out, but is seen.

GRIPE: Like, stop right there! You are so, you know, caught! You – come here. (Gestures at Whinge who drags him down by the arm.)

BUTTONS: What do you want?

GRIPE: That's more, like, respectin of our new position. You know what I, you know, really want?

BUTTONS: No, I don't – you know – know. If I did, you know, – know – I wouldn't – you know ask. You know? Like?

WHINGE: Is you, like, dissin' me and my sister and I? Is you, like, showing disrespect to me and my sister.

BUTTONS: Not never! I is like totally, you know, not never, you know, like dissin, like. You know?

GRIPE: Er, (confused) that's cool then. I know! You can get us something - cool!

WHINGE: Yeah! I think, like, I would like an ice-lolly to lick. Go and fetch me one, quick like.

BUTTONS: You, like, would like a licky lolly, like. And you, (to Gripe) would you, like, like a licky lolly, like?

GRIPE: Er, (confused) No. I'll have a, you know, cream cake. Any sort. (Suspicious) But one I'll like – nothing horrid!

BUTTONS: Like, you know, a cream cake, you <u>know</u> you will, you know, like, like? Or, like, a cream cake you <u>don't</u>, you know, <u>know</u> you will like, like, but, like, <u>might</u> like anyway, like? You know?

GRIPE: Aaaah......

WHINGE: Just get it! And be quick! (Boots him as he runs off through door.)

GRIPE: This is the life. (Settles into chair.)

WHINGE: I wish I'd asked for a cream cake. I'll go and, like, tell him to get me one.

She goes toward the door but it flies open and hits her in the face.

BUTTONS: Cream cake! (Runs forward, slaps it into Gripe's face. Runs off out door again. Slams shut.)

WHINGE: (rubbing nose. Comes forward) Is it nice?

GRIPE: What do you mean, is it nice?! Look what he's done! I'll get him!

WHINGE: Yeah – let's get him! (Confused) What shall we do?

GRIPE: Here – take this. (Hands her heavy object) You stand by the door. I'll get him to bring another, you know, cream cake and when he does – you whack him over –

WHINGE: - over the rainbow?

GRIPE: No! Over the head!

WHINGE: Head! Right! Wicked plan, like!

Gripe goes to the door, partly opens it and shouts:

GRIPE: Buttons! Buttons! Get me another cream cake! (Shuts door and rushes to seat.) Are you ready?

WHINGE: (Runs to stand by doorway but on wrong side). Ready! Ha! We'll show the little...

BUTTONS bursts through door, slamming onto Whinge **(sound fx: thump/crunch + Aargh!),** who holds it shut. Buttons runs to Gripe to slam cake into face then runs off leaving door open. Whinge slowly lets door drift shut to show her holding nose & groaning.

GRIPE: The horrible little... We'll get him! Do it again!

WHINGE: Yeah – do it again!

Gripe goes to the door, partly opens it and shouts:

GRIPE: Buttons! Buttons! Get me another cream cake! (Shuts door, rushes back to seat.)

WHINGE: (Runs to stand beside doorway on the wrong side). Ready! Here he comes!

BUTTONS bursts through door, slamming on Whinge **(sound fx)** and runs down to Whinge to slam cake into face. Buttons runs off leaving door open. WHINGE slowly lets door drift shut.

GRIPE: You were supposed to whack him over the head!

WHINGE: (rubbing nose & moaning) He's too fast, like!

GRIPE: OK. Change of plan.

WHINGE: What?

GRIPE: Exactly the same idea – **but** - I'll hide, inside this box. **YOU** call him! (Climbs in)

WHINGE: Brilliant. (Goes to the door, partly opens it and shouts) Buttons! Buttons! Gripe wants another cream cake! (Shuts door and stands back, beside doorway – wrong side). Haha! This time we'll show him he can't mess with... (or ad lib)

BUTTONS bursts through door, slamming on Whinge **(sound fx)** and runs down to box.

BUTTONS: GRIPE!!

GRIPE: (pokes head out of hole in top) What? (Gets cake in face)

BUTTONS runs off.

WHINGE: (Slowly lets door drift shut.) I don't think I like this plan. (Concussed)

GRIPE: One more go! You call him again!

WHINGE: (opens door) Buttons! Buttons! Gripe wants another cream cake!

Gripe goes back down into box. Buttons rushes in and crushes Whinge again **(fx)**

BUTTONS: (Taps on box) Is that you in there, Whinge?

GRIPE: (pokes head out) No it's me, Gripe! (Gets cake) (Buttons runs off). Aargh!

WHINGE: (slowly lets door drift) Do you have a slightly different plan we could try?

GRIPE: One more go! He won't trick me this time! (Gripe goes back down into box.)

WHINGE: Oh no! Not again. (Reluctantly) Buttons! Buttons! Gripe wants another cream cake!

Buttons rushes in and crushes Whinge. He has TWO cakes.

BUTTONS: Oy! Gripe! Do you want cherry cake or chocolate cake?

GRIPE: (pokes head out) Chocolate! (Gets both cakes, one each side) (Buttons runs off).

WHINGE: (slowly lets door drift shut) I really think this plan isn't good; I give in.

GRIPE: Nonsense. All I have to do is stay inside the box. Whatever he says I will NOT come out! One more try!

WHINGE: (opens door) Buttons! Buttons! Gripe wants another cream cake!

Gripe goes back down into box. Buttons rushes in and crushes Whinge. He has a very large cake (open, hollow base but filled with cream/foam) and a large winding handle. He puts the cake on top of the box where Gripe will pop out. He fixes the winding handle to the side of the box and starts turning slowly. Sound fx: music box: 'half a pound of two-penny rice'. At the last note Gripe pops up, pushing head into cake and stands up with it on her head. Buttons may need to press it down, then runs off.

WHINGE: (slowly lets door drift shut) (coming forward dizzy) Why have you got that hat on? (Or "necklace" if it goes right down) (Helps her out of box) Do you think we could change places? I keep getting bashed on the nose

GRIPE: Bashed on the nose?! How?

WHINGE: I don't know! (Runs back) I'm standing here, like this and ...

GRIPE: THIS side!

WHINGE: No. I'm standing here, like this ...

GRIPE: Then stand THIS side?! You idiot! Stand THIS side! (Blank face) Give me that. Let me show you how to do it. I will stand THIS side! You just sit over there and watch the master at work! (Gripe goes to the door, partly opens it and shouts) Buttons! Buttons! Get me another cream cake! (Shuts door on 'safe' side and raises club.) Watch this, now you'll see…

Buttons rushes in. This time the door opens with hinges on the other side (second frame) and crushes Gripe. **(New fx: crash/crunch + Aargh!)** Buttons runs to a relaxed Whinge, splats giant cake in face and runs off. Gripe lets door slowly swing away from her, says "ha-ha!" and falls forward onto floor. **BLACKOUT**

SCENE 3: IN THE GARDEN

Cinderella is sat peeling potatoes at a stool by a long table (with a long cloth on it). Mrs McChucker is there in another awful disguise as a bush. Mother enters haughtily in fancy clothes. She is wearing an elaborate hat.

MOTHER: So – this is where you're hiding, is it? (Comes down steps) Out here by yourself? Answer me girl? (Hat on table) Out here by yourself?

CINDERELLA: Yes. Just me – and the mice of course.

MOTHER: Mice? (Whirls around angrily) Mice?! I see no mice? (Puppet mouse through hole in wall) (To aud) You! Yes, you peasants! Do you see any mice? (Mouse goes) I see nothing! I tell you – there are no mice here! (Repeat. Oh yes there are, etc – 3x) Nonsense! If there are mice, where are they?! (Puppet mice appear again – in different places.) Where?! Where?! (Business) Enough! (To Cinderella who is caught encouraging audience) Girl! Are you mocking me, for if you are – let me tell you – I will not … (as she talks her hat starts to move on its own) What is going on here?! What are you doing, girl?

CINDERELLA: Me? Nothing. (Mother lifts hat to show mouse. Squeak!)

MOTHER: Grr. Stand back. (She gets a piece of wood and raises it.)

CINDERELLA: No – don't hurt it! Look out little mouse! (WHAM!!)

MOTHER: There. (She looks at the ruined hat then picks it up.) Nothing! (Glares at Cinders. Puts hat down again). I don't need this stress! I don't need you making me look like a fool. Do you understand? I said – do you understand?

CINDERELLA: Yes – you don't need me to make you look like a fool.

MOTHER: Precisely. (Thinks) I'll be watching you. (She picks up the ruined hat. There is now a mouse on the table. Mother screams, leaps back, stares at the mouse again who squeaks, then she exits out gate screeching.)

CINDERELLA: Well done little fellow – you taught her a lesson. Would you like to see something secret? You would? (To aud) Can you keep a secret from that horrid woman? You promise? You can? Then I'll show you. (She lifts a suitcase and brings out a ball gown) I hid it out here so those "sisters" don't take it from me. (She carefully folds it into a suitcase). I'll hide it in the garden until the ball tonight. I might even get to meet the Prince!

BUTTONS: (ENTERS from house in a rush, carrying 2 cream cakes he puts on the table) Waah! Quick – hide me – those awful sisters are after me.

CINDERELLA: Behind the bush! Not that one! It's Mrs McChucker! (Mrs M slouches off despondently) The other one!

BUTTONS: What?! (Goes to hide but Cowslip is there) Whoah!

COWSLIP: You is not to be alarmed, bro! It is me! Fairy Godmother Cowslip!

BUTTONS: Well we are alarmed! You should warn people if you plan to turn up suddenly like that: I have delicate bowels at the best of times!

COWSLIP: Yes! You is totally right. It was very thoughtless. That shall now be our new policy (notebook/phone) - Note: 'Do not frighten the pants off the customers'.

CINDERELLA: Is it just you today?

COWSLIP: De uvvers is on da way. Ah! Here – I shall tell them of our new 'Do not frighten the pants off the customer' policy. Hang on a tick. (Mobile phone) Ere, Nutmeg – Nutmeg? Nutmeg (loudly) Hold it de other way up! Yeah, dat's better. It is me…. Cowslip. …… Cowslip the Fairy. ….. Cowslip wiv da (colour) jacket. ………. And da (colour) wings! ………… Nutmeg! Give da phone to Peasblossom! …to Peasblossom! …… (Exasperated pause) …. About (height) …. (Colour) wings …. NUTMEG! She is probably standing next to you! ……. (To others) A slight problem wiv my staff. Peasblossom! Ere – listen. We is dealing with some <u>very nervous types</u> here. Do <u>not</u> suddenly appear and alarm them. Arrive in a <u>friendly</u> and <u>not threatening</u> manner. What? I dunno – think of something! (Closes phone) Sorted.

CINDERELLA: Did you find who you were looking for the other day?

COWSLIP: Ah – well. We checked our files and it definitely said this address for a girl who is called Ginderbready – Umberella – sumpin like dat.

CINDERELLA: Well – my new mother calls me 'Cinderella' but it's not my proper name.

COWSLIP: Dat is it girl! Cinderfeller! Proper wicked! If dat is you, den we is here to be helpin' you!

CINDERELLA: Help me? Super! How can….? (There is a knock at the gate)

PEABLOSSOM: (offstage: loud and slowly, as if speaking to an idiot) Do not be alarmed – it is just the man to read the electricity meter. Do not be alarmed in any way!

BUTTONS: Man to read the electricity meter?

COWSLIP: It's Peasblossom. Come in you fool! (Peasblossom enters dressed as a clown – top half only - but with a fairy skirt on below & wings) Why is you dressed up like a clown?

PEABLOSSOM: Well – you remember your phone call, yah? So Nutmeg and I thought we would dress up in not-frightening disguises, so as not to alarm folk.

COWSLIP: I is knowing all that – but you said you wuz the elec-trickery man and in fact you is wearing the top half of a clown costume.

PEABLOSSOM: Ah – well spotted! On reflection I felt that a clown was <u>very</u> safe and not likely to frighten!

COWSLIP: (rising irritation) But you <u>said</u> you wuz the elec-trickery <u>man</u>!

PEABLOSSOM: Yah. Duh! Why would a clown be knocking on the door?!

COWSLIP: But why not dress as a elec-trickery man? Who would be frightened by the elec-trickery man?!

PEABLOSSOM: OoooH! My Great Aunt Veronica was <u>very</u> badly frightened by the electricity man!

CINDERELLA: Oh my!

PEABLOSSOM: Yes! And - coincidence - I understand <u>he</u> was only wearing the top half of HIS uniform as well! (Looks from others)

COWSLIP: I is dealing with idiots. Never mind all that – I 'as found this Sindy Dolly.

BUTTONS: Cinderella?

COWSLIP: Dis is da one. Right here before your eyes!

PEABLOSSOM: Oh splendid. (Checks instructions. Very excited) So, first we have to get her tickets for the ball.

CINDERELLA: Oh – I already have some tickets. Sorry.

COWSLIP: OK – but second, we 'as got you a really wicked dress to wear so that … (fades as the dress is held up then put away in the suitcase).

PEABLOSSOM: How about a carriage to take you there?

CINDERELLA: It's not far to the palace– I'll be OK to walk if I set out in good time. (Fairies deflated)

COWSLIP: Shoes? (There is nodding from Cinders)

PEABLOSSOM: Oh. (Sad) Right. (Inspired) Here – have this deodorant foot-spray! I always need it when I go dancing! (Confidential) Bit cheesy, you know?

CINDERELLA: Lovely. How thoughtful.

COWSLIP: Job sorted. Done something right at last! Have a lovely time!

BUTTONS: Hang on! Where's the other one? The other fairy?

PEABLOSSOM: Nutmeg? Lost again I expect. Happens a lot.

NUTMEG: (OFF) Ho-ho-ho. (they all look up and round) Ho-ho-ho!

They look under table and pull. Nutmeg's legs appear in Santa Claus outfit.

COWSLIP: Nutmeg? Is dat you under there?

NUTMEG: (off) I don't know – it's too dark to see.

PEABLOSSOM: Nutmeg? What are you <u>doing</u> in there?

NUTMEG: Me? Well – mostly I am lying in mouse poop.

BUTTONS: Is she alright?

COWSLIP: No, dopey-as, pal. (Meaningful look) She's from (unpopular town).

BUTTONS: Ah! Er... Shall we help her out?

COWSLIP: (shrugs) Suppose we'd better. Come on – give a hand. (They just pull Nutmeg's trousers down to show amusing long-johns/bloomers.)

CINDERELLA: Oh my! This is embarrassing!

NUTMEG: (off) I have suddenly got cold draughts in unusual places. What are you doing out there? Is that you Derek? (They pull trousers up then tug again and she slides out with Santa beard & hat)

COWSLIP: What is you dressed like that for?

NUTMEG: You said not to look frightening, so I thought...

COWSLIP: You is a half wit!

NUTMEG: Don't you go at me – I never wanted to be a fairy. Even my mother was against me being a fairy.

BUTTONS: She was?

NUTMEG: She was. I remember the day I left home; she said to me: I didn't spend fourteen years changing your nappies so you could go off and be a fairy! (All think about that: horror)

PEASBLOSSOM: Here! Who is this 'Derek', eh?

COWSLIP: Never mind all dat now – we 'as done our job 'ere and can go.

NUTMEG: (worried) Have we killed anyone?

PEABLOSSOM: No – not this time. Not even their granny. Gone remarkably smoothly really!

MOTHER: (has appeared at gates and watched the last bit) And WHO are these people?

They all jump in appropriate ways.

CINDERELLA: These people are ... er ...

BUTTONS: From the village!

COWSLIP: That is it; we is just - village people!

MOTHER: Hmm. If you are indeed "Village People" – then sing something!

COWSLIP: What?

MOTHER: I said, if you are the Village People – then sing something!

COWSLIP: Err...

NUTMEG: (brightly) I can sing you something: (Big breath)

A wizard had a magic bean. T'was really rather **class**

Twas small and brown and wrinkly, And he kept it in a **glass**,

... (knowing look at aud)

But people tried to steal it; now he couldn't let that **pass**

And so they wouldn't find it, well, he stuck it up his...

PEABLOSSOM: COWSLIP: Nutmeg!!

NUTMEG: … up his nose. They spoilt my song then!

BUTTONS: I think she is rather expecting something by THE Village People – you know - the 70's group?

Whinge & Gripe enter from house.

WHINGE: Not that I care but, like, what is going on? Are we missing something?

GRIPE: Yes – you, Butt-face.

BUTTONS: Buttons!

GRIPE: Whatever. We said – what are we missing?

BUTTONS: Hard to know where to start: (counts on fingers) brains, good looks, clean teeth, deodorant…

MOTHER: Enough! Sing. Now!

COWSLIP: Come on; we can do this. Village People: YMCA! All together. (Music)

NUTMEG: Stop! Stop! I'm not quite sure I know that one. What are the words?

COWSLIP: Words? (Disbelief) Y-M-C-A.

NUTMEG: Right. (Stands in position) (Music) Stop! Stop! What's the first word again?

PEABLOSSOM: Y.

NUTMEG: So I can sing it.

COWSLIP: It is da letter 'Y'! Now – is you ready?

NUTMEG: I am ready …. (Looks nervous as they all watch her. Eventually ...)

A wizard had a magic bean. T'was really rather ….

PEABLOSSOM: No! Just follow us. And don't forget the actions.

NUTMEG: There are actions for "magic bean". Do you want to see them? A wizard had a magic bean. T'was really rather ….

COWSLIP: Just start without him.

It's fun to stay at the Y-M-C-A

(As they do this Nutmeg is plainly forming the wrong letters with arms: T.W.I.T.)

BUTTONS: Hang on. Hang on! Hang on!! Those aren't the right letters. Nutmeg, do them again.

NUTMEG: (sings) Y-M-C-A (signs T.W.I.T.)

PEABLOSSOM: Do them again. T-W-I-T. That spells 'twit'!

NUTMEG: Does it? It's the way my mother taught me. (Grins) 'Twit' was her nick-name for me.

COWSLIP: Good grief. Let's just get on with it. Come on you lot – you can all join. Yes – (Gripe and Whinge) you two with the faces like monkeys' bottoms. Come on.

All except the mother join in. Gripe and Whinge stand either side of Nutmeg (who is in the CENTRE).

With the first Y & the A (or T & T) Nutmeg repeatedly slaps both sisters in the face. They cry out.

GRIPE: Stop! Stop!

MOTHER: What is it my dumpling?

GRIPE: This fool keeps hitting us!

MOTHER: Does she now?

WHINGE: Yes, she does.

MOTHER: That is easily solved, girls – change places.

The sisters simply swap and the action repeats exactly the same.

WHINGE: (very loud at music) Stop!

MOTHER: What is it my now, my little teacake?

WHINGE: (sobbing) She's still, like, hitting us!

MOTHER: Then move right away from her.

They now stand: Buttons, **Whinge,** Cowslip, <u>Nutmeg</u>, Peasblossom, **Gripe**, Cinderella.

COWSLIP: Are we all ready? (They are)

This time as they sing YMCA only Whinge and Gripe do YMCA. All the rest do TWIT. The sisters get battered.

MOTHER: Stop this nonsense! Move around. There! (They now stand: Nutmeg, Cowslip, **Whinge**, <u>Buttons</u>, **Gripe**, Peasblossom, Cinderella.) And if these morons swing their arms around, all you have to do is duck! (Shows them how – by leaning forward)

(Meanwhile the audience see that Buttons now has the 2 cream cakes behind his back.)

COWSLIP: One last try!

They all sing. Chorus runs twice. On the very last A (or T if you are doing the TWIT version) the sisters duck forward and get the cakes in the mug. Much wailing and fuss.)

COWSLIP: Right – that's our cue. Everyone out! Come on! Cheers Cinders! Good luck!

PEASBLOSSOM: So lovely to meet you all! (They exit very fast)

GRIPE: (eating cream) I'm, you know, hungry. When's dinner?

WHINGE: Me too. Like, very hungry. I want dinner and supper together!

GRIPE: I bet she's, you know, hiding food in here. (Suitcase)

CINDERELLA: No! That's mine! I mean – there's no food in it!

GRIPE: (Opens suitcase) Oooh!

MOTHER: What is it?

WHINGE: Is it, like, food?

GRIPE: No – look!

MOTHER: A ball gown? (Slow & menacing) What on earth do you need that for?

GRIPE: For this! (Finds ball tickets)

MOTHER: (calmly looks at tickets) Three tickets! My, my! For a ball – tonight, at the palace!

BUTTONS: Give them back – they're Cinderella's!

MOTHER: But she doesn't need them. After all, she doesn't have anything to wear. (Nods at girls. They slowly rip the dress in two. Sisters exit into house waving tickets, pushing Buttons before them.) Oh – and another thing – if you are tempted to find another dress and somehow get yourself into that ball at the palace – that is fine by me. (Smiles horribly) But when you get back – don't expect to find your friend Buttons still has a job here. (She goes up steps but at top stops and turns back). Oh – and one other thing.

CINDERS: What?

MOTHER: (smug pause) Ha! Ha! **BLACKOUT**

SCENE 4: THE BEDROOM

Peasblossom & Cowslip appear through the door. Mrs McC is there badly camouflaged.

PEASBLOSSOM: Shushy-shush!

COWSLIP: I is not shushy-shushin'. If you 'ad not left our make-up at 'ome we would not be sneakin' around in 'ere; like, nicking some!

(They look round and spot Mrs McC)

PEASBLOSSOM: Look!

COWSLIP: What is it?

(They sneak closer and reveal Mrs McC's face)

PEASBLOSSOM: Hello.

COWSLIP: Can we help you?

MRS McCHUCKER: Muriel McChucker. Security. Licenced to kill.

PEASBLOSSOM: Really?

MRS McCHUCKER: Indeed. (Holds up one finger) This finger could kill.

COWSLIP: That finger?

MRS McCHUCKER: (now unsure) Or ... or maybe it's this one?

COWSLIP: OK. So how could it kill, exactly?

MRS McCHUCKER: Ah-er. Yes! Look! If I lick it (does) and then push it in an electric socket! BAM! I will be dead in two seconds!

PEASBLOSSOM: Er - doesn't 'licenced to kill' usually mean 'kill other people'?

MRS McCHUCKER: Really? Oh – YES! Well; if there was a bad villain I would lick HIS finger then get him to push – it - in ... (Realises flaw in plan) I'll be off then. (Exits)

COWSLIP: Bizarre. Remind me – why are we here?

PEASBLOSSOM: I am not going to the ball without makeup! Look – they've tons of the stuff. Midnight Mystery, or (topical / local name)? Gosh; look! (Gasps & holds up botox needle) They are – druggies!

COWSLIP: Not wiv dis dey aint. Dis is 'bum-tax'.

PEASBLOSSOM: (pause) Botox?

COWSLIP: That's it! You sticks it in your face and it freezes da muscles so they can't move - to make your face all smooth and loverly. (Gives her the needle. Stretches face to demonstrate) Here – sit down. (Pushes her into chair with back to audience) I will give you some!

PEASBLOSSOM: You certainly will not! Take it away at once! (She tries to pass it back but instead stabs COWSLIP in the leg)

COWSLIP: Ow! Be careful. That was my favourite leg!

PEASBLOSSOM: Stop moaning, and do my makeup.

COWSLIP: Alright – let's see what they is havin' in here. You'll need plenty of ... ooer (as she walks her leg goes numb and floppy)

PEASBLOSSOM: Get on with it! I'm going to shut my eyes and then you can surprise me when I'm done. Here – take this filthy bum-tox stuff. (This time it sticks in Cowslip's arm – same result)

Cowslip has to fetch make-up from the dressing table with one dead leg and apply masses of it to Peasblossom with one dead arm that she has to flap about like a paintbrush. She explains what she is doing as she does it (ad lib) but her face shows rising horror. At end stands back and looks at her work in terror.

PEASBLOSSOM: All done? Right. (Turns to show audience) What do you think? Has she, like, done a good job? Am I beautiful? Eh? (ad lib) What? Let me see – fetch me a mirror.

COWSLIP: Aaaah... No mirror!

PEASBLOSSOM: There is – over there. (Has a look) Waah! Where's that needle?! I'll make your sorry! Come back here.

She chases the still floppy Cowslip off (maybe through aud?). Ad libs.

SCENE 5: THE GARDEN AT SUNSET

Garden at evening. Small lights are lit. Mrs Mc.M is there on hands and knees disguised as a bench. Cinderella and Buttons come out of the door. She has a rug for beating.

BUTTONS: Evening Mrs Muck-Chucker.

CINDERELLA: How are you today?

MRS McCHUCKER: (turns and leaves on all fours) I keep telling you!

McChucker!

BUTTONS: At least they've got a lovely evening for the ball.

CINDERELLA: Was it tonight? I don't really remember.

BUTTONS: You fibber. You know very well.

CINDERELLA: Anyway … (looks up) What's that noise?

BUTTONS: (Runs to the gate) It's the people from the village! They're all dressed up.

Villagers enter in their ball gowns etc. Even the children.

VILLAGER 1: Hello, Buttons. Aren't you ready yet?

CHILD 1: (runs to Cinders) Come on; we're here to take you both to the ball!

CHILD 2: Yes – you need a bit of cheering up.

BOY 1: I estimate that if you walk at three leagues an hour you will take fourteen minutes to reach the palace.

CINDERELLA: I'm afraid I've got too much work to do here. You can go, Buttons.

BUTTONS: er... they took the tickets.

PERSON: I've got a spare!

BUTTONS: Well – thanks, but I can't go and leave … I mean – what if the loo gets blocked again!

BOY 1: Should be OK. I went at home.

CINDERELLA: There! Now, no more excuses. You go to that ball.

BUTTONS: But –

CINDERELLA: If you don't go then who can tell me all about it in the morning?

BUTTONS: But –

CINDERELLA: (sighs) I'll be fine! Go!

They reluctantly leave but Boy 1 comes back.

BOY 1: Don't be sad! Statistically there's a one in three chance the ball will be boring, and a one in three thousand chance the palace will be struck by lightning! Cheer up!

MUSICAL CHORUS NUMBER: 'Always look on the bright side'.
All children and chorus & Buttons joining one-by-one.
Finally, Mrs McChucker disguised as child.

They all exit, Buttons & Mrs McC being forced to go by Cinders.

CINDERELLA: Have a wonderful time! Goodbye! (Waves them off) Right – what's next?

MOTHER: (appears at door dressed for the ball) What's next? Not enough to do? (reaches back in and throws out a rug) This needs scrubbing clean! (Grinds her foot on it) Hurry up girls or you'll be late!

Sisters appear in appalling ball gowns & wigs. Gripe has fixed grin & raised eyebrows.

MOTHER: Gripe? What on earth have you done to your face?

WHINGE: It's this (holds up botox jab) Botox! I told her not to use too much, like. And she's even, like, taking more of the stuff with her!

GRIPE: strange noises through gritted teeth.

MOTHER: What did she say?

WHINGE: She says you can give me her pocket money for the rest of the month.

MOTHER: How kind. Off you go then girls. Be quick – it will be starting soon! (Girls exit through gate) Enjoy your cleaning, Cinderella. (Pauses) Oh…. and if I find out that you have somehow made your way to that ball …… then remember, Buttons is out of here! (Exits through gate)

CINDERELLA: (walks to face audience) And if you think I am going to sing another soppy song about always being cheerful, well I'm not. I am really fed-up. Horrid rug. (Throws rug out of gate)

NUTMEG: (Enters fighting rug) Aaargh! Help! Monster! (Fairies enter wearing fairy ball "gowns")

PEASBLOSSOM: It's just a rug! (Takes it off & throws out gate again)

COWSLIP: Hello – we was just looking for Cinder … oh – it **is** you. Where's that proper good frock what you showed us?

CINDERELLA: Those sisters ripped it up.

COWSLIP: I is going off those two!

PEASBLOSSOM: Surely you have other gowns? Come on – we'll help you choose.

CINDERELLA: No – it's alright. They've wrecked all my nice clothes; and I don't have a ticket; and it's too late to get ready now anyway, and … and … if SHE finds out I've been to the ball then Buttons gets the sack!

NUTMEG: (nods wisely) My mum gave me a sack once. She said it was my school uniform, but it wasn't like the other kids'. (They look at her) Smelt of turnips, too.

COWSLIP: I fort dis job wus goin too easy like. I finks there is only one solution to dis crisis.

PEASBLOSSOM: (Hopefully) Gin?!

COWSLIP: No. Magic!

NUTMEG: Right. (Thinks) I'm not sure I got that. Run it past me again.

COWSLIP: We is going to do magic. Pass me the wand. Stand back! First – da dress! (Waves wand; drum roll) Poshyfrockium! Ahum … Poshyfrockium! Perhaps the batteries are flat? Poshyfrockium! (Angry) **Poshy-fffff** (Peasblossom stops her swearing) frockium! (Nothing) Grrr! Do not be worrying – it sometimes takes a couple of minutes to kick in like. (Pause) Any minute now. Er – (Gives wand to Nutmeg then stamps to Cinders & adds something to her, like a cheesy novelty apron etc.) Da-da! Lovely.

CINDERELLA: That's very nice of you. But they still might recognise me!

PEASBLOSSOM: Here – I have it! Glasses! (Turns Cinder's back to aud) Transform you. (Gives her joke glasses with big nose and moustache. Turns her back) Hmm. Something is not quite right here. Perhaps it's your hair?

CINDERELLA: (indicates the nose) I'm not sure this is the look I really wanted …

PEASBLOSSOM: Fair comment. Try these. (Hands her nice glasses but she does not put them on yet) They are only little but they are … (Magic music; they all look around in confusion) magic glasses! (Music again; more confusion) Nobody is like going to recognise you at all.

CINDERELLA: What does this tag say? (Looks at large dangling label)

COWSLIP: Er … (takes & reads) "Magic glasses. Best before midnight". (Music) Alright – we 'as it! Enough with the tinkly winkly! (Glares) I is remeberin'! You must be out of dere before de last chime of midnight or Buttons, he is history!

CINDERELLA: Midnight! Right. (Puts on glasses) Now what?

COWSLIP: Ere! Who is you? Wot as you done with Cinder-inder?

CINDERELLA: Look! (Glasses off) It's me!

NUTMEG: (looks close) I still don't recognise you.

COWSLIP: Dat is awesome. Put 'em back on! Perfect!

PEASBLOSSOM: Next! You need a horse to pull your carriage. Fetch me a mouse and I will turn it into a lovely little prancing white pony! Cooee? Mousey? Cinderella needs you! Can anyone see a mouse? (Mouse appears through a hole in the wall of the house, or near the edge of the stage) Come on! Cinderella needs a mouse? (Business) Super; hold still mousey. (To aud) Never done this one before. I'm thinking big, strong, fast. Here goes –

Mouseygrowbigeo!

Thunder and lightening. (pyro??) Small mouse goes and giant, ugly, snarling mouse appears in place. It pushes them aside and marches down into the audience, terrorises the kids and exits to sound of smashing and screaming. They watch it go in stunned silence.

PEASBLOSSOM: Do you want me to try again?

ALL: **No!** Snatch wand away. Peasblossom goes and sulks, sitting on the bench

NUTMEG: I have an idea. You see that pumpkin by the gate?

COWSLIP: Right ... stop! What is you planning? Our insurance is not covering major disasters. Not since that last thingy. You remember? That thing wot happened when we helped dat poor, cold, Little Match Girl who was sat in the doorway – a'freezin'? What did they call dat fing wot we did?

PEASBLOSSOM: The Great Fire of London.

COWSLIP: Dat wuz it.

NUTMEG: I am planning to turn this pumpkin into a means of transporting Cinderella to the ball! (Moves it in front of the bench. Peasblossom lifts her legs clear)

PEASBLOSSOM: I say – have you done this before, Nutmeg?

NUTMEG: Loads of times.

PEASBLOSSOM: Show me how many 'loads of times' is - on your fingers. Proudly holds up no fingers.

PEASBLOSSOM: That's what I thought. (Covers head with hands)

NUTMEG: Stand back. I'm not a very good aim!

Stage light is slowly dimming.

NUTMEG: Transportiamus!! (Nothing) (To aud) Here – you lot can help. When I wave the wand I want you all to say the magic word: transportiamus. Ready? (Practice as necessary) Right! Transportiamus!!

COWSLIP: Nuffink has happened yet.

NUTMEG: Try again. Louder! Transportiamus!! No? One more try!! Everyone! **Transportiamus!!**

Sound of magical rumbling grows.

PEASBLOSSOM: I say – what's happening?

The bench starts to wobble. Sound of engine revving then bench slides off with Peasblossom on it, screaming. They go & watch it vanish over horizon, her screams fading away.

NUTMEG: **You** were supposed to be on that! Oy! Come back! (Runs off after it.)

CINDERELLA: I was rather expecting a beautiful white carriage.

COWSLIP: Beggars is not to be choosers. Here... (Hands her magic wand) Hold that! Be back later! Hey! Wait for me! (Runs of after others calling after them.)

CINDERELLA: Bye then! (Turn to aud) Oh dear. And I did rather want to go to the ball, but everyone else has gone and I'm left here with an old pumpkin and a magic wand. What am I supposed to do with these? (Business with aud.) Me? Do Magic? Do you think I could? It's worth a try! (Carries pumpkin to back of stage by rear wall, puts behind bush. Returns to front with wand) Now – what was the magic word? What was it? Will you help me say it? You will? Super. Here goes! **Transportiamus!!**

Stage goes very dark except for spot on rear wall / or localised lighting effect. Smoke. CINDERELLA SLIPS INTO WINGS AND CHANGES INTO BALLGOWN. Smoke. Sound effect grows louder, music swells, rear wall splits along jagged brick lines **(sound fx)** and opens to show beautiful white carriage. Cinders is back in place by now and thanks audience for their help: she climbs in the carriage. Music peaks; if possible carriage moves off with her waving.

BLACKOUT: <u>END OF ACT ONE:</u> **CURTAIN: INTERVAL**

ACT TWO: **SCENE 6: PALACE BALLROOM**
Traditional lavish ballroom, with steps rear right. There is a very large cuckoo clock as part of one side wall (Stage Left). Chair/throne with red cushion. Trays of fizzy drinks on table.

DANCE: CHORUS, HERALD, Mrs McC, PRINCE and PRINCESS. Children.
Old-fashioned ding-dong door bell. Herald runs up the steps. Mrs McChucker frisks Buttons.

BUTTONS: Getting to quite like that! (Hands ticket to Herald)

HERALD: Your Royal Highnesses; Lords, Ladies, commoners & peasants. Mr – er – is that all? 'Buttons'

BUTTONS: Just Buttons.

HERALD: **Mister Just Buttons**! (Buttons enters)

BUTTONS: (Goes over to Prince and Princess) Hello again! Nice do!

PRINCESS: My brother and I are very pleased that you could come to our ball.

BUTTONS: Your ball? But – I thought? You mean – you're the Prince? (Prince grins, hands glass to Herald, who drains it, then Prince bows.) So that means you must be ...

PRINCESS: The Princess. (Hands drink to Herald – who drains it - then curtseys)

BUTTONS: Blimey. (To aud) Never saw that coming! Did you?

PRINCE: And your friend – the girl from your house – is she here with you?

BUTTONS: No. She really wanted to come but – bit of a problem at home.

PRINCE: Oh. That's a shame. I was hoping ...

PRINCESS: Oh dear. Don't worry – we'll think of something. (To Buttons) Come on – you can get me a drink. (Moves Buttons away.)

Doorbell rings. Herald finishes drink & runs. Mother and sister arrive. Mrs McC tries to frisk. Business.

HERALD: Royal Highnesses, Lords, Ladies, other people: Lady Table – Seriously? Lady Table?! Whatever. **Lady Table** and her daughters, **Gripe and Whinge**.

MOTHER: Here we are girls – where we belong – the royal palace. And I am feeling HOT! (She licks finger, bends and touches bum with Hiss! as in 'very hot')

WHINGE: You? I'm the hot one here! (Repeats action: lick, touch, HISS)

GRIPE: Yeah – like, me too. (She bends and touches bum <u>then</u> licks finger. Horrid taste and disgust. Others go Yuck)

MOTHER: Now – to work. The Prince is here somewhere: go get him!

GRIPE: Which one's the Prince, like?

WHINGE: Here – you! (To Princess. Buttons hides) Which one is, like, the Prince or whatever then?

PRINCESS: He would be the one with the crown on his head. (Points)

WHINGE: We knew that. Come on. (Goes over and does awful curtseys) Good evenings your Princey.

PRINCE: Princey?

WHINGE: Duh, yeah. Tradey, boatey – Princey!

GRIPE: (worse curtsey) Greetings, your ferrero rocher.

PRINCE: Er – a pleasure... ladies? (To Herald) Help!

HERALD: (Hands them tray of drinks) If you ladies will excuse us, I am about to call the first dance.

WHINGE: Good idea, like. Liven this place up a bit. (Drink to Herald; over the top dancing)

GRIPE: Princy wincy! Remember to save a dance for me! (Gives drink to Herald, puts down handbag, clears space then 'twerks', winking at Prince)

PRINCE: A dance? Why - I am sure that would be something I would never forget.

WHINGE: And, like, save the last dance for me, cute stuff.

PRINCE: I assure you that a dance with you will definitely be the last thing I do. Excuse me. (Pushes off her advances) (Sisters try to follow but Mrs McC blocks them)

WHINGE: I'm in there. He couldn't keep his hands off me.

GRIPE: He was brushing your dandruff off!

MOTHER: Don't argue - just get after him.

(Doorbell. Herald drains drinks & runs, breathless.)

HERALD: Ahem! Your highnesses, Lords, whatsits: The fairy god-mothers. Frisking business with Mrs McC: maybe find rubber chicken or similar?

PEASBLOSSOM: How could you have left without her? That was the whole point!

COWSLIP: It wuz not entirely our fault. It wuz all so fast like!

NUTMEG: We was worried about you!

COWSLIP: Look – here is that Buttons. Hello!

BUTTONS: (joins them, with Princess) Hello again. I was hoping you might have brought (looks around) you-know-who with you.

COWSLIP: Cinder-inder. No – bit of a muck up there really.

PEASBLOSSOM: But we can still put in a good word for her, with the Prince!

NUTMEG: Which one is the Prince then?

PRINCESS: He would be the one with the crown on his head.

NUTMEG: But so have you.

PRINCESS: I am a Princess.

COWSLIP: Oooh! A Princess! (Exaggerated bowing from both fairies)

PRINCE: (To all) Now – Herald Harold has an announcement! Herald? (No response) Herald? Your speech?

HERALD: (as if waking) I never really believed in herbal remedies but once I had taken Herbal Ignite it seemed to work for me. My wife was very pleased but the staff at Countdown say we can never go in there again, so we …

PRINCE: No! The letter from the King!

HERALD: Oh blimey. (Runs up stairs) Highnessesseses, Lads and – ah - Loonies. Pray silence. I have a message from his Majesty the King. (Coughs: reads, slightly drunk) My loving and happy pimple – er - people. I send you greetings on this very special evening and hope that you all have a really wonderful time. (Ripple of applause) To add to this special occasion, I wish to announce that tonight my son – you know, the whatsit… Him there! The Prince! – will tonight choose, from amongst you, the young lady who will become his wife. Yes; it could be you (attractive person who looks excited) or you (repeat) or (goes to point to sisters but cringes and goes back to first girl) or you! (Looks at paper) Blah blah – boring bit. Er … ooh – here's a good bit! **If** he is <u>unable</u> to find a suitable wife tonight then I will find one for him – that's the king, not me. Blah blah. OK. Have a lovely evening. The King!

PRINCE: What?! But …

PRINCESS: Did you know about this?

PRINCE: Of course not! (He is suddenly surrounded by females)

MOTHER: There you are girls – your chance to bag yourself some royalty! Go get him – but be subtle! (They grab Prince under arms & drag him backwards) SUBTLE!

Door bell. Herald runs very breathless now.

HERALD: Oy! You lot! (Wobbles slightly and stares at them for silence) Your Highs, Gents and Lavvies. Another one! (Looks at card in hand) Miss Ann Oni-mouse.

(Music. Cinderella appears at the top of the steps.)

PEASBLOSSOM: Look! I think it's her! I recognise the glasses!

COWSLIP: How did she get 'ere so fast?

Crowd parts; Herald escorts her down the steps and across to the Prince

HERALD: May I introduce you to Prince ...

CINDERELLA: You! But ... I mean ... you're the Prince?! (In panic turns to run but Cowslip stops her)

PRINCE: I think – I mean – (looks closely) Have we met before?

CINDERELLA: I – ah – I don't think so. Perhaps I just look like someone else?

PRINCE: (Uncertain) Perhaps – (smiles) perhaps in a dream? (Sisters groan in disgust)

WALTZ: CINDERELLA WALTZ (Disney) or similar

The sisters keep getting in the way and taking over the Prince. The fairies try to help by dancing with the sisters & getting Cinders & the Prince together but Nutmeg gets very confused and makes things worse. This will take a lot of practice & tight planning but is worth it. Music & dancing continues over:

COWSLIP: Here – this is awful. These freaks is getting in the way and Cinders is only havin' until midnight!

BUTTONS: Cinderella – you mean! Wow! I never recognised her!

PRINCESS: Who is it?

MRS McCHUCKER: What's this? Security breach?!

BUTTONS: Er – no. (Fairies signal to say nothing) just someone from the village.

PRINCESS: She's very pretty. I think my brother looks rather keen on her.

COWSLIP: Well, 'e only 'as till midnight! And those two is getting' in da way of true love.

PRINCESS: Midnight? Why?

NUTMEG: Magic spell. (Taps nose) Say-no-more!

PRINCESS: Wow! Midnight, eh. Right! Come on, Buttons – let's see what we can do! (They run to Herald and tell him to say ...)

HERALD: Oy! Supper time! Grubs on the table!

All EXIT except Cinders & Prince. Sisters run off, shoving greedily.

DUET: Cinders & Prince (the chorus can drift back in to support the song?)

At end the sisters split them up, carrying the Prince off in an amusing manner. Cinders runs after.

Princess, Buttons and Mrs McCHUCKER enter.

PRINCESS: I think you're right. Mrs M. Something going on here.

Mrs M presses ear-piece and speaks into wrist again.

BUTTONS: Does that thing actually work? I mean – who are you talking to? Let me listen. (He pulls the ear-piece out. Tinny music – I will always love you, from The Bodyguard.)

MRS McCHUCKER: Er...

People start to drift back in.

PRINCESS: We can't have that awful noise. Can you turn it off?

MRS McCHUCKER: Er ... not sure...

BUTTONS: Just push it back in! (He pushes it back her ear, very hard) (The music gets quieter but is still heard, with echo)

MRS McCHUCKER: Ah! You've pushed it right in! (Rolls head) I can feel it rolling round inside!!

PRINCESS: We can still hear it! (Presses finger on Mrs M's other ear. Music quitter but still heard)

BUTTONS: (leans close) It's coming out of your nose! (He takes Mrs M's forefingers and jams one up each nostril. Music stops.) Sorted.

MRS McCHUCKER: (unclearly) I can't stay like this all night!

PRINCESS: Neither can I!

Fairies & rest of chorus enter. They look at the odd trio, who shuffle aside.

PEASBLOSSOM: This calls for some cool thinking and cunning plans! (Pause) I'm going to give those sisters such a whacking … (Advances in violent fashion)

COWSLIP: (holds her back) Ere! Steady on – you is not in Local Place now!

NUTMEG: I know! I will do some magic! (Waves magic wand)

COWSLIP: No! You is not – you is never yet getting nuffink right! You is gonna kill someone!

PEASBLOSSOM: But look at the clock! The time!

NUTMEG: Hmm. Remind me again ….

PEASBLOSSOM: I keep telling you – when the big hand is on the…

NUTMEG: No – which one is the CLOCK? Is it the one with the little bird?

PEASBLOSSOM: Cuckoo!

NUTMEG: (smiles) Cuckoo! When I was born that was what my mum wanted to call me!

COWSLIP: The cuckoo! I has an idea! Peasblossom – we need a LADDER!

MRS McCHUCKER: (dismantles ear piece & breaks pose) Hold on! Health and Safety! Ladder? What's going on?!

COWSLIP: Right! listen! That clock must never reach twelve.

BUTTONS: You have a plan?

COWSLIP: I do.

PRINCESS: Super. What is it?

COWSLIP: No cuckoo – no twelve-o-clock! We is goin' to get that cuckoo out of dat clock! That's why we need the ladder!

MRS McCHUCKER: OK – hang on! (Exits to get ladder)

PEASBLOSSOM: Jolly good plan, Cowslip!

BUTTONS: Right – but will it work? (assorted responses)

PRINCESS: Is this an adventure?

BUTTONS: I think it's turning into one!

MRS McCHUCKER: (returns with ladder) Where do you want it? Here?

PRINCE: Now what are you up to?

MRS McCHUCKER: Er – security matter. Stand aside, your Highness!

At the clock Mrs M goes up the ladder trying to get the cuckoo out of its door.

PEASBLOSSOM: Do hurry up! It's almost midnight! Grab it when it comes out! (The clock reaches 12. **CUCKOO** 1).

MRS McCHUCKER: Aargh!! The little brute moves so fast! (**CUCKOO** 2).

PEASBLOSSOM: Hurry – it's going to … (**CUCKOO** 3).

BUTTONS: GRAB IT!

COWSLIP: Right!

MRS McCHUCKER: Ready! READY! (**CUCKOO** 4) Aargh! Missed! (Reaches inside door as it disappears) Got it! (Appears to have it in both hands. No more cuckoo appearances from clock)

PEASBLOSSOM: Jolly well done, you! Bring it down! We shall hide it! (**CUCKOO** 5).

COWSLIP: Aargh! No! It is still going! What is we to do?!

PEASBLOSSOM: I don't know! I don't know! (**CUCKOO** 6). Aargh! Do something!

MRS McCHUCKER: What?!

PRINCESS: Here! (Grabs cushion off chair and pushed over cuckoo)

COWSLIP: Good finking, girl! (**CUCKOO** 7 **muffled**). Aargh!

NUTMEG: I know!! **Eat it!**

MRS McCHUCKER: What?!

PEASBLOSSOM: YES! Eat it! (**CUCKOO** 8). Quick! (Pushes it into Mrs.M's mouth.) There. Sorted! (Looks at friend's awful expression.) Do you need a drink?

MRS McCHUCKER: (Opens mouth to speak) (**CUCKOO** 9 + **echoing burp**).

COWSLIP: Aaaargh!! That's nine! Stop it!

BUTTONS: Keep your mouth shut!

CINDERELLA: (enters and rapidly rushes over) What shall I do? It's almost midnight!

PEASBLOSSOM: (rapidly) Don't worry - he can't take his eyes off you!

CINDERELLA: Really?

PEASBLOSSOM: Really! Isn't that right, Cowslip!

COWSLIP: Not half!

BUTTONS: You OK, Mrs Muck Chucker?

MRS McCHUCKER: Opens mouth to speak: (**CUCKOO** 10 + burp).

PEASBLOSSOM: Aaargh! Ten! (Holds Mrs M's's nose.) Swallow it!

BUTTONS: (to Cinders) Quick! Get back to the Prince. You only have seconds left! (Cinders runs off toward Prince)

PEASBLOSSOM: Swallow! SWALLOW! (Big gulping sound.) ……. Well?

MRS McCHUCKER: (Cautiously opens mouth. No sound.) There. Sorted. Oh my …!

NUTMEG: What is it?

MRS McCHUCKER: Feeling rather strange – er – down below. Mmmm. Oh my goodness!

PEASBLOSSOM: Down below? Oh my – (to Buttons) For pity's sake – move the Princess!

(Princess is at the bottom end of MrsM. Buttons leaps and rescues her just before MrsM suddenly bends double. **Farting CUCKOO** sound (11). Fairies scream; hold cushion over Mrs M's bottom. Princess joins the chain. Drunken Herald joins end, for no obvious reason)

PEASBLOSSOM: <u>**Eleven! One to go!**</u>

COWSLIP: Quick – get her out of here! (Prince enters)

PRINCE: (to Cinders) Ah – there you are. I was afraid you'd gone. I was wondering if perhaps, if you weren't too busy tomorrow, you might like to … (the cushion-holding line moves). (Prince notices but tries to carry on) I was saying, I was wondering if perhaps, if you weren't too busy tomorrow, you might like to … (the cushion holding chain moves). My word! Is anything wrong? (They all very innocently answer "No!")

PRINCESS: Quick! Ask her out or something!!

PRINCE: (embarrassed) Well, that's a bit ... I mean.

ALL: Hurry up!

MRS McCHUCKER: (desperate) I can't hold it in much longer!!

PRINCE: Err …

MRS McCHUCKER: (Wails) My bottom's going to explode!

PEASBLOSSOM: (To Prince) Isn't this so romantic!

CINDERELLA: Yes; you were saying??

PRINCE: Tomorrow? Yes! Perhaps a picnic? (Cinders smiles and nods excitedly)

GRIPE: (SISTERS ENTER) Princey poohs! Don't forget you promised me a dance!

WHINGE: And me! (Pushes sister aside.) In fact – me first.

PRINCE: Ladies – as soon as I have a name and address of this young lady, so I may collect her for tomorrow's picnic, then I will be delighted ….

CINDERELLA: Name? (Looks at glaring sisters.) Address? Well …. Er …

COWSLIP: Do something!

PRINCESS: (loudly) I say – is that more champagne they're opening over there?

GRIPE: More bubbly!

WHINGE: Make way! (They rush off for booze. Mother stays watching from edge)

PRINCE: As I was saying; if you could let me have your name and address?

CINDERELLA: Why, of course, (tries to whisper so Mother does not hear) it's …

MRS McCHUCKER: It's too late! I can't hold it!

NUTMEG: She's going to blow!

BUTTONS: This is the last cuckoo! Midnight!

COWSLIP: Get Cinders of here NOW!

CINDERELLA: What?

ALL: RUN!! (**ENORMOUS FARTING CUCKOO**.)

Cinders half carried off by Fairies & Buttons. The crowd leap aside, amazed by the noise.

MRS McCHUCKER: Sorry about that; something I ate!

PRINCE: What's going on?!

PRINCESS: Not too sure really. But it's very exciting.

HERALD: I don't feel well.

PRINCE: Where has she gone? That girl? She's the one I want to …

MOTHER: So – your highness. This seems to be the end of the ball. And – as your father instructed – you have to choose your bride. (Pushes daughters forward)

HERALD: She's right. Just choose quickly. (Looks ill)

MOTHER: So – name your choice!

PRINCE: Very well –

WHINGE & GRIPE: Yes!

PRINCE: I name - the girl who just left!

MOTHER: So ... (Comes close to him, menacing) ... name her then. Go on – **what** is her name?! (Prince can't; neither can anyone else)

HERALD: Ann –Ony-Mouse! Hic!

MRS McCHUCKER: Ha! Anonymous! A false name!

MOTHER: Pah! You can't name her!

PRINCESS: Look! She left a shoe behind! A glass slipper! Really nice. Dolce and Gabana I think! I've got some that… sorry.

PRINCE: There! I know one thing about her! She has lost one glass slipper – and her feet are this size!

MOTHER: That's not a **name**!

PRINCESS: No – but if you remember – my brother has to select a bride tonight!

HERALD: Yesh!

PRINCESS: And the night will not end until...

PRINCE: **Dawn**! I will find her before dawn! Everybody! Quickly! Find the girl whose feet fit this slipper, for she is the one I will marry!

BLACKOUT

ACT TWO: SCENE 7: PART OF THE KITCHEN

The fairies, Buttons & Cinders (no longer in gown) rush excitedly into the kitchen.

BUTTONS: Quick – get everything back to normal before <u>they</u> get home from the palace!

NUTMEG: Shall I use magic?

ALL: No!

COWSLIP: OK. (Stops to think) So – what <u>is</u> 'normal' in this place?

BUTTONS: Ah – perhaps cooking the supper for their return?

NUTMEG: Oh no! The words 'panto' and 'cooking' is not good news! No way! I am not as stupid as I look!

PEASBLOSSOM: I'm afraid you are, dear. Never mind. Anyway, we really should get changed out of these things.

CINDERELLA: I don't really feel like doing any cooking. Perhaps they can have this custard pie? (On table)

NUTMEG: Panto – cooking – **custard pie**!! That's it – I'm off! (Runs away)

BUTTONS: Don't be sad; we all saw the way the Prince was looking at you. Even his sister noticed it!

COWSLIP: Yeah – you is in there!

PEASBLOSSOM: I did sense a certain electricity between you! (Cinders looks coy) I'm sure this will all have a happy ending. Come, fairies – away! (They exit off stage)

BUTTONS: Right then: I'd better get their bedrooms ready. Goodnight!

CINDERELLA: Buttons!

BUTTONS: Yes?

CINDERELLA: I think you were getting on really well with the Princess!

BUTTONS: Yeah – like <u>that's</u> going to happen! Goodnight! (Exits)

CINDERELLA: Goodnight! Right – better get this place clean. (Sings a tune from the ball)

MOTHER: (Enters and watches) I knew it. I knew it. It was you!

CINDERELLA: You made me jump! (Thinks) It was me what?

MOTHER: Don't play innocent, you scheming, ungrateful child! That tune! It was you at the ball. Admit it!

CINDERELLA: I don't know what you're …

MOTHER: You are a very poor liar. (Walks closer) It was <u>you</u> … at the ball – wearing those stupid glasses. Did you think <u>you</u> had any chance with the prince when my daughters were there to show him what <u>real</u> quality looked like?!

CINDERELLA: Me? At the ball … I mean ….

MOTHER: (suddenly thinks) Be silent! (Cunning) If it was **not** you at the ball, where are your glass slippers?

CINDERELLA: What?

MOTHER: You heard me! Where are those glass slippers?

CINDERELLA: I haven't got them – er - I mean, I …

MOTHER: As I thought. (Quietly and nastily) Your dainty feet will be the death of you, my dear. But … no time to do it now. (Thinks) I know. In … here! (Pushes Cinders into cupboard & locks door, leaving key in lock) Now nothing can stand in my way! Before tonight is out, one of my daughters will marry that prince! (EXITS laughing)

Silence. Buttons enters from side.

BUTTONS: What's going on in here? I heard noises? (To aud) What's going on? Where's Ella? Not all at once! (There is a sound at the door.)

PRINCESS (V.O.): Hello? Anyone home?

BUTTONS: (To aud) Hang on a second!

Buttons opens door. It is the Princess.

BUTTONS: But – what? How …?

PRINCESS: I knew this was the place! (Over shoulder) I was right! In here!!

She enters followed by Prince, Mrs M and Herald.

PRINCE: Hello again. Sorry to disturb you in the middle of the night.

BUTTONS: No problem, squire. How can I help?

PRINCE: Well: there was a rather lovely young lady at the ball with you earlier and – silly really – she ran off before I could get her name. So …

MRS McCHUCKER: So who was she? Real name needed. Legal reasons.

BUTTONS: With me? Well …. Errr … (To aud) If I tell them I'll lose my job! What shall I do? Shall I tell him it was Cinderella? (Business with aud) You're right – this is a horrid job anyway! Yes – I will tell you – the girl at the ball was …!

MOTHER: (Appears in doorway.) BE SILENT! Not another word. Your Majesties. (Curtsey) What an honour!

PRINCE: Lady Table - (Herald sniggers) – so sorry to disturb but …

MOTHER: No, no, no. In fact – I think I can be of assistance here.

BUTTONS: In answer to your question, your Majesty – the girl at the ball was...

MOTHER: **Enough**!! Thank you, Buttons!

BUTTONS: Buttocks! Bottom! Er! (Stamps) Buttons!

MOTHER: (nicely) That will be all.

BUTTONS: But …

MOTHER: THAT WILL BE ALL! Kindly leave us …. (Viciously but so others don't hear) **now**, or that girl will not live to see another morning. (He reluctantly exits) (She turns and is suddenly pleasant) If you are looking for the young girl to whom that slipper belongs, then look no farther. Come in, girls. (The sisters enter). Your majesty, my beautiful daughters. I believe you said that whomever that slipper fits - will be your bride? (To Herald) Mmm?

HERALD: (cautiously) Something like that; it's a bit of a blur to be honest. (Looks ill.)

MOTHER: First the fitting - then the wedding! Girls! CHAIR!

WHINGE: Me first – I'm not putting it on after her – she's got athlete's foot!

GRIPE: Well you've got bunions, corns, verrucas AND stinky feet!

WHINGE: (to prince) Mine might be a tiny bit stinky but hers are like stilton cheese smeared on a pig's bottom!

GRIPE: That's not true. Here (to Herald) you! Whose feet are the stinkiest?! (Perch on chair. Hold feet up)

HERALD: I can't really say. In fact, I can't really breathe!

MOTHER: Quick – the slipper!

HERALD: (kneeling woozily) Right, you first! (Gripe sits and the slipper is pushed hard)

GRIPE: Push harder you fool! It's almost on! There! (It is hanging off)

HERALD: Not even close!

MOTHER: (produces large scissors) Perhaps – without those toes …?

Mrs. M takes the glass slipper back and it is snatched by Whinge.

GRIPE: Yes. I'm sure those wiggly bits weren't there last night! Cut them off!

PRINCE: Enough! (Stops the amputation at the last moment)

WHINGE: (Suddenly lifts leg with shoe fitting) It fits! It fits!

PRINCESS: What? No way!

PRINCE: No! Let me see. That's not possible.

WHINGE: Well it does fit, matey; just you look! (Waves false lower leg with slipper under his nose)

PRINCESS: What a faker! (Looks round) There's something wrong here.

Where's the other girl?

PRINCE: Yes – I was here today and there was another girl! Where's the girl I met in the garden?

MOTHER: What? That girl? She's just a servant! She is nothing! Look: my daughters have charm, poise, breeding; Cinderella has <u>nothing</u> – she is just ...

BUTTONS: (dramatic entrance) Stop! Even if I <u>do</u> get the sack you must know the truth! The girl at the ball **was** the girl you met in the garden!

PRINCE: I suspected as much!

BUTTONS: But – **this awful old boot** said something nasty would happen to her if I told you! You've got to protect her!

PRINCE: So where is she? What have you done with her?!

MOTHER: (Calms) Cinderella? She left. Ages ago. Said she'd had enough. Was too lazy to do the work here, if you ask me. She left - <u>didn't she</u>, girls! (They agree)

WHINGE: Miles away by now, like.

GRIPE: No idea which, you know, direction.

BUTTONS: (to aud) Is this true? Did Cinderella leave?

PRINCE: Then where is she? (Business)

Cinderella is released from the cupboard by Mrs M. Heroic music.

PRINCE: Please. (Kneels) Will you do me the honour of ...?

HERALD: Your Majesty. May I remind you – "Whoever this slipper fits will be my bride" ...

PRINCE: I remember. (To Cinderella) Please....

CINDERELLA: I will gladly try on that glass slipper – but first, perhaps you would like the other, to make the pair! (Excitement. Hands him the other) (Cinderella sits and the slippers are fitted. Cheers.)

PRINCE: Yes! I was hoping it was you!

CINDERELLA: I always knew it was you. (Sisters groan etc.)

HERALD: Your Majesty – it's almost dawn!

PRINCE: Quickly – everyone - back to the palace!

MOTHER: (smarmy) My dear, loving, daughter. I could not be more delighted. (Pushes sisters aside) Get out of my way. (Curtsey) Allow me to be the first to congratulate you both. Now, for the wedding, I think we should...

BUTTONS: Oh – get real! (Quickly slaps cream pie on her. Cheers) To the palace!!

ACT TWO: SCENE 8: TABS (community scene)

OPTION 1: Herald Harold stays on/enters. He seizes the moment and starts his song. But Fairies enter in finale costume & stop him.

COWSLIP: Not now – we 'as to do da business and stuff!

PEASBLOSSOM: Super. My favourite bit. What shall we do?

NUTMEG: I've got a song (starts Bean Song, with actions)

ALL: NO!

HERALD: Well, we could always sing my song!

They all agree to this and get the kids up.

COWSLIP: Right then – we is going to talk to da kiddies then sing the song of Harold the Herald. Give 'im da microfonic thingy and he can starts us off. Ready then?

HERALD: Super (taps mike to test) Hello – testing. OK – here goes! (Starts but looks distressed) Oh no – all those drinks! Got to go! Sorry! Won't be a minute! (Runs off with microphone)

PEASBLOSSOM: I say – we need that microphone! Harold! Oh never mind.

NUTMEG: We don't need the microphone – we will be loud as anything! Here goes!

Before they sing they hear Harold run down stairs, door open & close, echoing steady stream of water (3 times, then drips), flushing, door, running up stairs. Embarrassed faces. They sing the song. Harold returns in time for end of song.

PEASBLOSSOM: You missed it!

HERALD: But I didn't hear anything!

COWSLIP: Maybe not – but we was hearin' you!

Herald looks at microphone in horror then runs off to get changed.

PEASBLOSSOM: What do you say, little kiddies – one more time for Harold the Herald?

Thanks and sweets.

(If time is short do not bother with the Herald business & fx in this scene)

OR 2: Business with any child dressed as fairies, princesses or princes.

SCENE 9: THE BALLROOM

Children then Chorus enter and take their bow and sit along front.

Herald and Mrs McChucker: (enter and take bows)

HERALD: My Lords, Ladies, and Gentlemen: His Royal Highness, Prince Charming and his lovely bride.

(Enter and take their bow)

MRS McCHUCKER: Er ... what is your real name, just for the security check?

CINDERELLA: My real name is just plain, simple, Ella.

PRINCE: I love it. Princess Ella.

HERALD: Please welcome her Royal Highness the Princess, and Mr Buttons.

(Enter and take their bow)

ELLA: There is just one thing …

PRINCE: Anything. What is it?

ELLA: My new mother – and my sisters. I know they were not very kind – but I do forgive them. Can they come to the ball? Just this once?

PRINCE: (shrugs) Alright. Just this once! Herald!

HERALD: Please welcome – the ugly old boot and her revolting stinky daughters!

(Enter and take their bow)

PRINCE: Anyone else?

ELLA: There were three others who tried really hard to help me.

PRINCE: Who was that?

ELLA: Well – they were fairies! (Prince shrugs and nods to Herald)

HERALD: Finally, please welcome the fairy god-mothers!

(Enter and take their bow)

PRINCE: Once more our ancient tale is told,

CINDERELLA: with an ending that is happy.

COWSLIP: So sing a song,

PEASBLOSSOM: But don't take long.

NUTMEG: I need to change my nappy.

(Music starts: "Sleeping Beauty waltz": I know you.)

RED RIDING HOOD: (enters and stands) Oy! OY!!(Music stops clumsily)

PRINCE: What? Who?

RED RIDING HOOD: Not so fast! It is me – Little Red Riding Hood! And I have a bone to pick with <u>them</u>!

(huge cannon rolled on: fuse is visibly burning – possibly a sparkler) Say your prayers, you miserable, low-down fairies!

PEASEBLOSSOM: My word! Somebody do something!

COWSLIP: Right! (Thinks) I shall panic!

NUTMEG: I shall wet myself!

MRS McCHUCKER: Stand back! I'll save you! (Grabs cannon and swings it round madly, as it points at people they panic and/or duck. Finally it is pointing at the audience. All stand back in silent horror and watch as it explodes and EITHER showers audience with confetti/tinsel.

FINALE SONG

BOW (including one for Red Riding Hood who has not had one yet)

CURTAIN

LIST OF TITLES

Click to select

1. CINDERELLA
2. ROBIN HOOD
3. DICK WHITTINGTON
4. SLEEPING BEAUTY
5. RED RIDING HOOD & THE 3 PIGS
6. THREE MEN IN A TUB
7. JACK AND THE BEANSTALK
8. HANSEL AND GRETEL
9. SNOW WHITE & 7 DWARVES

CONTACT INFORMATION
and PERFORMANCE RIGHTS here:

PANTOSCRIPTS.ME.UK

ROBIN HOOD - THE PANTO

From an original script by Chris Lane & Simon Dunn
Updated Chris Lane 2018

ACT ONE: SCENE ONE: SHERWOOD FOREST

A lush glade in Sherwood Forest; the home of the outlaws. There are trees on both sides and at the rear, where there is also a view of the Sheriff's castle in the distance. There is a pot over a fire upstage and assorted logs, etc, on either side downstage, to sit on. All the **MERRY MEN** are on stage, going about their normal daily routine. Some are making arrows, sharpening swords, mending clothes, etc. There are local wenches there.

OPENING NUMBER: ALL During the song the stage should be filled with busy activity, but not dancing. **LITTLE JOHN** and **FRIAR TUCK** are practising with staffs, banging heads, fingers. Sudden commotion. Will Scarlet rushes in.

WILL SCARLET: Quick! Stop all the singing! Soldiers in the forest! (runs out)

FRIAR TUCK: Soldiers! To arms! To arms!! (Little John kindly offers his 2 arms) No, Little John: get your weapons! Much! Quick! Douse the fire – they'll see the smoke!

MUCH: Right! (Grabs bucket and throws it toward fire but gets Little John, who points angrily at his wet face)

FRIAR TUCK: Little John! Your make up is fine! Much! Get that fire out!

MUCH: Right! (Repeat water over John who points at wet face)

FRIAR TUCK: Little John: we can't play charades now! And Much! Get that fire out!

MUCH: Right! (Repeat water over John who protests violently)

DEREK: Little John's gone mad!

MUCH: Not again! I know what'll cool him down! (Grabs bucket and throws on Little John, who stands in shocked stillness)

Will Scarlet returns cheerfully.

WILL SCARLET: Oops – sorry everyone! My mistake! Not soldiers! It's just Robin returning!

FRIAR TUCK: Not to worry! No harm done!

LITTLE JOHN: No harm done?! No harm?!

FRIAR TUCK: Stopping flapping about, Little John. And look at that fire – is that welcoming for Robin? Get it going again, there a good chap!

WILL SCARLET: (notices audience) And who are this lot then, Tuck? New recruits?

FRIAR TUCK: They're guests, Will, and we're ignoring them! (To audience) Good company! Welcome to Sherwood Forest! Home of the fearless champion of freedom - ROBIN HOOD!! (All cheer)

LITTLE JOHN: Here in Sherwood Forest we live the life of OUTLAWS! We rob! (Agreement)

WILL SCARLET: We eat! (Loud agreement)

LITTLE JOHN: We fight! (Louder cheering)

WILL SCARLET: We drink! (Loudest cheers)

MUCH: And nobody makes us change our pants! (Sporadic cheers & shuffling away)

FRIAR TUCK: But there is one thing which spoils our life here! (All agree)

LITTLE JOHN: Yes, yes ...Not half! Ha!... No Wi-Fi! (they look at him) No? What is it then?

FRIAR TUCK: Why, you know what it is, Little John; it's the wickedest man in the land

MUCH: The cruellest man in the land.

WILL SCARLET The ugliest man in the land! (General agreement)

LITTLE JOHN: Who's that then? SOMEONE LOCAL / TOPICAL like Donald Trump.

FRIAR TUCK: No - that evil devil - the Sheriff of Nottingham!!

MEN blow 'raspberries'.

(SOUND OF DISTANT HORN in traditional Robin Hood manner.)

MUCH: 'Tis Robin! (General excitement)

FRIAR TUCK: (to audience) That hunting horn means that our leader, Robin Hood, is returning to camp. We must welcome him in proper fashion!

WILL SCARLET: Yes, indeed! When Robin comes into the clearing, everyone must shout - as loud as possible: 'Hello - Robin!!' (Agreement) (to aud) And you lot - will you help us shout 'Hello Robin'? (Shield eyes & look out) Hello? Is there anybody there? I said, WILL YOU HELP ME SHOUT, 'HELLO ROBIN'?!

FRIAR TUCK: They're not very loud tonight (this afternoon), are they, John? Perhaps we should have a practice?

MAN: I know! Little John can pretend to be Robin, and when he comes on they can all shout 'Hello Robin'! (They look dubious)

FRIAR TUCK: Great idea! Go on then, John.

LITTLE JOHN: What?

FRIAR TUCK: You go off – then come back.

LITTLE JOHN: Right. (Goes off. Voice from wings) What was after 'Go off'?

FRIAR TUCK: Come back!

LITTLE JOHN: (enters) What?

All shout 'Hello Robin'.

FRIAR TUCK: Well, that wasn't very loud. We'll try that one more time, and I want everyone to shout their loudest. Try taking your sweets out!

WILL SCARLET: (shields eyes and looks at front row) No, dear, he said take your SWEETS out - not your TEETH! (Pretend to listen) What? No we can't put the lights on now; you can look for them in the interval. Right then, off you go again, John!

LITTLE JOHN: Make your minds up: 'off – on – off – on' ... (exits grumbling)

Little John enters. All shout 'Hello Robin'.

FRIAR TUCK: Much better! And now, get ready to shout again, because here comes our real leader - ROBIN HOOD!!

ROBIN HOOD: Enters: all shout.

ROBIN HOOD. What a welcome! What a day!

FRIAR TUCK: You seem excited, Robin.

LITTLE JOHN: Is it good news from the forest? Something valuable heading this way?

ROBIN HOOD: Yes! The most valuable of cargoes!

MUCH: I hope it's not another wagon-load of jelly babies? (General agreement & stomach clutching) I still see them in my nightmares – huge red ones, striding towards me (demonstrates briefly, frightening Derek)

ROBIN HOOD: No: not more jelly babies!

LITTLE JOHN: Is it gold?

MUCH: Jewels?

WILL SCARLET: i-Phones? (Strange looks from others)

ROBIN HOOD: No. Far better than any of these! It is the most beautiful maiden!

LITTLE JOHN: Oh no! He's going to get all sloppy! Blow that; who wants to see my scars again? This big one's from my <u>first</u> wife. And this one's... (All but Tuck and Robin move aside)

FRIAR TUCK: A beautiful maiden, eh? But steady on, Robin. Don't forget - we're outlaws. No decent girl is going to want anything to do with us.

ROBIN HOOD: I know all that, Tuck, but ... when I saw her face ...

OPTION FOR SONG: ROBIN HOOD, possibly Merry Men support as appropriate. Something like Monkees: 'I'm a believer' or James Blunt 'You're beautiful'.

FRIAR TUCK: Robin; was this maid travelling alone?

ROBIN HOOD: No, there were two others with her, and half a dozen soldiers, and a cart piled high with wooden chests - possibly full of (whispers) gold!

LITTLE JOHN: GOLD! (All MERRY MEN leap up and gather around)

ROBIN HOOD: Aye, Little John - gold! Well, men. What do say? Feel like a fight?!

MERRY MEN: AYE!

LITTLE JOHN: Shall we hit 'em with our staffs? (Action)

MERRY MEN: AYE!!

LITTLE JOHN: Shall we punch 'em with our fists? (Action)

MERRY MEN: AYE!

LITTLE JOHN: Shall we slice 'em and dice 'em?! (Waves knife)

MERRY MEN: Urgh, not likely. (Various noises & actions of disgust)

LITTLE JOHN: And I shall lead you into battle with our Marching Song!! (Strikes 'singing' pose. Band starts up 'Men in tights!' Or 'Give me some men who are stout hearted men')

ROBIN HOOD: Aah. perhaps we'll just creep up on them? Element of surprise and all that, eh, Little John? (Little John looks very disappointed) Oh, all right then. We'll sing - but just as far as the edge of the forest

MUSIC: part of SONG.' ALL EXIT

ENTER **ALAN A'DALE** He is dressed VERY boldly in a minstrel's costume, with tights, pointed red shoes, large Tudor padded 'bits' around tops of his legs. He has two large pockets on the front of his jerkin, & a mandolin which he can neither tune nor play.

ALAN A'DALE: 'Oh, green sleeves, on my left and right ('twang'), (mimes wiping nose on sleeves) ('twang') 'I must go and buy, a new hankie tonight'

This looks like the right place - it looks lived in!

(Wanders idly to the front of the stage where he looks up, surveys the audience, then does a 'double take' at seeing the audience and jumps back.)

Crikey! Where did you lot come from? Creeping up on me like that!

(Covers eyes to look at them)

Let's have a better look! (House lights rise slightly) OooOOooHH! Someone's been in here with the Ugly Stick! (Chance to abuse any local dignitary or notable in the audience)

Quick! Put the lights out again! That's better!

Perhaps you lot can help me? I'm the famous singer: Alan A'Dale. You might know my hit song: 'If I'd wanted an ugly girlfriend I'd have moved to (local place)'. No?

Anyway: I want to join Robin Hood and his merry men so I've come into the forest to find them. (Looks around) Is this where they live? (Business) Is it? Super! Nobody here: they must have gone shopping.

Never mind: while I wait for them to come back I'll sing one of my more popular songs –

BUT - if you see any outlaws you must shout and tell me.

Will you shout if you see any outlaws? (No response) Hello?? Are you DEAD? YOU'LL HAVE TO SHOUT LOUDER THAN THAT! Will you shout if you see any outlaws? (Response) Great! Here we go then. This is my version of (A current popular song that can be easily massacred)

SINGS. Two outlaws start to creep up behind him, very feebly disguised behind small, leafy branches as some sort of camouflage. They run off at the shouting.

ALAN A'DALE: Don't interrupt! I was just getting to the note I could play!
(Repeat action)
They don't do this for (current singer)!
(Repeat)
What is the matter with you people? You can't ALL be music critics! I'll give you one last chance to hear a bit of culture.
(Outlaws come on again but this time they crouch down behind their branches and stay on stage.)
What is it? What's all the noise about?
(Looks around but sees nothing. Behind his back the outlaws shuffle closer.)
What are you shouting about? Eh? What? Where?
(Has good look round but still sees nothing)
Outlaws?! I can't see any outlaws! Where are they? Where?
(Two 'shrubs' shuffle stage left)
Over here? (Looks Stage Right) (Then REPEAT IN REVERSE)
I don't think there's anybody here!
(Outlaws throw aside branches and creep right up to Alan)

No - I think you're just teasing me!
(Outlaws grab Alan and lift him up so his legs swing up and out toward the audience. He shrieks in alarm!)

   ROBIN HOOD :(ENTERS with **LITTLE JOHN, FRIAR TUCK** and few other men including children **Very LITTLE JOHN, Very Very Little John** and **DEREK**.) So! You've captured something too! What is it?

   ALAN A'DALE: Unhand me, ruffians! This one finger of mine can be deadly!

MERRY MEN: Ooooohh! (Drop him)

LOCAL NAME: One finger! Deadly?

ALAN A'DALE: Yes indeed - if I stick it in the electric socket! Bam!

LITTLE JOHN: Er - why are you dressed like that?

   ALAN A'DALE: I will have you know that I .... am a Wandering Minstrel!

   FRIAR TUCK: A Wandering Minstrel?

MERRY MAN: Sounds like a lost chocolate!

   LITTLE JOHN: Can you prove what you say?

   ALAN A'DALE: Most definitely! Ahum! (Clears throat; starts to sing & dance the Macarena – no choice; needed later in show!)

MERRY MAN 2: What on earth is that noise?

ALAN A'DALE: It's the Macarena - everyone's been doing it for years!

MERRY MAN 3: Not round 'ere they aint!

   ROBIN HOOD: Enough! How on earth did YOU get a job as a minstrel?!

   ALAN A'DALE: I don't know really - it wasn't my first choice. I just went into the Job Centre and said 'I don't mind what job you give me I know I'll be outstanding in any field! So they gave me a job as a scarecrow! (Adopts pose)

   LITTLE JOHN: Pah! Enough of this foolery! (Draws dagger) Quick now - tell us ... what brought you to Sherwood Forest?

   ALAN A'DALE. A number seven bus, but I had to change at (local town) and...

LOCAL NAME: No, he means WHY did you come here?

LITTLE JOHN: And answer true or (pulls finger across throat & makes horrid face)

   ALAN A'DALE: You'll take my scarf?

LITTLE JOHN: No! Just tell him!

ALAN A'DALE: Gulp! I.. I .. I've come to be an outlaw!

   ROBIN HOOD: Ah! And why do you want to be an outlaw?!

   ALAN A'DALE: So I can forget ... a woman!

      LITTLE JOHN: Ooo0Ooo0OOooH! (John turns aside wistfully)

FRIAR TUCK: Don't mind Little John. He came here came to the forest BECAUSE he forgot a woman!

LOCAL NAME: He forgot his wife's birthday! (All pull horror faces)

LITTLE JOHN: Do you want to see the scars?

FRIAR TUCK: Not right now, John.

Tell us; who is the maid who has driven you to this desperate step?

ALAN A'DALE: The fair Maid, **LUCY** of 'local name'.

FRIAR TUCK: Ah, I see - and she didn't love you?

ALAN A'DALE: Oh yes - not half! But it was her Uncle. He threw me out!

LITTLE JOHN: That sounds reasonable.

ALAN A'DALE: No! He threw me out the window!

ROBIN HOOD: Who is her Uncle?

ALAN A'DALE: He's that old misery-guts: The Sheriff of Nottingham!

(Much raspberry blowing, much to his alarm and he has to wipe himself off)

Bleugh! All I said was 'Sheriff of Nottingham'! (Repeat)

FRIAR TUCK: We don't use his name in this forest!

ALAN A'DALE: (to audience) Urgh! You could have warned me! I must make sure I don't say Sh... (all start to pucker up to blow, but ...)

Ha-ha! Fooled you! You thought I was going to say Sheriff! (Raspberries!) Arrr!!

ROBIN HOOD: Enough of these terrible tales. You'll soon forget your broken heart here.

I am Robin of Loxley, known in these parts as Robin Hood. And you?

ALAN A'DALE: I am Alan A'Dale. Known in these parts as 'Oy, you there!' And I recognise this fellow, (to **Very LITTLE JOHN**) you must be Little John.

ROBIN HOOD: No, that is **Very** Little John; this is **Very Very** Little John and THIS (to tiny merry man)

ALAN A'DALE: Let me guess. **Very Very Very LITTLE JOHN**?

ROBIN HOOD: No. .... **DEREK.** (indicates John) THIS is **LITTLE JOHN!**

ALAN A'DALE: Why do they call him **Little** John? Is it personal and embarrassing? Tee hee.

ROBIN HOOD: It's the name he was given in prison

ALAN A'DALE: Oh - so it's a 'nick' name'!

LITTLE JOHN: I heard that!!

ALAN A'DALE: My! Haven't you outlaws got big ears!

LITTLE JOHN: No. (To aud) Not since Noddy paid the ransom! Ba-boom! (All stamp and extend a hand in the traditional ba-boom manner!)

WILL SCARLET and **MUCH** ENTER

ROBIN HOOD: Ah! Will Scarlet. Meet our new colleague: Alan A'Dale.

WILL SCARLET: Do we call you Alan or do you prefer A'Dale?

ALAN A'DALE: Frankly, Scarlet, I don't **give** a damn!

MUCH: And I'm Much the Miller!

ALAN A'DALE: Ah, yes! I knew your twin brother - **MUCH the Same!**

ROBIN HOOD: Enough of this nonsense! Here come the prisoners!

ENTER **MAID MARION** and more **MERRY MEN**

MAID MARION: Unhand me you brute! (Swings punch; sends man holding her flying)

ROBIN HOOD: Woah! Stand back, men! We've caught a wild cat!

MAID MARION: Better a wild cat than a gang of APES, swinging through the trees!! (She swings a punch at Robin who ducks. It hits Will, who falls spectacularly)

MAID MARION: Out of my way! (Tries to walk away but Robin blocks her path. A moment to look into each other's eyes sloppily) You can't keep us here like this!

And where's my sister?

LITTLE JOHN: Sister?! You mean there's another one like this?!
Where is she? Robin! You must introduce me to the sister!

ROBIN HOOD: I'm not sure that's such a good...

LITTLE JOHN: Go on, Robin! Here – you can have my last jelly babies! (Gives bag)

ROBIN HOOD: Alright then! Bring the sister in!

ENTER **MAID BADLY with last Merry Man**.

MAID BADLY: OoH! A barbecue! Lovely! (Marches up to John and grins horribly at him. He jumps away in alarm then snatches jelly babies back from Robin. Badly spots the sweets.) Oooh! Jelly babies! I've heard about men like you. Come here and tempt me!

MAID MARION: Sister. Come away from them! You people are going to be very sorry! Do you know who we are?!

MUCH: (a moment's thought) You're not Spice Girls, on another reunion OR similar, are you?

MAID MARION: Certainly not! I am Maid Marion. (Robin bows deeply to her) And my sister - is Maid Badly.

LITTLE JOHN: You can say that again!

MAID BADLY: Watch it, matey!

MAID MARION: And we are on our way to stay with our Uncle who happens to be the man who is going to send all his soldiers into this forest to find us; because our Uncle is none other than the Sh...

ALAN A'DALE: Shhh....!

MAID MARION: None other than the Sh...

ALAN A'DALE: Shhhhhh.. shame about the weather today! (hissing to Marion) Don't say it!

MAID MARION: Don't say what?!

ALAN A'DALE: Don't say 'Sheriff'! (Raspberries)

ROBIN HOOD: You think that we're frightened of that old windbag?! Hah! We spit in his face!

ALAN A'DALE: (wiping face with large hanky from breast pocket) Well that's no idle threat!

ROBIN HOOD: Tonight you good ladies will be the guests of Robin Hood! Prepare the supper!

MAID BADLY: See, I told you it was a barbecue. What are we having?!

WILL SCARLET: Local produce - purloined steak!

MAID BADLY: You mean sirloin steak!

WILL SCARLET: No - purloined - we nicked it! (To aud) It's a panto, alright?!

MAID BADLY: I know what you big, strong, hairy men need! Home cooking! Where's my basket?

(From nearest wings is handed basket with cloth over top)

A lovely cake! Made with my own bare hands! Here you are!

(She hands one slice of cake to John, who, amazed at its weight drops it with a heavy thud.)

Never mind, here's another piece! (She hands it to Will. He struggles to hold it then hits it on the head or nearby man who collapses backwards)

How about you? (To Alan) You need feeding up!

(All watch in horror as Alan is about to eat it. At the last moment he suddenly gasps in amazement at something above and behind them all, so they all turn to look up. He then - with great flourish so the audience don't miss it - places the cake carefully in his breast pocket.)

ALAN A'DALE: Delicious!

MAID MARION: You ate it?! (Looks of respect from everyone)
(Lookout rushes in)

LOOKOUT: Soldiers! Soldiers coming!

MAID MARION: What did I tell you! Soon you gorillas will be swinging from the battlements of Nottingham Castle!

ROBIN HOOD: They have to catch us first! Arm yourselves, men! Good Friar: you and our new friend (Alan) stay here to keep an eye on our guests. We don't want them wandering off and 'getting lost'!

LITTLE JOHN: Let's go! (Starts to sing again)

ROBIN HOOD: Er ...on second thoughts, John - perhaps you'd better stay too.

All EXIT except a disappointed **LITTLE JOHN**, **ALAN A'DALE**, **MAID MARION**, **MAID BADLY**, **FRIAR TUCK**. Derek is nearby.

MAID MARION: Great ape.

MAID BADLY: I think he's rather cute.

MAID MARION: Well, he's still a thief and an outlaw!

FRIAR TUCK: It depends who you talk to. If you ask the ordinary people around here what they think of Robin Hood...

ALAN A'DALE: That's right. Everyone knows the famous song about Robin Hood!

LITTLE JOHN: Yeah! (Goes to sing but can't) Which one is that then?

FRIAR TUCK: I know the one he means -
Robin Hood - Robin Hood - Riding through the glen.
Robin Hood - Robin -

LITTLE JOHN: What's he riding through?

FRIAR TUCK: A glen! It's a Scottish valley! Let's try again -
Robin Hood - Robin -

LITTLE JOHN: What's he doing in Scotland?

FRIAR TUCK: I don't know - it's just a song. Now are we going to sing it or not?

ALAN A'DALE: Let's try again:
Robin Hood - Robin Hood - Riding through the glen.
Robin Hood - Robin - with his band of men, feared ...

LITTLE JOHN: What a cheek! No we're not!

ALAN A'DALE: No you're not what?

LITTLE JOHN: We're not bandy men. Look at my legs, they're not bandy!

(**DEREK** peeps through his bandy legs)

DEREK: Peep-oh!

MAID MARION: Good grief. What a shower!

FRIAR TUCK: Now stop this messing about. (To aud) I bet you lot know the song, don't you?!

ALAN A'DALE: If they were born before 1960 they will! (they look out)

LITTLE JOHN: Born before 1900 that one!

(option of screen with words here)

FRIAR TUCK: OK: it goes:
Robin Hood - Robin Hood - Riding through the glen.
Robin Hood - Robin Hood- with his band of men,
Feared by the bad, loved by the good,
Robin Hood - Robin Hood - Robin Hood.

ALAN A'DALE: Easy! Right. Then you can all to help with the chorus. Here we go. Music please!

They sing the song, taking turns with the verses. SONG AND COMIC DANCE

ROBIN HOOD: (ENTERS QUICKLY) Quick everyone! The Sheriff is coming!!

(Bustles them offstage, all BLOWING RASPBERRIES.)

Fanfare. Sound of horses. ENTER **SHERIFF**, **HUGO FIRST** and **GUY De TOURS**.

SHERIFF is being carried on a wooden horse (on wheels), supported like a litter by the soldiers. Behind comes **QUIPAT**, providing sound effects with two coconut halves.

SHERIFF: Gently! Gently! You're shaking my noble personage! One more bump and I'll have you both hung up by the... (Deliberate bump by men) Argh! (Pats horse) Whoah there, Camilla! (He dismounts and turns on the men.) I told you what would happen if you broke the speed limit in Nottingham again!

GUY De TOURS: We weren't going that fast!

SHERIFF: Fast?! QUIPAT! How fast were they going?

QUIPAT: Eh? Aaah... Un moment! (Spanish accent) (taps coconuts, faster and faster, jogging in time, until satisfied he has the right tempo) (With suitable accent!) About twelve leagues an hour!

SHERIFF: Exactly! Two leagues an hour over the speed limit!

HUGO FIRST: I appeal!

SHERIFF: Not to ME you don't! QUIPAT! Check the sat-nav!

QUIPAT: Eh?

SHERIFF: You know – the sat nav!

QUIPAT: Oh yes! (Lifts horse's tail and puts in hand OR taps imaginary buttons.) (here a voice could say 'Please make a U-turn now') (Looks in) It's here - twelve leagues an hour!

SHERIFF: You know what this means, don't you!

Men: NO! Not...!

SHERIFF: Yes! Two weeks, trying to collect taxes in 'local place'. HaHaHa!!

SHERIFF: Now, where are we? (Looks around) At that speed we should have met Marion and her hideous sister ages ago!

QUIPAT: (nervously, seeing that they are in the outlaws' camp) Perhaps they have been captured by .... by outlaws!

GUY DeTOURS: Outlaws! Har! (draws sword and stamps about) Come on then outlaws! Who wants a taste of cold steel?!

HUGO FIRST: Ooh! I'll have a taste! (Bites end off Guy's sword)

GUY DeTOURS: (stares at sword, bursts into tears) My mummy gave me that!

SHERIFF: Stop your wailing, you dismal dung-beetles! (Strides across the stage thoughtfully.) I hope that nothing unpleasant has happened to the Maid Marion!

QUIPAT: So do I - she's very nice! (could hold the coconuts to chest rather rudely?)

SHERIFF. Idiot! I care nothing for the girl! I have a pernicious plot!

QUIPAT: Oh dear; I am sorry to hear that. A what?

SHERIFF: A pernicious plot! Listen. I plan to kidnap Maid Marion, and then write a letter to her rich father, pretending to be that villain, Robin Hood!

QUIPAT: Her father is pretending to be Robin Hood?

SHERIFF. No, you fool! I will pretend to be Robin Hood - and I will say that I have captured Marion, and I will not let her go until he sends me a thousand gold coins. Then, when her father has sent the money, we (makes the double finger "quote" gesture) 'dispose of her'.... forever! Teehee!

QUIPAT: 'Dispose of her'? (Makes the quote gesture but upside down, which looks rather rude. Sheriff corrects him rather embarrassed) What about her sister - MAID BADLY? How many duck eggs will Robin Hood want for her?

SHERIFF: Badly?! I should think her father would pay to get <u>rid</u> of her! She poisoned him once with her cooking. They had to send for the doctor!

QUIPAT: What did he say?

SHERIFF: He said it was a severe case of 'Culinary Thrombosis'!

QUIPAT: And what's that then?

SHERIFF: A clot in the kitchen!

QUIPAT: So do we (Makes the quote gesture sideways) 'dispose' of her too?

SHERIFF: Silence! Here comes my niece - she must know nothing of this plot!

ENTER **LUCY** looking exhausted.

LUCY: Good grief, Uncle; how am I supposed to keep up with you! You know there's a speed-limit here! (Sherriff glares at men) (Lucy looks around) So why have we stopped here?

QUIPAT: Ha! Your Uncle was just telling me he has a persistent spot about him kidnapping the Maid M ....

SHERIFF: (Stamps on foot.) We were waiting for you to catch up, my dear child!

LUCY: Hmmm. (Does not believe him.) Really.

QUIPAT: She is still cross with you. (goes closer) I think she has guessed you threw her boyfriend out of the window.

SHERIFF: She's just over-sensitive. I did open the window first!

LUCY: But isn't this forest a bit dangerous for you? Isn't this is where those outlaws hang about?

SHERIFF: Outlaws? Dangerous? Pah! (Strolls casually to one side and stands next to a tree) My dear child, there isn't an outlaw within fifty leagues of here!

(Sound of flying arrow. Arrow lands with a solid thud beside ear. On a spring!)

ROBIN HOOD: (ENTERS with bow in hand. It has been done by swinging in with one foot in a loop on the end of a rope!) Not so. As you can see, we are far closer than fifty leagues!

SHERIFF: (jumping behind soldiers) Don't just stand there like a queue at (local establishment like Tescoes) Seize him! (As they step forward reluctantly **LITTLE JOHN, FRIAR TUCK & WILL SCARLET** enter. Soldiers step backwards and bump into Sheriff.)

ROBIN HOOD. It would seem we are equally matched - at least in numbers, Sheriff! (Loud raspberries from MERRY MEN.)

SHERIFF: I wish you wouldn't do that! And it's <u>Mr</u> Sheriff to you!

ROBIN HOOD: Whatever: but at least we have spoiled yet another of your evil plans!

QUIPAT: Ah! He heard you!

SHERIFF: (Shushing QUIPAT then crossing to Robin.) My evil plan? What can you be talking about? (quieter once close enough not to be heard by **LUCY**) What a rotten trick - listening to a chap's secret plots from behind a tree!

ROBIN HOOD: Not as rotten as your plan to blame me for your own foul crime! But I forgive you - because the girls will be staying here, in the safety of Sherwood Forest!

ENTER **MAID MARION, MAID BADLY**.

MAID BADLY: Look! It's Grotty Notty and his little chums!

MAID MARION: Now we'll see who has the last laugh! (Starts toward Sheriff but Robin stops her) Let go of me!

ROBIN HOOD. But you heard what the Sheriff was saying! You heard what he planned to do!

MAID MARION: I heard nothing! Did you hear anything, sister?

MAID BADLY: All I could hear was this fat oaf's tummy rumbling! (Hits Tuck)

MAID MARION: This is just some feeble trick to avoid the punishment you deserve! Look at this man (Indicates Sherriff who looks innocent) - does he LOOK like a kidnapper?!

MERRY MEN: Yes!

SHERIFF: Oh no I don't!

MERRY MEN AND AUDIENCE repeat business THREE times.

ALAN A'DALE: Enters rapidly

ALAN A'DALE: More soldiers coming! Dozens of them! (Sees **LUCY**)

ALAN & LUCY: You!

ROBIN HOOD: This isn't the end of this!

SHERIFF: No, there are another five scenes to go yet! (Nose to nose)

ROBIN HOOD: We'll be meeting again - very soon!

SHERIFF: (snarling) I can hardly wait! (Loud) Back to Nottingham! (To aud) I have an important letter to write! Hahahaha...sneer, hiss, etc EXITS

EVERYONE EXITS (Sherriff & Marion etc one way. Merry Men another), EXCEPT **ALAN A'DALE** AND **LUCY**.

LUCY: Alan! What IS going on?! I don't see you for days then you turn up here - with these cut-throats!

ALAN A'DALE. They're not cut-throats; they're the only honest people I've met since I came to Nottingham! Except you of course.

LUCY: I waited hours for you the other evening and you never bothered to show up.

ALAN A'DALE: That's because your Uncle threw me out the window!!!

LUCY: What is this? Be rude to my Uncle week? All these terrible stories about him.

ALAN A'DALE: Come off it! You know what he's like! Don't you remember the time he found that rude poem about him on the toilet wall? He changed all the loo-paper for sand-paper, and said 'That'll wipe the smile off their faces!'.

LUCY: Oh, yes. I remember that!

ALAN A'DALE: Anyone who could stoop that low wouldn't think twice about kidnapping!

LUCY: But, if you're right Marion and Badly are in terrible danger!

ALAN A'DALE: Robin Hood will have a plan to save them! But it might be (gulp) dangerous!

Suitable intro into DUET.

ENTER ALL THE **MERRY MEN, ROBIN HOOD,** ETC.

ROBIN HOOD: Yes! There he is! Oh! And the Maid LUCY! No offence - but can we trust her?

ALAN A'DALE: LUCY? I would trust her with something local/topical (Brexit?).

ROBIN HOOD: Good, because she is vital to my plan! With Lucy's help, YOU are about to lead our attack on Nottingham Castle to rescue Maid Marion!

ALAN A'DALE: Me?! I'm just a minstrel!

ROBIN HOOD: Exactly! And you have a stout heart - that is what counts!

SONG: repeat of marching song

ROBIN HOOD: (holding sword high) TO NOTTINGHAM!!

ALL WAVE THEIR WEAPONS AND CHEER AS THE CURTAIN CLOSES.

SCENE 2: SOMEWHERE IN THE CASTLE

QUIPAT, Guy and Hugo are lined up. Sheriff is pacing angrily to and fro.

SHERIFF: You cretinous creatures! You moronic maggots! When I send you out to collect taxes - I expect you to come back with that funny little round stuff called MONEY!! Not some pathetic story about 'poor peasants' and a load of old junk!! I mean - what on earth IS this?!

HUGO FIRST: (hands him bag of sweets) Errr...I think they're jelly babies!

SHERIFF: (snatching bag and poking about inside) What use are these to me?! Someone has already bitten the heads off!

QUIPAT! How Much have you collected?

(QUIPAT looks vague then suddenly remembers and produces a false leg and holds it up proudly)

What on earth is that?!

QUIPAT: It was the only thing one old peasant had left. He even threatened me - he said that if I took it, he'd take me to court!

SHERIFF: So what did you say?

QUIPAT: I told him he didn't have a leg to stand on and could hop it!! (Laughs & hops, gradually losing enthusiasm as ...)

SHERIFF: (slowly and menacing) Was that supposed to be a 'joke', QUIPAT?

QUIPAT: Oui.

SHERIFF: You know my views on 'jokes', QUIPAT.

QUIPAT: Oui.

SHERIFF: The usual punishment.

QUIPAT: Oui. (QUIPAT hits himself on head with leg)

SHERIFF: (Stares at Guy.) And what taxes have you brought me? Hmm?

Guy De Tours: Errrrr....

SHERIFF: I sent you out to get results, man! I expect results!

Guy De Tours: Nottingham Forest 3, Arsenal 4 (or similar). 'Local minor team' 8, Liverpool nil. (Gratefully receives stamp on foot) Thank you, sir.

SHERIFF: Has none of you got any money at all?!

Hugo First: I recently had a little windfall!

SHERIFF: Then you'd better open a window!

QUIPAT! I want some good news. NOW!

QUIPAT: Err... ah, oui! The new soldiers have arrived.

SHERIFF: Soldiers?

QUIPAT: Oui! You remember – from e-bay (or similar)

CHOICE HERE: OLDER LADIES (AMAZONS) OR VERY SMALL CHILDREN (BONSAI WARRIORS)?

CHOICE ONE: AMAZONS:

SHERIFF: What - the terrifying, bloodthirsty Amazon Warrior Women? That was ages ago! Are they here? Then send then to me!

(QUIPAT EXITS)

Ha - real warriors. Now Robin Hood will meet his match!

(Smartens himself up) Cor - WARRIOR WOMEN!

QUIPAT: (ENTERS embarrassed) Arr. Umm ... Here they are. Come in, er, Amazon warriors.

ENTER a string of very non-warrior ancient women in 'old lady' hats but with horns & Viking wings. They are busy knitting. The last has a walking frame, some have sticks.

SHERIFF: What?! Who are you lot?!

Woman 1: We are ferocious - Cough - ferocious - Cough - Oh, you tell him Mable.

Mable: We are ferocious fighting Amazons.

SHERIFF: (Drags QUIPAT to one side) What IS this?!

QUIPAT: It's not my fault! You know what it's like buying things off e-bay!

SHERIFF: Good grief. And what - pray tell me - experience you - Ahem - 'fighting warriors' have had?

Woman 2: Ooh loads. There was the Battle of 'Local' Village Hall Jumble Sale.

Woman 3: Nasty business that.

Woman 4: And Phyllis here (push her forward to show medal) she won that for something local

Woman 5: Yes, and there was that business in the Doctor's waiting room when that fellow tried to take the last seat, you know that man with the glasses, and you said to him, or was it ...

SHERIFF: Silence! You lot aren't warriors!

Woman 6: We are. We even got a fighting song for going into battle!

Woman 7: Show him girls.

SONG (stirring military thing, maybe changed words?)

SHERIFF: Enough! QUIPAT! Take them away!

QUIPAT: Right you are. Come on now, you old battle-axes! Off you go!

Woman 6: Don't you push us sonny - or you'll be sorry! Men Laugh

CHOICE 2: JUNIOR WARRIORS

SHERIFF: What - the terrifying, bloodthirsty Banzai Ninja Warriors from Japan? That was ages ago! Are they here? Then send then to me! (QUIPAT EXITS) Ha - real Banzai warriors. Now Robin Hood will meet his match! Cor - Ninjas! Banzaii!! (makes karate motions)

QUIPAT: ENTERS: Arr. Umm ... Here they are. Come in, er, Ninja warriors.

ENTER a string of very small Ninja-style children

SHERIFF: What?! Who are you lot?!

Very Small Child 1: We are ferocious Ninja warriors. (sucks thumb & cuddles teddy)

SHERIFF: What?! What?! Show me the delivery note! Quipat! I told you to order me fierce Banzai Ninja Warriors!!

QUIPAT: I did – I did! Look – it says here (number) Banzai Warriors!

SHERIFF: To: Sherriff of Nottingham: (number) Bonsai Warriors. Quipat! This says BONSAI warriors. Bonsai – like the tiny little trees!!

QUIPAT: Is that wrong? (looks at paper both ways up) It's not my fault - you know what it's like buying things off e-bay!

SHERIFF: Good grief. And what - pray tell me - experience you - Ahem - 'fighting warriors' have had?

Child 2: Ooh loads. There was the Battle of (name of local playing field or infant school).

Child 3: I hurt my knee. Do you want to kiss it better?

SHERIFF: No I do not want .... Quipat!! At least that one has a medal. Mmm?

Child 4: Finger painting. It was a boat and a cloud and the sun. I can't do bunnies.

Child 5: We are genuine Bonsai Warriors. If you keep us for 15 years we will grow into ..

SHERIFF: Fifteen years! Silence! You lot aren't warriors!

Child 6: We are. We even have a fighting song for going into battle!

Child 7: Show him kids!

SONG (stirring military thing, OR King Foo Fighting, maybe changed words?)

SHERIFF: Enough! QUIPAT! Take them away!

QUIPAT: Right you are. Come on runny nosed brats! Off you go!

Child 8: Don't you push us, granddad - or you'll be sorry! Men Laugh

QUIPAT: I'll push you if I want you freckle-faced toddlers! Ha ha! (Exits pushing them)

SHERIFF: Now then. (Terrible screams & crashes from wings. QUIPAT returns. He has soiled nappy on his head & a teddy in his mouth. He is limping and groaning) Stop messing about, you useless article! (Pulls baby bottle from Quipat's bottom)

END OF CHOICES

BACK TO THE MAIN STORY

QUIPAT: I'm sorry but I am paid to push! I am a highly trained shover. Ha ha! (Exits pushing them)

SHERIFF: Now then. (Terrible screams & crashes from wings. QUIPAT returns. He has scarves around his head. There are two knitting needles through his ears, and the walking frame or a bent walking stick is around his neck. He is limping and groaning) Stop messing about, you useless article! Come here! Let's get back to the plot! Have you written the ransom note to Marion's father yet?

QUIPAT: Yes, yes, yes! I've got it here! (Proudly) I wrote it myself! (Pulls out scroll and hands to Sheriff who reads it)

SHERIFF: QUIPAT - was orange the only colour wax crayon you had? (Sneers at happily nodding minion: if QUIPAT is French you can add: 'Orange, oui' with the sheriff saying 'Then you should drink more water!') What does it say? 'Dear Marion's Dad' (stares at QUIPAT) 'Me and the lads has got your 'door-turs', 'door-turs'?

QUIPAT:Non – dorturrrrs. You have to roll your R's.

SHERIFF: (Looks at own bum confused) Hmm, and - if you does not cough up the monkey. Monkey?!

QUIPAT: (checking scroll) Ah – that is a mistake. Money!

SHERIFF: ...cough up the money by next 'munff'. Idiot! There's only one 'f' in 'munf'! (To aud) You will never know how carefully I said that. (Back to letter), blah-blah-blah, yours sincerely, 'singed'. Singed?

QUIPAT: Signed!

SHERIFF: Signed Ruben the Hod. Who's Ruben the Hod?! Sounds more like a Jewish bricklayer! Never mind, I don't suppose the real outlaws can write any better; it'll fool Marion's father. Soon we'll have cart-loads of money! Hahaha etc.

SONG: eg Money makes the world go around, or Taxman by the Beatles: SHERIFF takes main verses with other three providing 'backing' & gradually taking it over, to his anger OR QUIPAT can start to dance, getting more and more bizarre until Sherriff yells at him when he stops, merely twitching his fingers.

SHERIFF: Enough! I have horrible things to do. Quipat! Take this scroll and see that it gets delivered. (EXITS passing scroll to QUIPAT)

QUIPAT: Me? (Looks around) Deliver this! (Passes it to Hugo)

HUGO FIRST: Deliver this. (Passes it to Guy)

GUY DE TOURS: Deliver this! (Passes it to **MAID MARION** who has just entered)

BADDIES EXIT. ENTER **MAID BADLY**

MAID BADLY: What've you got there, Marion? Is it a love letter for me from the Sheriff?

MAID MARION: Of course not! It's addressed to Father.

And it's from someone called 'Ruben the Hod'!

MAID BADLY: I recognise that orange wax crayon from somewhere! The same handwriting! It's the same as that poem on the stable wall. You know, the one that goes -

> 'Robin Hood needed arrows strong, so he went into town - and got 'em. (Pause)
> He saw the Sheriff bending down, And shot him in the ...'

MAID MARION: Badly! Family show!

MAID BADLY: Sorry! (Mouths and indicates 'bottom' to aud.) But what does the letter mean?

MAID MARION: I'm afraid that it means those outlaws were telling the truth after all. And to think what I called them!

MAID BADLY: You called them 'great, hairy ...'

MAID MARION: Yes, I can remember, thank you.

MAID BADLY: I told you they didn't look like baddies! You can always tell a baddy from his face! (During this **QUIPAT** ENTERS and stands to one side, listening)

Baddies never shave properly - they look like a cross between (unshaven pop-star) and an old coconut!

(QUIPAT examines his own chin and agrees)

Baddies have greasy, black hair (QUIPAT, ditto) and little piggy eyes like two lumps of coal in a pizza!

(QUIPAT goes cross-eyed checking his own face)

And a brain - a brain SO SMALL YOU COULD GET IT INSIDE A MATCHBOX!

(QUIPAT Looks amazed, then takes a matchbox out of his pocket, takes a small, walnut like object from it, then nods in agreement.)

QUIPAT: She's right you know!

MAID BADLY: Look out; it's the creature from the black lagoon / or topical!

MAID MARION: We must try to get a message through to Father! Badly - you stay here and keep him talking. We'll sneak down and get three horses ready!

MAID BADLY: But – but. (but the others have already EXITED) What am I going to do? Father won't pay a ransom for me! He still hasn't forgiven him for making him that great big bowl of 'baked bean and Brussels'-sprout surprise'!

He said he had to get out of bed twelve times in the night to put the duvet back on!

QUIPAT: (Seeing the scroll in her hands) What have you got there?

MAID BADLY: (patting ample curves) Well, if you don't know by now, Sonny, I'm certainly not going to explain it to you!

QUIPAT: No, not all that stuff! There in your hand!

MAID BADLY: (looking at wrong hand) Nothing!

QUIPAT: No - the other hand!

MAID BADLY: (transferring scroll to other hand) Nothing in that one either!

QUIPAT: Are you trying to make a fool out of me?

MAID BADLY: I couldn't improve on nature!

QUIPAT: Ah, gracias!

Hey! (Snatching scroll from her) Give it to me!

SHERIFF: (ENTERS) What's going on here? (Sees scroll) Haven't you sent that yet?! You must have a brain the size of a pea!!

QUIPAT: No, actually it's about the size of ... (Takes out matchbox but is booted off - EXITS

MAID BADLY: (to audience) This is my chance is to get in the Sheriff's good books! I'll use all my feminine charms on the old buzzard! (Vamps over to him) Hey, there, Big Fellow. Feel like a little female company?

SHERIFF: Why yes! Who's coming?

MAID BADLY: Don't be silly; wouldn't you like to go out with a girl like me?

SHERIFF: I suppose it would be better than staying IN with you!

MAID BADLY: Saucy! People say I have the skin of an eighteen-year-old.

SHERIFF: Well give it back: you're making it all baggy!

MAID BADLY: Oh now. What would it take, for you to give me a teensy weensy littley kissey?

SHERIFF: Chloroform'y'. HAHA!

MAID BADLY: Haven't you even got one good word for me?

SHERIFF: Oh yes, I've got a very good word for you, it's...

QUIPAT:(ENTERS quickly) There's something in the stables!

SHERIFF: Well, that's not the word I was thinking of, but it is quite good!

QUIPAT: No - in the stables! They're taking the horses! The girls are trying to escape!

SHERIFF: So! No more Mister Nice-Guy! Raise the drawbridge! Lower the portcullis! Those girls won't leave this castle - at least, not alive! Hahahahaha!!

(ALL EXIT, TWO OF THEM LAUGHING HORRIBLY)

SCENE 3 THE KITCHEN OF NOTTINGHAM CASTLE

A very old kitchen with stone walls and tapestries. Doors up Left & Up Right. At the back of the stage (Up Right) is a sturdy kitchen table containing cooking utensils which include a heavy-looking frying-pan, a bag of flour and a large box of matches. Up Left is an oven, either a real one stripped down for lightness or a dummy one. Either directly behind, or in the top of, the cooker is a 'thunder flash' pyro (or improvise with sound effects, smoke and things falling over). Inside the oven, fixed to its floor, is a large sponge liberally coated in black powder. Down Left and Down Right are cupboard doors. OR just have one door, for the cupboard, and use the wings as other entrances) Inside the cupboard are three large packets of macaroni and a pie.

The curtain opens to reveal **MAID MARION** and **MAID BADLY** running across the room, looking for a way out. They try Stage Left.

MAID MARION: No - this door's locked. Can you see a key anywhere?

MAID BADLY: Nothing! What are we going to do? The drawbridge is up and this is the only other way out of the castle!

MAID MARION: There must be a key to this door somewhere!

MAID BADLY: Well, find it QUICK, the Sheriff's coming this way!

MAID MARION: Then YOU must keep him busy until we can find the key!

MAID BADLY: Me again? Perhaps I could cook him something - that would slow him down!

MAID MARION: Experience actually suggests the opposite.

SHERIFF: (OFFSTAGE) You look down there, QUIPAT - I'll look in the kitchen!
Marion dives behind Badly who holds her skirts out as if dancing. When the Sheriff enters: Right, Badly turns, keeping Marion out of sight as he crosses Left. They she dives out Right, unseen. Badly continues to dance - not knowing they are gone)

SHERIFF: What's going on in here? What are you doing dancing around at a time like this? Are you as daft as you are ugly?!
(Eyes her suspiciously and tries to see behind her but she keeps turning)
I've no time for this! I – er – I'll look in the dungeons!
(Pretends to EXIT RIGHT but reappears, spying)

MAID BADLY: Phew! He's gone - you can come out now!
(She turns but Marion has gone. In confusion she lifts her skirts and examines her petticoats, eventually revealing her vivid bloomers.)
What are you lot staring at?! Oh dear, I'm all of a fluster. I know, I'll cook something; that always makes me feel better. Let's see -what have we got here?
(Goes behind table)
FLOUR! Splendid.
(Lifts the frying-pan and starts to flour the table. The Sheriff sneaks up behind her to peer over her shoulder)
Whoops! Spilt some! Never mind - over the shoulder for luck!
(Throws a handful of flour over her shoulder into the Sheriff's face. He shrieks and dives down Left. Badly whirls Right to see what the noise was.)
What was that noise?! Sounded like a GHOST!
(Turns back as Sheriff straightens up with white face)
Waaah!! A ghost!

SHERIFF: Grrrrrrr...! I'm not a ghost, you silly old fossil!

MAID BADLY: I know that! Now stop messing about and fetch me some milk. In that cupboard - over THERE. (Gestures with the frying pan, smacking the Sheriff in the face with a good loud 'CLANG!')

SHERIFF: AA!! (Staggers forwards, to knees.)

MAID BADLY: Well if you're just going to play about I'll get it myself!

(Marches forwards, dangling the frying pan so it catches the Sheriff on the back of the head. He falls forwards, slowly recovering himself in time to be hit on the way back.)

SHERIFF: Bleugh... (Sheriff crawls round to the Left of the table and tries to pull himself up with one hand on the table just in time for Badly to slam the pan down on the table and his fingers)

Wah!!

(In rage the Sheriff shakes his bruised fingers, sucks them, then - straightens up onto his knees in time for Badly to sweep all the flour off the table into his face)

MAID BADLY: Don't you find cooking wonderfully relaxing?

SHERIFF: Grrr! (snatches rolling pin and hides it behind his back) The kitchen is no place for one as delicate as you, my dear. Why don't you go and take all that enormous weight off your feet?

(Badly turns away from him, he raises the rolling pin above her head, only to whirl it out of sight again as she turns back to him)

MAID BADLY: But what about dinner?

SHERIFF: I'll cook you something, my little blossom. (repeat action)

MAID BADLY: Why are you being so nice all of a sudden?

SHERIFF: I'm only bad until ... (Checks theatre clock/watch and says real time) then I'm just adorable! (Repeat action) Shall we dance? (Grabs her)

SONG: COMEDY DUET

SOUND: HIDEOUS GURGLING SCREAM AND GIANT TOILET FLUSHING

MAID BADLY: What on earth was that?! (Runs off in fright)

SHERIFF: It's just the front door bell! (ENTER **QUIPAT**) What is it, QUIPAT?

QUIPAT: It is the front door bell!

SHERIFF: Yes, I know. We've just done that joke. I mean - who is AT the door?

QUIPAT: It is very strange. There are two wandering minstrels asking to come in and entertain us!

SHERIFF: TWO wandering minstrels? Hmm. This sounds rather suspicious. Let me take a look at them. Quipat, you stay here and clear up this mess - I don't buy good food just to feed the MICE! (EXITS)

QUIPAT: I TOLD YOU - THERE ARE NO MICES IN THIS CASTLE! (TO AUD.) I got rid of all the mices here myself personally! There are no mice!

(As he talks he clears up and throws stuff into wings. As he turns a baby mouse tacks on straight behind him and follows him across the stage to the other side, etc. This goes on, to and fro, gathering more mice)

I made noise like the pussy cat and frighten them all away. .miaow .. see? That soon got rid of them, I can tell you. There aren't many castles round here that are free of mices like this one! Here!

(Stops and mice stop in line behind)

What you all looking at? What is it? Eh? Mices? No - I just tell you! There are no mice here! Oh no there aren't! (etc) Where are they then, these mices?

(As he turns right they all scuttle round behind him)

Nothing! You pulling my legs, eh? Where are these mices now then? (Repeat left) Nothing! You should all go to the Specky-Savers (or local opticians), I think! (Turns to see mice) Aaah!!

(Mice squeak to scare him)

And squeaky-squeak to you to! I am not frightened by mices!

(He crouches low. GIANT MOUSE ENTERS and stands behind QUIPAT. It squeaks or taps him on the shoulder.)

Another one of you mice! Well, (turns, then slowly rises from crouch) Oooh .....

miaow? (Mouse squeaks) Arrr! EXITS!
MICE DANCE. AFTER THIS THEY EXIT
SHERIFF: QUIPAT! (ENTERS) QUIPAT! Pah! Where is that idiot? Turns and shouts into QUIPAT's face) QUIPAT!!

QUIPAT: Errrrrrr (looks around nervously) Has it gone?

SHERIFF: Has what gone?

QUIPAT: The m.m.m.m. mouse!

SHERIFF: Mouse? A grown man afraid of a tiny little mouse?!

QUIPAT: Non! It was not a petite little mouse! It was GIGANORMANTIC! (Holds hand as high as possible)

SHERIFF: Nonsense! (Draws QUIPAT Down Centre) You don't get mice that big!

(Giant Mouse casually saunters across behind them, watched open mouthed by QUIPAT who points in despairing horror)

What are you doing, Quipat?

(IF the audience shout 'look behind you' QUIPAT can say 'What he/she/they said')

And ... listen carefully. Did you recognise those two minstrels we just let into the castle? (QUIPAT is still staring after the giant mouse)

Are you listening to me? Those two minstrels - did you see through their pathetic disguise?

QUIPAT: Minstrels? (Very vague) Disguise?

SHERIFF: Can I have a LITTLE intelligence please, QUIPAT? (Looks at him and QUIPAT shrugs & shakes head) This isn't (TV show with stupid people). (Looks around) Those two minstrels were none other than my niece, Lucy, and that idiot minstrel, Alan A'Dale!

QUIPAT: Minstrel?

SHERIFF: Good grief. Pay attention now and I will tell you my plan!

(Giant mouse crosses back again, into cupboard, seen only by QUIPAT who is speechless in hysterics and claws at Sheriff to turn and look)

Stop pulling my arm! What is the matter with you? Now then - my plan is to DISPOSE OF THE MINSTREL ALAN A'DALE ONCE AND FOR ALL!

(He goes to the cupboard the mouse has just exited into)

In this cupboard ... what on earth is the matter with you? Why are you looking like that? (Opens cupboard but with door between himself and the mouse who is standing in there. QUIPAT screams, runs & slams it shut)

Quipat?! Control yourself! (QUIPAT grabs crotch with both hands)

(Sherriff opens it again. Takes pie from mouse and closes door, not noticing it)

You see this pie. Well... (Stops - thinks - looks back in cupboard that is now empty- shakes head).

Now then. Next ...

(QUIPAT angrily marches to empty cupboard, yanks open door. Mouse is now there. Screams, slams door and shakes, holding it shut.)

 Quipat! Come back here and take this pie. My plan is to place this pie in this gas cooker. (Goes to it and puts pie in)

Then... we turn on the gas. Like this. (Sniffs) Then we tell that minstrel there is a LOVELY pie for his supper - IF he will just light the gas for us! And as soon as he sticks his head in the oven - and lights the gas –

(during this QUIPAT has been nervously listening at the cupboard door; he slowly creeps next to the Sheriff in time for...)

KABOOM!! MINCED MINSTREL!! Have you got that? Never mind - here they come now! Quick! Look normal!

(QUIPAT scratches bum and looks stupid. Sheriff hits him then spends time adjusting the gas, during which :)

ENTER **ALAN A'DALE** and **LUCY** both badly disguised.
ANOTHER CHOICE HERE:
In our 2010 production the director changed this to Strictly Come Dancing, with pairs of
dancers and the Sheriff & QUIPAT making comments and holding numbered paddles.
Equally you could adapt some other program. Or just stick to this one ...)

LUCY: (whispering) This will never work! He's bound to recognise us!

ALAN A'DALE: But it's the only way. All we have to do is to get the keys off the
Sheriff's belt. Look! These keys! (Gets them off Sheriff's belt, shows her, then
puts them back) Then, we take the keys over to the kitchen door, open it, and
Robin and all his men will run in and rescue everyone!

SHERIFF: Ah! Good minstrels! (Looks suspicious.) And what are you called?

ALAN A'DALE: Ah - we're called -umm.

LUCY: The Spice Girls! You must have heard of us! We are having another reunion!

SHERIFF: Yes - but I thought there were five of you!

ALAN A'DALE: We've been ill. I mean - I ... ooh ...errr We're in trouble now, **LUCY**!

ENTER **MAID MARION** dressed as Spice Girls, with wigs.

MAID MARION: Ah, there you are. I thought we'd lost you.

SHERIFF: Hmm .. but let me see, 1, 2, 3,...?

ENTER **MAID BADLY** - dressed as another one.

MAID BADLY: Well you know what I want, what I really, really want. (To Aud.) Do
you like it - can you guess which one I am?

SHERIFF: Old Spice?!

MAID BADLY: Cheek! As it's Xmas you can call me Min.

SHERIFF: Min?

MAID BADLY: Yes - Min-Spice. Gettit?

SHERIFF: Bah! Go on then!

ALAN A'DALE: What?

SHERIFF: If you're Spice Girls - SING something!

SONG OR DANCE

END OF OPTIONAL BIT

SHERIFF: Enough! I have decided what I am going to do with you!

LUCY: I don't like the sound of that.

SHERIFF: You will need to freshen up after your long journey. But perhaps if ONE
of you could stay here and help prepare supper?

(During this he bends forwards to stare closely into **LUCY**'s disguise. Behind him
Alan tries to get at the bunch of keys on his belt. Sherriff turns his head round to
see Alan with both hands reaching for his bum. Alan realises he has been seen
and embarrassedly pretends to be warming his hands by the Sheriff's seat.)
Perhaps YOU would help cook supper?!

ALAN A'DALE: But I need to clean up too and ...

SHERIFF: No you don't! Now, you ladies run along to the Guest Rooms - I'm sure
you will know where they are. Off you go. (Ushers them off)

ALAN A'DALE: I'll be alright. Don't worry!

SHERIFF: Now then, QUIPAT; what food do we have to offer our guest?

QUIPAT: (no idea) How about a nice - hot - plate - of -- pasta?!

SHERIFF: Yes..pie. Eh? What?! Pasta?! You idiot! (Hits him) I'm so sorry - he
means 'A nice hot piece of pie'!

ALAN A'DALE: Actually I do quite fancy some pasta!

SHERIFF: Well we don't even HAVE any pasta! It'll have to be pie!

QUIPAT: Oh yes we do! (Takes large bag of macaroni from cupboard) Look!

SHERIFF: What?!

QUIPAT: Here - look! A bag of MACARONI!

MUSIC: ENTER VERY SMALL MOUSE DOING MACARENA
The mouse dances right up to the Sheriff then stops and look up at him. Squeak!

> **SHERIFF:** Not Macarena, you miniscule rodent! MACARONI!! (Mouse tries one more dance) OUT! (Mouse squeaks pitifully) OUT!! (Mouse turns and leaves sadly)

QUIPAT: Ahh – isn't he cute.

> **SHERIFF:** You blithering idiot! (Grabs Quipat's throat) Remember - we make him light the oven to cook the pie!
> (While he talks the giant mouse strolls on, takes the macaroni out of QUIPAT's hand and strolls off. Nobody notices)
> So just get rid of that bag of pasta and ... where's it gone?
> **QUIPAT:** What?

SHERIFF: That bag - (almost speechless in confusion) - that bag of <u>macaroni!</u>
(MUSIC: ENTER 2 MORE MICE DANCING MACARENA twice around stage.)
SHERIFF: STOP THAT DANCING!! (General sighs of disappointment and they wander off)

> Anyway, (struggles to regain composure) we <u>DO</u> have a pie ready in the oven, just waiting for you to light the gas.... (leads Alan to the oven)
> **QUIPAT:** (In cupboard) Well, what a piece of luck! Here's another bag of pasta!
> **ALAN A'DALE:** Lovely!
> **SHERIFF:** (To Quipat) You! You!! If they'd invented the microscope I'd get your brain examined!
> **QUIPAT:** Gracias! (Repeat action with big mouse stealing bag)
> **SHERIFF:** Now get rid of that ... IT'S GONE AGAIN!!

QUIPAT: What's gone again?
SHERIFF: That bag of maca .... No - you don't get me to say that word again.
ALAN A'DALE: What word?

> **SHERIFF:** Macaroni.
> (MUSIC: more mice dance on. **Alan** and **QUIPAT** join in.)
> **SHERIFF:** Aargh!! OFF! OFF!! OFF!!! (MICE exit. Sheriff grabs Alan) Now just take this box of matches, open the oven door and light the gas! Go on!
> **QUIPAT:** Well - would you believe it?! (Pause) Here's ANOTHER bag of pasta! Isn't it funny - weeks with nothing to eat and this was in the cupboard all the time!! Isn't that fun - fun -fun (clearly the Sheriff does not find it amusing.)

SHERIFF: Grr!! (Snatches bag, holds it away but while the giant mouse is taking it from him he, turns, snatches it back from the Giant Mouse. Sheriff turns to QUIPAT, slowly realises what he has just seen, then jumps.) Erk! (Giant Mouse exits without pasta)
ALAN A'DALE: That was a biggun!
SHERIFF: Right - no more interruptions!! Now then:
ENTER 'Amazon Women' or Bonsai warriors
Number 1: Ooh, hello again!
SHERIFF: Argh! Now what?!
EITHER:
Amazon Woman 2: Now don't be like that. I don't suppose you've got any Valium? Corn-pads.
Amazon Woman 3: Dotty's is having a bit of a problem.
SHERIFF: Bit of a problem!! I'll show you bit of a problem!!
Amazon Woman 4: Don't you speak to us like that, young man.
Amazon Woman 5: Invite us here and then don't even have the politeness to feed us!
OR
Child 1: Have you got any ice cream and jelly?
Very Small Child 2: I don't really like jelly. It makes me burp.
THEN, FOR EITHER:

SHERIFF: **You want me to f**eed you! Even if I had some food I'd rather stick it...

SOMEBODY: Well you've got some food right there - in your hand.

SOMEBODY ELSE: Yes! You've got a whole packet of maca...**SHERIFF:** Stop! Don't say it! DON'T SAY THAT WORD!! Go on then - take the whole packet! I don't even LIKE macaroni! AARGH!

MUSIC. MICE & HUGO & GUY ENTER DANCING.

Everyone on stage joins in, even dragging in the Sheriff.

SHERIFF: STOP!!!! OUT!!!!! THROW THEM ALL IN THE DUNGEONS!!!

(all exit except Sheriff, Alan, Quipat)

Now - what was I doing? Oh yes! The cooker!

Listen! You take the matches, open the oven door, look inside - light the gas! Off you go!

ALAN A'DALE: O.K. (goes to oven and looks in. Meanwhile Sheriff & QUIPAT scuttle downstage and crouch with fingers in ears. Alan looks puzzled then walks to the men, peers at them, and then taps them on shoulder.)

Hey! (They leap in alarm)

Where do I light the oven?

SHERIFF: You light it inside, at the back. Go on; look very closely. Try again! (REPEAT ACTION) Waaah!! Now what's wrong now?!

ALAN A'DALE: What temperature do I need it?

SHERIFF: Don't worry about that - just light the gas! (REPEAT ACTION except SHERIFF & QUIPAT giggle excitedly)

ALAN A'DALE: I still don't see how you light it!

SHERIFF: You moronic minstrel! Look! You take the matches ... (He does it himself.) You open the oven door.

(Here QUIPAT realises what is going to happen, drags Alan behind the table and dives down with his hands on his head.)

Then you light the match...

KABOOM!! COOKER EXPLODES. After a second for the smoke to lift the Sheriff pulls himself out of the oven, staggers toward the audience backwards then turns to show a very black face and staggers to the front of the stage. While he wobbles from side to side Alan grabs the keys off his belt and, waving them to show the audience, runs to the door.

ENTER **MAID MARION**, **MAID BADLY** and **LUCY**

MAID MARION: What was that noise?

MAID BADLY: What's happened?

ENTER **ROBIN HOOD** and all the **MERRY MEN**.

ROBIN HOOD: (Sees Sheriff's black face) Wo! Haven't seen anyone do that in a panto since 1978 – and even then it was (Name of unpleasant place)

MAID MARION: Robin! You were right! (Runs across to Robin but is grabbed from behind by the Sheriff who has a knife/sword)

SHERIFF: Not so fast! Drop your weapons - or I run her through!

LUCY: (jumping behind Sheriff and doing same) Drop YOUR weapon, Sheriff - or I run you through!

QUIPAT: (behind **LUCY** the same) Drop YOUR knife or I run YOU through!

MAID BADLY: (using spoon in place of knife) Drop your knife or I run YOU through!!

HUGO FIRST: (ENTERING) Right then! Everyone drop their weapons or I run YOU through!!

ALAN A'DALE: (joining seventh onto the line) OK then everyone; that's enough. Release the girl - or I run through you!

HUGO FIRST: Run through me?!

ALAN A'DALE: Run over you?

ALL: Run over me?

ALAN A'DALE: (wandering off in confusion) Run under you? Run ...er ...?

GUY DeTOURS ENTERS

ALAN A'DALE: What's the phrase I'm looking for?

(Absent-mindedly he gives his knife to GUY. The baddies gather the knives & spoons of the confused outlaws.)

SHERIFF: So, Robin Hood! Once again the game is mine! Take them ALL to the dungeons. No more messing about! It's the axe for them! They're all on tomorrow's 'chopping' list!! Hahahahahahahahahahahah!!!!!

ACT 2

SCENE FOUR: THE DUNGEON OF NOTTINGHAM CASTLE

The dungeon is a dark, dirty cellar. At the back are a flight of stone steps up to a strong wooden door and, high up is a barred window. Part of the rear wall is either a large movable panel or gauze with the front camouflaged as part of the wall and the rear (unseen at present) a moonlit landscape.

All around the edge of the stage are piles of old rags for bedding. Beneath one pile is hidden Potty Pat. The Amazon Women/Bonsai warriors are hiding in the shadows out of sight.

Lighting is low, but will need to get even lower later. There could be 'torches' flickering, but when the curtain opens light is coming through the open doorway, where the **SHERIFF** is standing.

QUIPAT is onstage, pushing people farther into the dungeon. **ROBIN HOOD** and all the **MERRY MEN** plus **MAID MARION, MAID BADLY, LUCY,** are spreading out, as if they have just come through the door.

LITTLE JOHN: Stop your shoving!

QUIPAT: I am sorry but this is what I am paid to do.

MAID MARION: You can't hope to get away with this!

SHERIFF: But I already have! Ha ha ha!

ROBIN HOOD: We're not finished yet!

SHERIFF: Maybe not, but you WILL be at dawn! Sweet dreams! (EXIT laughing)

QUIPAT: Hahahaha! (Backs to steps laughing, then realises he is locked in too and starts to pound on door) Hey?! Help!! (Door opens and Sheriff grabs him by the neck and yanks him out just before John can throttle him)

FRIAR TUCK: Well, Robin; we've been in some pickles before, but this looks serious!

ROBIN HOOD: That just makes it more interesting! Now let's look around and see if there is any way out of here! (They do this)

MUCH: We don't appear to be alone in here! **CHOICE HERE** (Amazons/Ninjas come out of shadows)

ROBIN HOOD: Good evening ladies! [OR] You are the smallest prisoners I have ever seen.

Prisoner 1: If you're looking for a way out - don't bother.

Prisoner 2: We've searched every corner of this place and found nothing but bones!

ROBIN HOOD: Have no fear. My MERRY MEN and I have escaped from worse than this. And you shall all come with us.

Prisoner 3: Oh what a nice man. How charming. [OR] Even teddy? (Robin nods)

Prisoner 4: You wouldn't happen to have any wool with you? I want to get this finished for my niece's baby and its due soon so I... [OR] Have you seen my cuddle cloth?

ROBIN HOOD: Let's see what we can find.

MAID MARION: Oh, I feel so guilty. I should have believed your warning about the Sheriff, then none of you would be here now!

ROBIN HOOD: There's only one person to blame for this - and that's the Sheriff.

LUCY: He is an evil man. Even if your father sends the ransom, the Sheriff will never let you go.

ALAN A'DALE: The worse thing is that we're all going to be parted so soon.

WILL SCARLET: (to Aud.) Kids. There's a soppy bit now, so if you're easily upset this would be a good time to go for a pee or something. (Ninja may attempt to do this against his leg causing him some alarm. Hey!)

MAID MARION: Yes; just when we were getting to know each other.

Suitable intro into **SONG**

ROBIN HOOD: We must try to get some rest. We'll need all our strength in the morning.

MAID MARION: I suppose you're right; but who could sleep in here?

ALAN A'DALE: First, find somewhere dry.

LUCY: This looks like a good place. (Pokes at rags)

POTTY PAT sits up angrily.

POTTY PAT: Eh!! What's going on?! Find your own spot!

LUCY: I'm sorry: we thought you were a pile of old rags!

POTTY PAT: Charming, I'm sure! Just because you don't wear this year's fashions people think you're something to sit on!

LITTLE JOHN: (everyone gathers round the tatty old woman) How long have you been here?

POTTY PAT: Longer than you - so don't go saying you picked this place first - 'cos you didn't, see!

ROBIN HOOD: No, he meant how long have you been a prisoner here? We wouldn't dream of taking your place.

POTTY PAT: (regaining her dignity and straightening her rag clothes) Oh well, that's different then. Let's think-I've been here for ...... well, since... something local or topical that happened several years ago so ....

LITTLE JOHN: That was years ago! What do you do for food?

POTTY PAT: Oh, food's no problem. (Pulls bowls from under rags) Here, try this.

LITTLE JOHN: Hmm, not bad. What is it?

POTTY PAT: Minced slug. (Reaction from John) Or you could try one of these - a rat on a stick.

MAID BADLY: You don't really eat that, do you?

POTTY PAT: Oh yes - bats, rats, anything!

ROBIN HOOD: Lovely. So why were you put in the dungeons?

POTTY PAT: Oh, that's a tragic tale. (Summons them around her) I used to be the Sheriff's chamber maid!

MAID BADLY: You used to clean his bedroom?

POTTY PAT: No - I used to warm up his CHAMBER POT for him! Potty Pat they call me! First thing every morning I had to see that his chamber potty was nice and warm before he sat on it. Especially in the winter!

LITTLE JOHN: You mean you actually...! (Makes squatting motion!)

POTTY PAT: Bless you, no! I used to warm it in the oven! Two minutes at Gas Mark Two. (Looks sad) Except the morning I got a bit confused.

MAID MARION: What happened?

POTTY PAT: Well, instead of two minutes at Gas Mark Two - I gave the potty TEN minutes at Gas Mark TEN! (Shrugs shoulders sadly) You should have heard the noise when the Sheriff sat on it! They say he still bears the mark to this day! (Draws potty-sized circle in the air)

MAID MARION: So what crime did they charge you with?

POTTY PAT: (looks at audience sadly, pauses ...) Arson.

LUCY: Oh dear, so they locked you in here, all alone, for all those years?!

POTTY PAT: Ooh, no dear! Not alone. Once, this place was FULL of people. There was even one fellow dressed entirely in dead leaves!

MAID BADLY: What was he in jail for?

POTTY PAT: Rustling.

ROBIN HOOD: So where are all these people now?

LITTLE JOHN: (holding up a bone) Argh! She said she'd eat anything!!

POTTY PAT: Nah! I was never that desperate! Plenty of worms down here! No - they all escaped!

MERRY MEN: Escaped?! Where? How? (Start to look around)

ROBIN HOOD: Tell us! How did they escape?!

POTTY PAT: Oh, don't ask me, dear. I was always asleep when they went. They always seemed to go in the middle of the night!

MAID MARION: So you've no idea at all how they got out?

POTTY PAT: Well... (Slowly moves centre. Lights start to dim; mystic music?) There were stories... stories of something strange happening when the moon rises!

It's said, that whenever a full moon rises above the walls of the castle, then the Queen of all the Mice dances, following an ancient and magical track that runs through this very spot from a time even before the castle was built 'ere!

And that when the Queen Mouse dances - the very walls of the castle open before her! (General sounds of awe) But- there might be one small problem...

MAID MARION: What's that?

> **POTTY PAT:** I think I ate
> her five years ago!

MERRY MEN: Groan.

MAID MARION: But can you be sure? What if it's true? When's the next full moon?

ROBIN HOOD: Does anyone know?

ROBIN HOOD: Where's Friar Tuck? He knows about these things. Tuck!

FRIAR TUCK: (dragged over) Bleaugh! This is a disgusting place! I just saw a horrible creature with five legs!

ALAN A'DALE: Bet his trousers fit like a glove! (Tuck glares at him)

ROBIN HOOD: Tuck - you must tell us when the next full moon is!

FRIAR TUCK: Why?

MERRY MAN: Because the Queen Mouse dances then!

FRIAR TUCK: Have you been those mushrooms again?

MAID MARION: This is important! Our only chance to escape is if tonight there is a full moon!

FRIAR TUCK: Well then, it must be tonight!

MAID MARION: Why?

FRIAR TUCK: Well if it wasn't this would be the end of the story, and we've got loads to go yet!

ROBIN HOOD: So there IS a chance! All we have to do is to stay awake until the moon rises!

LITTLE JOHN: Well I don't know about this. 'Queen Mouse' dancing. Pah! (Yawns)

ROBIN HOOD: But we must believe! (Others are going off to sleep)

MAID MARION: They're all going to sleep! What can we do to persuade them to stay awake?!

LUCY: (tugging at Alan's sleeve) Stay awake, Alan! You must sing to them - nobody could sleep through that!

ALAN A'DALE: Cruel but true, though it's not singing you need - it's convincing! Nobody here believes that story about a 'Queen Mouse'!

ROBIN HOOD: Well I do! We have to believe it!

Or suitable intro into SONG: like I BELIEVE I CAN FLY. Or similar

POTTY PAT: LOOK! THE MOON! (The full moon has just risen behind the bars of the window)

ROBIN HOOD: Quick, everyone! Out with the lights! Hide - but be ready to move!

Lights go down and everyone dives into the wings, though some can be seen watching. (Dry Ice/smoke?). Music starts. From the darkness appears the Queen Mouse, wearing a small crown and a cape. She dances magically. At the end the back wall of the dungeon 'opens' to reveal a moonlit landscape with stars twinkling and a path. The mouse dances out.

ROBIN HOOD: This is it! Everyone! Follow that mouse! Quickly- before the wall closes!

Everyone rushes out except for **LUCY**, who has caught her dress. Alan stays to help her.

ALAN A'DALE: Lucy! Come on! We'll be left behind!

LUCY: I'm can't! I'm caught on something!

Suddenly the dungeon door is thrown open by the Sheriff in his nightgown & cap.

SHERIFF: What on earth have you lot got to sing about at this time of... AARGH! They've all gone! (Comes half way down steps) Ah-ha! Not all gone!

ALAN A'DALE: Oo-er! Come on, Lucy!

SHERIFF: So! It's you – (topical unpopular singer). Well, at least one outlaw shall die before this night is done! (Draws sword and advances)

ALAN A'DALE: Stand clear, Lucy (Grabs bone. Short duel, Alan outmatched)

SHERIFF: Enough of this! I want to get back to my beauty sleep; not that I need it of course. (Sneer. He stabs Alan in the chest. Alan staggers backwards then falls to the stage, 'dead'. Lucy rushes to him.)

SHERIFF: And you ... you can spend the rest of the night here to teach you a lesson! Hahahahahah! EXITS

LUCY: Oh no! Alan; you weren't a fighter. If you hadn't stayed behind to help me....

ROBIN HOOD: (off) They were right behind us! (ENTERS) What...?! No!

LUCY: The... the Sheriff! (Sob sniff)

ROBIN HOOD: This time he shall pay!

LUCY: My poor Alan. So brave, so gentle. (She supports him in her lap. He opens one eye and looks at the audience, smiles, then closes it again)
So patient, so kind (he opens both eyes and smiles at audience, then pretends to be dead again)
So willing to help, so generous, so.., so..

ALAN A'DALE: So good at singing.

LUCY: So good at s....What?! (Throws him off her lap angrily) Hey! You're not dead!

ROBIN HOOD: What's going on here?

ALAN A'DALE: (Sitting up and reaching into breast pocket) The Sheriff's sword hit this! (Produces slice of cake left there since Scene One)

MAID BADLY: Ooh! That's a slice of my sponge cake!

ALAN A'DALE: That's right! Nothing could get through that!

MAID BADLY: Cheeky devil!

WILL SCARLET: Robin! The wall is closed again!

LITTLE JOHN: But look! The Sheriff didn't bother to lock the door behind him!

ROBIN HOOD: That mistake will be his last!

FRIAR TUCK: What shall we do to him?

LITTLE JOHN: String him up!

MUCH: Draw and quarter him!

LITTLE JOHN: Stretch him on the rack!

LOCAL NAME: Tell him he looks a bit like. (Someone horrid or who does look like the actor)

> **ROBIN HOOD**: Aye - all of these things! But one thing is certain -   it is his turn to pay the price!

> RUSH OFF DRAMATICALLY OR SONG: CHORUS NUMBER: such as 'He shall die' (Emilio the Toreador song? One chorus?) (The song takes time and is often omitted but give it serious consideration)

CURTAIN

SCENE FIVE (half tabs with front tabs a quarter closed for entrances): ANOTHER PART OF THE CASTLE

SHERIFF: (RUNS ON) (If there is booing:) Silence, you dogs!

If there is no booing, then use this time to get the booing going; either way use the time to play with the audience. Suggestions: insult their booing; compare it unfavourably with your granny; split them in two to see who boos loudest; use the 'Hands up' hands down' 'volume control' idea controlling them. Why? So the stage crew have time to change the scene!

SHERIFF: So, those obnoxious outlaws have escaped from my dungeon, have they? No matter; this castle is a maze of secret tunnels! They will never find me in my special hiding-place, in the THRONE ROOM! (He suddenly remembers the audience)

Curses! I forgot you lot were there, sitting in the dark, crunching your sweets! I just hope for your sakes you didn't hear me say I was hiding in the Throne Room! Rats! Said it again! Grrrr! Well - if Robin Hood or any of those bone-headed outlaws ask you where I've gone DON'T YOU DARE TELL THEM I'VE GONE TO THE THRONE ROOM! Or I'll come down there - and SORT YOU OUT! Grr! (EXITS ANGRILY)

ROBIN HOOD: (running from other side) There's no sign of him here!

MAID MARION: (ENTER) Well, he can't be far away; the castle is surrounded and we've searched almost everywhere!

ROBIN HOOD: Perhaps these good people can help us? Excuse me; I don't want to interrupt, but do you know where the Sheriff is? Where? The Throne Room?! So, we have him trapped! Marion, you wait here until its safe.

MAID MARION: No way! I'm not going to miss a good punch-up!

ROBIN HOOD: I think it best that you miss this one. The Sheriff could use any cowardly trick - and, well, I don't think I could concentrate properly if you were in the room.

(To aud) If I leave Marion here with you, will you warn her if there's any danger? Will you warn her? You will? You stay here then, Marion.

Remember – warn her if there's any trouble! (EXITS)

MAID MARION: Don't you worry about me! You just take care of yourself, Robin! (SHERIFF appears behind her and starts to creep up horribly. He shakes his fist and retreats if there is a lot of shouting)

I wish I'd gone with him. I hope he's safe. (Repeat action)

I'd show that miserable Sheriff a few tricks! (Repeat. This time he grabs her)

SHERIFF: What sort of tricks, eh, girl?!

MAID MARION: You cowardly devil! How could you draw your sword on a woman!

SHERIFF: That's nothing! (To aud) At school I drew the teacher on the board!

But enough of this pleasant chit-chat! I knew these sweet-crunching yokels would give away my secret hiding place! But this time YOU are coming with me and NOBODY, not even these brainless bozos, will know that we've gone to the STABLES! Hahaha!

(BOTH EXIT)

QUIPAT: (ENTERS followed by ALAN & LUCY) Alright! Alright! Keep your tights on! I am a goody now! But how am I supposing to know where the Sheriff is hiding? He could be anywhere!

ALAN A'DALE: Well somebody must have seen him! (To aud) Hey, you lot! Which way did the Sheriff go? This way? (Points wrong way) This way? (Right way)

Thanks - then we'll go THIS way! (Faces wrong way) I'm not giving him another chance to make ME a kebab!

OPTIONAL BIT WITH KIDS (CAN MISS THIS OUT)

QUIPAT: But I'd be with you this time!

ALAN A'DALE: YOU?! What use would you be in a crisis?

QUIPAT: (THINKS) I can make a noise like a pussy cat!

LUCY: Oh anyone can do that!

QUIPAT: No they can't!

ALAN A'DALE: They can too. They can make all sorts of animal noises - like dogs and sheep and - Hey! Let's find out. Are there any children out there who can make different animal noises? Come up and show us! BUSINESS WITH CHILDREN asking the usual questions. Animal noises. Maybe a short song?

ALAN A'DALE: A big hand to all the children who helped us!

BACK TO THE PLOT

SHERIFF ENTERS with MARION in tow

QUIPAT: (diving behind Alan) Erk! It's old cod-piece!

ALAN A'DALE: Release the girl at once!

SHERIFF: (jumping back in alarm) What?! What magic is this? Are you a ghost? I ran you through with this very sword! Stand back, ghost of Alan A'Dale!

ALAN A'DALE: Not this time, Matey. Now you're trapped!

LUCY: That's it - you tell him!

MAID MARION: You'd better give in; you bully! You'll not escape now!

SHERIFF: Moron!

QUIPAT: Ci?!

SHERIFF: You think YOU can beat ME? Why, this castle is riddled with escape tunnels! It's got as many holes in it as ...er..

ALAN A'DALE: As your old pants?

SHERIFF: As my old ...grr! Fools! If you block one way then I just go another! (Indicates audience)

QUIPAT: Boss! You can't go down there! There are creatures down there! You can see the glistening of their beady little eyes! (If you can identify one then single them out: 'there's a green stripy one!')

LUCY: He's right! You can hear the crunching of their sweets!

ALAN A'DALE: You can smell that little boy we frightened with the exploding cooker!

SHERIFF: Pah! They don't scare me! (He goes down into the audience IF SAFE!!)

ALAN A'DALE: There's no escape that way!

QUIPAT: Come on, let's get help!

They exit calling for help.

SHERIFF: Stop your booing! I'll have the last laugh! Hahah...erk!

ROBIN HOOD: (appears blocking his path) That wasn't a very long last laugh, my dear Sheriff!

SHERIFF: Hood! Rats! Time to make a speedy exit, I think! GANGWAY!!

ROBIN HOOD: Stand and fight like a man!

SHERIFF: Not likely! I'd rather run like..., er, something that runs really fast! Marion EXITS.

Sheriff & Robin back on stage. Sheriff is stopped by the Curtains.

ROBIN HOOD: Nowhere left to run to now, eh, Sheriff?

SHERIFF: Nonsense! A real baddy always has a devious trick up his sleeve! One click of my fingers and these curtains will magically open! (CLICK!! Nothing happens. CLICK! CLICK! Eventually he stabs his sword into the wings, there is a surprised shriek from Stage Manager, and the curtains open)

SCENE SIX: THE THRONE ROOM OF NOTTINGHAM CASTLE

The Throne Room must be a spectacular set, with rich drapes or tapestries and vivid stained-glass windows at the back. Following the gloom of the dungeon scene this scene must not be too pale or wishy-washy. At either side are trick candles.

SHERIFF: Hood; I shall beat you if it's the last thing I do!

ROBIN HOOD: My dear Sheriff – I will be happy to make sure that it IS the last thing you do!!

SHERIFF: I could fight you with one hand behind my back! (Puts hand with sword behind back and tries to fight with empty hand & finger but gets very confused)

ROBIN HOOD: Fighting with one hand eh? (Picks up tankard, drinks and fights)

SHERIFF: Pah! Anyone can do that!

(Picks up sword and second tankard and copies, but Robin taps his own sword against his tankard while the Sheriff flails wildly in front of him drinking. Robin then circles behind the Sheriff, and - after much conspiring with the audience - pokes the Sheriff in the seat, making him splurt drink everywhere.)

ROBIN HOOD: Nothing has happened yet, Sheriff. Perhaps your blade needs sharpening?

SHERIFF: Ha! Just watch this! (Swipes at large candle but appears to miss)

ROBIN HOOD: Ha! Missed!

SHERIFF: Ha ha! (Goes to candle and lifts/pushes top off, showing it sliced in two)

ROBIN HOOD: Easy! (Swipes at large candle but appears to miss)

SHERIFF: Ha missed!

(Repeat but this time the candle stick-holder has been sliced in two OR similar depending on your technical team, such as paper chain of dollies, candle falls apart to reveal sculpture, etc. Fight continues. Robin's sword is knocked from hands. Sheriff gloats.)

SHERIFF: Now you have nothing to fight with. Victory is mine!

ROBIN HOOD: Don't gloat too soon, Nottingham!

SHERIFF: Why not? The only way I could lose now is if I was complete idiot and threw away my sword! (Does this) Whoops!

As he runs to get it Robin gets his and is ready when the Sherriff turns back. The Sheriff is forced to his knees

ENTER EVERYONE EXCEPT **MAID BADLY**.

FRIAR TUCK: Bravo, Robin! Well fought!

ROBIN HOOD: It was no contest; you know that evil will always be defeated in a fair fight!

LITTLE JOHN: And what shall we do with this miserable worm, eh, Robin? Shall I find a nice, long rope?!

SHERIFF: Oh no! Mercy, I beg you! I know I've been a bit naughty. .

MAID MARION: 'Naughty'?!

SHERIFF: Unkind?

Potty Pat: How about 'cruel'?

SHERIFF: Alright, cruel.

ALAN A'DALE: And mean.

SHERIFF: And mean.

MAID BADLY: And treacherous!

SHERIFF: Yes, and treacherous.

QUIPAT: (appears from side or trap-door) And hideously ugly!

SHERIFF: And hideous...Here! Whose side are you on?!

MAID MARION: But you promise to be a good boy now?

SHERIFF: Oh yes!

ROBIN HOOD: And you'll cut the taxes?

SHERIFF: Yes - I'll cut taxes to twenty percent! Er... fifteen? Alright! Ten percent, but that's my last ... (gulp as John produces rope) Five! I mean five percent!

ALAN A'DALE: And you'll let the villagers hunt in Sherwood Forest whenever they're hungry?

SHERIFF: Yes!!

Amazon Woman: And you'll do the teas for the Women's Institute?

Bonsai warrior: You'll sing us to sleep every night?

SHERIFF: Yes, anything!

FRIAR TUCK: And you give your permission for your nieces Maid Marion and the Maid Lucy to marry whoever they wish!

SHERIFF: What?! Married?! <u>DO</u> they wish?

MAID MARION and **LUCY**: (taking the arms of Robin & Alan) Oh yes!

Merry Men: Good grief.

SHERIFF: Yes, yes, yes, yes .... anything.

FRIAR TUCK: Then I think that's everything! You may get up.

LITTLE JOHN: But he must have SOME punishment for the things he's done!

ROBIN HOOD: Then what do you suggest?

LITTLE JOHN: Something awful!

WILL SCARLET: Something really terrible!

MUCH: The most dreadful thing we can think of! (All think hard)

ENTER **MAID BADLY**: in awfully tasteless costume.

MAID BADLY: Coee! Sheripoos!

MERRY MEN: 'Sheripoos'?

MAID BADLY: (hugging Sheriff) Take no notice of them, my Naughty Nottie Nightcap! They don't know there's something between us!

MAID MARION: Sister - you mean you actually LIKE this villain?!

MAID BADLY: Well, just between you and me, he's not exactly Prince Charming, but I think he's probably better than nothing. And anyway - it's somebody to PRACTICE MY COOKING ON!!

SHERIFF: AARGH! NO!! WHERE'S THE ROPE?!

ROBIN HOOD: That settles it! Tuck, good friar - we must away; Nottingham will see THREE weddings this happy day! (THREE COUPLES AND TUCK EXIT)

LITTLE JOHN: (To **QUIPAT**, **HUGO** & **GUY** who are trying to tip-toe away) And what about these miserable wretches? What about their punishment? I hear that some people actually ENJOY it on the rack! (Advances on them)

QUIPAT: Well some people will go to any lengths for a joke! Errr...Why not enjoy the relaxurious facilities here in the castle?! It will make a nice change to the middle of the forest! I can show you where everything is!

MUSICAL NUMBER: possibly part of 'consider yourself' or similar.

Music changes to 'SWAN LAKE' and all the men form the classic ballet line with interlinked arms. (Left hand across in front of the person on your left to hold onto the right hand of the next person. This will take more co-ordination and practice than the whole of the rest of the panto and may well end in violence.)

QUIPAT, Guy & Hugh may need to leave early to change. One variation is to get QUIPAT to vanish off the end into one wing to reappear joined on to the other end in the opposite wing (it has been done).

LAST CHORUS - ALL BOW AND PULL BACK TO EDGES OF STAGE. ENTER:
MICE
AMAZON WOMEN / BONSAI WARRIORS,
UN-NAMED MERRY MEN
POTTY PAT
HUGO FIRST and **GUY De TOURS**
WILL SCARLET, GORDON and **MUCH**
LITTLE JOHN,
QUIPAT (with Giant Mouse creeping behind him)
FANFARE IN **ROBIN HOOD** TRADITION

LITTLE JOHN: And here they come, let's wish them luck! First: newly promoted Bishop Tuck!

FRIAR TUCK: (ENTERS in splendid bishop's robes and mitre)
Happy endings? We've not forgotten 'em,
Here's another – set in Nottingham.
The first to end our comic tale
The lovely Lucy with Alan A'Dale.

ALAN A'DALE and LUCY ENTER AND BOW.

FRIAR TUCK: And now Maid Badly – though rather grotty,
Not half as bad as her husband Nottie!

BADLY: ENTERS in outrageous wedding gown.

SHERIFF: dragged on

BADLY: Do you like the wedding dress? Would you like to see my train?! (Whirls round to show large face of Thomas the Tank Engine on her rear.)

FRIAR TUCK: And now three cheers would be quite good
For our hero Robin - and Mrs Hood!

ROBIN HOOD and **MAID MARION** ENTER (small page carrying sword; small bridesmaid carrying flowers in front of them.)

ROBIN HOOD: This tale has found its happy end, & I have found a bride and friend.

MAID MARION: With taxes cut and forest free,

LUCY: The countryside lives happily.

ALAN A'DALE: No more will evil rule this land,
QUIPAT: But work together - hand in hand;
SHERIFF: (after nudge) Supporting right and fighting wrong!
LITTLE JOHN: Enough! It's time for feast and song!
FINALE NUMBER

LIST OF TITLES

Click to select

1. CINDERELLA
2. ROBIN HOOD
3. DICK WHITTINGTON
4. SLEEPING BEAUTY
5. RED RIDING HOOD & THE 3 PIGS
6. THREE MEN IN A TUB
7. JACK AND THE BEANSTALK
8. HANSEL AND GRETEL
9. SNOW WHITE & 7 DWARVES

CONTACT INFORMATION
and PERFORMANCE RIGHTS here:

PANTOSCRIPTS.ME.UK

DICK WHITTINGTON

© Chris Lane 2018

THE GRASSY KNOLL
To the side of the stage is a grassy hill with daisies. A dusty path winds over the top
& curves down/across to join the main stage. (or Dick enters through the
audience)
Milestone: LONDON 5 MILES
MUSIC: DICK appears, his bundle on a stick over his shoulder.
DICK: Come on, Cat! Look! Look at this milestone! Only 5 miles to London! We're
almost there! Come on! (CAT appears at a leisurely pace, looks at the milestone,
then starts to groom.) How can you be so calm? We've walked a hundred miles
from Gloucester and now we're almost there!
London – they say it's as big as all of Gloucestershire, and is so rich the streets are
paved with gold! (He settles down by the milestone, rests his pack and
daydreams) Can't you just see it, Cat? Can't you just imagine it? London!

SCENE ONE: LONDON
Upstage Centre is Alderman Fitzwarren's shop. This can be a free-standing
structure. Beyond is the skyline with the dome of St Paul's etc.
It is market time & the street is filled with brightly clothed people.
VIGOROUS OPENING NUMBER.
A crack of thunder & flash of lightening threaten rain; the chorus exit calmly.
DICK: Come on, Cat! What are you waiting for! Come on – I'm off to find my fame
and fortune!
He runs down the hill / onto the stage. Cat slowly follows. When he arrives the
stage is now dark, gloomy & foggy. An old man/woman coughs past with a
ragged child who runs over to beg but is dragged away coarsely.
DICK: Oh – this must be wrong – this can't be London. We must be in the wrong
place. I'll ask someone.
(Another ragged figure enters)
Excuse me – can you tell me the way to London?
(He is laughed at. Some urchins appear and he asks the way to London. They start
to taunt him then run off when Cat shows its claws.)
Be nice, Cat. Be nice now. We're just in a bad part of town, that's all.
(There is horrible laughing offstage: Rattigan)
Ahh … best move on I think.
(More laughing)
Let's just go over here and – err – hide! (to side of stage)
TWO RATS ENTER: RATTIGAN & SCABLEY.
RATTIGAN is obviously very rich & posh and carries a sword stick.
SCABLEY is dressed in plain black and carries a wooden club. They have long pink
tails.
RATTIGAN: Here it is. Fitzwarren's shop. The very place I told you about. Now –
how long to wait? Mmm? Scabley?
SCABLEY: What?
RATTIGAN: Time.
SCABLEY: What?
RATTIGAN: Time!
SCABLEY: OK – on your marks – get set – GO! (Looks up to see where Boss has

got to. Can't see him. Peers.) (Jumps when tapped on shoulder) Wow – fast!

RATTIGAN: No – let me **have** the time.

SCABLEY: Certainly. (Folds arms and looks at him) All the time you want, guvnor. What do you want to tell me?

RATTIGAN: No! (Angrily gestures at wrist) Watch!

SCABLEY: I'm watching. Ready when you are, guvnor!

RATTIGAN: My dear Scabley. (Slowly) Look - (indicates wrist) - tell me what it says!

SCABLEY: (looks carefully) It says: "I VOTED FOR BREXIT". (OR SIMILAR. Twangs rubber strap)

RATTIGAN: Scabley; (into his face) do you have the slightest idea why we are here?

SCABLEY: (nose to nose) No – I do not have the slightest idea.

RATTIGAN: Stop. Think. Look in your hands – wooden club. Look over there – posh shop full of gold coins – and in a minute those gold coins will be carried out here by a young girl. Got it? Wooden club? Girl with gold coins?

SCABLEY: (slowly) I is going to take my wooden club ...

RATTIGAN: (slowly) Yes ...

SCABLEY: ... and sell it to her!

RATTIGAN: Yes. NO! You are going to club her and take the money! You and your evil smelling friend .... and ... (looks round) ... where is s/he?

SCABLEY: Who?

RATTIGAN: OK. Stop. Listen. Evil smell. Hideous ugly face. Breath like an open sewer. Hair like a badger's bottom .... well?

SCABLEY: (slowly) Whoever called you that – they was not nice. But you is takin' it very well. Sticks and stones may ...

RATTIGAN: Where is your stinky friend – Winnet?

SCABLEY: Oh – just coming.

RATTIGAN: I trust s/he will have brought a club – I did explain what we were going to do.

SCABLEY: Here's Winnet now.

WINNET enters in disco clothes.

WINNET: Hello then. (Shows clothes) How about this then – I remembered what you said, Mr Rattigan.

RATTIGAN: And what was it that I said?

WINNET: You said get prepared –

RATTIGAN: Yes ...

WINNET: ...as we was going - clubbing! (Does disco moves)

SCABLEY: You never told me that – I'd have put on something nicer! You said ...

RATTIGAN: Quick! Here comes the girl! Masks on! No – on the front of your heads! Too late! Hide!

ALICE FITZWARREN comes out of the door of the shop, locks it behind her and comes downstage with a wicker basket on her arm. The rats creep toward her.

DICK: Look out! It's a trap!

ALICE: What? What do you want?!

DICK: It's a trap – they're going to attack you and steal your money!

ALICE: Who are?

RATTIGAN: We are ... we are going to steal all your money!

DICK: Get back! (Waves stick at them)

RATTIGAN: My word. How very brave; don't you agree, lads?

(Other rats agree)

Now then – (pulls sword from stick) - let's see how brave you are after we have removed your...

(Suddenly Cat leaps out and flies at them)

RATTIGAN: Aargh! A cat!

(He flees. The other two hesitate then flee screaming with Cat after them)

DICK: (checks they have gone) I think they've gone. Are you all right?

ALICE: They'll be back.

DICK: You know them?!

ALICE: I don't know who they are, but they've robbed us so many times nobody will work for us now. That's why it was me who had to close the shop tonight. If you hadn't been here …

DICK: (Suddenly embarrassed) Just happened to be passing through; we're on our way to London!

ALICE: On your way to London?

DICK: Yes indeed. (Proudly) Off to make our fame and fortune.

ALICE: But…

DICK: No – don't you try to put me off as well. I'm off to London where the streets are paved with gold.

ALICE: But – this IS London. And the streets are NOT paved with gold!

DICK: Oh. (Looks round disappointed) Well – what are the streets paved with?

ALICE: With 10,000 horses here – what do YOU think they're paved with?

DICK: (Looks at shoe.) Ah – ooh. (Looks around) London eh? Oh. (Miserably) Right then. Where's Cat? (calls out) Cat?!

ALICE: Is this all you've got – that little bag?

DICK: It's all I need. Actually, it's mostly Cat's things. Squeaky mouse, blanket, you know.

ALICE: No food? And where are you staying? With family? Friends?

DICK: My family are back in Gloucester. Haven't exactly got any friends – not yet – but …

ALICE: Well you have ONE friend now. Come on – let's get you into the shop and get some food in you. Well? Come on!

DICK: Just a moment – where's …… (Cat returns smugly) Cat! There you are! You brave cat!

ALICE: You certainly are a brave cat. You come in as well; I'm sure we can find some milk for you! They go up to front of shop and open the door

ALICE: Here we are; welcome to Alderman Fitzwarren's Emporium!

The front of the shop opens to reveal the inside of the shop. Inside is a counter backed by a huge wall of shelves filled with all manner of things. Standing behind the counter is ALDERMAN FITZWARREN.

FITZ: Alice. Back so soon! What happened? Was it those rogues again?! Are you injured? Who's this?

ALICE: This is a friend. He was very brave; he ...

DICK: It was nothing. I just gave your daughter a hand in …

FITZ: What?! You want my daughter's hand in marriage?!

DICK: What? Eh? No! I mean...!

FITZ: Well – you look a decent sort of fellow. Can always trust a man with a dog.

DICK: Cat.

FITZ: Oh, yes you can! Just got to ask you a few questions first before you can marry her.

ALICE: But father – he's not – I mean – he isn't - you can't …

FITZ: Shush now, Alice. Your poor dear mother told me this would happen one day and she told me just what to say. First: have to find out the size of something. What was it now?

ALICE: What?!!

DICK: Aaah. I don't really...

FITZ: Got it! Have you got a big **fortune**? You know – loads of money. Gold coins.

Land. Mansion-houses. Carriages. That sort of thing.

ALICE: Father!!

FITZ: Shush now. Well? Speak up? How much money have you got?

DICK: Well, sir. Err … nothing. All I have in the world is in this bag – and (indicates Cat) Cat of course.

FITZ: Nothing at all. Just a dog. Right then. What was the next question? Yes! What's your name?

DICK: Dick!

FITZ: (Ducks as dramatically as possible.) What?! What is it?

ALICE: He thinks you said 'duck'.

DICK: I see. (Goes to Fitz) No, Dick!

FITZ: What?

DICK: No, Dick!

FITZ: My word! I'm sorry to hear that. (Secretively) Does she know about this?

ALICE: (outraged & embarrassed) Father! This is really …

FITZ: Shush now – this is for your own good – you can't marry just anyone – you can't marry some Tom, Fred or Harry that walks in off the street.

ALICE: Dick!

FITZ: (Ducks dramatically.) What?! Is it another one?

ALICE: It's his name! His **name** is Dick!

FITZ: I must say that is a tragic and ironic twist of fate, under the circumstances. Now then – last question: do you have loads of money?

DICK: No. Like I said before I only have …

FITZ: No money? Well – in that case I don't think you can marry Alice. Sorry. Next customer!

ALICE: Father – that's awful! If I want to marry…. (Aside to Dick) Err, is that really your name?

DICK: It's short for Richard. Richard Whittington!

ALICE: OK. If I want to marry Richard, then I jolly well shall.

FITZ: You want to marry Richard?! Does Dick know?

ALICE: Father! Concentrate! You're saying I can't marry him if he's poor?!

FITZ: Nope. Not Richard OR Dick – not if they're **poor**.

ALICE: You – you – you are just – just a great - big - SNOB!

FITZ: Me?! A snob?! I'll have you know that I am an ordinary everyday cockney Londoner!

ALICE: You? A cockney? You don't even SOUND like a Londoner!

FITZ: Don't I? Oh - well. Er .. right you are then "my little bucket-full".

ALICE: Your little bucket-full?

FITZ: Bucket full of water – water – daughter. See! Cockney rhyming slang – like what us Londoner talk!

DICK: (to aud) I've heard about this. Rosy Lee. That means cup of tea! (to Fitz) Rosy Lee!

FITZ: Rosy Lee? Err ... Have a pee! There – see – a proper Londoner. Not a snob. You can't just marry any old Tom, Whatsit or Harry.

DICK: Dick?

FITZ: (Ducks). What?! Not again!

ALICE: I do not want to marry Tom or Harry!

FITZ: Have you told them yet? Tom and Harry? It's cruel to tease you know.

Now listen; we Londoners – we can't have just anyone popping wedding rings onto our daughter's finger! But enough of this – I'm off to bed. Goodnight! (Bobs down behind counter – Dick leans over to see where he has gone & Fitz bobs up rapidly) Don't forget to turn out the – oh! Who are you?

DICK: Me, Sir? Di… Richard. Richard Whittington.

FITZ: Splendid. You're here about the job then! Splendid. You look just the sort. Don't you agree, Alice?

ALICE: Mmmm?

FITZ: He looks just the sort!

ALICE: You mean brave, handsome …

FITZ: Spot on. So – Tom. You can sleep in the spare room and start work in the morning. Goodnight, Harry! (Vanishes again)

DICK: Wow! Only been in London for ten minutes and I've got a job!

ALICE: ... and a friend.

DICK: Er, yeah, and somewhere to stay, and ...

ALICE: ... and nearly got married! (Laughs shyly)

DICK: er – yeah. (looks awkward)

SONG

SCENE TWO
RATTIGAN'S DEN

RATTIGAN: You call that booing? My mother boos at me louder than that!

That's better. At least the front row was trying. (To victim – usually a boy) You were very good – what's your name? "Steven" (for example). (To aud) He'll be sorry he told me that! Now – back to the plot!

SCABLEY & WINNET appear

RATTIGAN: This is not good. (shows bandage on tail) The Alderman has got a new boy working in his shop and – come closer my evil little friends. Err, ... what on earth is that smell?! (sniffs around – end up staring at 'Steven' in the audience) Steven – is that you?! Are you sure. Hmm. Well it's either you or Winnet! Winnet. Go back. .... Back...Farther. Scabley: it's you!

Hmm – seems it wasn't you, Steven. But don't think you can use this as an excuse! Where was I? Yes! In the shop! The new boy! And (looks around) and … this **fellow** has got - **a cat**.

WINNET: (from a distance) What'd he say? I can't hear over here.

SCABLEY: He says there's a new boy in the shop and he's yellow and got a hat.

WINNET: Oh. I had a hat once. Wasn't yellow though.

RATTIGAN: I didn't say that!

SCABLEY: (loud) He didn't say that!

WINNET: He didn't say what?

SCABLEY: (leans in) What didn't you say?

RATTIGAN: I didn't say he was yellow and has a hat!

SCABLEY: (nods knowingly and taps nose) Right. Say no more. We didn't hear it from you. Got that Winnet? The new yellow chap with the hat – we never heard about him from the boss.

WINNET: I can't hear anything from back here.

SCABLEY: So, boss. What is your latest evil plan?

RATTIGAN: Simple. He will have to – hee-hee – disappear.

SCABLEY: Off you go then, Winnet. Your turn to hide. We'll count to snork, then we come and find you.

WINNET: There's no such number as snork!

SCABLEY: Isn't there? (Thinks) Well what comes after six then?

WINNET: Er … dunno. Just count to six!

RATTIGAN: Not him! It's not Winnet that's got to disappear!

SCABLEY: Oy! Winnet! Mistake!

WINNET: What?

SCABLEY: Not your turn! Whose turn is it then, Boss? You went last yesterday so it must be...

RATTIGAN: The boy in the shop! Him! The boy in the shop!

SCABLEY: The boy in the shop! Right! Winnet – the boy in the shop! It's his turn to hide!

WINNET: Right! (Looks around) He's very good – I can't see him anywhere. I reckon he's played before!

SCABLEY: Should be easy to find him. He's bright yellow and got a great big hat on!

RATTIGAN: He's not hiding!

SCABLEY: Who's not hiding, Boss?

RATTIGAN: Look. Just stop.

SCABLEY: Haven't counted to snork yet, Boss.

RATTIGAN: Stop! (Regains composure) Luckily I have hired ... professional help.

SCABLEY: Psychiatrist, Sir? About time, if you ask me.

WINNET: Plastic surgeon be more useful!

RATTIGAN: A sea captain! An old mate of mine. They call him – The Captain. But – a warning!

WINNET: What?

RATTIGAN: The Captain has only got one eye.

WINNET: That's right though, isn't it?

RATTIGAN: What are you talking about, Winnet?

WINNET: There's only one 'i' in captain – two 'a's, one 'i' - else it would be 'captaiiiiiin'.

RATTIGAN: Listen carefully. Just don't mention the fact that he's only got one eye.

SCABLEY: Why? (Comes closer) Doesn't he know?

RATTIGAN: Of course he knows!! But it's just not polite!

WINNET & SCABLEY: OooOOooH!

WINNET: Is **he** yellow as well?

RATTIGAN: What?! No! Just be tactful about the fact that he's got one eye!

SCABLEY: Trust us. (Thinks) Where does he keep it?

RATTIGAN: Where does he keep what?

SCABLEY: Where does he keep this eye? Is it like in a box, or in a jar of vinegar or...

WINNET: You wouldn't keep it in a jar of vinegar. One night you might think to yourself: "Oh, I fancy a pickled onion with this bit of cheese" and before you know it...

SCABLEY: Very wise words. Very wise.

WINNET: (has come closer now) Very wise.

RATTIGAN: Winnet – move back. Even for a rat you smell disgusting! Have you never had a shower!

WINNET: Did once.

SCABLEY: Standing in the sewers beneath Wembley stadium at half time is not what the boss would call a shower.

WINNET: Wasn't just me: there was this American with a ginger wig on sideways: Donald something. He was orange. Perhaps he's related to this yellow bloke.

RATTIGAN: I don't know why I bother. I could have been a singer you know.

SCABLEY: What – you mean a sewing machine?

RATTIGAN: Just listen. (to boy) This one's for you 'Stevie baby'.

COMEDY SONG ruined by Scabley & Winnet (possibly repeating final chorus making Rattigan sing it over again twice, despite him telling them to stop.) Rattigan exits angrily. Scabley & Winnet hiss to orchestra then do song again, starting quietly. Toward end Rattigan reappears, stands next them and at

SCENE THREE: THE SHOP THE NEXT MORNING
There are crowds of people in the street and in the shop. Musical chorus number

FITZ: Well, done – you are a natural salesman, Tom. Never seen it so busy.
ALICE: I think most of the customers are silly girls just standing around giggling!
 (Some are still doing it) (they wander off)
The three rats enter with the Captain. They do not have their masks on.
RATTIGAN: There he is. That's the boy.
CAPTAIN: Leave him to me. Five minutes and he'll be begging to get on board me
 ship in search of adventure, and - once we're out at sea – well, lots of **nasty**
 things can happen to a young feller, if you gets my meaning.
RATTIGAN: Most definitely.
SCABLEY: Yeah.
WINNET: Like – how nasty?
SCABLEY: I went on a boat once and got pooped on by an albatross. (Checks
 clothes) Still here somewhere.
RATTIGAN: Get on with it!
They wander closer to Dick.
CAPTAIN: (loudly; Rattigan repeats some of the key words loudly) That's right.
 Chest-loads of treasure. More than I could fit in me ship. Might go back for some
 more. It's not too far away. More of a cruise really. Sail to the island, load up with
 gold, and jewels, and – er – more gold, come back and buy myself another
 mansion.
RATTIGAN: (loudly) Treasure, eh! Wish I was a younger chap and could go with
 you!
CAPTAIN: It certainly is a young man's job, carrying heavy sacks of gold coins. But
 that's not the worst of it, you know.
RATTIGAN: Not the worst, carrying sacks of gold coins?
CAPTAIN: No the worst is - the girls.
SCABLEY: What – you have to carry them?
CAPTAIN: No. When you gets back a rich man – with a lovely healthy tan – and big
 muscles from carrying gold – well, the girls is all over you. All over you!
SCABLEY: Like a bucket of pig-swill.
RATTIGAN: What?
SCABLEY: I had a bucket of pig-swill all over me once.
CAPTAIN: No, all over you – like – err –
WINNET: Hair? Hair all over you? Like Swedish girls?
CAPTAIN: No – just - you know – following you around.
SCABLEY: Is that true?
CAPTAIN: Aye – they follow you ...
SCABLEY: No – about the Swedish girls.
RATTIGAN: Shh! This treasure hunting – it sounds wonderful.
CAPTAIN: It is. I just wish I knew a bright young fellow who wanted to make his
 fame and fortune. But it's not to be. I'll just have to keep looking.
They wander off
DICK: Did you hear that? Fame and fortune!
ALICE: Sounds suspicious to me. Nothing is that easy. There's always a catch.
DICK: Nothing ventured.
ALICE: A fool and his money are soon parted.
DICK: He who hesitates is lost!
ALICE: Many a slip twixt cup and lip!

DICK: err – You can take a horse to water but you can't make him a woolly jumper!

ALICE: Ha!

DICK: But if I was rich, then I could –

ALICE: Could what? Mmm? If you were rich you could ...??

DICK: I could – oo-errr – I mean –...

SONG about money, with chorus support

All leave except Dick and Cat.

DICK: That Alice is rather nice. I'm sure that if I really was a rich man she might ... but that'll never happen, working in a shop. Which way did that Captain go?! I think he went – hey – Cat! What's the matter? Out of the way! I want to find the Captain! Hey! Bad Cat! (Cat is upset and slinks offstage.)

RATS & CAPTAIN return at other side of stage.

CAPTAIN: Told ee. The boy is hooked by the gills and will soon be gutted and on a plate!

RATTIGAN: Disgusting turn of phrase – but I like your attitude. Come on – lets 'reel him in'!

CAPTAIN: (louder) So – back to the harbour I goes, off to search for treasure and ...

DICK: Ah-ha! There you are! I was coming looking for you!

CAPTAIN: Looking for me! Why – you're not a beautiful young woman after my vast fortune I hope!

DICK: No I'm a boy!

CAPTAIN: (surprised: to aud: points at eye patch) I should have gone to Specsavers. A boy are ye? Tell me, lad, what be your name?

DICK: Dick!

CAPTAIN: Now that's not nice! It were only a polite question!

DICK: It's my name – Dick Whittington!

CAPTAIN: Never mind – I'll call ee 'Lad'. Not worth the trouble of learning yer name really, you're only going to be around for a couple of... (Rattigan hits him)

RATTIGAN: So – young feller – you want to travel in search of fortune, do you?

DICK: How did you guess? Are you a sailor?

RATTIGAN: Me? No – I'm an honest businessman. In fact .... I am the favourite to be the next Lord Mayor of London!

DICK: Lord Mayor of London? What does he do?

RATTIGAN: Do? Err – not sure really. Rides around in a coach. Has a chain! Earns loads of money!

DICK: I'd like a job like that! Where do you apply?

RATTIGAN: Silly boy – you'll never be Lord Mayor of London!

DICK: I might!

RATTIGAN: Don't be so pathetic! You're nothing compared to me! You have no money – no aristocratic family – no great house – you're just a penniless little wimp!

DICK: I'll show you! One day I'll be a rich man – then you'll see – I'll marry Alice **and** be Lord Mayor of London!

RATTIGAN: You? Don't make me laugh. You – are – (hissed) nothing. And when it comes to Alice – let me tell you one thing.

DICK: What?

RATTIGAN: Only this very morning I spoke to her father and we have come to an arrangement. I think you will find that you are not going to marry Alice – because I am!

DICK: That's not true!

RATTIGAN: No? Ask him yourself.

FITZ: (wanders on absently)

RATTIGAN: Alderman Fitzwarren!

FITZ: Eh? What? Oh – it's you again my dear Mr Rattigan! (shake hands)

DICK: You know this – person?

FITZ: Eh? What? Know him? Of course I do – this fellow is going to be the next Lord Mayor of London and – more important – my future son-on-law!

RATTIGAN: Told you so.

DICK: But Alice can't...

FITZ: Of course she can. As soon as she's broken the bad news to Tom, Joe and Harry.

DICK: Dick!

FITZ: (Ducks again. The rats are alarmed and jump aside.) I'm glad you're here, Geoff. That one nearly got me! (sees Captain) And you're here too, Captain.

CAPTAIN: Morning Alderman. How be business?

FITZ: Very good. In fact, I need to talk to you about your next trip. Come indoors – I want more silk and spices. (They exit into shop)

RATTIGAN: (rubs hands together happily) Har-har-har! (same laugh as heard earlier)

DICK: Don't I know you from somewhere? Your voice sounds familiar.

RATTIGAN: How would a low life like you know someone like me? Now, we must be off.

DICK: Your tail. (points to bandage on tail)

RATTIGAN: What about it?

DICK: How did you get that injury?

RATTIGAN: That was your dratted cat! Vicious brute should be put in a sack and thrown into the Thames! (other rats try to stop him talking)

DICK: You! You're the one who was...

RATTIGAN: So what? Who's going to believe a homeless beggar like you? And if you think you can go and "tell tales" - let me tell you something (Winnet and Scabley appear behind him with clubs)

One word from you - just one little word - and your cat – and you - and Alderman Fitzwarren AND the lovely Alice - all of you – will end up in sacks at the bottom of the Thames! Glug – glug – glug! Now get out of here! Run!

(They chase Dick to the front corner of the stage by the grassy knoll)

Ha! (To aud) Now you've got something to boo about!

The rats exit, swaggering and laughing.

Cat enters and makes to chase the rats.

DICK: Cat! Leave them! It will only cause trouble for Alice and her father. Come on. They were right. I'm nothing. Nobody will believe me – (fetches his bundle) - nobody will even notice I'm gone! Come one. London's not what I thought it would be. Let's go back to Gloucester.

SCENE 4: THE GRASSY KNOLL

Dick & Cat wander up & sit at the top again. Cat tries to cheer him up.

DICK: It's all right, Cat. I don't really mind being a failure. Gloucester isn't that bad I suppose. I can help my dad in the blacksmiths.

(Distant church bells toll 'oranges & lemons'.)

Listen to that, Cat. (Laughs) They're so glad to see me go they're ringing the bells!

(Bells toll again)

I won't miss London. It certainly was not paved with gold! And the people weren't exactly friendly. (Cat looks at him knowingly) Well, one of them was. (Cat nudges him) All right – OK! I might miss one or two of them.

> The bells toll again: faint words can be heard sung over the oranges & lemons tune:
>> CHORUS: "Turn again Whittington, Lord Mayor of London."

> Dick looks up in surprise. Cat meows and Dick shushes her. He listens. The song continues with the number of voices growing until the full chorus is singing but gently to give a magical effect. Harmonies and rounds are an option. **This needs to be quite long to allow scene change.** Music carries on quietly through the following)

> DICK: Lord Mayor of London! Me?! Joke! To be mayor of anywhere you have to be one of the fat cats! No offence! (Cat starts to pull him back to London) You want me to go back? But I'll never make my fortune in that place! (Inspiration) I know! The treasure! I'll go on the ship with the Captain! That's what I'll do! I'll sail the seven seas and return a rich man – be Lord Mayor of London – and marry Alice!! Then they'll believe me about that evil rat! Come on, Cat! Don't hang around here!

(They run back down onto the stage and EXIT.) MUSIC ENDS.

> RATTIGAN: (appears from behind the knoll) Ha! You can boo louder than that! Ha! I knew it was wise to follow that boy. "Lord Mayor of London" indeed!

> But I don't want that meddling brat returning a rich man and taking my job – or even returning at all!

> My good friend the Captain will deal with him as soon as they're out at sea. If I can trust that sea-faring fool.

> I know! I'll keep following the boy to see the job is done properly – and of course I do like to see a nice bit of random violence!

(Follows after them, laughing horribly)

> SCABLEY & WINNET: (appear from behind knoll – very out of breath)
> SCABLEY: Now what's the boss up to?
> WINNET: I reckon the boss is onto a bit of money and don't want to share it!
> SCABLEY: That's what I'm thinking – come on – he's not cutting us out! Keep following but don't let him see us! (You <u>may</u> need to add extra business here to cover the scene change. Perhaps ask Steven what he thinks of the show so far?) (They Exit after Rattigan)
> ALICE: (appears from behind knoll) Where can he be? I was sure I saw him on top of this hill! Did anyone see him? (to aud) Hello – did anyone see a rather handsome young fellow with a cat? You did? Do you know which way he went? Where is he going? (business with audience) The ship! Oh no! That sounds too dangerous! I must follow him and make sure he comes to no harm! (Exits after them)
> FITZ: (appear slowly from behind knoll – so out of breath he cannot talk) (to aud) Oh – gasp – work it out for yourselves. (Exits after them)

SCENE 5: THE CAPTAIN'S CABIN

> This is made of three solid sides OR a series of doors in flats/boxes at edge of stage. It could easily be the back of the shop from scene one. To the rear are the main windows at the rear of the ship. At the sides are cupboards. Also at each side is a chest-type bench/table with cloth. These benches have false fronts that hinge at the top allowing an occupant to roll in & out. There is a small table with a white cloth over it. There is a double hook for coat and hat in the corner behind DOOR R.

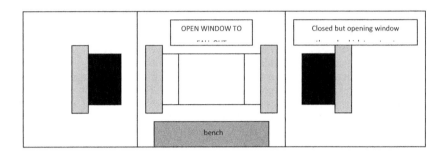

OPEN WINDOW TO
FALL OUT

Closed but opening window

bench

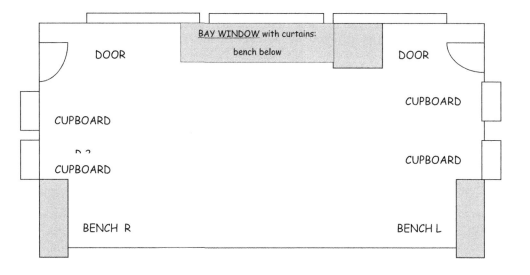

ALICE: (enters out of DOOR R) (to aud) Shh! It's me! I have smuggled myself on
  board. I just know that poor Dick is in danger, but he will be so cross if he knows
  I'm here! And if my father ever found out ... And what if that evil Captain finds
  out?! Perhaps this was not such a good idea? (She tiptoes back to Door R)
  Someone's coming! I'll hide! (She looks around then climbs into BENCH L)
SCABLEY & WINNET: enter (DOOR R)
SCABLEY: Quick – in here before they see us!
WINNET: In case who see us?
SCABLEY: Anyone! If the Captain sees us he'll throw us overboard. If that boy sees
  us he'll recognise us from the other day and know it's a trap!
WINNET: What about the boss? Can **he** see us? Or are we... (Spooky)...
  invisible?!
SCABLEY: What? No we are not... 'invisible' ... but the boss must NOT see us. I
  don't trust the boss – all this talk of treasure. What if it's TRUE?! We must get
  our share!
WINNET: (looks about) I've never been on a boat before.
SCABLEY: Ship! (both stand FRONT RIGHT to give maximum effect)
WINNET: No – it's true!
I wonder how far we are from land? (Runs over to the STAGE LEFT window)
  (Opens window & looks out. Huge wave drenches him. Staggers BACK CENTRE
  R.)
SCABLEY: Well? How far from land are we?
WINNET: Forgot to look.
SCABLEY: Clot. Go and have a proper look. (Repeat of action) Well? How far?
WINNET: Hard to say. Why don't **you** have a look? Go on! (Rubs hands and
  chuckles as Scabley goes to window, NO WATER)
SCABLEY: (returns DOWN R) Quite a long way – can't see land at all now.
WINNET: But ... (feels friend's dry clothes) ... what's going on? (Runs to window

and gets wet again. Returns slowly) (winks at audience) I think I can see an island! You go and have a look!

SCABLEY: (to window: dry; returns) No, nothing. You need your eyes testing.

WINNET: Right – I want you to come here (drags him, to window, pushes his head right out) and just wait until you can see something. (Waits giggling. Nothing happens)

SCABLEY: No, can't see any ...

WINNET: Get back out there and just wait! (Waits giggling. Nothing happens. Gets impatient) Anything yet?

SCABLEY: (at window) No. Just the sea .... and the sky ... and the waves ... and the .... Wow!

WINNET: What is it?!

SCABLEY: I think it's a mermaid!

WINNET: (runs back; drags him DOWN R, runs UP L and leans out) Let me see!! (Huge wave) (return DOWN L) I think I want to go home!

SCABLEY: Too late! Someone's coming! Quick! HIDE!

WINNET: goes to get into BENCH 1. Alice's head pops out but they don't see her.

SCABLEY: Not there – in a cupboard! (Both try to get into CUPBOARD L 1) Not you; you stinky rodent! Get your own! (He goes in but leaves his tail hanging out)

WINNET: Right! (Goes into CUPBOARD L 2)

RATTIGAN: (enters DOOR R) (to aud) (With mask on) So – you recognised me through my cunning disguise. You're not as stupid as you look, except for 'Steven' of course.

Yes, indeed - It's me – Rattigan! I have secreted myself – (pause, then withering look at audience) 'secreted'! It means hidden myself! You people...

I am on board this ship to see what that Captain does. I shall hide myself in his cabin and spy on him! Shh! Tell nobody! (Goes into CUPBOARD R 1)

FITZ: (enters DOOR R) Hello!! I say, hello? Oh! Nobody in here! I was sure I saw someone come in here! (To aud) I have no idea at all what is going on but I suspect foul play!

That Captain has taken a great deal of my money to buy precious silks and spices but I don't trust him! Tell you what – I'll hide myself and watch what happens! (Tries the 3 occupied doors but the rats stop them opening. He then goes across and goes into CUPBOARD R2)

CAPTAIN: (OFFSTAGE) Follow me! (Enters DOOR R.) Here we are, lad. (Pulls DICK in and shuts the door. Cat just gets tail inside in time) Me very best cabin (hangs coat on hook and puts hat on table) – and all yours for as long as you live. (to aud) About five minutes!

DICK: What?! As long as I ...?

CAPTAIN: Oo-ah – for as long as you LIKE! That's it – as long as you like.

DICK: Isn't it great, Cat? (Cat is nervous and appears not to like the captain) Hey! Calm down. Don't be so unfriendly. This is very kind of you, Captain. Wow! And look at the view.

CAPTAIN: The view! Yes. Do come and have a look out! Here – kneel on this bench. You'll get a much better view of the sea. (To aud) A much CLOSER view!

Dick climbs up onto the bench. He opens the window and leans out. Slowly the Captain moves to push Dick out. At the last moment the cat sees Scabley's rat-tail from the cupboard and goes for it. Scabley opens the door, whacks Cat on the nose, grabs tail back in & shuts door. At this noise the Captain jumps away and Dick jumps down.

CAPTAIN: Barnacles and winkles!

DICK: What is it, Cat? Come away – don't scratch the Captain's furniture! This is a lovely room, Captain, but where do I sleep?

CAPTAIN: Your hammock is through here. Follow me! (to aud) Next time! (They all go through DOOR L and close it behind them; Cat lingers suspiciously but is called through)

SCABLEY & WINNET: (both appear cautiously from L1 & L2 and move centre.)

SCABLEY: So – that boy's here.

WINNET: What – the yellow one? I didn't notice his hat.

SCABLEY: There is definitely something going … look out! (Rattigan starts to come out of R1. The two rats hide: Scabley <u>behind</u> cupboard door R1; Winnet under the table)

RATTIGAN: Well – it sounded as if he was trying to get rid of the boy and throw him into the sea – but I shall keep watch!

(Behind him Scabley darts across into L1)

RATTIGAN: What's going on? Something strange here.

(Goes upstage and puts sword down on table then returns centre)

What is going on? 'Steven' – what's happening? (if no response) So – that's your attitude is it? Don't come up here later expecting sweeties!

(Goes back to get sword but by now the table has moved across the room)

What?! But?

(Grabs sword and goes to stab under cloth but hears a noise)

They return! Oops!

(Dashes into R2)

CAPTAIN: (Enters)… and if you need anything, you know where I'll be.

DICK: (Enters) In the crows-nest at the top of the mast. I just put on a blindfold, climb up the rigging and find you.

CAPTAIN: That's it, lad.

(Reaches for hat but table has moved. Is suspicious. Gets hat off table and hangs it on hook above coat. Takes Dick down centre with arm around his shoulder.)

(While there Winnet gets out and dives into cupboard L2)

You see the table behind us – no, don't look! Do you notice anything odd about it? No? I have suspicions that something is... afoot! What do you think is afoot?

DICK: (joking) How about 12 inches?

CAPTAIN: (looking at him odd) I'm not sure what you're offering me, lad, but I must say you have aroused my curiosity!

(Pulls out dagger)

Wait here.

(Captain whirls at the table but it has moved.)

Barnacles and winkles!

(There is a click as Winnet closes door L2. The Captain hears it. He lifts eye patch and winks and nods at Dick who returns exaggerated wink in total ignorance)

There is something wrong here, lad. You just wait and see if I'm not right.

(Loud and clear) Right then! I am just popping out on deck for a bit of fresh air!

(He opens door, leaves it open, and makes stamping noise as if walking away. Instead he returns to Dick, checks his dagger for sharpness and giggles.)

(While he does this Winnet sneaks out of L2 and tiptoes across to stand behind the <u>open</u> door R.) (With a roar the Captain dives at cupboard L2 but of course it is now empty.)

DICK: This sailing stuff looks like fun! Can I have a go?

CAPTAIN: (confused, searching cupboard, leaves it open) What's that?

DICK: I say – this looks like fun. Can I have a go?

(Makes silly fierce noises then runs at cupboard L1 and yanks it open.)

(Scabley leans out, smiles at him and waves)

Yikes!

(Dick closes door quickly then gets Captain and hurries him down centre.)

(Scabley now swaps from L1 to L2.)
I think you may have... rats!
CAPTAIN: I think you may be right!
(Both nervously attack L1 but it is empty)
We must search the cabin. (rethinks this) You make a start – I'll get more weapons.
(He closes the open Door R. Winnet is standing behind it wearing the hat. The
    Captain takes the hat and dusts it off. Winnet smiles nervously at him.)
WINNET: Morning!
CAPTAIN: Morning. (He puts hat on and leaves, closing Door R.)
(Winnet now leaves the door and dives into the window seat.)
A second later the Captain returns in a rage and attacks the hanging coat still on
    the hook.)
Barnacles and winkles! Nothing!
Not feeling too bright today. I think it must be time for a tot of rum. (Wanders out
    Door R and closes it)
DICK: What fun! Better go and unpack! (Leaves through Door L)
FITZ: (comes out of cupboard) I think I am starting get seasick. Fresh air – that's
    the thing! (Goes over to window, climbs up on bench and sits on window sill)
SCABLEY: (comes out of Cupboard L2: stage whisper:) Winnet!
FITZ: Something is happening! I must hide! (Pulls curtain across in front of himself
    or blanket over head).
SCABLEY: Winnet! Where are you? Winnet?!
WINNET: I'm here! (bobs up in bench, raises lid and topples Fitz out of window.
(Distant yell and far off splash.)
What was that?
(Winnet looks out of window and gets soaked again)
I am definitely going off this cruising lark.
(Creaking sound as Rattigan comes out of R2)
Look out!
(Winnet gets back in box)
(Scabley has nowhere to go so eventually hides behind window curtain/blanket on
    top of box by window.)
RATTIGAN: (stage whisper to aud) I recognise those voices. And that smell! Only
    two creatures on the planet smell like that – one is 'Steven' – and the other is
    that fool, Winnet! (Louder) Winnet!!
WINNET: (bobbing up) What?!
(Scream etc as Scabley falls out window)
OOPS!
(Winnet ducks back down unseen)
(RATTIGAN panics and dives back into R2.)
(WINNET comes out again.)
WINNET: Scabley? Where are you?
SCABLEY: (distant drowning voice) I'm down here!
WINNET: Where?
SCABLEY: Look out the window!
(Winnet does and gets soaked again)
WINNET: This is not good for my complexion! (Gets back into box)
RATTIGAN: (reappears) Yes! Definitely the voice of those fools! But where are
    they? In here? (Goes to look in Box L but as he lifts the lid - and Alice appears
    ready to punch him - he turns, having heard Scabley.)
SCABLEY: (distant) I'll get you – you stinking rat! (keep repeating if noisy)
(RATTIGAN rushes to the window, kneels on box and looks out.)
RATTIGAN: I knew it! (Shouting) Is that you down there, Winnet?!

WINNET: (pops up) No – I'm in here.
(Rattigan falls out window into the sea.)
Oops. Was that the boss?
(Winnet rushes to the window and gets soaked again. He goes to dry his face with the tablecloth.)
(CAPTAIN returns. WINNET hides under table again.)
CAPTAIN: (leaps nervously around, searches coat) I've brought weapons! Barnacles and winkles! Where is the boy?
DICK: (enters from Door L) Here I am!
CAPTAIN: Time for some searching, lad. Here! (hands him weapon) Start looking! (He looks in window box then out window.)
 (Dick goes to Box L where Alice is. As he lifts the lid Dick is distracted by Captain shouting:)
CAPTAIN: Look! Something floating down there!
(During this Alice rolls out of the false front/cloth and crawls/runs across [wet] floor to roll into front flap of R1)
DICK: (searches box) Nothing in here.
CAPTAIN: Nor here. Tell ee what lad – we'll play them at their own game. You hide in here (opens window box) and we'll surprise em like!
(Dick gets in window box)
There. Now then – let's see you do your worst! (stands downstage centre)
(WINNET tries to sneak the table across the room but it bumps into the Captain's bottom who looks alarmed but does not turn. WINNET creeps out of the table but gets the tablecloth caught over his head. He stands up, as the CAPTAIN turns around.
CAPTAIN: Aargh! A ghost! (He dives out the window. Splash!)
WINNET: (Pulls cloth off) Who was that?! (Opens window, water)
(ALICE now starts to sneak out – WINNET hides in any cupboard.)
ALICE: I'm sure I heard Dick's voice.
CAPTAIN: (OFF) Help – I can't be swimming!
ALICE: A voice - in the water! What if it's Dick and they've made him walk the plank! (She goes to window and kneels on box to look out) Dick! DICK!
DICK: What? (As he bobs up from the box Alice flies out of window. Splash)
ALICE: (OFF) HELP! HELP!
DICK: Oh no! It's Alice – what on earth is she doing here? (leans out window) Alice! What are you doing in the water?
ALICE: (OFF) Drowning!
DICK: Oh, right. Drowning. DROWNING!! Oh no! (Leaps out to save her – splash)
Silence
(WINNET slowly appears.)
WINNET: All gone! The ship all to myself! Luxury! All alone. (Hums: 'Sailing') I shall sail the Snork Seas in search of treasure islands! Perhaps there's one out there right now! I'll take a look. (Goes toward window but stops at last minute) Oh no! (to aud) Not again! I'm not here for your amusement! I'll go up on deck where it's dry and have a good look round!
(Goes to Door Right and opens it. Huge bucket/s of water.)
WINNET: Enough! I can take no more! (Goes to window and jumps out yelling: Pinocchio!)
After 2 seconds all the cupboards and doors and boxes open and the chorus plus everyone else available, inc. stagehands, make up, wardrobe (the more the funnier) come out with suitcases etc. looking crabby & cramped.
PERSON: That's it – next time we fly Easyjet! (or similar)

ACT TWO
SCENE 6: THE PALACE OF THE SULTANA
A very richly appointed throne room glittering with silk drapes and gold.
The Sultana is raised on a platform with huge cushions, surrounded by
chests filled with treasure. She is being fanned by a slave.
EXOTIC MUSICAL NUMBER: Sultana & Chorus (not the 'rat' children)

SERVANT: Oh great and wise one; oh mistress of magical mysteries; oh splendid
spectacle of the starry skies; oh ...

SULTANA: Oh get on with it! What do you want you irritating little dung beetle?

SERVANT: Amazing things have occurred, oh wise and wondrous one!

SULTANA: (suggests something topical or local)

SERVANT: Not quite that amazing, oh fascinating fantasy of feminine fashion.
Firstly, a sailing ship has arrived in our harbour ...

SULTANA: So? That happens every day! I want real amazement, you festering blob
of beggar's earwax.

SERVANT: Indeed, oh all-splendid and all-seeing one; but this ship is completely
empty – not a single living soul on board.

SULTANA: some topical reference to e.g. luxury cruise ship with tummy bug – or
simply skip this line

SERVANE: But, oh sensuous siren of the shimmering seas, there is more! A
short way along the coast we captured spies trying to swim ashore

SULTANA: Spies! Bring them forth!

SERVANT: Right. Forth? Er – who do you want to see for the first three?

SULTANA: No – bring them here. Now!

SERVANT: Certainly, oh blessed breeze of balmy bliss. Two ticks! (exits)

SERVANT 2: Oh great one. Would you like a grape?

SULTANA: Hmm. What colour?

SERVANT 2: Colour? We have pale green, dark green, yellow, red, pink, purple, or
black.

SULTANA: I think I'll have…. blue.

SERVANT 2: Err, no – oh mistress of infinite appetite. Not blue.

SULTANA: No!! NO?! (menacingly) Grow some.

SERVANT 2: It shall happen as your mightiness commands.

SULTANA: Good. Or it's off with your head.

SERVANT 2: 'Ere – that's a bit harsh – just to grow some bloomin' grapes!

SULTANA: Executioner! (Enters with huge axe) Off with her head! (Watches them
go!)

SERVANT 2: Here – I've got rights too! I'll have the Daily Mail (Or similar) onto you!
(hits executioner and makes him back off nervously)

SULTANA: I'm bored. Where are my singers?

SERVANT 3: She who must be obeyed demands her singers!

VOICE OFF: FETCH THE SINGERS! Fetch the singers. THIS COULD BE
'DANCERS' OR 'MUSICIANS' – depends on the talent available.

Singers appear; 2 elegant operatic divas or similar, as available.

PERFORMER 1: We attend your majesty. What is your wish?

SULTANA: My wish is to be entertained without any interruption! Right – the rest of
you. You know the rules! None of you mention 'you-know-what'! Right? Good.
So – what are you going to perform?

PERFORMER 2: Well, your wonderfulness, she with the ears of gold, tonight we are
going to sing ..

SERVANT: (enters) Oh splendid one ......

SULTANA: You have disturbed my entertainment! Off with his/her head!

SERVANT: As you wish, but if I may finish: oh splendid one with the silhouette of a supermodel.

SULTANA: Ha! You worthless flatterer! Your words are like the fart of a bluebottle in the desert sands. (menacing & sly) Which supermodel?

SERVANT: er .... (Someone current)

SULTANA: That'll do nicely. What do you want, you worthless scraping from a camel's armpit?

SERVANT: The spies!

SULTANA: Alright! The entertainment can wait! Bring in the spies.

Rattigan, Captain, Winnet & Scabley are forced in.

RATTIGAN: Unhand me – do you know who I am?

SULTANA: Off with their heads!

RATTIGAN: What?!

SULTANA: Off with their heads!

RATTIGAN: Ooops! (makes them fall to their knees) Have mercy on us, oh great and powerful one! We are not spies – I am the Lord Mayor of London and these are – err – all rich and important people!

SULTANA: I have heard of this 'London'. Arise and tell me of London. Is it as modern as I hear tell?

RATTIGAN: Modern? London? Well, yes - it has every modern convenience – gas light, sewers, trams, and some houses are even getting loos!

SULTANA: Loos? What are 'loos'?

SERVANT: Your majesty! What have you said?!

SULTANA: Me? I just said 'what are loos'. Oh no!

RATTIGAN: I don't understand!

SULTANA: (in despair) You will! You will!

Sound of little feet steadily grows louder until MANY rats pour on stage and sing & dance to: Abba: WATERLOO. They exit squealing.

CAPTAIN: Barnacles and winkles! What on earth be that?!

SULTANA: It is our curse! Our land is over-run with rats – Abba singing rats! Any mention of a song by those screeching Swedish women and the rats appear!

WINNET: Are they covered in hair?

SULTANA: Rats – of course …

WINNET: No – these Swedish women.

RATTIGAN: Be silent you fool. (hits with tail)

SULTANA: I would give half my fortune to anyone who could rid me of this plague!

SCABLEY: Have you tried rinsing with mouthwash?

WINNET: Not 'plaque' – plague! Call yourself a rat and don't know what plague is?!

SULTANA: Rat? You are rats?! Off with their …

RATTIGAN: Ignore this poor fool, oh merciful one – s/he said 'prat' – which is glaringly evident!

SULTANA: Hmmm. Now tell me more about London.

SULTANA: I expect it is the same as here – everyone wants their bribe to get things done.

RATTIGAN: Very true, oh all seeing one – even in England it is gimme, gimme ...

SERVANT 5: gimme ... No! I couldn't help it! The tune is so catchy! I can't get it out of my head!

SULTANA: Well I have the cure for that! Off with her head!

RATS – ABBA SONG

SULTANA: I'm losing the will to live. Perhaps **now** I can hear a decent tune? Try again, singers/dancers; what have you for us tonight?

PERFORMER 1: Tonight, oh permed and tinted one, we shall be singing ...
SERVANT: (enters excitedly) Oh lustrous and luminous one!
SULTANA: You did it again, you festering flake of athlete's foot! Off with his/her ...
SERVANT: Hang on .... err .... Oh quivering queen of quiet, quality .... Oh heck. What else starts with a 'q'?
SCABLEY: The Harrods' sale? (or similar)
SULTANA: Just get on with it.
SERVANT: There are more spies!
RATTIGAN: (To aud & cronies) That will be the wretched boy and his cronies! I saw them swimming ashore farther down the coast! (Louder to Sultanna) Your wonderfulness!
SULTANA: You may speak, grovelling one.
RATTIGAN: I know of these infidels! They are indeed spies – sent by the King of ... King of .... Quick! Name of somewhere violent and primitive!
WINNET: [local town].
RATTIGAN: Good choice! ... the King of [local town]. - to spy on you!
SULTANA: Spies! I shall boil them in ....
SERVANT: No – don't say the 'o' word! We'll be up to our necks in Americans!
SULTANA: Good thinking. Bring the spies in!
 Dick, Alice & Fitzwarren are dragged in.
RATTIGAN: Yes – these are the very spies of which I warned you! (to executioner) Oy – chopper boy! Off with their heads!
SULTANA: Oy! I say that bit!
RATTIGAN: Sorry.
SULTANA: Right, No problem. Off with their heads!
DICK: Hang about – we're not spies! I am Richard Whittington of Gloucestershire and this is my friend Alice and this is Alderman Fitzwarren of the City of London.
FITZ: How do you do?
SULTANA: Very well thank you.
DICK: And who are you?
SULTANA: Me? You dare speak to ME in this manner! Off with his head.
DICK: Stop larking about. Who are you then?
SERVANT: (to Dick) This – oh doomed one – this monumental mountain of maiden-hood ...
SULTANA: Not sure I liked that one.
SERVANT: This – dazzling divinity of delights brought to earth to illuminate our insignificant existence.
SULTANA: Better. Keep them there.
SERVANT: ... she is THE SULTANA.
Dick giggles
SULTANA: Why do you laugh?!
DICK: "sultana"!
SULTANA: Boy! Why do you laugh?!
DICK: No .... "raisin"! (gets hysterical)
SULTANA: Do you mock me?
DICK: Not at all – to meet you is a 'grape' pleasure, my 'old fruit'!
SULTANA: Are you jesting?
ALICE: No – he means – to meet someone as glorious and important as you is super. Really super!
VOICE: TROOPER!
SULTANA: Who was that?! Off with their head!
ABBA SONG
SULTANA: Will nobody rid me of those rats?

DICK: I think they're quite cute?

SULTANA: Cute? You wouldn't think so if that's all you could hear every minute of every day? Having to watch every word.

WINNET: I wouldn't mind – not if I was as rich as you!

RATTIGAN: Ignore my feeble minded friend – all s/he thinks about is money, money, money! (As he says the last word there is widespread cry of dismay, but too late)

ABBA SONG

DICK: Ah – bless! Thank you, little rats – thank you for the music!

ABBA SONG

DICK: Ah – yes – I see what you mean. It could get on your nerves a bit.

RATTIGAN: Your imperial mintiness. Shall you not dispose of these spies?

SULTANA: Whatever. I've really lost all interest in being nasty to people.

RATTIGAN: No interest in being nasty?!! I'm sure that's not true. (goes and sits next to her to amazed gasps; takes her hand) I think you and I are very like in many ways; I'm sure we think alike. May I suggest that - knowing me, knowing you – the best...

ABBA SONG

RATTIGAN: Get off – filthy little things! I can't stay this cheerful forever you know!

SULTANA: And to make it worse – just look at my coat of arms!

CAPTAIN: What is it – a plant and a circle? What type of plant is it?

SULTANA: A fern.

RATTIGAN: The letter 'O' and a fern. What's wrong with that?

SULTANA: Think about it.

ALICE: I get it! Fern and O!

ABBA SONG

SULTANA: Does anyone want to chop their heads off? I've gone past caring.

RATTIGAN: I'd like to! Off with their heads! Don't look at me like that! It's not personal – it's just the name of the game!

ABBA SONG

SULTANA: (very angry) That's enough! Are you doing this on purpose? The next one to say an Abba song is in real – deep trouble – up to their necks – which will be just as far as their body goes! Do you get my drift? (sudden idea) Ah-ha! Right! I have it! A competition! Look – here is a huge pile of treasure. It is all up for grabs. The winner will be the first one to get rid of those singing rats and THE WINNER TAKES IT ALL! Aargh!!

ABBA SONG

SULTANA: That's it – everyone out. Bedtime! You have one night to get rid of the rats then in the morning it's off with ALL your heads. Night-night! Sleep tight!

(most exit) (Captain – who has been amazed by the exotic dancers/slave girls throughout chases these off.)

RATTIGAN: That Captain – he has an eye for the girls.

SCABLEY: Really? Where does he keep it then, this eye?

RATTIGAN: Where does he ... idiot! Come, fellow schemers, let us plot! (Villains leave)

Only Dick & Alice left

DICK: Well – what a set-up! And who would have thought I'd see you here? What were you doing on the ship in the first place?

ALICE: Following you. Making sure you were OK.

DICK: Really? Wow! You know – all that soppy stuff about getting married ... well – if I DID ask you – and I'm not saying I'm going to or anything. but ...

ALICE: How could I resist you?

DICK: Hang on. (Looks around) Isn't that in an Abba song?

They sing Mamma Mia but at 'how could I resist you' the rats join in quietly.
The rats stay at the end of the song

DICK: (to rats) You know – you fellows could make a fortune in London singing like that.

RAT 1: Love to mate, but if she thought we were worth money she'd never let us go!

RAT 2: No – if she knew people would pay to hear us ......!

DICK: Hmm! Listen carefully – I have a cunning plan! (all exit)

Rattigan returns L

RATTIGAN: (to aud) No – I think you will find that I am the one with the cunning plan!

Captain enters R

CAPTAIN: What are you up to now?

RATTIGAN: You'll see. Here it comes! Hurry along! Drag it in!

Scabley and Winnet fetch machine. This machine is like a wardrobe open at both sides, with an arrow on the front: OFF, STUN, DROP DEAD, AARGH!

CAPTAIN: So what is it?

RATTIGAN: This – is a rat-trap! Winnet has made it to my design. It is to kill baby rats!

CAPTAIN: Is it now? Barnacles and winkles – that was quick work! What does it do?

RATTIGAN: Very simple. Even the most stupid person on the planet can understand it, can't you 'Steven'.

RATTIGAN: (after every underlined word Winnet does the 'magician's assistant bit and repeats the word with an irritating flourish) First we get some cheese. Then I set this lever. Next (notices Winnet) I place the cheese on this spigot. (notices Winnet again and frowns) The trap is now fully armed. (notices Winnet again and glares)

CAPTAIN: How does it work then?

RATTIGAN: Aha! It is simplicity itself! (notices Winnet nibbling lump of cheese and glares) The cheese .... (eventually is handed to him) The cheese is placed in here, thusly. Into the trap the unsuspecting rat is lured. (glares at Winnet) The machine does its **diabolical machinations**! (Winnet looks vague and flaps arms vaguely) Then out the lifeless, mortified cadaver ... flops. (Presses finger to Winnet's lips. As he walks away Winnet says "Flops".)

CAPTAIN: Don't quite get it.

RATTIGAN: I'll show you. Scabley! In you go!

SCABLEY: What. Me again? In there? Not bloomin' likely!

RATTIGAN: Don't be such a baby. Look – I'll just set it to STUN. There – now in you go! (Pushes him in. Noise, shaking, shrieking etc from machine)

SCABLEY: (reappears as quick as possible – in a stunning dress, hat & sunglasses) There! Stunning!

CAPTAIN: 'Ee don't look lifeless!

RATTIGAN: Drat the machine. In you go again! DROP DEAD setting! (Grabs Scabley and thrusts him inside again the turns dial to DROP DEAD. Tells aud. what it says. More noise and screeching.

SCABLEY: (appears in even more amazing outfit) Wahey! Drop dead gorgeous!

RATTIGAN: That's not right! What's going on with this stupid machine!! Out of my way!

He pushes them aside, turns dial to OFF, strides inside.
Scabley wickedly turns the dial to AARGH!
A rising sound grows and grows, as does sounds of distress.

When the noise & vibration reaches a peak Rattigan appears in bizarre clothes. Chases rats off in rage. All exit with machine.

SULTANA and her minions reappear, followed by Fitz, Dick & Alice.

SULTANA: How can I sleep with all this noise?! Someone will lose their heads! You, boy – I blame you!

DICK: It wasn't me – I was busy with my secret plan for getting rid of the singing rats!

SULTANA: Get rid of the rats? Is this possible?

DICK: I think so! All we have to do is get the rats back and try it out!

SULTANA: How will we do that?

DICK: Well, your sultanniness; you are sort of the queen around here? (She agrees) Then come down here – don't be shy – follow us. (Dick & Alice start to dance – gradually the Sultana joins in and starts to enjoy it) Look everyone! Come and see your dancing queen!

ABBA SONG

In the middle of the song Cat appears and rounds up the rats, chasing them off. The rats pretend to be afraid. As the last one leaves Dick talks to it:

DICK: Meet you all on the boat like we planned! (Winks)

Last rat exits happily

SULTANA: Gone! They have gone! And all thanks to this amazing creature. What manner of beast is it?

DICK: This, is a cat! She has found her way here from the ship!

SULTANA: A 'cat'? Is it safe? (Nervously strokes cat) Truly magnificent!

Cat exits proudly.

FITZ: I'm not entirely sure what's going on here.

ALICE: This clever fellow has just solved the problem of the singing rats - and won all that treasure!

FITZ: Which clever fellow?

ALICE: Dick!

FITZ: (Ducks again.) This is not good for my back you know!

SULTANA: The girl is right! The treasure is now yours! And this day shall forever be named after you. Tell us your name that it may be written in the book of our history!

DICK: Dick!

SULTANA: Let it be known – for the rest of time this day will be a holiday, forever known as 'Dick Day'. (all look a bit concerned at this)

ALICE: Hmm. How about 'Spring Bank Holiday'?

SULTANA: Probably for the best. So be it! If that is agreed by you – er – Dick?

DICK: I can live with that. (Looks at Alice) And, Alderman Fitzwarren? If it's all right with you – there's someone else I wish to live with. (Nods at `Alice)

FITZ: Well, I do have a spare room.

DICK: No – not you, sir. With Alice!

FITZ: What? Like as in 'married'? (Alice & Dick nod) Right: I have to ask you some questions: first …

DICK: Yes – I do have an enormous amount of money and I also plan to be next Lord Mayor of London. Next question?

FITZ: I think that rather covers everything... but I've got the feeling I'm forgetting something important ….

ALICE: Like what?

Enter three rat villains – with swords. Dramatic music.

RATTIGAN: Like me! Your father promised that you would marry me!

ALICE: What?!

FITZ: That was it! Now I remember! Seemed a good idea at the time. Nice fellow, good prospects, bags of money.

RATTIGAN: Indeed. And even more money when I get back to England with this pile of treasure!

WINNET: There, Scabley – told you. We're going to be rich!

RATTIGAN: Not you two! You ruined my only song in this show! You're getting nothing! Nothing!

SULTANA: I say! That treasure is not yours, and you cannot have it!

RATTIGAN: And who's going to stop me?

SULTANA: (pointing at cowardly servant) (nervously) He/She is?

SERVANT: Oooer! Umm – off with his head! Hello? Anyone? Off with his ... umm.

RATTIGAN: Boo! (Servant cowers.)

DICK: Ha! I know someone who can deal with you. Where is she? Ca ... (Rattigan grabs him by the throat before he can call Cat)

RATTIGAN: No you don't! No four-legged flea-bag to save you this time! (To rats) You two! Start loading the treasure onto the ship! (menacing) I want to deal with this brat myself!

(Winnet a& Scabley exit)

ALICE: (runs toward to aud) This is awful. We must call for Cat. Will you all help me?

(During this Rattigan is still menacing Dick and shouting at the audience)

Will you help? When I count to three we must all shout 'Cat' as loud as we can! Ready? One-two-three. CAT!!

Nothing! Even louder! One-two-three!

Still nothing! Call again! Louder!

Cat runs down the hall/theatre onto the stage. She circles Rattigan but he has the sword & Cat can't attack.

Alice gets a long heavy object (eg. stick part of Rattigan's sword stick) to hit Rattigan but Fitz, very confused, is standing in the way.

ALICE: Dad! DUCK!

FITZ: What?

ALICE: DUCK!

FITZ: Ah-ha: you mean 'DICK' – you won't catch me with that aga ... (gets whacked on head)

Things look lost but Winnet wheels the rat-catcher box on.

Rattigan is forced backwards into the box, complaining loudly about the cat's sharp nails.

Scabley spins the arrow until warning lights flash.

Chorus enter to see what is happening.

Vibration & noise increase until machine explodes/collapses OR just breaks down. This time it is empty (Rattigan having crept out of the back into the crowd & exited).

FITZ: Gone! Nothing left but his tail! (holds it up)

DICK: And nothing left but to load the treasure on the ship and sail home to England!

PERFORMER 1: (They enter) Oy! Hung around here for twenty minutes like lemons!

PERFORMER 2: Let's at least have a bit of a tune before we all go home!

SULTANA: At last! Let the entertainment commence!

CHORUS: MUSICAL NUMBER TO END SCENE (some principals will exit to get changed)

SCENE 7: COMMUNITY SONG

Alice and Dick and Cat enter with suitcases / duty-free bags. Finale
costumes.

ALICE: So nice to be back in England again.

DICK: Yeah – I wonder what's (something topical / been happening in TV
show?)

FITZ: (enters excitedly with newspaper) Thank goodness I've found you! You
are the talk of all London. Everyone knows how you freed the Sultana from
the plague of rats, and won the treasure…!

DICK: Yes?

FITZ: AND – now that you are the richest man in the city there is talk of you
being the new Lord Mayor of London! (to aud) See: 'cash-for-honours'
even back in these days!

ALICE: This is wonderful. I'm so excited I must buy some new shoes!

DICK: (to aud) Nope – even in a panto that doesn't make sense!

OPTION: choose actors to do the rest of the scene.

BUSINESS WITH CHILDREN & COMMUNITY SONG.

SCENE 8: FINALE

Banqueting hall of the Lord Mayor of London OR back in London.
On stage: chorus, Fitz, Captain, Scabley, Winnet, Sultana & servants in fine
clothes. No rats yet.

FITZ: My Lords, ladies & gentlemen. Honoured guest – the Sultana of - er –
Sultana-land. Please raise your glasses in a toast - to the new Lord Mayor
of London and his lovely new wife: Lord and Lady Whittington!

They enter to applause

ALICE: This happy day has come at last.

DICK: And all my dreams have come to pass.

SCABLEY: No more crime – we know that's wrong.

WINNET: Just cut the chat – let's have a song!

SULTANA: No Abba songs – they make me sick!

ALICE: Those days are gone now, thanks to Dick.

FITZ: Thanks to who?

ALICE: Dick!

FITZ: Ducks. My word. They're flying low today!

SCABLEY: The world is free from that evil rat.

DICK: And all thanks to this splendid Cat!

WINNET: Our boss just got what he was due.

SULTANA: Indeed – he met his Waterloo! … OH NO!!!!!!

LIST OF TITLES

Click to select

1. CINDERELLA
2. ROBIN HOOD
3. DICK WHITTINGTON
4. SLEEPING BEAUTY
5. RED RIDING HOOD & THE 3 PIGS
6. THREE MEN IN A TUB
7. JACK AND THE BEANSTALK
8. HANSEL AND GRETEL
9. SNOW WHITE & 7 DWARVES

CONTACT INFORMATION
and PERFORMANCE RIGHTS here:

PANTOSCRIPTS.ME.UK

SLEEPING BEAUTY

© Chris Lane 2018

ACT I: SCENE 1: BALLROOM OF KING BRENDAN AND QUEEN FELICITY:
THE CHRISTENING OF PRINCESS BEAUTY

A magnificent ballroom with everybody on stage except Fairy Starglow, Fairy Toadlick and Yurinn.

King Brendan & Queen Felicity can be on their thrones, beside them are their guests King Peppin the 1st and Queen Petronella. Courtiers are dancing; royal children could be running about & playing with hobby horses, wooden swords, etc. There could be a jester.

OPENING NUMBER (virtually the full company.)

> KING BRENDAN: Greetings, people of Tintinabula! My wife, Queen Felicity, and I wish to thank you all for coming to the christening of Princess Beauty!
> Cheers.
> QUEEN FELICITY: Yes; King Brendan and I thank you all for being with us on this happy, happy day.
> KING BRENDAN: And a special thanks to our allies from over the seas: King Peppin of Pimplevania, and his beautiful wife, Queen Petronella. (All bow)
> KING PEPPIN: No, no, no – it is you, King Brendan that <u>we</u> must thank. With your friendship our two countries, Tintinabula and Pimplevania, have been at peace, and together we have stood strong against the tides of war that circle us.
> QUEEN PETRONELLA: Now – my ears don't wish to hear any talk of war; after all – they are the ears of a queen you know.
> QUEEN FELICITY: (ignores others raised eyebrows) Indeed. Well spoken, Queen Felicity. My ears are also those of a queen – and agree with you.
> KING BRENDAN: Very true, my dear. We even invited King Septimus to be here at this christening, but the old devil has a baby daughter of his own – called "Cecily" and – "coincidence" - she is being christened on this very day!
> KING PEPPIN: Really?! I am sure I received no invitation to that! Did we dear?
> QUEEN PETRONELLA: No, my dear; we did not.
> QUEEN FELICITY: I cannot believe that <u>anyone</u> of any importance has gone to that other christening!
> QUEEN PETRONELLA: Indeed. I mean – I am here and I am a queen! And look – (indicating audience) – even the common folk have made an effort!
> KING BRENDAN: (peering into audience) Not too sure about <u>that</u> one. There – that one. See? (They peer & agree)
> QUEEN FELICITY: Hush now. (Puts wifely hand on his arm) Herald!
> HERALD: (Has appeared directly behind them; shouts random words far too loud) Your **high**ness!!
> QUEEN FELICITY: (In alarm) Oh me. (Calms) Herald; do we not have the finest people from throughout the land?
> HERALD: In**deed**, highness. Not **one** person **of** Himportance has been left **out**. From the mightiest Kings **and** Queens (checks she is happy with that – she is) and also Princes, Princ**esses**, Lords, Ladies, ANYBODY IN AUDIENCE OF NOTE and ... by no means **least** ...fairies! Fairy Starglow! (They all turn to look for Fairy Starglow)
> FAIRY STARGLOW: (Enters flustered) I'm here! (To audience?) Hello all! Having a nice time? Right: do you want me to do the bunny trick now? (Starts to produce

bunny from cloak / bag. Music. Starts to do poor trick)

KING BRENDAN: (has seen the trick a lot!) Not at all! (Stops her) Fairy Starglow: your tricks are not needed! You are here as a guest!

FAIRY STARGLOW: Am I? Super! I am very pleased to be here, (wobbly curtsey) your majestics.

QUEEN FELICITY: (To Queen Petronella) Have you met our fairy? King Peppin, Queen Petronella, let me introduce you to the wisest and kindest fairy in the land: Fairy Starglow Pretty-Pretty Dew-Shine.

FAIRY STARGLOW: Oh – get on with you; I'm just an ordinary, every-day, working fairy. (Looks embarrassed) Are you sure you don't want to see the bunny trick now? (Tries again but is stopped; most people look relieved) No? Oh! Ah... Nearly forgot! I've brought a present for baby Beauty. (Looks in cloak / bag finding nothing) It's here somewhere...

PRINCE PEPPIN THE 2ND: (To King Peppin) Father! Father! Didn't we bring the baby a present?

QUEEN PETRONELLA: Peppin. Peppin! Your son is trying to tell you something. Take notice – he is the son of a queen, you know!

KING PEPPIN: What is it, Prince Peppin?

PRINCE PEPPIN THE 2ND: We brought the baby a present as well. Can we give it to her now?

KING PEPPIN: The present! How could we forget! How clever of you to remind me; what a clever little fellow. (To others, proudly) Prince Peppin the Second! (Prince Peppin bows) Yes; we brought her a present. Err. (Checks pockets) Where is it my dear?

QUEEN PETRONELLA: Your memory, dear. Luckily, I have the memory of a queen. Here.

HERALD: (loudly; frightening everyone) **We** shall now do the presen**ting** Hof the **gifts** to Princess Beau**ty**!

Queen P hands gift to Prince to put by baby's cot. Fairy Starglow has to be nudged again. She jumps, hurries to the cot with a small gift.

PRINCE PEPPIN THE 2ND: Is that for the baby?

FAIRY STARGLOW: Yes, it is, Prince Peppin.

PRINCE PEPPIN THE 2ND: Prince Peppin the SECOND!

FAIRY STARGLOW: Oh, right, Prince Peppin the SECOND. Yes – it's a present for Princess Beauty.

PRINCE PEPPIN THE 2ND: (shyly but meaningfully) I like presents.

FAIRY STARGLOW: Well that's a relief, I must say. I was afraid you didn't like presents. Because I've brought you one!

PRINCE PEPPIN THE 2ND: It's not that bunny trick again, is it?

FAIRY STARGLOW: (It plainly was about to be) Oh – have you seen it before? (He nods) Oh – right – then it's not that – it's a REAL present!

PRINCE PEPPIN THE 2ND: For me?! (Looks at parents who signal it is OK) Ooh – what is it?

FAIRY STARGLOW: What? (Thinks – teasing him. Takes bunny out of hiding place while she searches. Puts it back) Oh yes! Here! (If necessary she can signal to a page boy/girl to fetch beautifully decorated but clearly wooden sword)

PRINCE PEPPIN THE 2ND: (Holds it up) A sword! Look! A sword! (Flourishes it)

QUEEN PETRONELLA: And, if it is from Fairy Starglow, it will not be just any ordinary sword!

FAIRY STARGLOW: It's not? (Moment of panic) Oh no – you're right! Yes! Your mother's right. (Brings him closer to aud to tell him the secret) This sword has a magic power; it ... it.... (Teasing) ... can open a jar of Marmite! No.... when your hands are full it will scratch your bottom for you! No... ummm.

I remember! It can only be used once, (Peppin looks sad) BUT! But that one time will be to find the one true love of whoever carries it! (Looks proud)

PRINCE PEPPIN THE 2ND: (looks at it a bit disappointed) Oh. That's a bit soppy. (Brighter; waves sword a few times) Don't you have one that can chop the head off giants?

KING BRENDAN: (Alarmed by the vigorous waving near his nose) It is a wonderful sword; go and practice with it, Peppin – the Second! So, Fairy Starglow – what gift did you have for Princess Beauty?

FAIRY STARGLOW: It is just a book. I'm sure it's nowhere near as exciting or expensive (Rumbling / distant thunder starts) as all these fine things but I always say that a book is ... is... (Looks around in alarm as a rumbling sound gets louder)

KING BRENDAN: What on earth?! (They all cluster together, facing outwards) Guards? Guards!!

Depending on resources there could by a pyro or a brief black-out, or a guest could transform, or use a trapdoor or something magical but suddenly Fairy Toadlick is standing centre stage. Crash and flash of lightening. Evil burst of music / dramatic chords. All leap back in alarm. Any guards move toward her but she points and paralyses them.

FAIRY TOADLICK: (Looks around as if surprised) What is this? Some sort of ... party? Hmm?

KING BRENDAN: Well ... er...

FAIRY TOADLICK: And everyone in their finest clothes? (Takes closer look at someone in audience) Well – mostly. (Looks around) So – not just any old party I think?

QUEEN FELICITY: It is a christening. The christening of Princess Beauty.

FAIRY TOADLICK: Ah.... (Walks to look down at baby) Princess...... (Sneers) "Beauty". Mm? Hmmm. Perhaps the light in here is not good.

KING PEPPIN: (getting cross) Steady on now ... she is a beautiful baby! Who on earth do you think you are to...? (Advances on her)

FAIRY TOADLICK: Me? Who am I? (Smiles horribly and makes him walk back before her) Why – I am the one who can make every crop on your land wither and rot - and every beast in your fields fall and die. One-two-three – WAP! (With finger & hand gestures) (Smiles even more) Mmm? You were saying?

KING PEPPIN: You don't frighten me – you – you –

QUEEN FELICITY: (Quickly trying to defuse things) King Peppin, Queen Petronella, let me introduce you to the most powerful fairy in the land: the **wise** and (meaningfully, with a forced smile) **patient**, Fairy Toadlick Goat-Strangler.

QUEEN PETRONELLA: (Advancing on her) We are charmed to meet you, Fairy Toadlick. Of course I have heard of you, even in far off Pimplevania – **I** am a queen you know.

FAIRY TOADLICK: (Making her retreat) And I don't give a warthog's nose-picking whether you have heard of me or not. (Goes nose to nose) **I** am an evil fairy you know!

QUEEN PETRONELLA: Oh my!

PRINCE PEPPIN THE 2ND: Warthog's nose-picking! That's jolly funny! (Chuckles.)

FAIRY TOADLICK: Hmm. Some people know how to show respect! (Looks at Prince & seems to relax. Goes to him as if pleased, then jabs him in the eye. Cries from crowd & Starglow sneaks to help him) (Toadlick looks at the gifts by the cot) What **is** all this junk? (Teasing maliciously) Party bags? Do I help myself? (Picks one up)

QUEEN FELICITY: They are gifts! Gifts from our kind family and friends; gifts for our dear baby daughter.

FAIRY TOADLICK: Ah. Very tasteful – not! (Throws to ground and stamps on it. Audible breaking. Suddenly senses Starglow & turns slowly) Oh! You're here!

FAIRY STARGLOW: Er – (Nervously) hello, Fairy Toadlick.

FAIRY TOADLICK: (Sneering) Fairy Starglow 'Drippy-Drippy' Dewshine? So?! Are you the kiddies' entertainment? Mmm? Have you done the bunny trick yet? (Goes close menacingly & waves hands at hidden bunny then smiles) Oh dear! You left it a bit too long, I fancy.

Fairy Starglow pulls out the bunny again but now it is plainly dead (longer, limper, paler; maybe hanging by the neck?). Much shock from chorus.

FAIRY STARGLOW: You horrible woman!

FAIRY TOADLICK: Thank you. (Pause) How strange; (thinks) it must have got lost in the post. But the mail is so unreliable.

KING BRENDAN: What was lost in the post? You sent a gift?

QUEEN FELICITY: No – she means her invitation. My dear Fairy Toadlick; we never thought for one moment that you would be so gracious as to attend our simple gathering. You cannot imagine how delighted we are that you could find time to honour us with your...

FAIRY TOADLICK: (impatient) Oh, give it a rest. I was invited by King Septimus of Slugovia to the christening of his stinky little brat – "Cecily". (Horrid smile) But there's no fun going where you're wanted!

KING BRENDAN: Our deepest apologies, we never thought – I mean we...

FAIRY TOADLICK: Not a problem. (Another horrid smile) I'm not one to get upset over silly little things like: (Toward Herald) "Not one person of importance has been left out" – **except me**! (They look speechless and awkward but she silences them) No problem. In fact – to show there are no hard feelings ... I too shall give your little "Princess" a gift. (Goes to cot)

FAIRY STARGLOW: No! I don't like this; she's....

QUEEN FELICITY: Guards! Get her away from....

FAIRY TOADLICK: STOP! (With the flick of a hand she freezes the guards' feet again) My gift to a Princess?! What shall it be? Beauty itself? No – you seem to think she has that already.

Money? (Fingers gifts) Nope.

Love?! Ha. (Bitter) You don't need love when you're rich!

(Thinks) What then? (Thinks) I have it! (Sudden change from apparent reasonableness to rage) Princess Beauty – I give you the gift of...

(Dramatic chords from orchestra) (To orchestra)

Thank you. I give: the gift of - a curse!

(More chords)

Yes! Before the sun sets on the day of your 18ᵗʰ (?) birthday Princess Beauty I shall return – invited or not - and by my hand you shall die!!

(Nods at orchestra as if to say 'now'. Dramatic chords again. Lightning?)

General cries of horror.

QUEEN FELICITY: Fairy Starglow! Stop this! Take this curse off her!

FAIRY STARGLOW: What? Me? (They push her toward Toadlick who squares up to her) Ooer! But ... her curse is too strong... I don't know what...

FAIRY TOADLICK: There is nothing you can do! Nothing! Once a curse is spoken it cannot be broken.

QUEEN PETRONELLA: There must be something. (To terrified husband King Peppin) As a queen I command you to kill that woman!

FAIRY STARGLOW: No! (Stops him) A human can't kill a powerful fairy! Only some stronger magical creature can do that! There's no way you could...

KING PEPPIN: But, but, but there must be something!

FAIRY TOADLICK: Ha! This will teach you that I am not to be ignored! Perhaps next time you will...

FAIRY STARGLOW: Wait! (They stop and listen) My gift! I haven't given Princess Beauty <u>my</u> christening gift! (Approaches the cot) Princess Beauty; I cannot take away this curse but I can "bend it" a little – (looks around nervously) – you will not die – you will fall into a deep sleep; yes – fall into a deep sleep, never aging, until... (inspired) until woken by love's first kiss!

FAIRY TOADLICK: Grr. (Thinks) (suddenly) Yes; sleep... (Smiles horribly then gets cross) Sleep <u>for a hundred years</u>! (Cries of outrage) (To baby) Sleep for a hundred years until all those you love have died and withered and crumbled to dust and their very names are forgotten!

QUEEN FELICITY: But – you foul hag – you forget that if one of us gives her the lightest of loving kisses then she will wake long before a hundred years!

FAIRY TOADLICK: 'Foul hag' – I rather like that. (Walks calmly up to her) I'm afraid it is not so simple ... it has to be...

FAIRY STARGLOW: Love's first kiss.

FAIRY TOADLICK: (sarcastic) "Love's first kiss". Yes! Only true love's <u>first</u> kiss can wake her from this magic sleep. (They look confused) (Exasperated) Doh! From someone who has never been in love before, and who loves her, AND who is her first love!

QUEEN PETRONELLA: But, if she's asleep, how can she ever get to <u>meet</u> someone for them to fall in love with...?

FAIRY TOADLICK: It's a problem, aint it! And to make things worse – if she is <u>not</u> woken by love's first kiss - when the sun sets, on the last day of those hundred years then she will awake as normal – kissy or no kissy!

KING BRENDAN: Good!

FAIRY STARGLOW: No, bad. She means Beauty will be 118 years old and will die!

KING BRENDAN: This is a very complicated curse.

FAIRY TOADLICK: Yeah – tis a bit. Should have just turned her into a toad and got it over with. Never mind. Next time.

BUT! Whichever way you look at it – Princess Beauty is doomed! Ha-ha-ha! Oh! (She stops and talks to Herald) Were there any more of those little sausage rolls? No? Never mind. Ha-ha-ha! (Evil laugh and she vanishes, perhaps with another pyro or at least thunder; if none at least get to her to poke a small kid in the eye as she exits)

KING PEPPIN: That, that, that 'woman' – she, she, she...

QUEEN PETRONELLA: Not the time for anger. We must be cunning if we are to cheat that witch of her evil reward, and – as a queen – one thing I <u>DO</u> know is how to be cunning! Fairy Starglow. What if that evil woman cannot FIND Princess Beauty before that birthday?

QUEEN FELICITY: Yes; Fairy Starglow! Would that work?

FAIRY STARGLOW: Oo err. Umm. (Panics. Thinks) Well ... don't know; I suppose you <u>could</u> take Princess Beauty and hide her and then...

KING BRENDAN: Hide her?

FAIRY STARGLOW: What? Hide her: yes – far away; somewhere Fairy Toadlick can never find her.

KING BRENDAN: But...

QUEEN FELICITY: She's right; I shall take her and...

FAIRY STARGLOW: No. No! <u>You</u> can't! I mean - <u>you</u> could never hide, your highness; everyone in this land knows your face – it's all over the stamps! No, the baby must go without you; with someone else. (Lots of volunteers step forward) Someone brave: not afraid that Toadlick will find them, melt their ears off, turn them into slugs, and send them to live in LOCAL NAME. (Volunteers slink back farther with each threat) (Inspired) OH! I know! <u>I</u> shall take her!

KING BRENDAN: Nonsense. I have enough soldiers here to keep a whole army away, one miserable old woman could never...

QUEEN PETRONELLA: She already got past your guards!

QUEEN FELICITY: Yes; hiding her is the only answer. Terrible as it may seem; the safety of Beauty is our first concern.

KING BRENDAN: But – eighteen years!!

FAIRY STARGLOW: And the sooner the better. I shall take her away now and she will not return until it is safe. (She wraps the baby)

MUSIC STARTS

PRINCE PEPPIN THE 2ND: Why is she taking the baby away?

QUEEN PETRONELLA: Hush now, Peppin. Time to say goodbye.

SONG (like Spice Girls 'goodbye') **The baby is carried out**

BLACKOUT

ACT I: SCENE 2: THE TOWER OF FAIRY TOADLICK

This can be a half-tabs scene or a side stage built on a temporary rostra/stage blocks; it needs a door (but you can do without) and a table or shelves with several props: set of ancient bottles with no labels; a tub or old container for scooping 'antidote'; a range of glasses or tankers going from tiny to enormous; also a selection of plates with dragon patterns (they could be in a box or bag but better if on display throughout the show).

IMAGE: Axminster Drama Club.

FAIRY TOADLICK: There's no point all you peasants booing OR what happened to the booing? It's not even as if you're very good at it. Not a patch on last year's audience; real quality they were. For goodness sake people – have you never BEEN to a panto before? Look – (fetches or reveals very large sign saying BOO) I've had it printed out for you; Apologies to those of you from LOCAL NAME who can't read long words: it says "Boo".

I know – let's practice. First this side of the asylum. When I go "Ha-ha-ha-ha!!" you all go BOO as best you can manage. Ready or not. Ah-ha-ha-ha!!" (Looks at them in disgust) Pathetic.

(Looks around & sees other half) You lot over there. Yes, you; and for goodness sake put some effort into it. Ready or not. "Ah-ha-ha-ha!!" (Looks at them in disgust) Worse than that lot.

Oh – I give up. Next year I'll play ANOTHER TOWN – they appreciate wickedness! (Loud knocking, 3 different door bells and a large bell tolling)

(To person in front row or pianist)

Is that you? Is it time for your tablets? What? The doorbell? Who'd visit an evil fairy? (Opens door – if you have one)

YURINN: (very annoyingly perky) Hello, hello, hello!

FAIRY TOADLICK: Yes?

YURINN: I am here about (looks smug) - the job!

FAIRY TOADLICK: No, you're here about (starts to conjure) - to be turned into a frog.

YURINN: (disbelieving chuckle) No; stop messing about. Look – it says here (reads newspaper with difficulty): 'Wanted: enthusiastic, alert, intelligent delivery person: must have own transport and (pause for effect) a good sense of direction: based in (LOCAL NAME BUT SOME DISTANCE AWAY.) That's here, right?

FAIRY TOADLICK: (takes ad & reads, looking at him doubtfully) Enthusiastic?

YURINN: Yes! (To aud) My mum made me come.

FAIRY TOADLICK: Alert?

YURINN: (mindlessly looking about for EXACTLY 3 seconds; suddenly :) Sorry, what?

FAIRY TOADLICK: Alert?!

YURINN: Yes! A-lert! (Searches pockets) I have one here somewhere.

FAIRY TOADLICK: Hmm.... Own transport?

YURINN: (indicates legs) Da-dah!

FAIRY TOADLICK: Intelligent?

YURINN: (after a hesitation). Alert!

FAIRY TOADLICK: And 'good sense of direction: LOCAL NAME SOME DISTANCE AWAY. This is LOCAL NAME not DISTANT LOCAL NAME!

YURINN: Close, eh? Do I get the job then?

FAIRY TOADLICK: No, you do not. I have absolutely no need of.... hang on. (To audience) This foolish person could be just what I need. (To Yurinn) What is your name, fool?

YURINN: (recites carefully) Yurinn User Spacewaste.

FAIRY TOADLICK: 'Yurinn' – that's a very odd name.

YURINN: Duh! Everyone says that! I am named after the first person in space: the Russian Cosmo-Snot ... Yurinn Gagarin!

FAIRY TOADLICK: Yuri. (Yurinn is puzzled) Yuri Gagarin – not URINE! Never mind; (to band or aud) His/her mother must have been taking the pi...

YURINN: (quickly) And I worked out that my middle name is User.

FAIRY TOADLICK: User? How did you "work it out"?

YURINN: Ah-ha! Well, my mum's only book is a dictionary!

FAIRY TOADLICK: A dictionary?

YURINN: Yeah – and she always says, in her book I'm next to 'Useless', so...

FAIRY TOADLICK: So you looked it up and...

YURINN: Yep – next to Useless it said 'User'. Clever eh?

FAIRY TOADLICK: Good grief. You sound perfect: you've got the job. I am the Fairy Toadlick Goat-Strangler.

YURINN: (perky & too chummy) Can I call you Toady?

FAIRY TOADLICK: (also perky) Can I hit your head with a rock?

YURINN: (unsure) Is that part of the job?

FAIRY TOADLICK: (To aud) An idiot – perfect! Now listen; I am planning a special 'surprise' for a certain young lady and you can help.

YURINN: Super-duper pooper-scooper!

FAIRY TOADLICK: What?

YURINN: Super-duper pooper-scooper!

FAIRY TOADLICK: (hard stare then) Never EVER say that again.

YURINN: Oakeley-dokely! (Sees her anger and stops) Right. (Mimes zipping lips)

FAIRY TOADLICK: You see these bottles. They've been here so long the labels have all fallen off. I want you to try each of them for me.

YURINN: And tell you what flavour they are?

FAIRY TOADLICK: Err ... If you like. (To aud) One of them is the deadly poison for that foul Princess 'Beauty', the others are just magic potions, but I can't remember which is which.

YURINN: Super-dup... sorry. Eh?! Did you just say - 'deadly poison'?!

FAIRY TOADLICK: Err........ No. (Gets bottle) Here – try this one.

YURINN: Woh! I'm not as daft as I look!

FAIRY TOADLICK: Well, obviously. Nobody could be that stupid.

YURINN: (Pleased) Oh; thank you.

FAIRY TOADLICK: You're welcome. Go on; just a small sip.

YURINN: What if it does something horrid to me?

FAIRY TOADLICK: What in your life could possibly get any worse?

YURINN: Fair comment. (Goes to swig then has a thought) Here – have you got an 'anecdote' for this?

FAIRY TOADLICK: An 'anecdote'?

YURINN: Anecdote? Is that a word?

FAIRY TOADLICK: You mean antidote. (OPTIONAL SECTION) But funnily enough, I do have an 'anecdote' about this stuff. Quite funny really. Once I was asked to make two potions for two different people; one was for a rugby player who wanted big muscular arms to impress the other players after the match when they were in the showers, and the other was for a beautiful young woman who wanted – you know (makes large chest gesture by clawing both hands in front of her)

YURINN: What; arthritis?

FAIRY TOADLICK: No – you know. Big.... (Nods and flickers eyebrows meaningfully) to impress her boyfriend.

YURINN: (all silly & embarrassed) Oh you! So – what happened?

FAIRY TOADLICK: Put the wrong labels on. Swapped 'em over.

YURINN: Oh my. Were they cross?

FAIRY TOADLICK: Not really. She's now a bouncer at LOCAL DISCO - and he said it made him even more popular in the showers. (Looks thoughtful) Anyway – do I have an antidote? Doh, of course – here – a bucket full. (Indicates bucket and scoops out a tiny glass of it)

YURINN: Oh no – more than that. (Scoops larger glass) Larger. (Larger glass) Larger. (Larger glass) Nope. That one! (Indicates very large tankard or jug)

FAIRY TOADLICK: Are you sure?

YURINN: Best to be safe. Right. Here goes. (Swigs potion; looks increasingly odd, starts to twitch & grunt; Fairy grabs his rear - a tail appears.) Aargh! Quick – the anecdote! Anecdote! (She throws the tankard of liquid in his face) What? What?!!

FAIRY TOADLICK: Don't blame me – I was only going to use the small one.

YURINN: I thought I had to drink it!

FAIRY TOADLICK: Did I say anything about drinking it? (To aud) Did I? Be fair; did I? No. See. Here – try this bottle.

Drinks. This time an elf or goblin appears. Yurinn rubs eyes and more appear.

FAIRY TOADLICK: What is it?

YURINN: I can see – elves or goblins.

FAIRY TOADLICK: Ah.... (Writes on bottle; speaking slowly as she writes) Stella - Extra – Strong - Lager. What are they doing now?

YURINN: Doing? Well, one is showing me its bottom. Aaah! Now they're dancing!

MUSIC

They do a little dance. At the end another tankard is poured over Yurinn and the elves vanish.

FAIRY TOADLICK: OK. Two left. One is a love potion – whoever drinks it will fall madly in love with anyone THAT MOVES within the next ten seconds.

YURINN: And the other one?

FAIRY TOADLICK: (solemnly) Isn't. (Smiles at him) Just a warning though.

YURINN: Oh! (Concerned) What?

FAIRY TOADLICK: The warning's not for you; it's for them! (Indicates aud) If this fool takes the poison: dead in three seconds: (gestures; counting with finger then slamming hand down) one – two - three – WHAP! BUT! If it's – the 'other one' it will be instant love with the first person who makes ANY MOVEMENT so, if death doesn't strike within three seconds you all have to be very still - or else! Here – drink up!

Yurinn drinks but – despite looking very odd does not die as Fairy T counts down the three seconds. After three she signals everyone to be still. She freezes but uses fingers to count to ten.

YURINN: Who was that?! Somebody moved! (Down steps / house lights up a bit. After some noisy searching for their 'one true love' the person is found. It could be one of the Front of House team)

Ah! I have found you! (kneels in front of them)

Now tell me, my beloved, what is your name? (Repeats name several times in rapture) Surely that is the fairest name ever to walk the earth! At once I will get permission for us to wed.

Who are you here with today? (Finds out and asks their permission to marry. Suitable response – either: "Yes! Then it shall be this very day" or "No! Alas! Alack! Woe is me! But my love will not be defeated! We shall.... elope!" or ad-lib)

Until later my beloved; return to / stay here in the safety of your seat and I will make all the arrangements. (Helps them to the steps – or if still in audience Yurinn returns to steps)

But wait! Here! (Gets giant valentines card with sloppy heart in it: it says "This card can be exchanged for any item at Refreshments during the interval. Not a joke! Thanks for being a good sport!")

Farewell once more, my beloved!

FAIRY TOADLICK: Enough! (Yurinn is still waving & blowing kisses) Enough! I have evil deeds to do! Antidote! (Splash!) Go and get yourself dried off. (Yurinn exits) (To aud) So – now I have the poison; but how to get it to the child? I must find out where she is hidden and then – the slightest drop on her lips - or prick of her finger! - and it will be (Gestures) one – two – three – WHAP! DEAD!! Evil laugh. (Booing. Pause as exiting) Still rubbish!!

BLACKOUT

ACT I: SCENE 3: THE SECRET COTTAGE

A beautiful flower garden in a forest clearing. There is a picket fence at the back and a gate Up Left. Opposite the gate is a beautiful thatched cottage Up Right with porch and windows. There is a bench by the cottage. There are several hedges for skulking & hiding purposes. There is also a pig-sty Down Left and a well Down Right which both must have a low wall suitable for diving over purposes yet be deep enough for hiding! A rose arch leads off beside the cottage. (The easiest option is to build the well off the stage, on a rostrum; this means it is not clogging your wing space and does not mean moving – as it will be heavy – and is then deep enough to hide in but low enough to sit on. Easier than it sounds)

FAIRY STARGLOW: (appears from cottage with basket of washing.) Beauty?! Where is she? All this washing to do and not allowed to use any magic. (To aud) If I use magic then Fairy Toadlick would find us like a shot. Nearly eighteen years with no magic. Thank goodness for FAMOUS AGE-DEFYING COSMETIC.   OK – washing! Er…

She holds up at least one very distinctive & memorable brightly coloured dress or shirt. She looks around irritably, and then notices the well. Thinks. Humming she goes to well, one by one drops the washing in, including huge padded bra; watches it fall out of sight FX: delay then small echoing splashes. She notices empty basket in hands, thinks and throws that down the well. FX: second different echoing splash. She rubs her hands together.

FAIRY STARGLOW: Sorted!

PIG: (looking over sty wall; bit of a lout) Ere! I saw that. (The pig has thick round glasses & woolly hat in football colours but with pig ears) (To piglet) Oy! Cocktail! Did you see that?!

PIGLET: (bobs up: smaller but also thick round glasses & woolly hat; very clever pig) I most certainly did witness it!

FAIRY STARGLOW: Witness what? (Looks up in sky & all around pretending innocence)

PIG: You silly fairy! You knows perfick what I means!

PIGLET: Indeed – you fully comprehend to what we are alluding!

Beauty enters through rose arch and come to stand unseen behind the fairy.

PIG: Wait till Princess Beauty finds out what you've done!

PIGLET: I must agree! Her response when she finds out will be...

FAIRY STARGLOW: Well, Beauty won't find out. (Closer) Unless 'someone' does something... 'rash'!

PIGLET: Ha! Was that a rather crude threat involving a feeble play on the word 'rash' and the similar sounding word 'rasher' with its unfortunate pig-based implications?

FAIRY STARGLOW: (Closer & firmly) It certainly was.

PIGLET: (Shrinks back nervously) Oh. Gulp. Very clever.

Beauty enters from cottage.

BEAUTY: Beauty won't find out what?

FAIRY STARGLOW: Ooh! Beauty! Nothing at all! (Pigs grunt. To pigs) Shhh! (Back to Beauty) I'm off into the woods to collect bluebells; do you want to come and help?

BEAUTY: Not me – I've got some fishing to do!

FAIRY STARGLOW: Fishing? Lovely! You three - be good! (Exits through gate)

BEAUTY: (To pigs) She's thrown the washing down the well again, hasn't she. (They nod) I thought so. (Goes to well, picks up fishing rod – whose line is already down well) (To aud) Every week it's the same – ah! Got something! (Pulls out an item already attached to line) Good start (looks around) Now, where's the basket?

PIGLET: Bizarrely that has also been cast down the well!

BEAUTY: Oh really! (Looks down well) That's a new one. I'll see if I can find something else to put the washing in. (Exits into cottage)

FAIRY TOADLICK & YURINN appear outside gate. If there is booing shush them.

PIG: Aye-aye! Now what? (The pigs dip down and peep over the sty wall)

YURINN: What makes you think this is the place?

FAIRY TOADLICK: Look. (Pushes gate open or lifts sign so aud can read:) "Secret Fairy Hideaway".

YURINN: Ah. So - once more – we are here because...??

FAIRY TOADLICK: Good grief. Nearly eighteen years I have been explaining this to you! Listen. (Clearly) We are here so that I can carry out my curse and kill the princess with this deadly poison (Holds up cocktail). Follow me. (They creep into the garden)

PIGLET: Who's that? It's not the usual SALESMAN like 'Avon' lady.

PIG: Dunno. (Alarm) Might be Jehovah's Witnesses! Hide! (They duck down out of sight)

FAIRY TOADLICK: Get over here and listen. First – the 'special' cocktail! (Holds it up. Laughs)

YURINN: Oooh! Can I have a sip?

FAIRY TOADLICK: Well; do you want to turn green, have your eyes pop out, and then drop down dead? (Gestures) One-two-three-WAPP!

YURINN: (Thinks) Er... decisions, decisions...

FAIRY TOADLICK: Shush! Someone's coming! (Runs across. Places glass on bench. Runs back) Hide! There; behind that hedge! (She goes behind out of sight; Yurinn hides in front of the hedge; Toadlick pops up to look for him; drags him behind hedge)

BEAUTY: (Reappears with suitable old container) This will – ooh! (Puts down container) A drink! How...? (Looks around. Baddies duck down. Picks drink up and approaches audience) I know! It's my birthday tomorrow; I'm going to be 18 years old! It must be a surprise present from Fairy Starglow. Shall I try a bit? (To aud) What do you think – should I have one little sip? (Goes to sip) No? Not even just one little bit? (Closer to lips) No? You seem very certain. Alright. I don't want to upset Fairy Starglow. (Thinks) I know – I'll tell her it was so delicious I drank it all in one go! Where to put it...?

(Sees bush, walks to it, looks around, then empties glass behind hedge. There is a LOUD cry of distress from Toadlick.) What was that sound?! (Beauty runs downstage to aud) Something not right here. I'm going back inside! (She does that)

YURINN: (Slowly rises from behind hedge) That didn't work too well, boss. (Looks around; she is not beside him) Boss?

FAIRY TOADLICK: (Slowly rises from behind hedge with cocktail over head: growling angrily. It needs to be thick like custard or it won't show up. It does not have to be what Beauty actually poured! That could have been caught in a bucket then smeared on T's head & face)

YURINN: (Does double take)

FAIRY TOADLICK: Now it's getting personal. The secret weapon!

YURINN: You don't mean...?

FAIRY TOADLICK: Yes! (Fetches fake gateau from wings). Chocolate cake!

Toadlick drips poison on it, chuckles, Yurinn tries to take a taste but is slapped back;

she runs, puts cake on bench, chuckles, knocks at door, chuckles, and runs off behind hedge.

Yurinn is still at front of stage; she has to run and grab him. They hide just before -

BEAUTY: (Enters with poker in hand) Hello? Now I'm getting concerned. I was warned that – ooooooh: chocolate cake! It does look tempting – but I remember what Fairy Starglow once told me about another princess, and a poisoned apple. (To aud) What do you think? Should I have a bit? (Goes to taste) Not even just a tiny bit? (Goes to taste; pigs support aud in calling out)

No – you're right. (Marches to hedge and drops cake upside down behind it. Another terrible moan from Toadlick.)

That sound again! (Hurries back indoors)

YURINN: (Rises up) She's not an easy one to kill, is she, Toady. (No response) Toady?

FAIRY TOADLICK: (Slowly rises with chocolate smeared over head – not necessarily the cake Beauty dropped! Yurinn jumps.) Grrr... (marches to front) TRIFLE!

YURINN: (recovering from surprise) What?

FAIRY TOADLICK: Sherry trifle! NOBODY has ever resisted my sherry trifle!

Gets trifle. Drips poison on it, Yurinn tries to scoop a bit but is stopped. Toady chuckles, runs to put on bench, chuckles, knocks at front door, chuckles, runs off behind hedge.

Yurinn – still at front – smiles and produces a spoon and scuttles to eat trifle.

At last minute Fairy T stops him and they hide.

Pause. Sound of chuckling from unseen Toady.

BEAUTY: (Reappears) Now what? Oooooh – sherry trifle. (Brings it to front) My favourite! This must be a birthday treat from Fairy Starglow!

(Goes to taste) But... what do you kind people think? Eat it - or dump it in the hedge? Mmm? Eat?

(Goes to taste) Just a tiny bit.

(Goes to taste) Hedge? Eat? Hedge?

So – hedge it is!

(Marches to hedge and dumps it behind. Another terrible moan from Toadlick.)

That sound again! (Front – to aud)

I'm going to find Fairy Starglow! (Hurries offstage)

YURINN: (Rises) I really thought she'd go for that one, Toady. Toady? (Looks around)

FAIRY TOADLICK: (Slowly rises from behind hedge with trifle all over head. Yurinn shrieks.) (In rage) That's it – (She walks out & to front) I am going to...

YURINN: (follows) Someone coming!

FAIRY TOADLICK: Hide! Quick – in there! (Indicate pigsty)

YURINN: Not there! That's the.... (Too late; Toadlick climbs over wall into pigsty and disappears with a wail. Pigs throw out straw. Fx: squelch.) ... pigsty! (Goes to look in but the voices are closer so Yurinn runs off through rose arch)

FAIRY STARGLOW: This way! (Enters flustered) Nearly there! Here – 'Fairy Hideaway'. (Opens gate with much bowing & curtseying) After you, King Brendan; Queen Felicity. Come and see your daughter! Beauty is nearly fully grown now!

Brendan, Felicity & Peppin 2ⁿᵈ enter (he is now 18 years older of course!)

KING BRENDAN: Thank you, Fairy Starglow. (He is very serious. Comes through gate & looks around.) You remember Prince Peppin the 2ⁿᵈ of Pimplevania. (They come through gate)

FAIRY STARGLOW: Of course. (Smiles) My - you <u>have</u> grown since I last saw you.

QUEEN FELICITY: Eighteen years ago!

PRINCE PEPPIN THE 2ᴺᴰ: (Bows) I believe I was about five?

QUEEN FELICITY: And you see? He still carries the gift you gave him. (Indicates the sword)

FAIRY STARGLOW: Oh yes – I saw that. (To Brendan)

KING BRENDAN: Ah – this young man was visiting from Pimplevania when we got a message saying a suspicious pair have been spotted prowling around here!

QUEEN FELICITY: Yes; we must speak to Princess Beauty; she may be in danger.

FAIRY STARGLOW: Oh my! She's probably inside.

KING BRENDAN: Prince Peppin; tell the coachman we will be just a short while. (Peppin bows slightly)

They all exit inside except Prince Peppin who exits back through the garden gate. Yurinn appears.

YURINN: Who was that? (Creeps over to sty) Fairy Toadlick? (Looks round at cottage nervously) Fairy Toa... (Turns back just as Pig appears.) Waah! Toadlick??

PIG: Watcher bro!

PIGLET: (suddenly rising) Delighted to make your acquaintance.

YURINN: (approaches nervously) Toadlick? (She rises covered in "mud" and straw) Waah!! (Jumps back in alarm then has closer look.) Er.... which one is you?

PIG: Hey! Bloomin' cheek!

PIGLET: The nerve of it! (The pigs drop back in disgust)

FAIRY TOADLICK: Grr! Get me out of here!

Yurinn starts to tug her out but the cottage door opens & voices are heard; she gets pushed back into the sty with a wail. Fx: solid squelch.

Yurinn hides.

Beauty returns from garden.

BEAUTY: No sign of her anywhere. Better finish off here.
Beauty goes to the well and looks in. She gets the fishing line and fishes, deep in
    thought. Prince Peppin enters and strolls across to her. She catches something.
PRINCE PEPPIN THE 2ND: You've caught something.
BEAUTY: What?
PRINCE PEPPIN THE 2ND: I said, you've caught something.
BEAUTY: (Looks at him) Who are you?
PRINCE PEPPIN THE 2ND: Aren't you going to reel it in before it escapes?
BEAUTY: It won't do that.
PRINCE PEPPIN THE 2ND: Why not? (Peers into well)
Beauty reels in and a large pair of bloomers comes out, hitting Prince on face?
BEAUTY: That's why.
PRINCE PEPPIN THE 2ND: (He recovers his composure, smiles at the bloomers,
    holding them out or pointing to them. He grins) Yours?
(She pretends to look cross at the idea and puts the fishing rod away)
BEAUTY: And – you are...?
PRINCE PEPPIN THE 2ND: (Embarrassed & flustered) Prince Peppin the 2nd. My
    father is King Peppin the First, and my mother is Queen Petronella...
BEAUTY: Ah. (Looks down well again)
PRINCE PEPPIN THE 2ND: And you are, without doubt, Princess Beauty.
(He smiles again as she nods) I was at your christening; only five but I still
    remember it.
BEAUTY: (Sudden interest) My christening? You remember it?
PRINCE PEPPIN THE 2ND: Of course! Who could forget that?! (Imitates Toadlick)
    "Princess Beauty – I give you the gift of - a tragic and early DEATH. A terrible
    death - before the sun sets on the day of your 18th birthday!"
FAIRY TOADLICK: (Peers over wall) Nothing like me! (Ducks down quickly as they
    look round)
BEAUTY: So – it IS all true.
PRINCE PEPPIN THE 2ND: But don't be afraid – if that evil Fairy tries anything while
    we're here...
BEAUTY: You'll get her with your wooden sword?
PRINCE PEPPIN THE 5TH: Oh, this. (Looks a bit taken aback & embarrassed) I was
    given this sword at your christening. (Laughs at the silly idea) It has "magic
    powers" to help the owner get to "the one he loves". It's soppy. I shouldn't still
    carry it.
BEAUTY: I'm sorry; I didn't realise it was so special. (Looks ashamed) That was
    rude of me.
PRINCE PEPPIN THE 2ND: No. I suppose it is a bit odd; it should be a real sword
    and I should be with my parents, meeting our enemy in Slugovia.
BEAUTY: Your enemy?
PRINCE PEPPIN THE 2ND: King Septimus the Seventh and his horrible daughter
    'Cecily'.
BEAUTY: (Smiles) But then you would not be here.
PRINCE PEPPIN THE 2ND: You're right. And now I see that I don't need the sword
    any more. I mean (Gets embarrassed) I – er – it's soppy. (Takes it off. Idea!) I
    shall give it to someone younger.
(Looks into aud. Sees someone and goes down to them. Ideally a small boy)
Here; what is your name? (Repeats it) Then I use this sword to name you 'Sir ....'
    and I ask you, Sir ... to guard this sword; to look after it until it's needed. Will you
    do this for me?
(If necessary whisper or give note to boy & parent: "Look after this until we need it
    later on!")

(Returns to stage)

PRINCE PEPPIN THE 2ND: And! Tomorrow is your 18th birthday! Just one more day to stay out of trouble then you can return and become a real princess!

BEAUTY: I suppose. I don't even know what that means. What do real princesses do?

PRINCE PEPPIN THE 2ND: Err – they wave; and open schools; and buy frocks, and – err.

BEAUTY: Is that all?

PRINCE PEPPIN THE 2ND: No – they buy shoes as well!

BEAUTY: I have shoes. (Getting frustrated) Do they do nothing more – useful?

PRINCE PEPPIN THE 2ND: Well; (brightly) they marry handsome princes and then when they're older they get to be king and queen together!

BEAUTY: I want something more than that!

PRINCE PEPPIN THE 2ND: (Disappointed) Oh.

BEAUTY: No, I don't mean; I mean, oh, what do I mean? (Frustrated again) What do you want to do?

PRINCE PEPPIN THE 2ND: Me? Easy! I want to be a hero! Save the country, that sort of thing.

BEAUTY: Why can't a princess be a hero?! I want to be a hero too, and do things –

PRINCE PEPPIN THE 2ND: (cautious) Swim with dolphins?

BEAUTY: Yes! We can be heroes and swim with dolphins – even defy gravity if we want to!

SONG: possibly Defying Gravity from Wicked OR 'We can be heroes: David Bowie' (Selected parts) Change lines above to fit.

They exit through rose arch together.

FAIRY TOADLICK: (Appears again) Yurinn! YURINN! Get me out of here!

YURINN: (Scuttles back) hang on; right! Pull yourself up out of the.... That's it. (Looks at her filth and steps back holding nose) Oh my!

FAIRY TOADLICK: Don't start! You can blame those two! (Pig & Piglet pop up; she glares at them) Living in filth!

PIG: Here! 'Ang about! Aint my fault! Pigs don't choose to live in stinking filth you know!

PIGLET: (hand up) I do – I'm a teenager! (Both duck back down)

YURINN: Come over to the well and clean up.

FAIRY TOADLICK: (Follows to well; looks at shoes) These shoes are ruined! (to audience) Designer label! LOCAL SHOP

YURINN: Here – rinse them off. Sit on here. (Edge of well) That's it; now swing your legs over and I'll get water and – look out! (Cottage door opens; voices.) Someone coming! (Yurinn pushes her down well; fx: long echoing scream and distant splash.)

(to aud) Oops! (Looks down well; gives her feeble wave; fx: distant, echoing, indistinct swearing

(to Toadlick) **Shush!** (Yurinn quickly hides)

KING BRENDAN: (Enters) No – I say get Beauty back to the palace! (Queen Felicity follows him out; he talks to her in confidence at front of stage) In the village - not a mile from here - they told us they'd seen an ugly old woman!

FAIRY TOADLICK: Ugly old woman?!!

QUEEN FELICITY: (Looks around nervously) Yes; I think you're right. There is something strange about this place. (They all look round to see pigs waving at them) Beauty will be safer back in the palace, for just one day.

KING BRENDAN: We will keep her in the ballroom and guard her until sunset tomorrow.

FAIRY STARGLOW: Oh my! Perhaps you're right. (Idea) I could cast… (dances around them) …a circle of protection about her; it only lasts 24 hours but if she stays inside that she'll come to no harm. (Looks about) Where is she?

QUEEN FELICITY: Ah! Look! Over there! With Prince Peppin!

KING BRENDAN: Let's get her out of here. They exit through rose arch calling her name.

YURINN: (Scuttles to well) Are you still there?

FAIRY TOADLICK: No – I've gone jogging! (Yurinn nods and wanders off) Of course I'm still down here you moron! Get me out!

Yurinn reaches in and pulls Toadlick's top half into view. She is wearing the horrid bright item of clothing and giant bra seen being thrown down the well earlier. She spits out water.

YURINN: Oh! You look nice. Is that new?

FAIRY TOADLICK: Is what new? (Notices dress) Aargh! (Raises arms in horror and falls back down well – scream and splash!)

YURINN: (calls down well) I hope it's not dry-clean only! Come out now! Try again. (Pulls her up)

FAIRY TOADLICK: (Viciously to Yurinn) Not one word about the dress! Not-one-word!

YURINN: (Steps back. Zips lips to indicate his silence – letting her go in process. Scream. Splash.)

Oops! (She reappears)

Come on; don't let go this time! Look out! (Repeat as Fairy S appears. Splash) Yurinn hides behind well.

FAIRY STARGLOW: Wait for me! (Exits to coach)

YURINN: Quick! (Peers down well, searching) Coee! (Listens & peers) Stop messing about! Where are you? (Leans forward to peer in looking for her. Helps her up)

FAIRY TOADLICK: You – stand over there. I will get myself out.

Yurinn does as told but they hear the King returning. Toadlick falls back again. Splash

Starglow, Brendan, & Felicity enter.

KING BRENDAN: Come on you two – dangerous here. Quickly; into the carriage!

Starglow, Brendan, & Felicity exit through gate. Beauty & Peppin enter from garden.

BEAUTY: And will you be at my birthday party tomorrow?

PRINCE PEPPIN THE 2ND: Am I invited?

BEAUTY: Maybe. I think you might be. (Looks around sadly) I have been very happy here.

FAIRY TOADLICK: splashing and cursing sounds

PRINCE PEPPIN THE 2ND: I think we should get out of here! (They exit through gate)

Yurinn nervously approaches well, leans in, calls "Hello? Hellooo?!" then Fairy T's hands grab him and drag Yurinn in. Fx: double echoing screams & double splashes.

BLACKOUT

ACT I: SCENE 4: THE TOWER OF FAIRY TOADLICK

Goblins or elves appear among the audience with a lot of noise (so the other two get out the well, unseen in blackout if needed; or crawl away under stage/rostra through hole in well). The elves are carrying bits of equipment and start to assemble it on stage. They do this to music in a dance sort of way, with a lot of giggling. Depending on the complexity of the scene change and the drunkenness of the stage crew this dance can be extended to fill any gap in timing.

On stage now is a device. It has switches, dials and lights. It may still be in some packaging. Fairy T and Yurinn arrive.

YURINN: But you're out of the well and back home now, so stop moaning.

FAIRY TOADLICK: STOP moaning?! STOP?!! I'm just getting started!!

YURINN: What's this?

FAIRY TOADLICK: Ah-ha: it's arrived! (Quickly inspects equipment and looks at instruction book)

YURINN: Is it something to make you beautiful?

FAIRY TOADLICK: Mmm? No; it's – (Thinks) What do you mean by that?

YURINN: (Looks behind, confused) What?

FAIRY TOADLICK: Get over here. (Studies manual) This is a new invention – it is called Elec-Trickery. **Deadly**!! But (searches instructions) how do you use it to kill a princess? Pah! It doesn't tell you important stuff like that – not a mention! Not even got 'Princess' in the index! Can you believe it?! This thing is useless! (Throws instructions away) Right then. (Presses switch; lights come on; adjusts dial and there is a humming & dimming of the lights) I need to test it. (Looks thoughtful then slowly turns to see Yurinn & smiles.) Yurinn! Hold this! (Gives him handle on curly wire).

YURINN: Will this hurt?

FAIRY TOADLICK: (absent-mindedly) No; I won't feel a thing. (She turns the dial again; Yurinn looks alarmed then starts to twitch and YODEL. Lights flicker & the hum rises slightly.) Let's try the next setting. (Repeat but more; Yurinn makes a louder yodelling sound) Still not enough. (Repeat but even more). (To Aud) Children – be sure NOT to try this at home. One more go... (Repeat but lots more; higher yodelling notes).

YURINN: I'm pretty sure I've had enough now; thanks for the job but...

FAIRY TOADLICK: You get back there! I had an idea! Orchestra, please. Oy! Yes, you: musical name like Mozart. Music! You know what.

Orchestra plays intro to a yodelling song such as: 'The Lonely Goatherd' from The Sound of Music by Rogers and Hammerstein. Toadlick sings the verse; for the yodelling bit Fairy T turns the dial and Yurinn wails/yodels in distress. Much flickering and buzzing.

YURINN: That was horrid!

FAIRY TOADLICK: Don't be such a baby!

YURINN: You're right. No hard feelings. (Holds hand out to shake. At last Yurinn minute grabs the electric rod; much buzzing and light flickering; they both shake and wail and at the big conclusion there is an electric-style pyro or at least a loud bang, double scream, and a blackout.

BLACKOUT

ACT I: SCENE 5: BALLROOM OF KING BRENDAN:
THE BIRTHDAY CELEBRATION OF PRINCESS BEAUTY

Everyone possible on stage (not Beauty or villains).

HERALD: **Your** royal **high**nesses; my lords, ladies and gentle**men**; please welcome, after 18 years, the return **of** the Princess Beau**ty**! (Herald exits soon after this)

BEAUTY: Enters in posh clothes and all bow or curtsey. She curtseys to the King and Queen; then sees Prince Peppin.

PRINCE PEPPIN THE 2nd: (Bows) Princess Beauty – Happy Birthday!

KING BRENDAN: Welcome back to your home, Beauty! Come in! And – err, stay away from the windows.

Fairy Starglow! Come and tell Beauty about the – 'situation'.

BEAUTY: Situation?

FAIRY STARGLOW: Well – it's the Evil fairy's curse. It is only until sunset – about half an hour – but you have to stay in here where we can see you. Don't get too worried! (Dancing in big circle) I have put a circle of protection around this room, so as long as you stay in here Fairy Toadlick can do nothing to harm you.

QUEEN FELICITY: And we have eighteen years' worth of birthday presents to give you! (Holds up cuddly baby toy – the rest of the chorus could do the same – rattles, teddies, baby-grows, etc.)

BEAUTY: But first, I have a present for Prince Peppin, don't I father!

KING BRENDAN: Indeed, you do: here. (Hands her a real sword that she presents to Peppin)

PRINCE PEPPIN THE 2ND: For me?

BEAUTY: I was very unkind to you yesterday, about the wooden sword; I should have realised that it had special meaning for you. I hope that this sword will have special meaning of its own.

QUEEN FELICITY: (Happily) Very nice. (She leans toward Brendan) Can you not see? You don't have to be a queen to see what's at the end of your nose!

KING BRENDAN: What? What? What? (Petronella nods at Prince Peppin and Beauty) Eh? You mean… Peppin and Princess Beauty?

QUEEN FELICITY: Yes. Peppin and Beauty! (they smile)

The Herald rushes in.

HERALD: **Sires!** Ma**jes**ties! News! Great **news**! King Peppin and Queen Petronella are **here**!

KING BRENDAN: What?! Excellent!

QUEEN FELICITY: (Sees Prince Peppin who is engrossed with Beauty) Peppin. Prince Peppin! Your mother and father are here!

KING PEPPIN and QUEEN PETRONELLA: Enters excitedly.

Prince Peppin rushes across & greets in an appropriate way.

KING BRENDAN: You're back so soon, are you alright? Did the peace talks go well?

KING PEPPIN: Yes, yes, yes! Phew. Just let me get my breath back! (Herald pushes chair behind him and he sits: he sees Peppin talking with Beauty)

KING PEPPIN: Peppin! Peppin!

Peppin brings Beauty to meet his parents.

PRINCE PEPPIN THE 2ND: Mother: father – I want you to …

KING PEPPIN: But first! We have great news: that is what we are here! We have signed a peace treaty – and as part of it, you are to marry Princess Cecily of Slugovia: daughter of King Septimus the Seventh!

BEAUTY: Did you know about this?

PRINCE PEPPIN THE 2ND: What? Who? No! I've never met her! But I don't wasnt to…

KING PEPPIN: But you are royalty. You do not get to choose!

QUEEN PETRONELLA: It is all arranged. It will mean peace for all our lands!

PRINCE PEPPIN THE 2ND: Then I will not <u>be</u> a king!

KING BRENDAN: But the peace of all our lands – the lives of our people...
QUEEN PETRONELLA: Peppin – you must understand what this means.
KING PEPPIN: I – I - I don't know what to say. I just thought… I'm sorry. It never crossed my mind.
BEAUTY: (Holds Peppin's hands) We understand. (Smiles sadly) I understand.
KING BRENDAN: Peppin. It is for your country.
QUEEN PETRONELLA: It is for our countries we; must make sacrifices.
SONG such as the Anthem from 'Chess' by Andrew Lloyd Webber. **Started by Kings Peppin & Brendan then Queen Petronella and full chorus. The music continues quietly then with rising drama:**
At the end Beauty cannot take any more, sobs and flees in tears.
KING BRENDAN: Stop her! Stop her!
FAIRY STARGLOW: She's outside the circle of protection!
KING BRENDAN: Quick! Everyone! Find the Princess! (All exit quickly)
BLACKOUT

ACT I: SCENE 6: THE PALACE SPINNING ROOM (front tabs)
There are bulging sacks overflowing and clearly labelled 'wool', a stool and an empty spinning wheel. Suitable music throughout this scene and the next. Two stools for actors to sit on.
YURINN: Well? We've been hiding up in this tower all day, and now you've only got twenty minutes left to think of something.
FAIRY TOADLICK: (Snappy) I know! (Thinks) If I could only get this poison to her (shows bottle) – but that dratted 'goody-goody' fairy has her in a circle of protection. There's no way inside that.
Perhaps if I destroyed the whole castle?! But how? An earthquake? (Beauty has appeared perhaps in the aud or on the stage some distance away and Yurinn is trying to get Fairy T's attention to the fact)
Ah-ha! A dragon! Now ... that might be.... (Yurinn tugs her sleeve madly) What? What?! (Sees her) Yes! (To aud) I have her! (To Yurinn) Quick! Out of sight! (Bustles Yurinn off stage)
Fairy T quickly gets the poison, looks around and, inspired, sprinkles it on the spinning wheel. She then sits, starts to spin and sing a tune: the duet Beauty & Prince sang earlier- but very badly!
Beauty hears and looks to see who it is. She stays as far away from Toadlick as possible until the very last second to build up the tension.
BEAUTY: Who are you? (No reply) Do you work here in the palace? How do you know that tune?
FAIRY TOADLICK: I am just a poor, old wo… (look at audience) – just a gorgeous, young woman who spins.
BEAUTY: What is it that you spin? I see no wool on this spinning wheel. It is quite empty.
FAIRY TOADLICK: I do not spin wool, my dear. I spin dreams.
BEAUTY: Dreams? (Sadly) Dreams are just for breaking.
FAIRY TOADLICK: Ah; but this spinning wheel takes broken dreams and spins them back, whole and strong, to last forever. (Pretends to spin then stops) Do you have a broken dream you wish to spin whole and strong again, my dear?
BEAUTY: My dream is too badly broken to be mended.
FAIRY TOADLICK: Maybe true – maybe not. Come closer. See the wheel spin. Watch it spinning, spinning. See how sharp the spindle is. Just put your finger to it to share your dream. That's it. A little closer; yes – closer still. (Continue as necessary)

BEAUTY: Ow!

FAIRY TOADLICK: (Leaps up) Ha! You are mine, Princess Beauty! One hundred years you will sleep and then – at sunset on the final day – your ancient body will crumble to dust! Dust! Evil victorious cackling. Exits

Beauty staggers back onto the main stage and into the panic-stricken ballroom!

ACT I: SCENE 7: BALLROOM AT SUNSET
Some people on stage; the rest rush onstage in concern as soon as possible. Dramatic music.

PRINCE PEPPIN THE 2ND: There she is! She's back! Everyone! (Rushes to her) We were so worried! We thought – what is it? What's that? (Closer look at finger) Blood?

Beauty staggers.

FAIRY STARGLOW: (Rushes in) She's here!

PRINCE PEPPIN THE 2ND: Blood! Just a scratch, but...

FAIRY STARGLOW: No! Let me see!

KING BRENDAN: (Rushes in) Where is she? Is she alri...?! Oh no! What is it? What's the matter with her?!

BEAUTY: I'm alright. I'll be.... just let me.... (Collapses into Prince Peppin's arms. They lay her down)

PRINCE PEPPIN THE 2ND: Is she dead?!

FAIRY STARGLOW: No: it's Toadlick's curse!

KING BRENDAN: Where is that woman! Find me Fairy Toadlick! She shall die for this!

FAIRY STARGLOW: Too late for that! Quick – everyone!

QUEEN PETRONELLA: What can you do?!

FAIRY STARGLOW: She will now sleep for one hundred years.

PRINCE PEPPIN THE 2ND: Don't be stupid. How can anyone...

FAIRY STARGLOW: There's no time to explain. King Brendan – you still want to follow our plan? (Without waiting for reply) Yes? Good. (Turns / crosses quickly) Peppin – you and your parents must get out of here – now!

KING PEPPIN: But...

PRINCE PEPPIN THE 2ND: I don't understand! No. I'm not...

FAIRY STARGLOW: Get him out of here!

KING PEPPIN: But...

PRINCE PEPPIN THE 2ND: No! I'm not leaving until...

KING PEPPIN: But...

FAIRY STARGLOW: (To crowd) Anyone not in the royal family – this is your last chance, get out of the castle NOW! (Some servants run out) (To Peppins) I'm so sorry. OUT! NOW!!!

King Peppin & Queen P drag a protesting Prince off.

FAIRY STARGLOW: Everyone – choose: leave now and never return to this castle again, or stay here and sleep for a hundred years. Choose now. (They all call out "we stay!")

Music and lights change. Fairy S dances magically. Recorded voice, as creepy as possible:

"One hundred years this castle sleeps, with magic hid, its secret keeps;

One hundred years no creature wakes; Until true love its silence breaks.

Sleep..... Sleeeep.............. SLEEEEEEP...."

They all slowly fold to the floor and sleep. Lights dim. Fairy S exits.

In the centre of the room one of the sleeping figures slowly rises with its back to the audience. It turns to show that it is Toadlick. She laughs madly into the slow blackout, her voice echoing on in the dark theatre. Dramatic chords; curtain closes.

ACT II: SCENE 8: THE BIRTHDAY CELEBRATION OF PRINCE PEPPIN
5th

A large inn/hunting lodge in the alpine style, filled with barmaids, drinkers, soldiers, student-types. Also on stage can be the actors who played King Peppin & Queen Petronella (who died years ago) – in disguise as bar staff! On stage is Prince Peppin **the 5**th (Same actor as the 2nd but with/without a moustache or whatever) plus the entire chorus. Hanging in full sight is a large portrait of King Peppin 1st (as seen in Scene 1).

Lively song (Drink, drink – from Student Prince, or similar)

FRIEND 1: A toast to Prince Peppin **the 5**th on his 18th birthday!!

ALL: Prince Peppin **the 5**th!!

PRINCE PEPPIN THE 5TH: I thank you all. And another toast!

FRIEND 2: Yes! (Eagerly gets new drink)

PRINCE PEPPIN THE 5TH: And a toast to the very first Peppin! (Indicates the portrait) King Peppin the First – my great, great, grandfather!

ALL: King Peppin the First!!

PRINCE PEPPIN THE 5TH: And...

FRIEND 2: Another toast! (Knocks back last drink & gets another – getting tiddly)

PRINCE PEPPIN THE 5TH: Why not?! A toast from me – to thank you all for this party! And for the gifts!

FRIEND 1: Ah-ha! And there are more gifts! (Exits to fetch them)

FRIEND 2: Indeed there are! From your father, King whatsisname – Peppin the – the –ah ...!

FRIEND: Fourth.

FRIEND 2: Yes! King Peppin the Fourth. (Drunken confidence) Why didn't they call them Derek or Wayne or something easy?

PRINCE PEPPIN THE 5TH: More gifts? But I already had the horse and the...

FRIEND 2: Your father said these were 'less formal' gifts.

FRIEND 1: (Returns with a parcel wrapped in plain cloth) Here!

PRINCE PEPPIN THE 5TH: (Unwraps) A sword! And a scroll. (Looks at sword) This is beautiful; an antique; it must be a hundred years old! (Friend takes it to look at) What's this? An old scroll? (Prince Peppin the 5th comes to the front with friends). It is a letter from – how amazing – from King Peppin!

FRIEND 2: But **which** King Peppin – 4, 3, 2...?

PRINCE PEPPIN THE 5TH: (Looks) Err... King Peppin the 2nd!

FRIEND 3: Peppin the Peacemaker – you know: the romantic one! (Dramatic & emotional) Forced to give up the Princess he loved to marry someone else, to bring our countries a hundred years of peace.

FRIEND 4: They say the Princess died of a broken heart! (General 'aahs' from the sad chorus.) And her whole family sealed themselves away in their castle, never to be seen again! (General 'oohs' from the chorus.)

FRIEND 3: Yeah – like THAT happened!

FRIEND 2: Is the sword his?

PRINCE PEPPIN THE 5TH: Yes – yes, it was. Listen; 'My dear descendant...

(At this point it would be very cool and not too hard to show a projected film or large TV screen of King Peppin the 2nd – AS AN OLD MAN – on a suitable disguised screen at the side of the stage, or at the rear. The letter's writer could then read it out. If not, then a recording of voice of Peppin 2nd as an old man OR OR just get Peppin the 5th to read it.)

KING PEPPIN THE 2nd: "My dear descendant; in your hand is a sword that was given to me by a beautiful and brave young woman called the Princess Beauty.

The fates meant that I should marry her – but the powers that run our land said that I must marry another. ('Aahs' from the chorus.)

"I am sure you have heard this sad tale, about the girl dying of a broken heart. (Pause) But she did not die; she still lives, not as an old woman, but in an enchanted sleep. And you have the power to wake her! (Pause)

"Through the years this sword has been passed on – together with this letter – to each prince of the royal family when they reached 18 years old. Now it passes to you! (Smiles)

PRINCE PEPPIN THE 5TH: Me?!

KING PEPPIN THE 2nd: "Yes, you! If you receive this sword, then it must mean that others have tried and failed. As soon as you can – you alone, find a way into the castle of King Brendan in the Kingdom of Tintinabula and wake the girl!

"But if you do not, should the hundred years come to an end, she will wither and die and be nothing but dust. (Pause) Her fate is now passed into your hands.... (Fades)

PRINCE PEPPIN THE 5TH: (Reading) P.S. Don't bother taking this sword. Its power is useless against the terrible evil that waits for you there. Good luck!

FRIEND 1: Wow!

FRIEND 2: Freaky. What are you going to do? Do you even know where this castle is?

PRINCE PEPPIN THE 5TH: Heard of it but... look, (shows scroll) there's a map!

FRIEND 1: Err – you wouldn't want us to come too?

FRIEND 2: Gulp – it clearly said "you alone", (Glares at Friend 1) so... I'm sure you alone can cope with (stress to Friend 1) that "terrible evil"

PRINCE PEPPIN THE 5TH: But I'm not the hero sort – I mean ...

SONG: SOMETHING LIKE Bonnie Tyler – Holding out for a hero?

ACT II: SCENE 9: THE TOWER OF FAIRY TOADLICK

The boredom scene. The dragon plates.

Yurinn and Toadlick are sitting looking very bored. Toadlick is unchanged but Yurinn has very long hair over face.

YURINN: What's the time now?

FAIRY TOADLICK: Ninety-nine years, eleven months and 30 days. Now stop asking me the time every ten years!

YURINN: (Looks bored again.) I spy with my little eye…

FAIRY TOADLICK: groans. Not again!

YURINN: Something beginning with...

FAIRY TOADLICK: (Groan) Hair!

YURINN: I didn't say the letter yet; how did you know it was hair?

FAIRY TOADLICK: Because you've said nothing else but 'hair' for the last sixty years!

YURINN: Because that's all I've seen for the last sixty years! (Sulks) Your turn!

FAIRY TOADLICK: Alright! Er... (Looks around bored – they will need to read this off something suitably hidden from the aud though it WAS learnt in Axminster!) I spy with my little eye, something beginning with:

M.I.A.W.T.T.H.G.T.A.P.A.A.S.I.F.A.H.D.A.N.I.W.W.H.P.C.U.O.T.

YURINN: (reading slowly and phonetically.)

M.I.A.W.T.T.H.G.T.A.P.A.A.S.I.F.A.H.D.A.N.I.W.W.H.P.C.U.O.T. ... Hmmmm..... (To aud) Any suggestions? No? Ummm... Ah-ha! Gottit! Man In Audience Who Thinks That Taking His Girlfriend To A Panto Is A Suitable Idea For A Hot Date And Now Is Wondering Whether He Put Clean Underpants On Today.

FAIRY TOADLICK: (Sulks for a moment) Yes! (Looks up at aud, possibly name someone who you know is there with his girlfriend) And – no, dear – he didn't put on clean pants; not since last Sunday.

YURINN: Clean pants once a week, eh? There's posh. (Long bored silence) I had a bath once.

FAIRY TOADLICK: (Slightly surprised) What – on purpose?!

YURINN: (Thinks) No. More – 'thrown in' really.

FAIRY TOADLICK: (Finding it hard to believe) You mean you actually had a bath – in real water – and you still...

YURINN: Oh no; it wasn't in water!

FAIRY TOADLICK: Then what was it?!

YURINN: Don't know really. (Reflects) It had things floating in it!

FAIRY TOADLICK: Good grief.

Bored silence

YURINN: A hundred years is a long time. (More boredom) I think I might pick my nose again tomorrow.

Fx: STRANGE SOUND, RATHER LOUD. AN ALARM OF SOME SORT. They both leap up.

YURINN: What?!!

FAIRY TOADLICK: It's the castle! Somebody is trying to get inside! Quick! The magic mirror!

If you have been using a projector, then this is a chance to use it again. A film of Peppin the 5th climbing through brambles / over rubble – ideally not in bright sunshine!

If not using a projector, then they peer into something magical & pretend.

YURINN: Who is it?

FAIRY TOADLICK: No idea.

YURINN: (Pause) What's he trying to do?

FAIRY TOADLICK: Stop asking stupid questions! (Keeps staring intently)

YURINN: Right. (Pause) Where does he get his hair cut?

FAIRY TOADLICK: I know who that is! It's that Prince from Pimplevania! Peppin the - whatever.

YURINN: He's got lovely short hair.

FAIRY TOADLICK: We must do something! (Looks at Yurinn)

YURINN: (Nods) I could ask him where he gets his hair cut!

FAIRY TOADLICK: No! (Dramatic pose) Release the forces of evil!

YURINN: What?!

FAIRY TOADLICK: Release the forces of evil!!

YURINN: Do they do hair cutting?

FAIRY TOADLICK: No; they'll stop him getting in and waking the princess! Release them now!

YURINN: What – all of them?

FAIRY TOADLICK: Yes – all of them. (Sudden idea) And we will be there to stop him!

YURINN: What? Go out like this? (Indicates hair)

FAIRY TOADLICK: You will at last see Mighty Blood-Flow Razor-Claws the Skull-Crusher!!

YURINN: (Goes close & confidential) That's not a promising name for a hair-dresser. Is he in LOCAL NAME?

FAIRY TOADLICK: Yes. What? No, it's not a hair-dresser! Razor-Claws is a dragon!

NB: if you can't manage a dragon then Razor-Claws is the leader of the gang of goblins seen earlier. All references to the dragon then become an attacker by goblins! The plates have goblins on them Though the dragon is easy and

looks good!

YURINN: I've not noticed him around here? Where is he?

FAIRY TOADLICK: He's doesn't <u>live</u> here! I have to use my evil powers to conjure him from the depths!

YURINN: Super-doop.... Sorry. Forgot.

FAIRY TOADLICK: Quick! The dragon plates! (Yurinn looks vague) Those! (Indicates plates that are painted with Chinese style images of a dragon) Throw them into space! (Yurinn goes to fling the plates into the audience but Fairy T hisses "Health and Safety" so he changes and throws them either out of a door or window or into wings.) Ha-ha!

YURINN: Ha hah hah hah. Now what?

FAIRY TOADLICK: Now we go and watch! Ha hah hah hah. Exits.

YURINN: Right! Ha hah hah hah. Can I get my hair cut now? Exits

ACT II: SCENE 10: OUTSIDE THE ANCIENT CASTLE OF KING BRENDAN
The rescue scene

This can be done with mostly black curtains, with some cut outs of ruins and perhaps the odd dead tree. A wall of foam blocks ready to be pushed over? Light smoke. Eerie music / sound fx.

Prince Peppin the 5ᵗʰ is there, looking rather nervous.

PRINCE PEPPIN THE 5ᵀʜ: I know the sword would be no use here – but I'd feel a lot happier if I'd brought it! What's that? Who's there?!

FAIRY TOADLICK: (Wrapped in black cape) Turneth back, brave Prince Peppin. Do not throweth away your life here. Turn-eth back I say! Turn-eth back or face the forces of evil! Hahahahah!

PRINCE PEPPIN THE 5ᵀʜ: (to aud) Is that LOCAL OR FAMOUS PERSON?

FAIRY TOADLICK: Turneth backeth, I sayeth to ye! (Conjuring motions to scare him) Evil cometh! EEEvil cometh!!!

YURINN: (Enters casually, crosses & shakes Prince's hand) Hello.

PRINCE PEPPIN THE 5ᵀʜ: (To Yurinn) Hello. Are you the forces of evil?

YURINN: Nah – just need a hair-cut. Think I might have got dandruff though! Look – can you see any flakes? (Hair checking and chatting about hairdressers)

PRINCE PEPPIN THE 5ᵀʜ: Can't see anything; you should use a good conditioner though; I use NAME OF CONDITIONER

FAIRY TOADLICK: Oy! OY!! Spoiling the moment! Trying to get an atmosphere of fear and tension here!

YURINN: Sorry.

FAIRY TOADLICK: (Resumes menacing posture & tone) Be-eth warn-ed!

PRINCE PEPPIN THE 5ᵀʜ: Be-eth warn-<u>ed</u>?!

YURINN: She means 'be warned'.

FAIRY TOADLICK: No I don't; that's how you say it at times like this. Now shut-eth up-eth!

YURINN: Ok-eth! Fair enough-eth. <u>I</u> am off-eth! NAME OF CONDITIONER eh? (Exits)

PRINCE PEPPIN THE 5ᵀʜ: Look – I'm sure you mean well (Toadlick splutters in horror at this) but I'm on a mission so, if you'll just step aside, please, old woman.

Before she can respond he exits. She looks disbelievingly at aud, and then runs into wings. A second or two later she reappears, pushing him back onstage and holding him tight.

FAIRY TOADLICK: Yes!! A mission that lead-eth to your horrible death-eth! Be-eth warn-ed (Glares at him) – those who venture-<u>eth</u> within these curse-<u>ed</u> walls will surely...

PRINCE PEPPIN THE 5ᵀᴴ: OK, OK – I've the idea. Thank you for helpful advice, it was very nice of you.

FAIRY TOADLICK: What?! "Helpful"?! "Nice"?!! I have never been so.... grah! You wait, matey – you're going to get yours– **eth**! (Stamps off in rage)

PRINCE PEPPIN THE 5ᵀᴴ: My – what a grump. Anyway – if she is the worst that... hang on. Now what? (The elves come on menacingly with music) Elves! (Or goblins if you prefer)

ELF/GOBLIN DANCE. **This is spooky and menacing, circling the Prince, but he is not alarmed.**

PRINCE PEPPIN THE 5ᵀᴴ: Very nice. Thank you very much. Have you tried Britain's Got Talent OR similar?

(The elves/goblins look crestfallen and dejected. They exit bowed.) Oh dear; I hope I didn't upset them? This is all very interesting but I don't really have time to hang around. If this is the best that the "forces of evil" can manage then... (fx: significant thud and crash. Echoing heavy footsteps) Ah! Now this sounds a bit more worrying! (He pulls back)

Flickering flame effects light up the side of the stage and a large shadow appears; fx: heavy breathing and growling as well as the footsteps and crashing. DRAMATIC MUSIC THROUGH ALL THE FOLLOWING.

FAIRY TOADLICK: (appears amongst the smoke) Destroy him! DESTROY HIM!

The dragon (or goblins!) appears. It should be as big as possible. This can be just the front half, supported on light black-painted rods by puppeteers in black. Its body and legs should be strings of disks, modelled on the plates from the last scene, strung on rope or lengths of dowel hooked together. The head should have an opening jaw and possibly eyes that light. It needs one hand or wing that can look as if it can 'grab'.

There must be just enough smoke. No honest – it's not that hard!

fx: load roar. Dramatic music / percussion. Quieten for the next bit.

FAIRY TOADLICK: Ha-ha! (Yell!) Now you trembleth before the forces of evil!

PRINCE PEPPIN THE 5ᵀᴴ: Well, yes; I do-eth rather. (He tries to get past the dragon but each time its head swings down and almost gets him, with much roaring and smoke. He throws bits of wood or rock at it but to no effect. The elves/goblins could also appear in the smoke to add to the spectacle if safe.) (To aud) **If only I had a sword!**

PRINCE PEPPIN THE 2ⁿᵈ: (Voice recording or projection again) "There was a sword! A magical wooden sword! A hundred years ago I gave it to one who was young; a young warrior. Ask them! Ask if they still have the sword!"

PRINCE PEPPIN THE 5ᵀᴴ: A sword?! (To aud) Was there a wooden sword? Does anyone still have this sword?! What? Who? Where?!

Runs into audience to fetch the sword OR summons the child to come up on stage to one SAFE side to watch him stab the dragon/fight off goblins. It rears up with a terrible roar then buckles and crushes down.

PRINCE PEPPIN THE 5ᵀᴴ: Dead! (Kneels to young person) Who are you, brave warrior? (Repeats name; if they forget to say "Sir..." then add it in now) I will be forever in your debt, Sir...

Accompanies young person back to their seat while scenery changes.

PRINCE PEPPIN THE 5ᵀᴴ: And for your reward, Sir.... you may keep this magical weapon! Something to keep forever to remind you of your bravery this dark night! Good people! Hail the hero of the day! Sir... (All applaud child) (Prince moves back toward stage.) Now – which way?

ACT II: SCENE 11: INSIDE THE CASTLE

Music from their duet plays in the background. As he approaches Peppin sings a bit from the song, softly. Beauty is asleep behind lace or curtains or a piece of scenery that pull back to reveal her on a flower-covered couch (cobwebs?). It can roll on in front of half-tabs / cloth (stick some wheels under it). Suitable music, smoke, light.

The Prince is amazed.

PRINCE PEPPIN THE 5ᵀᴴ: This must be her. (Approaches nervously) A hundred years old? I don't believe this – but then I never believed in dragons/goblins either. (Goes closer) Hello? Cooee? (Closer) She's very pretty. Hello? Wakey-wakey, Princess! (Closer still) (To aud) She looks very familiar; like I've met her before!

I can see why Peppin the 2ⁿᵈ was so upset not to marry her. She is rather amazing! (Takes her hand gently) Hi there! (To aud) She's a very heavy sleeper. I must wake her slowly.

SINGS PART OF THE DUET FROM EARLIER. (Music carries on) Nothing. (To aud) What shall I do? Shall I slap her face? (Listens) What? Give her a kiss?! Don't be so soppy. (Listens) Really? Well, maybe a little one – on the hand. (He lifts her hand and gives it a polite peck. She starts to stir and he steps back, then, nervously:) Hello?

BEAUTY: Hello? (Slowly) What? Where? (Looks at him) You? Prince Peppin!

PRINCE PEPPIN THE 5ᵀᴴ: Why – yes; I am! How did you – Oh, I see. No – I'm not that Peppin; not Peppin the 2ⁿᵈ. I am Prince Peppin the 5ᵗʰ!

BEAUTY: What?

PRINCE PEPPIN THE 5ᵀᴴ: Yes. Err – you have been asleep – for a hundred years.

BEAUTY: Asleep? A hundred years? (Thinks & realises) You woke me up! With a kiss?

PRINCE PEPPIN THE 5ᵀᴴ: On the hand! Little peck! Nothing – you know...

BEAUTY: (Suddenly realises) My family! Where are they? Help me up. The ballroom. Quick; this way.

He supports her as she is wobbly and they go upstage through the tabs / cloth to:

ACT II: SCENE 12: THE THRONE ROOM OF KING BRENDAN
The waking up scene

Everyone from the end of Scene 5 is asleep on the floor (obviously not Queen Petronella or King Peppin the 1ˢᵗ who are long gone) King Brendan and Queen Felicity are asleep on thrones.

PRINCE PEPPIN THE 5ᵀᴴ: Are they dead?

BEAUTY: I don't know. (They check) No – asleep!

PRINCE PEPPIN THE 5ᵀᴴ: You're right; and is this your father, King Brendan? Hello! King Brendan!

KING BRENDAN: (Starts to wake) Who's there?! What? I'm not asleep; (gets up) just resting my eyes; (walks forward) heard every word of the meeting! (is woozy) Oo-er.

Everyone else starts to wake slowly, with suitable noises & stretching. There could be a fart and a lone voice of "Sorry!"

KING helps the QUEEN awake.

PRINCE PEPPIN THE 5ᵀᴴ: King Brendan; Queen Felicity. (Bows) I am honoured to meet such a famous and historic figure (Bows to King)

KING BRENDAN: Historic? What are you talking about, Peppin? Historic! (Suddenly) Beauty! Quick! That evil fairy is around; you must stay here, in the magic circle!

BEAUTY: The evil fairy's curse is over; one hundred years have passed!

QUEEN FELICITY: My word. (OPTION: To aud: And you've all been sat there 100 years?! Have you got numb bums? OR SOMETHING TOPICAL such "Is .... still married to ...?" or have they sorted Brexit yet or similar.)

BEAUTY: And this is who we must thank: Prince Peppin the 5th!

KING BRENDAN: Peppin the <u>Fifth</u>?! What happened to the other four?

PRINCE PEPPIN THE 5TH: A 100 years have passed?

KING BRENDAN: A hundred years? (Sudden realisation)

QUEEN FELICITY: That foul Fairy Toadlick! She is to blame for this!

HERALD: **She** may well have **died** years **ago**.

PRINCE PEPPIN THE 5TH: An evil fairy? Is she the DESCRIPTION TO FIT ACTOR one? (They nod.) She's still alive – I saw her around here just minutes ago.

KING BRENDAN: My word! Guards! She will pay for this! Guards!!

FAIRY STARGLOW: (enters) Hi all! What's happening?

BEAUTY: Fairy Starglow! (Crosses to her excitedly) You don't look a day older!

FAIRY STARGLOW: (touches face; with secrecy) Bit of work – you know...
Oh! But watch out – Fairy Toadlick's curse is broken but she will not be happy!

PRINCE PEPPIN THE 5TH: But, this Fairy Toadlick. Surely there is no need to punish her – her curse has caused no real harm; and if it wasn't for her ... (looks soppily at Beauty)

FAIRY STARGLOW: Wisely spoken; but don't forget she still has her magic powers. May be best to leave her in peace!

KING BRENDAN: I agree, Fairy Starglow: will you find out what Fairy Toadlick is up to now? We will all relax more if we know she is not plotting some other wickedness!

FAIRY STARGLOW: Indeed. (She bows & dances off)

HERALD: **Perhaps**, Highness, a cele**bration** is more in ord**er**?

KING BRENDAN: Indeed – a celebration! Ooh – but first – a hundred years eh? (Looks uncomfortable) I really do need to go... you know… (Hurries off) Chorus / sleepers show same reaction and hurry off. Only Prince & Beauty left.

BEAUTY: Just before I woke up – a dreamt I heard someone singing.

PRINCE PEPPIN THE 5TH: Singing? Er – well – that might have been me. Trying to wake you up.

BEAUTY: But the song – how did you know it?

PRINCE PEPPIN THE 5TH: That song? It's something our family have sung for...

BEAUTY: For 100 years?

SHORT REPEAT OF DUET

BLACKOUT / HALF TABS

ACT II: SCENE 13
Community song / kiddies' scene

Yurinn (in finale costume, with hair cut) is in Toadlick tower packing evil plates into a sack or bag. Good Fairy Starglow enters.

FAIRY STARGLOW: Oy!

YURINN: Wo! Made me jump! Who are you? Do you like my hair?

FAIRY STARGLOW: I am the Good Fairy Starglow and – what? Your hair?

YURINN: I went to ANOTHER LOCAL HAIRDRESSER

FAIRY STARGLOW: Er – very nice? (Goes closer suspiciously) Who are you?

YURINN: Me? Nobody. (Guiltily seems to notice plates in bag) Er – I am from – er – TV AUCTION STYLE SHOW and we ... er

FAIRY STARGLOW: Hmm. So where is Fairy Toadlick?

YURINN: Not here! I'm getting out – and taking all her magical stuff so she can't cause any more trouble!

FAIRY STARGLOW: That's very good. (Looks at bottles) What are these? Magic spells! Anything worth keeping? (Reads) "Look like FAMOUS UGLY PERSON/Donald Trump" (Shudders and throws in bag) "Have a body like FAMOUS ATTRACTIVE PERSON OF APPROPRIATE SEX" (goes to drop in bag but Yurinn takes it and puts in pocket OR is given to pianist / usher or local notable in audience) Ah – here's a good one: "SING LIKE A POP STAR; JUST ONE DROP ON YOUR HEAD". (Goes to have a drop on head but Yurinn is staring & shaking his head) What?

YURINN: You can risk it if you like, but the labels are not always right. Test it first – oh no – not on me! Get a volunteer. (Nods at aud.) Down there; but – ah – only get a small one. If it turns them into an ogre it's easier to deal with small ones. Trust me: got the scars!

FAIRY STARGLOW: Small volunteers. I don't know. Are there any small volunteers down there who would like to come up here and see if this magic potion will turn them into a wonderful singer?

BUSINESS WITH KIDS such as singing

FAIRY STARGLOW: A big clap for our volunteers. Thanks. See you all later! (Exit)

ACT II: SCENE 14: THE THRONE ROOM OF KING BRENDAN

The Finale

All the royal family from Scene 12 in their finest costumes.

KING BRENDAN: It's going to take a month to finish dusting this place! And have you seen the size of the spiders?!

HERALD: **No** – but I have noticed **one** thing. I think it is just a matter of **time** before we have another union bet**ween** two royal fam**ilies**.

KING BRENDAN: Eh? A union?

HERALD: A marriage? Uh?! Beau**ty** and Pep**pin**! You **must** have not**iced**!

KING BRENDAN: What – romance?! My word! Are you sure? Shush! Here they come!

Beauty and Peppin the 5th enter with Yurinn.

PRINCE PEPPIN THE 5TH: King Brendan! Fairy Starglow found this person lurking. They claim to be a former worker for Fairy Toadlick!

YURINN: Never got paid though. All I've got are these old plates.

KING BRENDAN: Even worse if you helped that evil woman for no reward! I shall throw you in the dungeon. Guards!

BEAUTY: But wait! That is not the face of an evil person. (Yurinn looks as un-evil as possible. All look at the very daft smile) I think we can be forgiving. After all, we have our happy ending and nothing can spoil that now. Nothing at...

EVERYONE SUDDENLY FREEZES EXCEPT YURINN (maybe magical note from orchestra to coordinate?)

YURINN: That is very gracious of you, you majestic princessness. I thank you from the heart of my.... heart of my ... what is it? What are you playing at? Is it a party game? (Mimics them freezing then looks alarmed) That's enough. Stop messing... (Can play with one actor's face at end of line, flicking nose & lips etc. trying to make them laugh. Walks along the line of guests until...)

FAIRY TOADLICK: (Is already on stage, back to audience; spins to confront Yurrin) Ha!!

YURINN: Wa!! You?! Now what? Leave them alone! The curse is over. You lost; just move on; get some therapy!

FAIRY TOADLICK: Lost? Lost?! Me? I don't think so! (Reveals bottle of poison) There is more than enough left in this poison bottle. One drop on each of their lips will stop them laughing at me ... just one – tiny - drop. (Dips poison on her finger and moves toward Beauty) You first I think, my dear.

YURINN: That's not nice; she was kind to me!

FAIRY TOADLICK: (mimics nastily) 'She was kind to me'. Pah! Step aside. (He refuses) What are you going to do, you silly little human? No mortal can harm me! You're certainly not going to stop me!

YURINN: Yes. Yes – I am. (Goes to side of stage and clearly throws the plates into wings)

FAIRY TOADLICK: (She pulls Yurinn back and stands with back to wings) What are you doing, you fool? (Looks alarmed as fx: sound of dragon rises)

DRAMATIC MUSIC. Dragon's head/goblins appear amidst smoke. Suddenly her spell is broken, the trance stops and everyone is awake, some shrieking. The dragon/goblins grab at Toadlick.

YURINN: Destroy her! Now! One-two-three-WAP!!

With a terrible wail fairy Toadlick is dragged off to her doom. Lights back to normal.

YURINN: (Triumphant) Super-dooper pooper-scooper!

KING BRENDAN: My friend; (gets sword which alarms Yurinn) kneel, tell me your name and you will arise a knight!

YURINN: My name? My name is - Yurinn!

KING BRENDAN: Then arise, Sir... Sir... Is 'Yurinn' really your name? (Thinks) Perhaps I'll just buy you a drink instead, what do you say? (They agree)

HERALD: I think we could all do with a drink – (To principals)

REPRISE OF DRINKING SONG?

WALKDOWN

LIST OF TITLES

Click to select

CONTACT INFORMATION
and PERFORMANCE RIGHTS here:

<u>PANTOSCRIPTS.ME.UK</u>

RED RIDING HOOD AND THE THREE PIGS
By Chris Lane
ACT 1: SCENE 1: DINGLY DELL COTTAGE

This is a traditional interior of a fairy-tale cottage.Stable door and window with long curtains Stage Left. A sink with tap and a table Stage Right.A couple of wooden chairs. A small wooden table.At rear: door to cupboard. Space for bed (with secret flap in rear wall behind bed)It should be filled with children, washing-up, laundry, etc. Fit on as many people as possible, mostly children (**optional**: Chorus of adult delivery people.)

Onstage: 3 Pigs. Chorus. Children. Kids are stealing tools. Mate in cupboard.

SONG: (such as? 'THE HIPPO SONG'): CHORUS & Pigs.

GRANNY ENTERS

GRANNY: (To Aud) Welcome to Dingly Dell – my humble home in the country. I'm Granny Hubbard (gives aud a look)

CHILD 1: We've finished cleaning, Granny Hubbard.

Child 2: It was fun!

CHILD 3: It was jolly hard work!

GRANNY: Ah! But you know what they say: 'Hard work never did anyone twice in the same place'!

GAMMO: Wise words, Granny, wise words! 'Hard work should never take place twice'!

CHILD 4: Right then, Granny; what's next on the list of jobs to do?

GRANNY: No idea (Name of Clothes). Red Riding Hood has the list; where is she?

CHILD 5: BIG Red Riding Hood or LITTLE Red Riding Hood?

GRANNY: Er – BIG?

CHILD 6: She's in the garden. (Opens top of door and calls) BIG Red Riding Hood!

RED RIDING HOOD: (Looks in) What is it, (Name of Clothes)?

SPAMMO: Red Riding Hood! What is the next task on the list?

RED RIDING HOOD: (Enters) The list? Here it is, Spammo.

SPAMMO: (CHECKS LIST) Ooh! Oh yes! One – clean floor. (Spits on floor and rubs with foot.) Done! Two – do dusting! (Flicks kids with duster) Done! Three – err – can't read the handwriting. (Covers one eye) It looks like it says '**attack cyclists**'. Yes; attack cyclists.

RED RIDING HOOD: Attack cyclists?! Are you sure? It doesn't sound...

HAMMO: Attack cyclists: You two – outside – and if you see any cyclists – attack them! Go! It's a jolly good idea – they're a menace to road users!

Squeal of bicycle brakes, yell, breaking glass, cheers from kids. 2 kids reappear with bicycle wheel. Cheering.

GAMMO: (grabs list) No – look! It doesn't say 'attack cyclists': it says, er: '**take out Red Socks Kid**'.

GRANNY: OK. Red Socks Kid?! (Red Socks Kid looks alarmed) There he is!

RED RIDING HOOD: Here! Put him down! Let me check that list. (READS) No – you silly pigs! What it actually says is: '**take out recycling**'!

GAMMO: Durr! Sorry Red Socks Kid.

RED SOCKS KID: (Dazed) No problem.

RED RIDING HOOD: OK – everyone – recycling OUT! Come on! (exits)

Some kids follow with recycling. Two are about to throw Child 7 out.

Mother enters, in business-suit and with clip-board, and is furious.KIDS FREEZE.

MOTHER: What on earth is going?! Why are you all here?!

CHILD 7: Hello Mother!

MOTHER: Put (Name of Clothes) down! (Looks around) Why are you all here?! Granny) I left the children a clear memo of (today's date), saying 'clean the house': meaning OUR house, not yours and...! (Looks around in disbelief)

CHILD 3: Yes, Mother. We got your memo, of (today's date). We did OUR house – and it was such fun we decided to do Granny's house too!

MOTHER: Oh – well; that's acceptable then. But – if you've left OUR home in the same state as this one...!

GRANNY: This is fine! As long as we all have fun! Remember, dear: 'All work and no play makes a man healthy, wealthy and stinky'.

GAMMO: Yes – wise words yet again, Granny! 'All work and no pie makes a man Grumpy, Sneezy and Dopey.

SPAMMO: Wrong panto. That's the one with the – you know (indicates dwarf height. Gammo points at kids questioningly. Spammo shakes heads) Bit like them, but with beards. (to aud) And quieter.

MOTHER: Having fun is NOT a lesson I want my children to learn, thank you. I want them to follow my example of hard work, not the pointless 'games' of a silly old woman!

Gran gets sympathy.

GRANNY: Well! At least I know the names of all my children! I don't have to call them by the clothes they're wearing!

MOTHER: You only had the one child! Me! Remember?

GRANNY: Vaguely.

MOTHER: Go on then; what am I called?(Granny confused; child whispers to her)

GRANNY: (proudly) Mother!

MOTHER: I give in. (Looks at clip-board) For a start: 'Item one: clean floor'. Just look! (Stands and looks down tutting and shaking her head. 3 pigs are lined up beside her doing same) It looks like a herd of pigs have been 'dancing' on it! (Pigs start simple dance moves. Mother slowly turns to look at them) What?! (Pigs slowly stop dancing) Don't tell me you three are in here again!

HAMMO: Spammo, don't tell her we're in here again.

SPAMMO: Right. Gammo – don't tell her we're in here again.

GAMMO: I shall say nothing. I am the master of silence.

MOTHER: (To pigs) I cannot believe you three are in here AGAIN!

The pigs relax.

HAMMO: It's OK, Spammo; she can't believe we're in here again.

SPAMMO: Really? Gammo: She doesn't believe we're in here. Tee hee.

GAMMO: Tcha! She has only to look!

GRANNY: Should have gone to Specsavers! (agreement from pigs.) Remember: 'There are none so blind as those who don't have a pot to pee in'!

GAMMO: Indeed; wise words, Granny: 'Pull the blind before you pee on a nun!

MOTHER: (crosser; to pigs) Well? ARE you three in here again?!

HAMMO: Dunno. Bit confused now. (aside) Spammo; are we in here again?

SPAMMO: I'm not sure any more either. (confused) Gammo? Are we in here again?

GAMMO: (Pompous) Yes – I can definitely state – we ARE in here again.

MOTHER: OUT! OUT!!! Pigs in a domestic dwelling, despite the 2012 Health and Hygiene ruling on the matter!! Out! Get back in the pig-sty! OUT! OUT!

The pigs try to say something but are bustled out.

MOTHER: (about to confront Granny) And as for you... (Granny looks alarmed)

ROB (enters): Look here – misses! I'm trying to fix the plumbin' (Shows large wrench on pipe above the sink) but every time I put me tools down some little blighter nicks them!

The kids all look innocent and hide tools behind their backs.

MOTHER: Is that right? Now! Listen! You are all clearly in breach of Domestic Regulation Number 326, namely: 'You shall not borrow without asking'. So, who has got Bob's tools?!

ROB: Rob.

MOTHER: What?

ROB: Rob – not Bob. ROB the Builder. Rrrrob.

MOTHER: Are you sure? Not 'Bob the Builder'? (Looks disbelieving as he is dressed as Bob) Hmmm. Anyway. So, 'Rob', what do these missing tools look like?

ROB: (unpleasantly sarcastic) They look like tools – hammers, wrenches!!

MOTHER: Hammers, wrenches! Come on! Who has them?

Crowds hand over tools.)

ROB: You little perishers! (Grabs tools) And where's my mate gone?

MOTHER: Who?

ROB: My mate! He's gone too!

MOTHER: (sighs) What does he look like?

ROB: My mate? (Describes him in a few words) He's from (place with strong dialect)

MOTHER: OK. I am waiting! If you remember from that incident? The one with the unfortunate person from Jehovah's Witness? I told you! Kidnapping is against Domestic Regulations 39 A, B AND C! (Guilty children release Mate from cupboard)

MATE: Complains at length in unintelligible regional dialect. No swearing!

ROB: I know, I know! Now keep away from them kids like I told you!

MOTHER: That's it! I am now using an 'Emergency Evacuation Order': ALL OUT! (They groan and turn to leave)

GRANNY: Off you go then, kids. Big thanks – and - remember – 'Children should be seen and not not live by bread alone'!

GAMMO: (pops head in to say:) Wise words: "Children are obscene and shouldn't be bred at home".

ROB: Hear, hear.

GRANNY: See you tomorrow kids!

MOTHER: (To Granny) And you! Out! Leave the workmen in peace.

GRANNY: Me? But I live here! And it's raining!

MOTHER: Then go with the pigs into the pigsty! (Pushes them all out)

GRANNY: (making dignified exit) Remember – 'People who live in glass houses should put the toilet in the basement!I bid you farewell!

MOTHER: OUT! Right – that's better. (Sees Rob and Mate leaving, with tools still in sink) I say! Bob!

ROB: Rob!

MOTHER: Whatever. Where are you off to?

ROB: Emergency Evacuation Order!

MOTHER: But you haven't finished!

ROB: Can't ignore an Emergency Evacuation Order! Come on! (Mate and Rob EXIT)

HAMMO rushes back in as the builders leave.

HAMMO: Raining out there!

MOTHER: Don't care. (ushers him out)

SPAMMO: (rushes in) Cold out there!

MOTHER: Don't care. (ushers him out)

GAMMO: (rushes in) No wi-fi out there!

MOTHER: Don't care. (ushers him out)

GRANNY: (rushes in) No gin and tonic out there!

MOTHER: Don't care. (ushers her out)

LITTLE RED RIDING HOOD: (rushes in with wicker basket) Hello there!

MOTHER: Don't care. (ushers her out)

LITTLE RED RIDING HOOD: But...!

MOTHER: Oh, it's you – er – Little Red Riding Hood. (Lets her in)

LITTLE RED RIDING HOOD: Are you getting stressed again, Mother?

Mother loudly bolts the top half of the stable door.

MOTHER: Not at all. Just following safety regulations. (Checks door won't open then looks at list) Little Red Riding Hood: did you get the decorations for the party?

LITTLE RED RIDING HOOD: Here you are. (Hands over basket)

MOTHER: (Ticks item off list) And you're sure they meet the Fire Safety Code?

LITTLE RED RIDING HOOD: Yep. Look.

They go over, to the side away from the door, to examine decorations. One by one Hammo, Spammo & Gammo then Granny knock at the door. Each time mother goes and opens the top half, they look pleading but Mother just says 'NO!' then shuts the door. As she walks away one at a time they crawl in through the bottom half, closing it behind them, then hide. Needs to be fast!

LAST KNOCK ON DOOR.

MOTHER: (angrily opens top of door) I told you ...! OH!

The WOLF is standing there. The pigs all give small screams.

MOTHER: Yes?

WOLF: Good morning, Madame. Can I interest you in topical item?

MOTHER: No, you can't. Sorry! (shuts door)

PIGS: general panic and cries of 'a wolf'!

MOTHER: (Sees them all indoors and is shocked) How?! What?! What 'wolf'? There's no wolf! Look!

Mother opens top of door and Wolf is still standing there.

WOLF: (slow & sleazy) Hello.

PIGS: Wolf! (in terror they point)

GAMMO: (To audience member) You look sensible. It IS a wolf, right? (Business)

MOTHER: Hmm. (Listens to business then looks closer) Are you, in fact, a wolf?

WOLF: Me?!! Ha-ha! No-no-no! Not at all.

GRANNY: He looks like a wolf to me. You know what they say: 'If the cap fits – shepherds warning'!

WOLF: No, no, no! I am - er - a meerkat. (Makes meerkat squeak) (Wolf opens door and walks in to look at pigs) My, what lovely children you have. So – tender and juicy! (Licks lips and wrings hands)

Pigs hide behind LRRH.

MOTHER: Children?! They - are pigs!! Rudeness! OUT! Come on, I'm too busy for this. (Steers him to door)

WOLF: (Talking as walking) But madam; can I interest you in double glazing? Solar panels? Cheaper firewood? Faster broadband? Raffle tickets? Lucky heather? Anything off TV. (Starts to sing TV advert jingle. Door slammed in his face.)

LITTLE RED RIDING HOOD: He did rather look like a wolf.

HAMMO: He

SPAMMO: certainly

GAMMO: did!

LITTLE RED RIDING HOOD: What do you think, Granny?

Granny carries on singing the advert jingle.

MOTHER: I'm too busy to argue about mammalian classification. I've got a birthday party to sort out.

GRANNY: Remind me. Whose birthday is it today? (Little Red puts her hand up & waves but is not noticed)

MOTHER: No idea. Always one of them. Anyway; I'm going to collect the cake; I'll take whatshername... you know, the other one with the red riding hood, but taller.

LITTLE RED RIDING HOOD: Big Red Riding Hood. She's doing the recycling.

MOTHER: (Ticks item off list) OK. Did you get the balloons?

LITTLE RED RIDING HOOD: Here. (Holds them up. Non-inflated.) (Mother ticks item off list) I'm not very good at balloons though.

MOTHER: OK. No problem! You four (pigs and granny) – you _can_ stay in here _IF_ you help – er – LITTLE Red Riding Hood? get the balloons ready. (Ticks item off list. She goes to door then turns) But no mess!

GRANNY & PIGS: Got it! No mess! (Mother exits)

LITTLE RED RIDING HOOD: Now, if you're going to help you've got to stop messing around and get organised! (They look outraged) Hammo, you blow up the balloon; Spammo you tie it up; Gammo put the ribbon on it, Granny – you hang it up. (She passes balloons and then checks party things in basket)

HAMMO: Blow!

SPAMMO: Tie!

GAMMO: Ribbon!

GRANNY: Hang! Got it!

HAMMO blows up balloon, passes to SPAMMO. POP! They all jump.Granny late.

HAMMO blows up balloon, passes to SPAMMO, passes to GAMMO. POP! Jump.

HAMMO blows up balloon, passes to SPAMMO, to GAMMO, GRANNY. POP! Jump.

LITTLE RED RIDING HOOD: How are we doing?

GRANNY: Better than I expected to be honest.

LITTLE RED RIDING HOOD: Oh you! Try again.

They repeat very carefully with a long thin 'flying' balloon. – but don't tie it. Duiring this blowing up:

GRANNY: Reminds me of my Gerald. He'll be looking down on us now. He's not dead – just very condescending.

At the end Granny lets it go and it flies off into the audience. Ad lib with audience.

GAMMO: Almost perfect! Let's all be jolly careful. (They manage to blow one up and tie ribbon.) Excellent!

GRANNY: (Carefully carries balloon to window while pigs each blow up and hold untied balloons.) I'll hang this one up here. (At the window it pops. Pigs shriek and let go of balloons.) (Granny rips the curtains down in alarm.)

LITTLE RED RIDING HOOD: Granny! Your curtains!

(Granny hands curtain to Hammo who holds it up at the window.)

GRANNY: Not a problem! Just need a Hammer! (Runs to sink.) Saw one here! Yep!

LITTLE RED RIDING HOOD: That's not a hammer!

GAMMO: That tool is, in fact, a wrench.(Blows up balloon and hands to LRRH)

GRANNY: Whatever. It'll do. (Pulls it from sink. Water squirts. Shriek. She stops the flow with her hands.)

LITTLE RED RIDING HOOD: Now what are you going to do?

GRANNY: Not a problem! (Gets squirted again) Can somebody get a cloth?

HAMMO: Here!

(Hammo takes curtain down & sees wolf looking in, licking lips.)
HAMMO: WOLF!! (Hammo quickly REPLACES CURTAIN by hand)
SPAMMO: What?! (Hides behind mop handle)
GAMMO: (Who has found a bucket) WOLF! Where?! Let me see.
(Gammo pulls curtain in Hammo's hands aside. Looks. Turns back) Nothing there.
   (Hammo lowers curtain to see MOTHER glaring in) Waah! (Hammo runs across room
   with curtain and hides under it.
(GAMMO sees MOTHER and puts empty bucket over head to hide.)
GRANNY: What's all the noise? (She turns. Squirt.) Aargh!
MOTHER: (Enters carrying large cake) What on earth is...?!!
(The pigs are standing under curtains or bucket. Granny is fighting the water. All
   freeze.Moment of silence.All balloons are released to fly off into audience. Mother
   watches it go in disbelief.
MOTHER: Where is the Health and Safety in THAT?!
The pigs start to shuffle nervously away.
MOTHER: Stand still! Do not move!
Granny freezes but keeps getting squirted until she hits it with wrench.Mother carefully
   puts cake on a chair then moves to stand by open door. Without speaking she angrily
   points that they are to leave by the door.
HAMMO: But – the wolf!
MOTHER: Meerkat!
Hammo nervously exits.
SPAMMO: The rain!
MOTHER: It's stopped!
Spammo cautiously exits.
GAMMO: Where can we go? (Glares at Gran) Our sty is full of empty gin bottles!
MOTHER: Build your own houses!
Gammo sadly exits.
GRANNY: You can't throw them out! It's MY house! If they go – I go (Mother opens door
   wider for her) Very well. 'A nod's as good as a wink before they're hatched'! (Exits with
   dignity)
LITTLE RED RIDING HOOD: Oh my! Will they be alright?
MOTHER: It'll teach them a lesson. (Locks door) Peace at last: kids outside; pigs gone; no
   Granny. Perfect! A nice cup of tea and a relax, I think. Tcha! That builder has left his
   tools in the sink! (Before LRRH can stop her MOTHER lifts the wrench. SQUIRT IN
   FACE. Yelping she retreats backwards, water in eyes, as far as chair then sits heavily
   on cake with a screech.) **BLACKOUT**

SCENE 2: A CLEARING IN THE FOREST – tree profiles
Enter WOLF
WOLF: Look, before the next scene – can I just make one small complaint. Not normally
   one to complain – but I am, quite obviously, THE STAR OF THIS SHOW – and I have
   just been on-stage five minutes!! Five minutes!!
And another thing! I bet you imagine my dressing room is, like, really posh – with a star on
   the door and my name: 'B.B. Wolf', and so on. NO! I have to, like, SHARE!!
And – they haven't even fed me! Not even a bowl of peanuts! Starving I am. STARVING!
   (Drools) I could eat a whole... (Scans front row of audience) ...Hmmm. (approaches
   looks hungrily) No – you lot are safe. (to aud) Looks like the front row contains nuts.
   Allergic.
OK – so (shields eyes and scans) Anyone here gluten free?

So, anyway, before they come back – first I would like to sing a selection of hits by NAME. Music please...

Music starts. Some small children come on: juggle, dance, or unicycle then exit. (We had a five-ear old on a tiny bike with a small puppy in the basket.)

WOLF: What was THAT all about?! Not even part of the story!! That's it – I'm going to see the idiot they call the 'director' of this drivel! This is no way, no way to treat a star! (Exits R)

Enter L: Prince, Rob and the Builder's Mate.

PRINCE: Is this the place?

ROB: Indeed, your Highness. A perfect site for a palace, sir!

PRINCE: But it slopes and...

ROB: Split level palace: very modern. Interior - exterior flow. Entertainer's delight.

PRINCE: Isn't it a bit – boggy – I mean: the ground here is...

ROB: Perfect for water features! And soft soil – much easier for digging. Isn't it, Mate? Oy! Cloth ears (Clips around ear)

MATE: replies.

Nanny McSpreader enters.

NANNY: (speaks as if he was still 5) Watch out there! Mind where you're treading, , Highness. New shoes, remember!

Rob takes Prince aside.

ROB: And who exactly is she, sir?

PRINCE: That's my Personal Assistant. All Princes have one.

ROB: Seriously?

PRINCE: Well, she used to be my nanny and her contract says she's employed until I'm 21, so...

NANNY: I don't like this place, dear. Very damp: you'll catch your death of cold. And sloping: you could easily take a tumble and hurt your knees! (She passes him a tissue for his nose)

ROB: All easily solved, highness. AND I know the owner of this site – you can get it for next to nothing; all you have to do is sign here. (Holds up papers & quill)

PRINCE: Really? How much?

ROB: Just ten thousand gold coins.

PRINCE: Ten thousand?! That seems a lot!

ROB: Not at all. Not for (name of posh area) A bargain! (Prince doesn't take it)

PRINCE: Well... who is the owner?

ROB: Nobody you know, highness. (Mate points at Rob & mumbles but is silenced)

PRINCE: Well, I don't know... (Takes quill and Rob looks excited)

MATE: Sniggers and says something probably vulgar! They look at him.

PRINCE: What did he say?

ROB: (Glares at mate) He was just saying, if he was you, he would stay in the Royal Palace with all those lovely young ladies - princesses and the like.

NANNY: That is exactly what I've been saying: stay where its warm and cosy.

PRINCE: Ha! Being at court is not what you'd think. Princesses are so boring! (Mimics vain/'chav' girls) "I found this super new place that does my nails (examines nails). Have you see Alexandra's hair – what IS she going as? And who in their right mind voted for SOMEONE TOPICAL OFF TV SHOW?!" (shudders in horror)

Yuck! They might look OK but their heads are totally empty except for gossip and fashions and... and they are so NASTY to each other, the other day one of them...

ROB: Alright, alright! Chill! Sorry I mentioned it! Anyway: if you could just sign: here

PRINCE: Sorry. Get a bit worked up. (About to sign then stops) But it's awful! You know, I really believe if I found one girl that was ordinary and down to earth I'd marry her on the spot!

ROB: What spot?

PRINCE: Eh? It's just an expression: on the spot?

ROB: Ooh! I wouldn't marry someone with spots if I was you. No way. Might be measles: or the plague!

NANNY: Very true. You don't want any more spots again: you remember when you were fifteen you were one mass of...

PRINCE: Right. OK!

MATE: mumbles and points to bum.

ROB: Oh yeah! Mate here. He's got a HUGE spot! Ooh – nasty it is; as big as... (Mate starts to pull down seat of pants)

NANNY: No! (Rushes Prince off) Horrid! Come on. Time for your walk!

ROB: (Clips Mate around ear) Idiot! He didn't want to see it! (Looks at it) Yuck: it looks like name! Put it away!

Never mind about the Prince; he'll be back. That track just goes round in a circle. (to aud) Perfect – ten thousand gold coins for this bit of waste-land!

MATE: says something about a palace falling down

ROB: What if the palace does fall down. You think I care? I'll be long gone! Plenty of dozy princes like that one; half a dozen in England alone!

OPTIONAL: song about money They EXIT right.

Enter RED RIDING HOOD and LITTLE RED RIDING HOOD: stage left

RED RIDING HOOD: (to aud) Hello again. Alright?

LITTLE RED RIDING HOOD: (to aud) We've got this basket of food for Granny but she's wandered off again; have you seen her at all? No?

Enter 3 PIGS and GRANNY Stage Right.

RED RIDING HOOD: Ah – there you are!

GAMMO: Indeed we are!

LITTLE RED RIDING HOOD: We've got some supplies for you!

GRANNY: Very thoughtful, love.

SPAMMO: Lovely.We're starving!

HAMMO: Yum!

GAMMO: Food! We have been forced to live off what nature provides.

SPAMMO: Berries and stuff.

GAMMO: Like in those 'survival-in-the-wild' TV programs – Ray Meers, Bear Bum...

LITTLE RED RIDING HOOD: Bare bum?!

RED RIDING HOOD: Bear Grylls. Grylls!

GRANNY: No – no grills out in the wilderness; no ovens or barbecues of any sort! All you have to cook with is just ... a handful of dry twigs. (mimes rubbing sticks together)

SPAMMO: No house! Just ... a handful of dry twigs to shelter under. (mimes)

GAMMO: No furniture! Just ... a handful of dry twigs to sit on. (mimes)

HAMMO: (sees it's his turn and thinks. Suddenly-) No toilet paper! Just a handful of dry twigs to w...... er... well, maybe some toilet paper.

RED RIDING HOOD: Grand Designs! Seen that? You can build a shelter from things you find: rocks, mud, straw bales, and ...

GRANNY: Indeed! Build your own! Remember – (she strikes a noble pose) 'Rome wasn't built – ah - on the cart before the horse'!

GAMMO: Wise words, Granny. Must remember that one: (noble pose) 'Aromas should be blamed on a fart from a horse.' They all look at him.

HAMMO: She's right! We will be pig-survivors! I'll make a house of... I know! That field back there was full of left-over straw – I'll make a house out of that!

RED RIDING HOOD: That's the attitude! What about you, Spammo?

SPAMMO: Ah... yes! I shall make a house of – worms!

LITTLE RED RIDING HOOD: Worms?

SPAMMO: Yep. Worms. Bigguns. (Shows size with hands)

RED RIDING HOOD: Don't you think that worms might just - wriggle away?

SPAMMO: Ha! But I will use specially trained worms!

RED RIDING HOOD: OK. But - what if birds eat the worms?

GRANNY: You can be so negative at times, dear.

SPAMMO: No; she's right... I know! I shall use twigs! Big, solid twigs.

LITTLE RED RIDING HOOD: That's a much better idea!

RED RIDING HOOD: But - how will you join the twigs together?

SPAMMO: I shall tie them together! With worms! (Acts out the tying)

LITTLE RED RIDING HOOD: Brilliant!

GRANNY: Sorted! Gammo? Your house?

GAMMO: Quite traditional me. Happen to know where there's a pile of bricks been thrown away, so...

RED RIDING HOOD: That sounds sensible; but straw, twigs, worms?! They sound rather 'flimsy' to me! I suggest you choose more appropriate materials? And maybe ...

GRANNY: Nonsense; positive attitude! Just start building! Remember: 'Never put off tomorrow - until the fat lady sings'!

(Marches them off)

GAMMO: (as he exits) Wise words, Granny; wise words. Must remember that one: 'Never pull off tomatoes until ... when was it? (Runs off confused)

LITTLE RED RIDING HOOD: Oh no! They've forgotten the basket! (Runs off) Granny!

RED RIDING HOOD: Granny is so thoughtful, wanting to help those silly pigs build their own houses. Sighs. Sometimes I think it would be nice to have a little place of my own.

SONG: Such as: WOULDN'T IT BE LOVELY (My Fair Lady).

Prince enters

PRINCE: Hello? Are you lost?

RED RIDING HOOD: Lost? No – I know exactly where I am. Do you?

PRINCE: Ah – no; not really. I was with some people, but I'm not sure...

RED RIDING HOOD: Well – (she looks at his shoes). Bit muddy here. Your shoes ... well not very 'sensible' for walking in the forest, really?

PRINCE: Ah – right. (smiles & looks at feet) No. Suppose not. More for wandering around palaces, really. (to aud) Nanny will go mental!

RED RIDING HOOD: Sorry?

PRINCE: Ah.... nothing

RED RIDING HOOD: (awkward pause) So; I guess you're The Prince?

PRINCE: Yes. Good guess! And you're called...?

RED RIDING HOOD: My name? Well, I'm usually called 'Red Riding Hood'.

PRINCE: Red Riding Hood? Well, I can see you're wearing one, but, do you have a real name?

RED RIDING HOOD: Yes, thank you. Do you?

PRINCE: Er – yes, of course. I'm The...

RED RIDING HOOD: I know you're 'The Prince'. But that's not a REAL name either.

PRINCE: I suppose not. (smiles again) You are very 'practical' aren't you. So... your real name first...

RED RIDING HOOD: Charlotte Emily Louise. But my friends call me Lottie.

PRINCE: Charmed (bows). And my name is Maximillian Alphonse Ludovico Horatio, the Tenth. (sees her raised eyebrows) Max.

RED RIDING HOOD: Pleased to meet you, Max.

PRINCE: And I am very pleased to meet you, Lottie. (bows)Actually we might be neighbours soon. I'm here to plan a new building! A palace!

RED RIDING HOOD: Really? Lovely. Well, don't use worms

PRINCE: Worms? Er – any special reason why not?

RED RIDING HOOD: Birds, of course! Eat them!

PRINCE: Gosh! You seem to know a lot about building. (thoughtful) Is your father a builder?

RED RIDING HOOD: Not all. He climbs beanstalks for a living. (pause for this to sink in) HeI just worked it out for myself.

PRINCE: Do you often work things out for yourself?

RED RIDING HOOD: Of course. Don't you?

PRINCE: Er no; I have people to do that sort of thing for me. Perhaps you could help me – you know - with ideas for the new palace?

RED RIDING HOOD: Help you? Palace? Well...

SONG: duet: such as duet from Frozen

They both get closer. Nanny enters L.

NANNY: Ah! There you are, you young scamp? (She separates them and wipes his face and hands with a tissue.) Don't touch the peasants, dear. You've no idea where they've been. (smiles nicely at RRH) Now: nearly time for your nap! Off we go! (start to exit) I'm sure she's a lovely girl, but I suspect she's just after your crown jewels.   BOTH EXIT R.

RED RIDING HOOD: OK. Not sure what happened then. I need time to absorb this. (Exits R)

WOLF: (Enters down steps) Thank goodness they've gone. Now – let's notch the quality up. First I would like to sing you a...

ROB ENTERS L

ROB: Ah! There you are. Been looking all over.

WOLF: Yes – here I am. And getting hungry! Do you have anything...?

ROB: I might have something here...

WOLF: (To aud) Some lovely, juicy, pork chops would be... What's this?

ROB: Closest I could get.

WOLF: Smokey bacon crisps?!

ROB: Like it or lump it. Anyway: I have another job for you.

WOLF: (shovelling crisps in) Go on.

ROB: The Prince wants to build himself a new palace, and I have the perfect site for it – HERE. Now, 'coincidentally', I happen to own it but I am prepared to sell it: for ten thousand gold coins! But - there's one, small problem...

WOLF: (shovelling crisps in) Mmm?

ROB: There's an old cottage on the site already. (Indicates) Over that way. Dingly Dell. Owned by an old Grandmother with an awful family.

WOLF: (checking empty bag for crumbs) So? Kick her out!

ROB: You know the law: I can't just throw people off! At least, not while (looks around furtively, speaks meaningfully) not while the owner is still ... alive.

WOLF: So... ?

ROB: So... she has to go.

WOLF: And you want me to...?

ROB: To do whatever it takes to get rid of her.

WOLF: Like – ask her to leave?

ROB: Ah. Tried that.

WOLF: Pay her to move?

ROB: Tried that too. The old boot won't go.

WOLF: (inspired idea) What if someone should - accidentally - tip her into a big cooking pot and make her into a delicious stew with red wine - and herbs - and little baby onions! And... then – by mistake of course – accidentally ... eat her!

ROB: How terrible! Ha! Whatever it takes! (Gives him bag of gold coins) And more when the job is done. Just get it sorted! (Exits)

WOLF: Splendid. (Checks coins) Now: for a feast! Ha ha!!!! (Call that booing?! Evil exit)

SCENE 3: CLEARING IN THE FOREST
THE HUFF AND PUFF SCENE

Houses slide onstage: straw, twigs and bricks. They are very badly built.

The straw & twig houses need not be more than cut-outs, one on either side to be pulled off-stage later, but the central brick house needs a door that works.

SONG: Pigs & Granny plus the Riding Hoods & Junior Chorus: such as OUR HOUSE.

ALL EXIT except Granny and pigs.

HAMMO: There – finished!

RED RIDING HOOD: They don't look very – er – solid. Shouldn't you have used – I don't know – concrete and nails and stuff?

GRANNY: Nonsense! (Taps one and it wobbles) Why waste money? Remember: 'Take care! A penny earned is thicker than water'!

GAMMO: Wise words, Granny. Take care when you spend a penny if it might be more than water! (Exits into his house)

HAMMO: Better get the furniture now.

(The pigs exit)

RED RIDING HOOD: (secretly) Granny! Psst! PSST (To one side)

GRANNY: No I'm not! Eh? What is it? You can tell your Granny.

No – hang on – let me guess: you met a really handsome chap in the woods and you have both fallen madly in love with each other BUT he is a fabulously rich Prince and you're a just a poor girl from a poor family: "Scaramouche, Scaramouche will you do the fandango' ....

RED RIDING HOOD: (pause) NO.

GRANNY: What do you mean 'No'?

RED RIDING HOOD: Sorry? (laughs) I meant 'Yes'! Silly me!

GRANNY: Good grief.

RED RIDING HOOD: So: in love with a prince. What can I do, Granny?

GRANNY: I shouldn't worry, dear – after all, this is only a panto. Just wait and see. (Quoting with deadpan expression:) "I'm sure the writer will think of something".

RED RIDING HOOD: "Yes, he's a very clever fellow".

GRANNY: (To wings) So, what's he written next for us?

PERSON: (stagehand looks at script) It says: 'They exit to have cup of tea'.

GRANNY: G and T! Perfect! Come on! (They exit LEFT together)

ROB Enters RIGHT with Mate, Prince & Nanny

ROB: So that's agreed then.

PRINCE: I think it's a lovely spot: lovely views of the forest.

NANNY: Squirrels.

ROB: Sorry?

NANNY: Squirrels. He's afraid of squirrels.

PRINCE: No I'm not! Apparently one jumped in my pram and I cried!

ROB: Recently?

PRINCE: No! It doesn't mean I'm still afraid now!

NANNY: We shall see. We shall see. Don't blame me if you open the window of your shiny new palace and there, on the lawn, is a huge squirrel with blood dripping from its fangs and - in its claws - a dead badger.

MATE: sounds of agreement and fear

PRINCE: Shall we just sign it?

Rob eagerly gives contract and quill. Mate sneezes.

NANNY: What was that noise?!

ROB: I think it was a squirrel!

Nanny panics and runs off, dragging Prince.

PRINCE: Sign it later! (Exits)

ROB: So: soon I shall have ten thousand gold coins. As soon as that old woman is gone and her cottage is pulled down and... (looks around and sees new houses) What?! WHAT?! Where did these come from?!

MATE: Explains what straw and twigs are, briefly.

ROB: Yes, you idiot, I know what straw and twigs are! (Hits) But who built them?!

GAMMO: (Enters LEFT) Hello! Oh: I know you from somewhere, don't I?

ROB: Er – ah – maybe. Perhaps you've seen us on the telly!

GAMMO: Telly? Are you someone on TV yet very unlikely or very unpopular?

MATE: abusive tirade against that person with odd recognizable words slotted in.

ROB: No – no – we're ah ... we're filming these houses - for a TV program!

GAMMO: What program?

ROB: It's – er – 'Grand Escape Homes Designed Under the Sun'!

GAMMO: Oh? (Suddenly gets suspicious) So where's the camera?

ROB: Er... it's up there. (Points out into back of audience)

GAMMO: Ooh. (Turns and stands grinning moronically toward 'camera')

MATE: mutters something then does the same, by his side.

ROB: (to aud.) I have to destroy these houses, or those gold coins are gone! Gone! (He touches huts) Pathetic structures! (To aud) Look! These two are only made of straw and twigs: you could almost blow them down! Ah-ha! I know! Matches!! Tee hee! (searches pockets & finds a box)

SPAMMO: (Enters) Hello! Who's this then?

GAMMO: Ohh! They're from Grand Escape Homes Designed Under the Sun! Here to film our houses! The camera is up there. (Both stand grinning with Mate)

ROB: These matches are useless, have you got...? Here, stop that, you twerp! (Clips mate round ear) Have you got any matches?

Mate finds a box and passes it to Rob, who takes it, giggling, & tries burning houses again. The others watch him with apparent lack of understanding/concern.

HAMMO: (Enters) Ooh, hello! Here: haven't we met that bloke with the matches before?

GAMMO: He's off the telly?

HAMMO: The telly?

GAMMO: Yeah! Grand Escape Homes Designed Under the Sun!

HAMMO: No!

GAMMO: Yo! The camera ... is ... (points) (They turn and stand still, grinning moronically toward 'camera'; Mate & Spammo join them in a line)

ROB: These aren't even matches – they're stale Twiglets! (or similar stick-like sweet or nibble) How long have you been carrying these around?!

MATE: mutter

ROB: Since your fifth birthday?! (Disbelief; Clips around ear) Are you mental?!

MATE: (produces certificate proudly) Yes!

ROB: Grr. I know! I'll rub these two sticks together. (Breaks off house and rubs)

GRANNY: (Enters) I bought you some cushions for your new homes; no – don't go all shy; as I always say: 'It is better to give than to arrive'! Here you go. (Looks around) Don't I know these two from somewhere?

GAMMO: Off the telly! Here to film us for Grand Escape Homes Designed Under the Sun!

GRANNY: Get away! (Preens) So, where's the – you know... (many hands point) (all except Rob, one by one, turn and stand still, grinning moronically toward 'camera', ignoring the frantic stick rubbing and muttering from Rob)

ROB: These sticks are damp. I need some kindling. (Looks at them all) What's the matter with these people? Here! Does any of you have any scraps of paper, for starting a fire?

They all look in pockets etc.

GRANNY: Here's a receipt from local shop for gin (Huge long list)

GAMMO: I've got a newspaper clipping: something silly, topical or old-fashioned.

SPAMMO: I've just got my birth certificate, passport and baby photos!

ROB: They'll do. (Takes them) How about you?

HAMMO: Nothing. Though according to the labels these local shop clothes are highly flammable!

ROB: OK. (Rips significant clothes off Hammo) Thank you. (Starts to build fire by straw hut, watched by others)

GAMMO: (Getting suspicious) Have any of you seen this TV program before?

HAMMO: Oh yes; this is what they do every week.They still just watch.

BIG RED RIDING HOOD: (Enters) Hello.

All shush her.

GRANNY: On the telly. (Nods at 'camera') Grand Escape Homes Designed Under the Sun! (all except Rob, turn and stand still, grinning toward 'camera')

WOLF: (Enters) It's no good – I've looked everywhere but I can't find Granny's cottage. What on earth...

GRANNY: Shh! Telly!

(Wolf joins the line of posing idiots)

ROB: Nothing is going to light. I give up. I ... ooh; what's happening? (Joins the line)

MOTHER: (Enters with clipboard) Ah! So – this is where you're all hiding! I knew you wouldn't have gone far from...... what are you all doing?

ALL: Shhh! We're on the TV!

MOTHER: No. No you're not. That's Bob the Builder and his mate. Come on! Things to do! (She exits with LRRH)

ROB: Rob! Rob the Builder! Oops!

PIGS & GRANNY: Ah! What a con! Etc....

They all EXIT L & R except Rob & Wolf and Mate.

WOLF: Listen – I can't find that Granny's cottage anywhere.

ROB: Ha! There are four buildings to get rid of now!

WOLF: What? Four?! (Holds up 3 fingers)

ROB: Grah! Four! (Mate shows 6 fingers) These three and Granny's cottage!

WOLF: These? These?! They're made of – junk! You just need to blow hard!

ROB: Then do it! I don't care if you blow them DOWN or blow them UP! Just get rid of them! Come on! (Drags Mate off RIGHT – still grinning at camera.)

The 3 pigs reappear LEFT. Wolf sees pigs coming and exits RIGHT.

Pigs do intro into brief song:

SPAMMO: I hope that wolf isn't around anymore!

HAMMO: Hah! Are we afraid! No!

PIGS: SONG: 'Whose afraid of the big bad wolf?' (Chorus: only!)

Wolf appears and joins in. One by one HAMMO & SPAMMO notice the wolf and dive into their houses until it is just Gammo & Wolf dancing. Gammo finally realizes.

WOLF: Well: that little piggy went to market, and that little piggy stayed at home – is this little piggy going to go 'wee wee wee' all the way home? (Evil smile.

GAMMO: Er: I think I've started already, actually. (Shakes leg) Oh dear! (into house.)

WOLF: So – little piggies. Where to start? Hmm. The house of straw I think; just to warm up. Hellooo? Anybody home in there?

HAMMO: (through small window) No! Go away!

WOLF: Let me in, little pig, let me in; or I'll huff and I'll puff and I'll blow your house in!

HAMMO: (in window) Not by the hair of my chinny-chin-chin! I won't let you in!

WOLF: 'Not by the hair of your chinny-chin-chin'? I'm here to eat you! Not shave your 'chinny-chin-chin'! What on earth are you talking about?

HAMMO: (opening window) I don't know; it's traditional. Now clear off!

WOLF: (To aud) Now I'm getting cross. I'm going to huff – and puff – and BLOW this house in. (So he does)

The house 'blows' offstage exposing Hammo who shrieks and runs into Spammo's twig house.The WOLF goes to Spammo's twig house.

WOLF: This seems to be held together by – yuck! – worms! Never mind. OK: Let me in, little pig, let me in; or I'll huff and I'll puff and I'll blow your house in!

SPAMMO: (out window) Not by the hair of my chinny-chin-chin! I won't let you in!

WOLF: 'Not by the hair of your chinny-chin-chin'? What is it with you pigs and your 'chinny-chin-chins'?!

SPAMMO: (out window) It's what pigs say to drive off the big bad wolf!

WOLF: Well it doesn't work! I am now going to huff and puff and blow your house in! (He does)The house goes exposing Hammo and Spammo who shriek and run into Gammo's brick house.

WOLF: Hahaha! Too easy; one more to blow in, then off to sort out Granny! Right! Let me in, little pig, let me in; or I'll huff and I'll puff and I'll blow your house in!

GAMMO: (Opens door and looks out) Bog off (or similar)!

WOLF: (Stunned shock) What?! 'Bog off?!' Hang on; that's not right. You're supposed to say: "Not by the hair of my chinny-chin-chin!"?!

GAMMO: What?

WOLF: "Not by the hair of my chinny-chin-chin!"

GAMMO: I have no idea what you're talking about. I don't HAVE a hair on my – what was it? – "chinny-chinny-chinny"?!

WOLF: 'Chinny-chin-chin'!

GAMMO: Whatever. Bog off! (Slams door)

WOLF: I have never been so .... Right here goes. I will huff ... and puff .... And huff ... and - phew – puff ... and huff ... hang on. Gasps. Need to rethink this plan. (Thinks.) Aha! If I can't blow it down... (Runs into wings and returns with bomb: black ball with indoor sparkler in it) ...I'll blow it up! Oy – let me in!

PIGS: No!

WOLF: Let me in NOW!

PIGS: Oh – alright then!

The pigs run out of the door. The wolf then runs inside, laughing triumphantly.

Gammo pulls door shut. The pigs retreat across the stage and watch as the laughing from inside changes from manic to unsure.

WOLF: "Oh no! Little pigs! Let me out! Let me out!".

PIGS: Not by the hair on your bummy-bum-bum!

Explosion. House lights brightly from inside; sound fx; smoke.

Door slowly opens and smoke billows out. Wolf staggers out with torn, black, smoking clothes and hat.

GAMMO: Quick – off to Granny's house! (The pigs exit)

WOLF: Granny's house! Yes! All I have to do is follow them! Ha ha! Then ALL the houses will be destroyed. And very soon I shall be enjoying Granny casserole for my dinner. Yum-yum! HAHAHA! EXITS L

BIG RED RIDING HOOD enters R carrying cushions.

BIG RED RIDING HOOD: I've got some more cushions for the pigs so that – OH! What happened here? Business with kids in audience.

That's terrible I must get help! I know – the Prince. Look – it'll take a while to get there and I am NOT going there like this! I know – why don't you all have a break – and I'll meet you at the palace in – oh about twenty minutes? Great! See you later!

INTERVAL
ACT II: SCENE 4: IN THE FOREST – tree profiles / cloth
TAKING THE BASKET TO GRANNY SCENE

Optional Jr CHORUS NUMBER dance. (Fairies? Elves? Mice?) Chorus EXIT

MOTHER and LRRH enter.

MOTHER: Right – this is where the path splits in two. Now: I've still got a birthday party to organize (Checks clipboard) – though I must say I can't remember which one of you it's for. (LRRH tries to indicate that it is her, but is not noticed) I'll be glad when your father gets back down from that beanstalk.

So: you'll have to take this basket of food to Granny's house.

LITTLE RED RIDING HOOD: OK.

MOTHER: And be sure to stick to this path (indicates) It's the quickest and safest.

LITTLE RED RIDING HOOD: Right. (Is not looking – instead is peering into basket)

MOTHER: And – if there IS a wolf about – not that I'm saying there is – then he'll be hiding in the dark parts of the forest, so avoid them. Have you got all that?

LITTLE RED RIDING HOOD: Yes! Yes! Yes; of course. I'll be perfectly fine.

MOTHER: Off you go then. Oh: first … sign here to confirm I warned you about the wolf. And the date. OK. Remember what I said! The safe path! (Exits)

LITTLE RED RIDING HOOD: (to aud) Hello again! Enjoy the interval? OK: so - I've got another basket of goodies to take to Granny. And I'm going to go through the forest this way (points wrong way) so I can pick some wild flowers for her. She'll like that!

But – this way is a bit dark and gloomy. Do you think it'll be safe? What do you think?

This way, or that way? Well – there are no wild flowers that way. Look: if I go this way I won't be afraid, not with you all here.

BUT! If you see a wolf will you shout and warn me? You will; thanks.

I've got loads here in my basket; I've got … bread, cheese, gin, butter, more gin, tonic, lemon, gin, …

As she discusses the contents the wolf appears, fleeing offstage when shouted at. Each time LRRH stops, looks around, sees nothing, continues. This happens 3 times then LRRH sees him

LITTLE RED RIDING HOOD: Ha! So – Mr Wolf. Trying to creep up on me! (To aud) Thank you for the shouting! (Approaches and slaps his hand) You are a wild and wicked wolf!

WOLF: Meerkat? Squeek.

LITTLE RED RIDING HOOD: Get real. (Taps foot & folds arms) What is it you're up to, you mangy, malevolent mammal?

WOLF: Me? Nothing at all! What is it you're up to!

LITTLE RED RIDING HOOD: Me? I am taking this basket of food to my granny. And NO (pokes again) you can't have ANY of it! Now I'm going and YOU cannot even think about following me, you loathsome lupine!

WOLF: (sarcastic) Oooh!

LITTLE RED RIDING HOOD: (To aud) And if he tries to follow me – will you all shout and warn me? Yes? Thanks then; see you later! (Exits)

Wolf tries to follow, hopefully shouting, then...

WOLF: Alright! Enough with the shouting! I don't need to follow that little brat! This trail only goes to one place – and it's not the quickest way. If I go this (points) way, I'll get there long before that – that 'scarlet squirt'! See – she's not the only one who can do alliteration! Ha-ha! (Exits laughing)

ACT II: SCENE 5: GRANNY'S COTTAGE
GRANNY AND THE WOLF SCENE Full stage

Interior of Granny's cottage. There is now a short bed with its head against the rear wall and blankets that reach the floor (secured in place). At its foot is a large, top-opening linen chest (with no back so that cast can crawl out of it, under the bed and off stage) The bottom of the chest is well-padded! The front stable-door and a cupboard as before. There is a large broom.

ALTERNATIVE: INSTEAD OF THE LINEN CHEST HAVE A SECOND CUPBOARD

An activity is taking place such aerobics with chorus, led by berserk Granny.

Chorus exits.

GRANNY: Same time next week!Granny is wearing glasses, a shawl and a 'mop cap'. Still humming / singing to herself she folds up 'things' and puts them in the linen chest, to show how the lid works. Suddenly Gammo bursts in. NB: a second cupboard can be used instead. E mail for help!

GRANNY: Oh my!

GAMMO: Granny Hubbard!

GRANNY: What on earth is it, Gammo?

GAMMO: It's the wolf!

GRANNY: No! Where?! (Looks outside, either door or window)

GAMMO: He just blew down Spammo and Hammo's houses then blew mine up!

GRANNY: My word! Are the others safe?

GAMMO: I think so! They ran off. I came here to warn you!

GRANNY: Right! What to do? Think-think-think... Ah-ha! A wolf trap!

GAMMO: A trap?

GRANNY: A trap!

GAMMO: A trap! How?

GRANNY: Ahhhh.... Breadcrumbs! A trail of breadcrumbs to this cupboard, then we push him in, with this broom! Trapped! (Sits on chest triumphantly)

GAMMO: Brilliant! Er ... do wolves eat breadcrumbs?

GRANNY: Ah. See your point. (Thinks. To aud) 'The best laid plans of mice from little acorns grow'!

What we need is some proper bait! (Looks about) So – what DO wolves eat? (Slowly turns to look at unsuspecting Gammo)

GAMMO: (Eventually understands) What? Me?! No way! (Heads for door)

GRANNY: (intercepting him) You'll be fine. Look: you get in the bed. That's it. (She opens cupboard door ready for the wolf) I'll hide behind the curtain with the broom. (Acts) 'wolf-wolf-wolf-broom-broom-push-slam'. Sorted.

Now: safety goggles! (Puts on old style flying goggles or similar) What can go wrong? (feels her way around blindly) Come on – remember: 'Faint heart never one way to skin a cat'! Shhh! I can hear him coming!

She hides with broom.Gammo hides under blanket: ears & hat still visible.

SPAMMO: (Enters quickly and sees Gammo) Gammo!

With a battle-cry Granny charges with the broom, pushing Spammo into cupboard.

GRANNY: Got him!

GAMMO: (Reappears) Are you sure?

SPAMMO: (echoing) Help! Help! Let me out!

GRANNY: Listen! Hear that wolf wail!

GAMMO: That's not the wolf! That's Spammo!

GRANNY: Are you sure?

Nervously she opens door. Spammo pops out angrily. They jump back in alarm.

SPAMMO: You silly old woman; pushing me in there and... (knocking at the door)

GRANNY & GAMMO: The wolf!

Granny pushes confused Spammo into the linen chest and waits as before.

HAMMO: (Enters quickly and sees Gammo) Gammo!

Granny charges, pushing Hammo into cupboard, slams shut.

GRANNY: Got him!

GAMMO: Where is he? (Granny indicates) In there?!

GRANNY: Look!

Gammo jumps out of bed and Spammo leaves linen box and together they nervously open the door. Hammo pops out angrily, making them shriek again!

HAMMO: What did you do that for?!

GRANNY: We thought you were ... (loud knocking at the door)

ALL: Aaargh!

WOLF: (Offstage; slimy voice) Hello – anybody at home?

ALL: The wolf!

GRANNY: Quick – hide in there!

She rushes Hammo and Spammo into the linen chest. Gammo has had enough.

GAMMO: I've had enough. Not doing that again! (Gammo gets into chest with others but lifts two safety blocks to keep lid partly open)

The door starts to open a crack.

GRANNY: You have to be in the bed!(Tries to get him out of the box)

WOLF: (Voice) Hello?Hello? Anyone at home?

GRANNY: Too late!

Granny closes the lid but Gammo's arm is still hanging out (arm-sized cut-out to avoid injury!)Granny goes to tuck the arm in but the door opens too soon and she is forced to sit on the box. The arm is now hanging between her legs.

WOLF: (Enters) Ah; so you are at home, Granny Hubbard. (Looks around suspiciously) I am very pleased to meet you again.

Wolf walks across with hand held out for shaking. Gammo's arm comes up from beneath Granny's skirt. Wolf shakes it as if normal.

WOLF: How do you do. What a very nice cottage you have here.

Wolf walks away as he talks, then suddenly realizes what happened and spins back but by now Granny has jumped up, pushed the arm back in and returned to lie provocatively on the box. (Pigs now escapes unseen from back of box and off under the bed to get into cupboard.)

WOLF: Yes – a very nice cottage. A shame it's built in the wrong place.

GRANNY: Built in the wrong place? What do you mean?

WOLF: Very simple, my dear woman, this land is owned by Rob the Builder – and he plans to build the new palace for the Prince here. But, sadly, your cottage is in the way – and will have to go. (He goes facing away from cupboard and examines wall.) Shouldn't take much to knock it down: just like those horrid little sheds those pigs built.

The pigs make offstage shouts of angry protest and try to come out of cupboard.

GRANNY: What? How did you get in … never mind! Get back in!

Granny pushes them back in the cupboard. Wolf hears but turns late.

WOLF: What's going on in here? Are you trying to make a fool of me?

GRANNY: Not at all! You're doing a very good job of that yourself.

WOLF: Thank you; how kind. But this seems suspicious. (Business as he circles and Granny tries to hide the cupboard from him) Stand aside – what is in there?

GRANNY: Nothing. Nothing at all! Ooer.

Wolf pushes her aside, flings open cupboard door. He sticks his head in and looks. She gets broom and is about to push him in when he turns: she strokes him with broom: he likes that. He turns and she brushes under his tail, in disgust. He likes that too. He looks in cupboard and shuts door.

WOLF: Hmm. Empty.

GRANNY:?!

Pushes him aside and leans in. She then looks at audience in amazement then starts to secretly searching, including under the wolf or his cloak.

Wolf starts to prowl around, looking in the bed etc. Finally, Granny opens the linen box and a pig pops up but Wolf is looking around.

He is suspicious and hurries to look in the box. Empty. A pig appears in cupboard as door swings open. Gran rushes across, slams the cupboard door and stands against it.

WOLF: This is most peculiar. (He sees her hiding the cupboard) Stand aside!

He pushes her aside, dramatically opens door to show empty wardrobe. Granny is shocked. Wolf steps inside the cupboard to search and Granny slams door on him, wedging it with the broom under the handle.

GRANNY: Psst. (Stage whisper as she looks around for the pigs) Where are you?!

(She looks in most unlikely places, including under blankets, in coat pockets, in jugs. Finally, she checks the linen chest again and the pigs pop up, making her shriek) Get out of there. Quick now! (they get out)

Gammo is carrying a large chamber-pot (potty)

GAMMO: Where's the wolf?

GRANNY: In there. (Sees potty) Oh – thank goodness you found that! I'm desperate! (She goes across to potty and gets bottle of gin out; sips: looks at it) Oh: must have taken the wrong one to the doctors. (Finishes it anyway)

HAMMO: What will you do with him?

GRANNY: No idea. OK! I need you three to run to the palace and get help.

SPAMMO: Why don't you come with us?

GRANNY: Me run? Ha! 'You can't teach an old dog to suck eggs'.

GAMMO: Well... (uncertain)

GRANNY: Run along. I'll be fine! (They exit and run off.)

Granny goes and listens at the cupboard door but hears nothing. She checks the broom securing the door then adds a wooden chair. While she is doing this, behind her back, the lid of the chest slowly opens and the wolf appears. He climbs slowly out, gesturing to the audience to be quiet. He creeps to stand beside Granny.

GRANNY: (she glances at the wolf but is confused) Here; you help. (She grabs him so he is helping her lean against the door) That should do it. (She walks away then suddenly realizes her mistake) Oops!

WOLF: Haha! Now – what to do with a tough old bird like you? If I had a big slow-cooker perhaps...

LITTLE RED RIDING HOOD: (Offstage) Granny! Granny!

GRANNY: Little Red Riding Hood!

WOLF: Ha! A much tastier snack! (Grabs Granny and bustles her into cupboard) You – Granny – will have to wait! In here you go!

He pushes her in, slams the door, and then uses the broom to block the door.

Quickly he finds spare glasses, shawl and mop-cap, pulls window curtains (dim lights) and climbs into the bed, pulling blankets up under his chin. He giggles and signals the audience to be quiet.

LITTLE RED RIDING HOOD: (Offstage) Granny! Granny! Are you home?

WOLF: (Granny voice) Why yes, my dear. Just open the door and come on in!

The door starts to open and Little Red Riding Hood is seen standing there.

BLACKOUT

SCENE 6: AT THE PALACE Throne and guards with flags.

PAGE: (Enters with RRH) In here, Madame. The Prince will be with you shortly.

RED RIDING HOOD: Wow. Super. Thank you. (Page bows and exits) This is jolly posh here. It must be a bit like NAME'S house.

Page returns and bows, followed by the Prince.

PAGE: His Royal Highness, Prince Maximillian of Tintinabula. (Stays on stage)

PRINCE: Ah ha! Lottie, I was hoping it would be you.

RED RIDING HOOD: (Curtseys) I wasn't sure you would remember me.

PRINCE: Oh yes – I certainly remember you. Would you like tea? Coffee? (Gestures to Page who steps forward) Perhaps we could sing another duet?

RED RIDING HOOD: Oh no; no thank you. Perhaps later? No – I came here for help!

PRINCE: Help? Why – of course. Help with what?

RED RIDING HOOD: Well, it seems a bit petty really, but we're having some trouble with a wolf.

PRINCE: At your house?

RED RIDING HOOD: No. My friends, the Three Pigs, have built houses – on that land where I met you? (He nods) But for some reason a great, hairy wolf has been and destroyed their houses and now he's off to my Granny's house to destroy that!

PRINCE: Wolves don't normally do that sort of thing. (To Page) Get the Chief of the Guards and his best men; assemble them in the courtyard.

(PAGE bows and exits)

RED RIDING HOOD: Wow. That's really kind of you, I mean...

PRINCE: It's the least I can do, and when that's done perhaps...

PAGE: (Enters in a rush; quick bow)

PRINCE: What is it?

PAGE: There are three – er – 'pigs' outside, your Highness. They seem very 'agitated' and want to 'speak' to you.

PRINCE: Will that be your friends?

RED RIDING HOOD: I expect so. Talking pigs aren't really that common.

PRINCE: Send them in. (Page exits) I hope it doesn't mean worse trouble!

RED RIDING HOOD: Granny!
PRINCE: Don't panic – we'll sort things out. Here they are.
But NANNY enters.
NANNY: My word: still up at this time of night? Whatever next? Visitors?
PRINCE: Ah…
PIGS enter in panic.
GAMMO: Your royalness! There's a … Red Riding Hood! You're here!
RED RIDING HOOD: What is it? (Alarmed) Is it Granny?!
SPAMMO: Yes! That wolf! He's at her house!
NANNY: A wolf?! Oh my! (She faints: Hammo catches her and lowers her into sitting position, holding her upright.)
HAMMO: It's alright – she has him trapped in a cupboard! (He steps away from Nanny and she rotates to fall back with legs in the air. Hammo is oblivious. Others look at raised bloomer's, point, and Hammo realises and presses feet down to rotate her back sitting upright)
PRINCE: In a cupboard!
GAMMO: But she needs help to deal with it.
PRINCE: This is the mystery wolf? The one that knocks houses down for no reason?
SPAMMO: Yes! But he does have a reason!
HAMMO: He's doing it for Rob the Builder.
GAMMO: He's got the wolf clearing everybody off the land!
SPAMMO: Rob wants to sell the land for ten thousand gold coins to some dopey
  Prince!Awkward moment.
PRINCE: Now it makes sense! The cad! We must get there fast! Can you ride a horse?
GAMMO: (raised eyebrows and a sarcastic response) I'm a pig.
PRINCE: OK – yes, right; then follow us as quick as you can!
NANNY: What? It's freezing out there! Ride – in the dark! I mean…
PRINCE: I'll be fine! You get some nice, hot cocoa (or similar) ready for when I get back.
NANNY: Cocoa? Yes – cocoa!
PRINCE: Quick! Granny's cottage! (to aud) I hope we'll not be too late!
ALL EXIT except Nanny.
NANNY: Cocoa, cocoa (she dithers then hurries through the audience muttering)

SCENE 7: GRANNY'S COTTAGE
THE RED RIDING HOOD AND THE WOLF IN THE COTTAGE SCENE
Knocking on door.
WOLF: Come in my dear. I'm not feeling too well - cough, cough! Having a bit of a lie-down.
LITTLE RED RIDING HOOD: (Enters) Oh dear. Well, I've got a lovely basket of goodies for you Granny.
WOLF: How very kind. Bring it a little closer, my dear.
LITTLE RED RIDING HOOD: It's only the usual stuff; gin, cheese, gin, bread, gin. I'll put it over here for you.
As she turns her back to put the goodies down the wolf starts to crawl from the bed toward her. As she starts to turn back he dives back under the blanket. If the audience make a noise LRRH will have to ignore them, though the wolf can pull faces and wave angrily.
WOLF: Come closer so I can see you, my dear.
LRRH moves a tiny bit closer but stops and stands looking at the bed.
LITTLE RED RIDING HOOD: You do seem unwell, Granny. You're not looking yourself!
WOLF: I'm not?
LITTLE RED RIDING HOOD: No. I mean – (Squints at him) What big EYES you have,

Granny.

WOLF: Tee hee. All the better to SEE you with, my dear.

LITTLE RED RIDING HOOD: Oh. (Thinks) And – what big EARS you have, Granny.

WOLF: Tee hee. All the better to HEAR you with, my dear.

LITTLE RED RIDING HOOD: Oh. (Thinks) And – what a big NOSE you have, Granny.

WOLF: Tee hee. All the better to SMELL you with, my dear. (To aud) Here it comes, folks –
(points to teeth and mouths 'teeth')

LITTLE RED RIDING HOOD: Oh. (Thinks) And – what big EYEBROWS you have, Granny.

WOLF: Tee hee. Eh? What? Eyebrows?! Err... All the better to LOOK SURPRISED with,
my dear. (Looks surprised) Anything else? (Shows teeth) Mmm?

LITTLE RED RIDING HOOD: Oh. (Thinks) Yes! What big WHISKERS you have, Granny.

WOLF: Eh? What? Whiskers? Whiskers?! What is she talking about? This isn't in the
script! Err... Whiskers .... ah ... All the better to ... to ...? Look – all Grannies have
whiskers; just get over it, eh?

LITTLE RED RIDING HOOD: OK. I'll be off now then.

WOLF: What?! Hang about! Hang–a–bout! Haven't you forgotten something?

LITTLE RED RIDING HOOD: Forgotten? Don't think so. Cheese, bread, gin. All here. Ta
ta!

WOLF: No! Oy! OY!! Teeth! Don't forget Granny's teeth!

LITTLE RED RIDING HOOD: Oh yes! Silly me! Laughs. You want me to get your teeth for
you, Granny! Are they in this glass? (Goes to shelf/table)

WOLF: No! Look! Look at my BIG teeth! Are they not huge?! What do you have to say
about THAT, eh? Eh?

LITTLE RED RIDING HOOD: Oh yes; now you mention it they do look a bit different?
(Thinks) My...

WOLF: Here it comes!

LITTLE RED RIDING HOOD: My, Granny, what big TEETH you have!

WOLF: (leaping up and throwing off glasses and hat) Ha! Yes! ALL THE BETTER TO EAT
YOU WITH!!

The door bursts open. The Prince!!

PRINCE: Not so fast, Mister Wolf!

Strides in with Red Riding Hood, Page, 3 Pigs and armed soldiers/vigilantes.

WOLF: What?! You cannot be serious! This is my big moment!!

Granny wails and rattles cupboard door.

The pigs rush to let Granny out of the cupboard.

GRANNY: Something wrong with the toilet in there: the flush doesn't work.

PRINCE: That animal ... belongs in a zoo! (Wolf wails and hides back under blanket)

GRANNY: (flustered but composes herself when she sees the Prince) Ooh. Your majesty.
(Wobbly curtsey) Er – could I trouble you to just pass me my handbag?

PRINCE: Er – your handbag? Why, certainly... (It is passed to him) Here.

GRANNY: Thanks.

She gets more composed then turns and batters the living daylights out of the wolf with her
handbag. Wolf flees yelping and howling – Granny does battle cry then pursues Wolf
off. Maybe through audience?

MOTHER ENTERS (with Little RRH if no scene between)

MOTHER: I don't understand any of it. So, start again; there was a wolf in Granny's bed.

LITTLE RED RIDING HOOD: Yes!

MOTHER: And this is really the Prince?! (He bows) And you're here because?

PRINCE: I'm here, because I want to ask permission - to marry your daughter.

NANNY: This is so emotional!

MOTHER: Marry my daughter? Certainly. Which one? I seem to have several.

PRINCE: Lottie.

MOTHER: Lottie? Oh. Ah. Which one's that?

LITTLE RED RIDING HOOD: Red Riding Hood. (Mother looks surprised) No – the old one – I'm LITTLE Red Riding Hood.

RED RIDING HOOD: Me! (Looks lovingly at Prince)

MOTHER: Right. Got all that. Wolf. Prince. But why are we all here?

GRANNY: It's one of your children's birthday! Remember?

MOTHER: Oh yeah. Which one is it again? (She checks her clipboard)

LITTLE RED RIDING HOOD: Me!! I am AGE today! Look (shows large birthday cake)

Knock at the door.

GAMMO: I'll get it!

ROB is at the door. Granny hides.

ROB: Ah! They said the Prince was down here! (Goes straight to Prince, with Mate following) Been looking all over for you, Highness. Here are the documents for the sale of that land that you signed. A few minor obstacles have been … 'removed'. I just need the ten thousand gold coins and the land is yours.

PRINCE: OK. Just ONE little thing...

ROB: Mmm? What's that then?

PRINCE: What about the house that's already on the site? A cottage I believe? In fact – this one!?

MATE: unintelligible words agreeing.

ROB: Oh that! (Hits mate then gets smarmy again) Not a problem. I understand that – tragically – the old woman who lived here has had a terrible accident. So – your majesty; if you'll just sign HERE.

RED RIDING HOOD: A terrible accident?

ROB: Mmm. Yes.

Granny comes and stands behind him.

GRANNY: Eaten by a wolf.

ROB: Yes. (Looks around at her and nods) Eaten by a ... (double take) YOU!

GRANNY: Yes – me. So – NOT eaten by a wolf, after all.

PRINCE: And I will NOT be buying any land off YOU. (Rips up contract & hands back) As all these good people are very soon to be my in-laws, they will be living in the new palace – which will be built right here! (Indicates cottage)

ROB: OK – that's a plan. But it'll take years! Where will all these horrible little brats and stinky pigs live while I knock this cottage down and build the new palace?

MOTHER: They will all be staying with you, at your house! (Kids swarm around Rob; he wails)

PRINCE: And! **You** will NOT be building the palace for me! I am promoting your Mate here to be the new Royal Builder.

MATE: Oh – how jolly kind of you! Super!

ROB: What?! What about ME?!

GAMMO: You – are going to be the new 'builder's mate'!

MATE: Ah-ha! Revenge! (Clips Rob around ear who yelps)

LITTLE RED RIDING HOOD: (Walks up to Rob, smiling) Happy birthday, Bob the Builder's

Mate.

ROB: It's ROB! ROB the Builder's Mate. I am sick and tired of telling you stupid people! ROB!! And it's NOT my birthday!

LITTLE RED RIDING HOOD: I think you'll find it is! (Points over Rob's shoulder.)

Others move back. Rob turns just as Granny splats the birthday cake in his face. Cheering as he is led off.

GRANNY: Ha! 'He who laughs last –farts longest!'

ALL: Wise words, Granny! Wise words.

ON-STAGE BOWS

<div align="center">SONG: something like extract from 'FLASH BANG WALLOP WHAT A PICTURE?'</div>

RED RIDING HOOD © Chris Lane 2016www.pantoscripts.me.uk

LIST OF TITLES

Click to select

1. <u>CINDERELLA</u>
2. <u>ROBIN HOOD</u>
3. <u>DICK WHITTINGTON</u>
4. <u>SLEEPING BEAUTY</u>
5. <u>RED RIDING HOOD & THE 3 PIGS</u>
6. <u>THREE MEN IN A TUB</u>
7. <u>JACK AND THE BEANSTALK</u>
8. <u>HANSEL AND GRETEL</u>
9. <u>SNOW WHITE & 7 DWARVES</u>

CONTACT INFORMATION
and PERFORMANCE RIGHTS here:

<u>PANTOSCRIPTS.ME.UK</u>

THREE MEN IN A TUB

© Chris Lane 2018

ACT ONE

'Introduction'

Three toys appear through the audience: two any sort (beware: some kids have a clown phobia so appearing in the dark might cause screaming: soldier & doll?), one teddy-bear.

Toy 1: (pompous) This way! Come on! Just follow me!

Toy 2: (nervous) It's awfully dark. Are you sure this is the right town?

Toy 1: Of course I'm sure! I've got the address of the toy-shop on this bit of paper!

Toy 2: I'm not sure I like this... And who are all these people?

Teddy: Don't worry! I'm sure they're friendly.

Toy 2: But they look a bit.... **frightening**.

Teddy: No they don't.

Toy 2: They do - look at this one! (they stop and look)

Teddy: Well, perhaps that one does. But the others look fairly normal. Hello! Hi there!

Toy 1: (from stage) Stop hanging around down there, you two!

Teddy: (to Toy 2, going up steps) Just stick by me. I'll look after you.

Toy 1: Right; we're nearly there.

Teddy: What's the name of the shop?

Toy 1: Ah... (studies paper) Majestic Toy Shop. It's a brand new one. Not even open yet!

Toy 2: I hope a nice child buys me.

Teddy: Me too! Someone who likes lots of cuddles!

Toy 1: More likely some little horror who'll pull your arms off! (Goes to explore in front of curtains. Is snatched away through curtains by villains HENCH & TOADY.)

Teddy: Take no notice. Most children love their toys

Toy 2: Now which way is it? Hey! Where's he/she gone?

Teddy: Let's look over here. I hope it's not far. It's nearly time for my milk and biscuits. (Toy 2 is snatched.) If I don't... Here! Don't mess around! Where are you?! (to audience) Which way did they go? (Walks and points Left) This way? (Hands try to grab him as he passes) How about this way? (Repeat: Right) I give up. (Returns Centre) Where did they go? What's that? Pardon? (Leans down to hear. Grab again & miss) Hold on; I think my cotton-wool is coming out. (Wiggles paw in ear and steps back) Oops! (Is snatched)

Boss: Appears from Left. Ah-ha! The last one! NO toys for the Majestic Toyshop! Soon all the toyshops **in the world** Will be mine ... MINE!! **Ha-ha-ha-ha-ha!** But first --- I must take these toys to my secret island...**and DESTROY THEM!!** (Exits laughing madly)

Scene One: OUTSIDE THE MAJESTIC TOYSHOP

A street in a port; quaint buildings but neat and attractive.

CHOP'S FAMILY BUTCHER (UR with opening door), WICK'S QUALITY CANDLES (UL), BUNN THE BAKERS (DR With opening door) and MAJESTIC TOY SHOP (DL) With its sign under a cloth.

SONG: **Whole company** on stage as townspeople/pirates. (Not Boss, Teddy, Toys) Adults wander about then exit except children. Child PJ runs across stage to corner. They look at the shop with the hidden sign (toy shop)

Child 1: It's so exciting!

Child 2: What kind of shop is it going to be?

Child 3: A sweet shop!

Child 4: Yes - a sweet shop!

All children: Hooray! Yippee!

Child 5: No! I know - a TOY shop!! (STICKY: adult baker: enters DR With tray of buns)

Child 6: YES! A toy shop!!

All children: HOORAY!!

Sticky: Nah. It's going to sell hard Maths books! (groans from children)

Children: (Suddenly see him.) Hiya, Sticky!

Sticky: Hi there, kids! (to aud) and a big hello to all of you! I'm Sticky Bunn the Baker. Look at these! (holds up tray) Made too many again! Here - who wants a bun? (Help themselves. One child, PJ, is too shy) One bun left. (Teasing) Hmmm. Perhaps I'll just eat it myself. No - I'm not hungry. (To audience) Who shall I give it to? This boy here? This girl? This one? This one? (Gives to PJ)

PJ: For me? (Amazed look) All of it?

Sticky: Yes, all of it. Go on! Looks like you haven't had a good meal for ages!

PJ: (With mouth full) Ages!

Mr Chop: (adult butcher: enters UR during above) Ha! In that case what you need is MEAT! Not a chunk of pastry! Here - have a sausage!

PJ: Wow! Thank you very much, sir. (not sure what to do With it)

Sticky: That was really nice of you, Mr Chop.

Mr Chop: Nah! (secretly: to Sticky) Poor little thing is from the orphanage. They're always hungry up there, Sticky.

Sticky: (to aud) This is Mr Chop the Butcher. (to Mr Chop) Say hello to the nice people.

Mr Chop: Hello there. Bit quiet aren't they?

Sticky: Well - I didn't like to say anything, but they are a BIT shy.

Mr Chop: Soon sort that out. How about a DECENT "Hello, Mr Chop"? Let's see if you can manage that. **Hello!!**
(to Sticky) What do you think?

Sticky: One more try?

Mr Chop: Right you are. **Hello!!** That's more like it. See you all later!

ALL EXIT STAGE RIGHT

The pirates, MR HOO & MR WYE, enter Down Left and check nobody is around.

Mr Hoo: All clear, Mr Wye.

Mr Wye: Still can't remember the rest of the song, Mr Hoo.

Mr Hoo: What song?

Mr Why: The pirate song! You know:
Yo-ho-ho and a bottle of **milk**,
fifteen men on a dead man's ...er, dead man's ...
Er ... What rhymes with 'milk'?

Mr Hoo: No -no - no, Mr Wye! That's wrong! It's not milk! It's: Yo-ho-ho and a bottle of ....er, now I can't remember! We'll have to ask someone. (Look at audience) Here, you lot are sat doing nothing. Anyone know what comes after: 'Yo-ho-ho and a bottle of ...'? Eh? What? Wine gums? Plums? What? Rum? That's it! (looks out) You can spot the boozers!

Mr Wye: Oh, **rum**, is it, Mr Hoo? Well, I never knew that. Thanks. (Clears throat) Yo-ho-ho and a bottle of **RUM**,
fifteen men on a dead man's **bum**!

Mr Hoo: No! Not 'bum'! **CHEST**! Fifteen men on a dead man's CHEST!

Mr Wye: Chest??! That doesn't rhyme with rum!

Captain Watt: (PIRATE CAPTAIN: enter UL; striding forward with the Bosun) Stow the noise, yer scurvy dogs!
We is here, a-secret like! A-stocking up on grub and grog.

Bosun: (unintelligible pirate: glares at Dag) Skurvin whelks 'n skrimshaw!

Mr Hoo: What did he say?

Mr Wye: He said 'let's see if they sell organic goat's cheese.' Come on!
The pirates move to look in the shop windows. Some ladies enter and stop to chat. Sticky & Mr Chop enter and see the pirates.

Sticky: Aargh! Over there! No - don't look! (drags him down stage) Aren't they ... **pirates?!**

Mr Chop: Which ones?

Sticky: WHICH ONES?! There: those ones in the long dresses and make-up of course! What do you mean 'Which ones?'! The ones with the swords and wooden legs and eye-patches and parrots on their shoulders?

Mr Chop: Hard to say, really. You could be right! I'll ask 'em!

Sticky: No! Don't do ... (but Chop has already gone) (to aud) Oh no! Pirates give me the willies!

Mr Chop: (pulls Bosun to front) Here we are. Now; my friend - the baker here - he says that you're pirates! Ha ha! What do you have to say to that?

Bosun: Avast! Swab me mizzen with a wet lanyard, ye lubbers.

Mr Chop: Eh? What's that in English?

Bosun: Strap the fo'c'sle cat and float me gunnels! Ye scurvy weevils!

Mr Chop: (to Sticky, confidently) I think he's from Somerset (or another rural area/town nearby).

Captain Watt: Ahoy there, shipmates! What in the name of Captain Flint be the mutiny that's a'goin on over 'ere, eh?

Sticky: Oh no! Now we're for it!

Mr Chop: Hello there! I was just asking your chum here ...

Captain Watt: Askin'? And WHAT h'exactly was ee askin', if'n I may make so bold?

Mr Chop: I was asking him if you were pirates!

Captain Watt: (pretends surprise) Pirates! Why -I'll be keelhauled! Whatever next? Pirates eh? Har-har! Now then, matey; does we LOOK like pirates? (they pose) Eh?

Mr Chop: Well (looks) yes. Not that I've ever seen a REAL pirate before but ... you do. A bit?**Captain Watt:** Now that's a first; stuff me parrot if it isn't! No, no, no, no, no ... Me and my chums is ... Um ... (sees feather in Bosun's hat) ... Feather collectors! That's it - we're feather collectors.

Sticky: Feather collectors?

Captain Watt: That's it, me bucko. Plenty of pieces of eight to be made collecting feathers from the far corners of the Seven Seas.

Sticky: Really! Where do you get these feathers from then?

Captain Watt: Where from? Er. Well ... Um ... Birds' bottoms.

Mr Chop: Birds' bottoms?

Captain Watt: Er, yes; that's it. Right then, we've got some thieving – SHOPPING!

– shopping, to do. Come on, mateys!

Bosun: Gaah! Scuppers 'n bilge! (Pirates Exit Down Left)

Mr Chop: There; told you they weren't pirates!

Sticky: But - but - but ...

MR WICK (older candle-maker) enters and pauses, Up Left, checking local paper:
    headline: PIRATES SPOTTED IN (name of place or shop).

Mr Chop: Look out; here comes old Wicky.

> **Sticky:** It's Mr Wick, the Candle-stick Maker. When he says 'hello' I want you ALL
> to give him the BIGGEST EVER 'hello Mr Wick'! Get ready! Wait till he says
> hello ...

> **Mr Wick:** (Is a gloomy fellow. Comes centre, looks at audience) Hello. Aargh!!
> (throws paper in air and leaps back) What's the matter with you people?!
> Shouting like that! Frightened the life out of me!

> And why aren't you two in your shops? No customers to serve?

> **Mr Chop:** Loads. Shop-full! Mrs Chop is behind the counter while I get some fresh
> air.

> **Mr Wick:** Hnn. (gloomily) Mrs Chop? Is that ... wise? She'll probably slice a
> customer's nose off, or some other vital part of their body.

> **Mr Chop:** Nah: can't happen twice in a week!

> Sticky and Wick look at each other then move on.

Sticky: So, how's the candle business, Mr Wick?

> **Mr Wick:** Not what it was. The business is failing fast. It's all these new-fangled 'oil
> lamps' and 'gas lights' nowadays. (Sighs) It can only end badly.

> **Mr Chop:** People Will always need candles! For birthdays - and dinner-parties -
> and - you know - that new thingy: aroma therapy.

Sticky: Eh?

> **Mr Chop:** Aroma therapy: it's where they rub warm oil all over your body.

Mr Wick: What on earth for?

Mr Chop: It helps you relax. (Secretly) Mrs Chop tried it on me the other night.

Sticky: Ooh! Did it work?

> **Mr Chop:** No. Can't say that it did - but next time she'll take the chips out first.

> **Mr Wick:** Hnn. More interesting; I've just sold some candles to - a **pirate!**

Mr Chop: Oh, he's not a pirate! He's a feather collector!

Sticky: He's a PIRATE!

Mr Chop: Nah!

Mr Wick: He paid me in these gold coins. (shows)

Sticky: Pieces of eight! (Madly) **The man's a pirate!!!**

Mr Chop: OK! OK! Hold onto your hot-cross-buns!!

> **Mr Wick:** Indeed. If you carry on like that you'll do your insides a mischief.

> **Mr Chop:** You're too stressed out! What you need is a good woman to look after
> you! Why - when I was your age I'd been married for YEARS! Tell him about
> being married, Wicky!

> **Mr Wick:** Well (glumly) where does one begin to expand on the joys of matrimony?

Sticky: How long have you been married Mr Wick?

> **Mr Wick:** I married young - I was only 17. So I've been married for 13 years.

> **Sticky:** (doing sums on fingers) So you're only ... er ... thirty. You're only **thirty**?!
> But you look at least fifty!! How come you look so old and worn out?

> **Children:** (enter Right in a **long** line, tallest first, ending with a pram. All say to Mr
> Wick:) Hello dad; Hello dad; Hello dad... (There is a silence from the pram, they
> all look at it. It burps. The children exit Left)

Sticky: I think that answers my question.

> **Mr Chop:** No, it's not the kids that wear him out: it's the worry!

Sticky: What worry?

    Mr Chop: Worry his wife'll find out! Ha ha!! (The 2 wives enter Up Right) Oops - speak of the devil!

Mrs Chop: (not bright) Here they are, Mrs Wick!

Mrs Wick: (rather sharp) As I thought, Mrs Chop, - messing about again.

Mr Chop: Who's guarding the shop, my little pork pie?

    Mrs Chop: It's alright - I'm not stupid; I left a note! I thought of something **very clever** to write and left it on the cash register.

    Mr Chop: What's that then?

    Mrs Chop: It's like a little drawer with buttons where we keep all the money.

Mr Chop: Brilliant, my little dumpling.

Mrs Wick: Good grief.

    Mr Wick: I trust, Mrs Wick, that you have left our shop with a more secure arrangement.

Mrs Wick: Of course, Mr Wick. I closed it.

Mr Wick: WHAT?!! **Closed it!** With all these people in town?! (runs off UL)

Sticky: You really closed it?

Mrs Wick: Of course not. (Looks sour) It was a joke.

    Mr Chop: Mrs Wick! You are a laugh! (She gives him a miserable look. He thumps her on the back and laughs) I could stand here joking with you all day - but that won't get the sausages stuffed! See you all later! (Exits UR)

Mrs Chop: (to Sticky) Have you left a note on your till too?

    Sticky: No. Sold out! Next batch is still in the oven. (Pulls them slightly aside) But you ladies shouldn't be out here!

    Mrs Chop: Why not? I've got me winter thermals on.

Sticky: No! (looks around) Pirates!

Mrs Chop: Ooh! How exciting!

    Mrs Wick: You silly woman! What do you mean: 'How exciting'?

    Mrs Chop: Pirates! Just like in the stories. Ooooh! Pirates is the handsomest (The shortest, ugliest, dirtiest pirate in the world sidles up between them),

Mrs Chop: most dashingest, most glamorous, most romantikest of people.

Ugly Pirate: disgusting snorting sound and rubbing of legs.

    Mrs Chop: (looks hard at him) Perhaps I'm thinking of train drivers.

    Pirate: (Wipes nose on sleeve with a snort) (To Mrs Wick) Hello, gorgeous... are you married?

Mrs Wick: Hello, Smelly... are you human?

    Ugly Pirate: Very good! Not heard that one before. 'Are you human?'. Very good! My sort of woman. (Wanders off Right chuckling)

Hoo and Wye enter Down Left.

    Mr Hoo: Didn't I tell you, Mr Wye. Best place for finding girls!

    Mr Wye: About time, Mr Hoo. After three months at sea I need to see a pretty face -

Mr Hoo: Let's take a look around. (stroll upstage)

Ladies overhear the pirates

Mrs Chop: Hear that? You'd better watch out, young Sticky!

Sticky: What for?

    Mrs Chop: Well ... With your girlfriend, Loraine, being - you know - the most beautiful UNMARRIED girl for miles around, and with all these romantic train drivers in town ...

Mrs Wick: Pirates.

Mrs Chop: What?

Mrs Wick: All these romantic PIRATES in town!

Mrs Chop: See - I knew you felt the same way. (Nudges) You sly little minx you!

Mrs Wick: Good grief.

Mrs Chop: (to Sticky) If I was you, I'd ask her to marry me quick - before some pirate sees her!

Sticky: Don't tease!

Mrs Wick: It'd be your own fault! You keep making up excuses not to get married.

Sticky: I don't make up excuses!

Mrs Chop: Oh no?

Sticky: Not at all!

Mrs Wick: So why don't you ask Loraine to marry you this very evening?

Sticky: Well ... I really need to clean out the rabbit hutch, and ...

Ladies: Pah!

Mrs Chop: Don't you blame us if these pirates find out there's a beautiful, SINGLE girl on the loose around here!

Mr Hoo: What's that? (both come down between Sticky & ladies)

Mr Wye: A beautiful young wench cast adrift in these waters?

Mrs Chop: (to Sticky) Ooh! We warned you!

Mr Hoo: I said we'd come to the right place! (to Sticky) Here, pal: any luscious lovelies on the loose hereabouts?

Sticky: No - none! No girls at all around here!

Mr Hoo: What's her name?

Sticky: Loraine. Oops!

Enter Loraine, Right, to stand behind Sticky.

Mr Hoo: Now, tell me about this ... Loraine. (Looks past him at her) Does she have beautiful, silky hair?

Sticky: Silky? Noooo ... like straw; all sticky up. Nits! And dandruff!

Mr Hoo: But I'll bet this Loraine has bright, sparkling eyes!

Sticky: She squints! Eyes like a little piggy. Thick glasses!

Mr Hoo: Smooth, white skin?

Sticky: Sandpaper! And spots! ... BOILS!

Mr Hoo: But I bet my best sea-boots she's got a good sense of humour.

Sticky: Loraine?! Pah! Miserable old witch! Wouldn't know a joke if she saw it crossing the road.

Mr Hoo: So ... this Loraine is spotty, bad-tempered, piggy-eyed, with hair like a scarecrow?

Sticky: Sounds like you've met her already. Still interested?

Mr Hoo: Nah; if we'd wanted girls like that we'd have gone to (local town/area) ! Pirates move upstage

Sticky: Ha! There! I showed him! (Sees ladies signalling to him) What? What's the matter? (Turns) Loraine!!

Loraine: (Hits him.) So - I'm spotty (hit), bad-tempered (hit), piggy-eyed (hit), am I?!!!

Sticky: Hold on! Hey! I was just ...

Mrs Wick & Mrs Chop: No - don't. Don't hit him! Poor little chap! Hugs him

Smoke puffs from bread shop.

PJ: (running on) Hey, bun-man! There's smoke coming out of your shop!!

Sticky: The bread! Ooer! (Runs off into shop DR)

Loraine: Grrr!

Mrs Chop: Don't be like that. He means well.

Mrs Wick: I don't know why you put up with him.

Loraine: Neither do I.

Mrs Chop: Yes you do. You're in lo...

Mrs Wick: Good grief. Don't use the 'L' word! You know that always sets her off.

(Possibly not in show /matinee if time is short)

Mrs Wick: Before you can say "Mills & Boon" she'll start singing! (Music starts) There! What did I tell you? Quick - everyone - FLEE! (Move aside)

Song: Possibly something like On My Own (Les Mis)

Mrs Chop: (In tears) Oh, bless! It's so sad! SOB!

Mrs Wick: (Also in tears) SOB! Don't be so soft.

Sticky: (Runs back in. Swerves away from Loraine and over to others.) Has she calmed down? I was only trying to... (They hit him)

Mrs Chop: You rotter!

Mrs Wick: Horrid, **horrid** little man!

Sticky: Hey! Gerrof! (He flees back into shop)

Mrs Chop: How about a nice cup of tea?

Mrs Wick: Lovely! (The two exit into butchers)

Loraine: (To aud) Hello! Sorry; it's not **always** like this here. It's just that there's a new shop opening today, and there are so many strangers in town. (Boss, Toady, Hench enter Up Left) Look at this lot. Never seen them around here before. Don't like the look of them. I think I'll get back home. (Exits Down Right)
(Villains walk down centre)

Boss: Splendid progress. Soon my plan Will be complete! Now, (loudly and pompously) fetch me ...

Toady: ... a bedpan?

Hench: ... a plastic surgeon?

Boss: No, no - fetch me the toyshop owner! (They scuttle off into Toyshop DL) (to aud) This is all going so very well. The last of those disgusting, soppy, "cuddly" creatures are on board my ship. **There is not one, single toy left!** This shop will never be ab open and they'll be forced to sell it to me! Ha-ha-ha! (to aud) Be quiet, you booing buffoons; there is more to my plan!

When I own **every** toyshop they'll sell only MY toys: guns, and swords, and grotesque monsters, and fighting figures, and (something topical)! That's what children REALLY want - things that frighten and KILL!
(children run on and race around Boss).

Urgh! Get away! Scat! Filthy little things! Clear off!
(They run off)

Bleurgh! Foul vermin! Hate those things! They should keep them in cages until they're big enough to work! (sneer at aud)

Hench and Toady return DL with the toyshop owners and their child.

Mr Majestic: Unhand me, you ruffian!

Mrs Majestic: (vigorously hitting out with walking stick) Let go of him, you horrid brutes! (Sends Hench flying forward with whack on back)

Boss: Good shot, Madam!

Mr Majestic: I told you - we are not going to sell you our shop!

Boss: So (goes close to him, "friendly") your toys have arrived, have they?

Mr Majestic: Well, no; not yet.

Mrs Majestic: Any time now!

Boss: Wonderful. (Smiles horribly) But ... if they don't arrive?

Mrs Majestic: We've made our own toys.

Mr Majestic: Yes indeed!

Boss: How enterprising of you. Hench, Toady - don't you think they're so terribly ...

Hench: ... old?

Toady: ... smelly?

Boss: CLEVER! (Smiles again) Perhaps you would like to show me some of the "toys" you've made? Mmm? (The three go off DL) (becoming angry:) We can't let them make their own toys! If they get away with this then I am...

Hench: ... ugly?

Toady: ... incontinent?

Boss: No ... I'm ruined!

They return with their 'toys'. These are awful - an old mop with odd eyes stuck on; a sack shaped into a teddy, a puppet made of loo rolls, etc. There is a moment's silence as they all study these proudly-displayed monstrosities.

Mr Majestic: Of course these are just prototypes.

Boss: (smiles horribly and takes puppet from child) How charming. And did it take you long to make? Whoops! (pulls head off toy, hands back) Har-har-har. (suddenly angry) You stupid shopkeeper! (Dashes toys aside) **There are no toys for your shop! And there never will be! So sell me the shop!!** (children run on again and circle baddies) Get them away from me! Eurgh! Repulsive reptiles! (Children move away but stay on stage)

Mrs Majestic: We will never sell the shop to the likes of you! NOT .... NOT FOR A HUNDRED POUNDS!

Boss: Good - because I was only going to give you **five** pounds!

Mr Majestic: Five pounds?! Never!

Mrs Majestic: WE ... are going to make **more** toys! (Exit, DL, hitting Hench)

Toady: Oh no, Boss! They're going to make more toys!

Hench: What shall we do?!

Boss: Ha! You two are a pair of ...

Toady: ... socks?

Hench: ... pants?

Boss: - Idiots! Even if they **did** make anything that looked **half** like a toy then we'd steal that as well, and take it to ...

Toady: ...the cinema.

Hench: ...McDonalds.

Boss: ...to the island! You do **remember** the island? Mmm? You know - the place with our toy factory?

Toady: Oh yeah! The toys will like it there!

Boss: Like it? **Like it?!** Do you think they'll "like it" when we push them into the transforming machine?!

Hench: Yeah!

Boss: No they won't! (Grabs by throat) Now get back to the ship - we've cuddly toys to destroy! Ha-ha-ha... (turns to exit Right)

PJ: (jumping in front of them, Right) **Oh no you don't!**

Boss: Urgh! Keep it away! (Hides behind Hench) What does it want?

PJ: I heard everything you were saying! You can't steal all the toys! I'll tell!

Boss: (mimics) "I'll tell." Oh Will you? We'll see about that! Grab the creature!

Toady: (grabs PJ) Now what shall we do with it?

Boss: Do with it? Why - there is only one thing we CAN do with it! We'll take it with us on the ship, back to the island. And, when we're there, we'll just have to ...

Hench: ... play with it!

Toady: ... buy it sweets!

Boss: No! .... **dispose of it! Ha-ha-ha** etc... (All exit DR laughing horribly)

Child 1: (appears from where they were all listening) What can we do?

Child 2: Who were those people?

Child 3: What shall we do?

Child 4: We could panic. You know, sort of run around screaming, sort of thing?

Waaah! (They stop him/her)

Child 5: No - we must tell someone!

Child 6: Yes! Quick - tell somebody!

The 3 shop-owners enter from their shops

    Mr Chop: What's all this noise? Sounds like a hedgehog in a nudist camp!

    Mr Wick: I might have guessed it was you lot! Do be quiet!

    Sticky: Hold on! What is it? What's the matter?

    Child 1: They've stolen all the toys!

    Child 2: They're going to change the cuddly toys into **horrid things**!

Child 3: On an island - With a toy factory!

Mr Chop: Who's done all this?

Child 4: We don't know - they were dressed all in black!

Mr Wick: Now don't drag **us** into your silly games.

Child 5: It's not a game. It's true!

Child 6: And they've taken PJ!

    Mr Chop: PJ? What that cute little kid from the Orphans' Home?

All Children: Yes!!

    Sticky: (dubious) So, some men in black have stolen all the toys, taken them in a boat to an island and kidnapped an orphan? Hmmm...

    Child 1: It IS true!

Sticky: (To audience) Did you see any of this?! Is it true?! Is it?!

Mr Chop: It must be true! This is terrible! Wicky! (Grabs) Run for help!

    Mr Wick: Me??!! (gloomily) No point. By the time we get help, it'll be too late. This can only end badly.

Sticky: But we've got to do something!

Mr Chop: We'll go after them ourselves!

    Mr Wick: Oh yes? And what shall we do - swim after them?

Sticky: There must be a boat somewhere we can borrow!

All look thoughtful

    Mr Chop: (inspired) I know where I can get a boat! Get your things together and meet me at the harbour!

Sticky: It's not that pirate ship is it?!

    Mr Chop: No - no - no! (To aud) Never thought of that! No - much better! You wait and see! (Exits)

Sticky: Crikey!

Mr Chop: This can only end ...

Sticky: ... I know ... badly! (Mr Wick exits)

    Child 1: Take us with you!

Child 2: Can we come?

Child 3: Do let us come too!

    Sticky: Not a chance! You stay here! Tell everyone where we've gone!

    Children: Come on! Let's find someone! (all run off)

    Sticky: (To audience) I hope Mr Chop gets a really safe boat - I'm not a good sailor! (exits) (Curtain)

Scene Two: ON THE HARBOUR
In front of main tabs

Pirates enter: Dag, (left) Wi & Bosun (Right)

Mr Hoo: It's a disaster! A terrible, t-e-r-r-i-b-l-e disaster!

Mr Wye: What ... (something topical or local)

Mr Hoo: Nooo! About the ship!

Mr Wye: It's sunk?!

Mr Hoo: No, not today!

Bosun: Barnacle, splice me bilge 'n mizzen!

Mr Hoo: It's been stolen?

Mr Wye: Don't be so daft! Who'd want that old hulk? No - it's the crew!

Mr Hoo: What about them?

Mr Wye: Tell him, Bosun.

Bosun: Arrrr, bilge'n, crowsnest of Davey Jones, eave-ho-me-hearties, flogging, grog, har-harr, iron pigs'n jumpin kangaroo to leeway off Montevideo, that nest o' pukin' queen rats on starboard, top-sail unfurlin' and vast Winnetndward exit of yellow-bellied zombies! (note: words are in alphabetical order!)

Mr Hoo: No!

Mr Wye: Aye! Every scurvy dog has jumped ship! Said they'd found the perfect job on dry land!

Mr Hoo: The perfect job for a load of twisted sadists who can't even read and write? What job is it?

Mr Wye: They've gone to be OFSTED School Inspectors (or MPs or similar local / topical).

Mr Hoo: Oh yeah. ... Never mind! There's always plenty of lads wanting adventure on the High Seas!

Mr Wye: Blow me down, you're right! Bosun: off you go! Get us a rough, tough crew!

Mr Hoo: Females would be nice! Ha-ha!

Mr Wye: Good joke, there Mr Wye.

Bosun: (Spits) Splice me bilge 'n mizzen. (Exits)

Wye and Hoo move to look in shop windows)

Mrs Chop: (enters Right) Ooh! Lawks! Mrs Wick! Mrs. Wick!

Mrs Wick: (enters Right) What?!

Mrs Chop: Those idiot husbands of ours! Gone to sea! What do they know about ships?!

I don't know about your Mr Wick, but there's only one thing my Mr Chop ever did in the sea!

Mrs Wick: What's that?

Mrs Chop: It's a lot of water - like a puddle, only bigger.

Mrs Wick: Good grief. No, not the sea! What was the one thing he ever **did** in the sea?

Mrs Chop: I don't want to go into the details - but he had a funny smile on his face!

Loraine: (enters Right) What's going on? Has Sticky really gone in a boat after some kidnappers?!

Mrs Chop: That's what the children say!

Loraine: So - what are we going to do about it?

Mrs Chop: We must get **another** boat and go after them!

Mrs Wick: Who do we know with a boat? (Heads slowly turn to the pirates)

Mrs Chop: Ahoy there, fish pastes!

Mrs Wick: Shipmates.

Mr Hoo: Is she talking to us?

Mr Wye: Go and see! (Pushes him toward them)

Mrs Chop: Avast behind up your poop! Will you sea-cats ...

Mrs Wick: ...dogs!

Mrs Chop: ...sea-dogs come and share a glass of frogs?

Mrs Wick: Grog.

Mr Wye: What do you want, my good woman?

Mrs Chop: You have a fine sailing vessel.

Mr Hoo: We do?

Mr Wye: Yes - we do! What about it?

Loraine: We want to borrow it.

Hoo: What?! Why on earth do you want a pira... (Wi hits him) ... a feather collecting ship?

Mr Wye: (pushes him aside) Can you cook real food?

Mrs Chop: Yes.

Mr Wye: With no fish-heads in it?

Mrs Chop: Yes!

Mr Wye: And can you do washing and ironing and such-like?

Mrs Chop: Yes!!

Mr Wye: Then it's a deal!

Mrs Chop: Done! (They spit on their hands, slap them, splatting Mrs Wick in the eye) There! We're off to sea!

Not vitally needed in matinee (if scene changing permits)

Loraine: My father would be proud! He was a great naval man!

Mrs Chop: What, you mean he had a big naval?

Mrs Wick: Urgh!

Loraine: No - he was a sailor! You know what they say - you can always tell a naval man!

Hoo: She's right!

Song: (Possibly: 'He's a naval man')

Child 1: (two children run on) Mrs Chop! Mrs Chop!

Mrs Chop: What is it now?

Child 2: There's water pouring out of the upstairs window of your house!

Mrs Chop: What?!

Child: Yeah! Someone's stolen your bath-tub! (Holds up rubber duck)

Mrs Chop: Who would want to take a great-big bath like that?! (ladies look at each other as truth sinks in) No! They wouldn't!

Mrs Wick: Yes, they would!

Mrs Chop: Quick! The ship! Let's get after them! All exit L & R.

Child: Giggle! I'm going back to watch the butcher's shop get flooded!

Scene Three: IN THE TUB
(Tabs Scene)

Poking from the wings Left is the end of an old jetty with mooring post & lifebelt. Beside it is a huge tub, with large taps and empty mast. Low wave profile across front of stage. Mr Chop is in the tub. Mr Wick and Sticky are standing nervously on the jetty.

Mr Wick: What on earth is this thing?

Sticky: It looks like a bath-tub!

Mr Wick: It looks **exactly** like a bath-tub!

Mr Chop: So now you're both experts on **boats**?!

Mr Wick: Then tell us, what sort of boat **is it**?

Mr Chop: Er.... It's a bath-tub!

Mr Wick: Where on Earth did you get it?

Mr Chop: Where do you think I got it? In the bathroom of course!

Mr Wick: And I'm sure you remembered to turn the water off before you ripped it out?

Mr Chop: Ha-ha! Did I remember to turn the water off! Ha-ha! Ummm... (briefly serious) No. (Brightens up) Never mind - place needs a good clean. Come on! All aboard! (Sticky climbs nervously in.)

Mr Wick: This is going to end very badly. (He gets in)

Mr Chop: That's the way. First Mate Sticky Bunn, cast off the lines!

Sticky: Eh?

Mr Chop: Untie that bit of string.

Sticky: What? This?! It's all that's keeping us afloat! (Does it anyway; the jetty moves away) I feel ill already.

Mr Chop: Ahhhhh - the open sea!

Sticky: Uuuuuu - the open sick-bag.

Mr Chop: Full steam ahead!!

Mr Wick: We didn't **bring** any steam.

Mr Chop: Well ... **hoist the main sail!**!

Mr Wick: Have you **got** a main sail?

Mr Chop: Of course I've got a main sail - do you think I'm an idiot?

Mr Wick: (nods) Yes.

Sticky: So where **IS** this sail?

Mr Chop: On top of the oars!

Sticky: And the oars are where?

Mr Chop: Under the sink.

Sticky: (looking around) And the sink is ...?

Mr Chop: Doh! Stupid! Next to the fridge!

Sticky: And the fridge is ...?

Mr Chop: Where do you think? In the kitchen!

Sticky: This bath has a kitchen?!

Mr Chop: Of course not! The kitchen behind the shop! (They stare at him as the facts sink in) Oh!

Mr Wick: This will end very, very badly.

Sticky: (to Mr Chop) Are you wearing a vest?

Mr Wick: That's it; he's gone mad.

Mr Chop: I'm a butcher! Butchers always wear a vest!

Sticky: Good! (Sticks hands up back of Chop's shirt and tugs; a very large vest comes out.) There! (Hangs it on the cross-bar of the mast.) Off we go!

Slow blackout. Sounds of the sea.

Slow lights on again. The men are sprawled in the boat looking near death.

Mr Chop: Groans. Water .... water!

Mr Wick: I can't stand it! Manic laugh. I say we draw straws. Whoever gets the short straw ... gets **eaten**! (Advances on Sticky)

Sticky: For goodness sake! We've only been here for ten minutes! Have another custard cream. (Passes biscuits)

Mr Chop: You're right. We must pull ourselves together. I know - we'll sing a rousing song. (Takes heroic pose at prow of ship) **Sings: Near, Far, wherever you are...**

Sticky: Hang on; hang on! (To Mr Wick) Can't you sing something more cheerful?

Mr Wick: (pompously) I would sing you a song ... but I had a nasty experience once, and it has left me unable to sing in public.

Sticky: Oo-er! What happened to you?

Mr Wick: Well, in my youth I was a professional actor. Then, one terrible night, in front of a crowded theatre, I was about to sing my big solo when suddenly the rotten wood beneath my feet gave way and I hurtled down, with a terrible scream.

Mr Chop: Oh, (trying not to laugh) that was just a stage you were going through!

Mr Wick: (Scowls at Mr Chop's hysterics) Hnn!

Sticky: Come on, Mr Wick. You can do it. Everybody sings in the bath! (taps side of bath) Give us a tune to lift our spirits!

Mr Wick: Very well. (Cough to clear throat. Dramatic pose.)
Sings: For those in peril on the sea. (two lines)
Sticky: Stop! Don't either of you know something NICE?!

> **Mr Chop:** OK. How about 'The Wild Rover'? I'll sing the verse and you two join in the chorus: "no-nay-never-no more". You know? (They nod agreement) Right; here goes. (sings: I've been a wild rover, for many a year, etc)
> While he stands in the bow, singing, Sticky is in the stern. A large octopus appears and wraps its arm around Sticky's neck. He misses the chorus. The octopus sinks out of sight. Nobody else sees it.

Mr Chop: You missed it! It was your turn to sing!
Sticky: Choking noises, gasping and pointing
Mr Wick: Do make an effort; it was your idea.
Repeat of song (second verse) and octopus business.

> **Mr Chop:** For goodness sake, Sticky! Look, all you have to do is sing the chorus; alright? Now. Try again.

Repeat yet again. (third verse)
Mr Wick: I was singing, but someone else **wasn't**!
Sticky: (pointing) But ... but ... but!
Mr Chop: Everyone sings when they're in **my** bath! One last chance!

> **Sticky:** Hold on! You stand here - and **I'll** go **that** end! (They swop) Right. Now YOU try to sing! (Repeat of action, but this time a giant shark rises beside Sticky; it's mouth opens to show its teeth.) **AAAAAAHHH!!!**

Mr Chop: No - not AAAAAAAHHH. It's (sings) La - la - la - laa....

> **Sticky:** That's it! **You** go **here**, and **you** go **there**, and **I'll** stand in the middle!

(Mr Chop & Mr Wick sing the verse; octopus and shark appear. By the chorus Mr Wick is in the arms of the octopus, Mr Chop bashing nose of the shark. Sticky is the only one to sing the chorus, which he does with a flourish.)
Sticky: Land ho!

Main Tabs Close

Scene Four: ON THE PIRATE SHIP (the confusion scene)
In front of the main curtains.

Mr Hoo & Mr Wye enter Left, followed shortly later by Mrs Chop & Mrs Wick.
Mr Hoo: So, Mr Wye, at least we've got **three** females on board the ship!
Mr Wye: Yes indeed, Mr Hoo. Captain Watt will be surprised! (Girls arrive)

> **Mrs Chop:** Ooh - I've never been on a ship before. Where do you drive it?
> **Mr Hoo:** Up the top. There's a sort of big round thing. But that's the captain's job.
> **Mrs Chop:** I'd like to meet the captain! You'd better tell us his name.

Mr Hoo: Watt.

> **Mrs Chop:** I said ... I' d like to meet the captain! Tell us his name!

Mr Hoo: Watt!

> **Mrs Chop:** Good grief. This one's deaf.

Mrs Wick: Let me have a go with the other one. (To Mr Wye) **Who** is the captain?
Mr Wye: No, (laughs) **Dag's** not the captain! Watt is.
Mrs Wick: (slowly) What is the captain's name?
Mr Wye: (very slowly) Yes. That's right.
Mrs Wick: (even slower) What's right?
Mr Wye: (slower still) Yes. Watt's right.
Mrs Wick: OK - (pushes Mrs Chop forward) - your turn again.

> **Mrs Chop:** Let's start with easy questions: (to Mr Hoo) First - you are **who**?

Mr Hoo: (chirpy) Yes! How did you know?

> **Mrs Wick:** (to Mrs Chop) Breathe deeply ... Stay calm.... Let me try this one. (To Mr

Wye, in a very slow, clear voice) Tell me <u>your</u> name!

Mr Wye: (slow and clear) Wye.

    Mrs Wick: Because I want to **know**! Just tell me what people call you!

Mr Wye: Wye.

    Mrs Wick: (Grabs Wye by scruff and pulls face to face) Listen to me VERY CAREFULLY. (Points to Dag) Tell me **HIS** name!

Mr Wye: Hoo!

Mrs Wick: (speechless rage for two seconds) **Him there!!**

Mr Wye: **Hoo!!**

Mrs Wick: (shaking him) **Are you blind as well as deaf?!**

    Mrs Chop: Let him go! **Shaking people** is **never** the way to get things done! Now then (dusts him off); slowly - and - clearly, tell me the name of the man who runs this ship.

Mr Wye: Watt.

Mrs Chop: This ship - this boat - **Who** runs it?

Mr Wye: No he doesn't.

Mrs Chop: What?!

Mr Wye: Yes, **HE** runs the ship! We've already told you that!

Mrs Chop: Then **what's YOUR** name?!

Mr Wye: No, it's not!

    Mrs Chop: Grrrraahhh!! (starts shaking him worse than before)

    Mrs Wick: One - more - try. (Deep breath. To Mr Hoo) Who are you?

    Mr Hoo: Yes! You've got it! Bad grammar though - it's not "Hoo are you", it should be 'You are Hoo. (laughs) If you talk like that you have to say: (points to Winnet) 'Wye is him'.

Mrs Wick: Why is him what?!

Mr Hoo: No - he's not Watt; he's Wye. I'm Hoo!

    Mrs Wick & Mrs Chop: (attacking them with renewed vigour, beating to floor and sitting on them) Him who, me him, you why, me us, them those, AARGH!!

    Loraine: (enters) Stop! What are you doing?! Leave Mr Hoo and Mr Wye alone! Heaven knows what Captain Watt Will say if he catches you!

Mrs Wick: Mr Hoo?

Mrs Chop: Mr Wye? (Let go of pirates)

Loraine: Yes.

Mrs Wick: Captain Watt? Oh ... good grief. (dusts off pirates)

    Mrs Chop: Ooh! Not **THE** Captain Watt, the terrible scourge of the seven seas?! (Captain Watt is standing behind them. Main Curtain opens. IF the scene is ready – if not keep going into Scene 5 until ready)

Scene Five OUTSIDE THE CAPTAIN'S CABIN
The Pirate Ship: below decks.

At rear centre is a double door with CAPTAIN on it.

On Rear Left flat is cut a round porthole at face-level, that opens. Rear Right flat is a cupboard. At the base of both front flaps is a box with a water pump or hose pipe in, directed upwards and holes for squirting more water through. There is a trapdoor in the centre of the rostra stage-extension OR a flap in a flat.

Loraine: YES! That Captain Watt! And you know what I heard?

Mrs Chop: No - what?

    Loraine: He's so fierce - he's got a wooden leg, a hook, one eye and one (looks around, then whispers in her ear)

Mrs Chop: No! A wooden leg, a hook, one eye and one ... (whispers back)

Loraine: Yes!

Mrs Wick: And does he look like ... that? (She nods at Watt. They look round)

Loraine: Yes! (look away, then look back)

Both: Wahh!

> **Watt:** Be still, women! Arr... Be you the three wenches what has hired my trusty vessel?
>
> **Mrs Chop:** Arr! Arrr -arr -arr-ar! We be they three wenches who has ironed your vest and truss. Arr ... Arrr ... Arr. Who be you?

Mr Hoo: This is ...

> **Mrs Chop:** Not you! (Slaps hand over Hoo's mouth) We're not going through all that again. (Mr Hoo starts to speak. She points menacingly at him) No!
>
> **Watt:** I be the fearsome piii ... er ... feather collector, Captain Watt!

Mrs Wick: You can't be! Captain Watt has got a wooden leg.

> **Watt:** Aye; that be right enough! Dag! (Mr Hoo goes to wing and fetches wooden leg) There; got that from a mullato in the South China Seas. Killed him with my bare hands.

Mrs Chop: It says here: 'Property of LOCAL NAME Hospital'!

> **Mrs Wick:** I don't think you're Captain Watt. Prove it! Show us your hook!

Watt: Now that I CAN do! I've had the hook for twenty years!

> **Mrs Chop:** Oh yeah? Hands up everybody who's got a .... hook! (Watt puts his hand up) No - the other hand. (Watt changes hands) There! You do NOT have a HOOK!
>
> **Watt:** I do too. Look! (Turns to show hook of coat-hanger sticking up at the back of his neck)

Mrs Wick: (pulling it out of his coat) It's a coat-hanger!

> **Watt:** Arr! That feels a mite better! It's been a'sticking in there ever since I bought the coat, twenty year ago!
>
> **Mrs Chop:** There's still the matter of the one eye, and the one ... (whispers in his ear)
>
> **Watt:** Ooh arr, they're real enough. Here, I carry them in this bag. (Produces small pouch and passes it to her.)

Mrs Chop: (looking inside) Mmmm............. which one's the eye?

> **Watt:** (looks inside for a minute, thoughtfully) It's that one. It's just got a bit of fluff on it.

Mrs Chop: Where did you get that, then?

Watt: In LOCAL NAME, in a chip shop, in a jar of pickled onions.

Mrs Chop: And the ...er ...

Watt: That? (points in) That's all that's left of me old mate, Black Dingus.

Mrs Wick: All that's left?

> **Watt:** You've heard of The Horse Whisperer? (They nod) Well Dingus was a'goin to be the world's first **shark** whisperer. (They look in bag sadly) And this bit 'ere was what I was a' holdin' 'im by when we lowered 'im into the water.

Loraine: (looks in bag) Just the one?!

Watt: I was a'holdin' both of em at first, but I 'ad to scratch me nose.

> **Loraine:** And all you have left of him is this one (reaches in and lifts it out) ... big toe. (to aud) Come on - family show.

Mrs Chop: Oh dear. So, anyway, you really are Captain Watt?

> **Watt:** Indeed, I am; and I'll have no nonsense on my ship! Now, I'm a'goin to have me tea, but while you're here you ladies must work your passage. (Stamps off into his cabin)

Mrs Chop: Is he allowed to say that?

Mrs Wick: What does he want us to do?

Mr Hoo: Just a bit of laundry.

Mrs Chop: No problem.

Mr Wye: But .... one word of warning...

Loraine: What?

    Mr Wye: Whatever you do (glances nervously at Captain's door) NEVER mention the Captain's family! (Points to paintings on wall)

Mrs Chop: Why not?

Mr Wye: He **hates** them! They were all useless pirates!

Mr Hoo: Feather collectors.

Mr Wye: Feather collectors! Yes! Useless. Don't even say their names!

Mrs Chop: No problem with that - don't even **know** their names!

    Mr Wye: Good. So, let's get your first lot of washing! Come on! (Exits with Mrs Chop and Mr Hoo.)

    Lorraine: (They look around.) Oh, look! There's a little window!

Mrs Wick: Porthole.

    Loraine: No need to be rude. (Opens porthole and looks out) It's so pretty, With the sun sparkling on the sea and the waves splashing!

    Mrs Wick: (crabby) Don't be so soppy. (soppy voice:) Let me have a look. (Goes to look out. Wave splashes in porthole onto her. She staggers over to Loraine.)

    Loraine: Laughs. What HAVE you been doing? You're all wet!

Mrs Wick: Think it's funny, do you? You just come here! (Takes her to porthole)

Loraine: Lovely. (No water comes in)

Mrs Wick: (pushes her aside) Let me see (Splash!)

Loraine: Ooh - you're even wetter now! Come on - let's get you dried off. **Both Exit.**

Mrs Chop and Mr Hoo enter, Mr Hoo carrying vest.

    Mrs Chop: Here, I've got the ... oh, they've gone. Never mind. I can do a bit of washing by myself. (to Mr Hoo) What've you got?

Mr Hoo: Here's my very bestest vest!

Mrs Chop: Your bestest vestest. What's all this down the front?

    Mr Hoo: Which bit? Oh - that's prawn curry served to me by a beautiful girl in Thailand; **that's** Daddies sauce from a little pub in LOCAL NAME, OR NAME OF LOCAL PUB the night I first met my old mate Mr Wye; **that's** chocolate milkshake from my nephew's third birthday party - he's married with three kids now! And that's ....

    Mrs Chop: I get the idea. Are you sure you want to wash away all these memories? It's like a pirate 'This Is Your Life'.

Mr Hoo: Just be sure you don't damage it! (Hoo exits Right.)

    Mrs Chop: I think the dirt's all that's holding this together! Never mind. Now - where's the washing machine? (looks around - sees porthole. Sings as she opens port-hole and throws vest through.)

    Mr Wye: (Enters Left) More washing for you! (Holds up a short sleeved shirt.)

Mrs Chop: I must say this is very clean already!

    Mr Wye: My mother left it to me in her will. I don't know what I'd do if I lost it. It's for wearing when I go out with young ladies.

Mrs Chop: You must be a neater eater than Mr Dag.

    Mr Wye: No - I've just never ever been out with a young lady! (Sobs & exits right)

Mrs Chop: How sad. Better wash it for him though. (Porthole)

    Bosun: (Enters Left - holds up large, horribly stained and holed underpants.) Scrapin' barnacles ye starboard spinnacre!

    Mrs Chop: Oh my! (Staggers back) Don't tell me - these were left to you by your mother in her Will?

Bosun: Arrr... keelhaulin bulwarks on yer jetty!

    Mrs Chop: I see ... they remind you of her. (turns it round to show stains make ugly face on seat) I see what you mean. Don't worry - nothing can possibly happen to them.

Bosun exits Left, swearing. Mrs. Chop throws pants through the porthole.

Captain: (enters from cabin) I be 'aving some washin for ye! Somethin' more precious than all the treasure of Captain Kid.

Mrs Chop: What is it?

Captain: This. (Holds up huge bra).

Mrs Chop: Don't tell me - left to you by you mother! All you have to remember her by!

Captain: Not exactly. Me father! Ee was a much misunderstood man for 'is times.

Mrs Chop: I see.

Captain: (menacingly) I would take it very BADLY if anything should 'appen to this 'ere item.

Mrs Chop: Don't you worry. (Ushers him back into his cabin) What could possibly happen to it in a washing machine?! Laughs (throws it out porthole)

Mrs. Wick and Loraine enter R.

Mrs Wick: I don't think this ship is very safe. It's full of holes.

Loraine: Don't worry. We haven't got to go far.

Mrs Chop: I've done the washing! It's in this machine!

Mrs Wick: What machine?

Mrs Chop: This one. (They run to porthole. Loraine looks out and groans; Mrs Wick looks out: gets wet again)

Loraine: You're all wet again.

Mrs Chop: You shouldn't open the machine in the middle of the cycle!

Loraine: Come on; let's dry you off again. (to Mrs Chop) And you come too; before you do something else!

Mrs Chop: (Follows them off) Hey! What do you mean 'Do something else'?

They exit Right. Hoo & Wye enter Left With a list. Bosun follows them.

Mr Hoo: Bosun, so you mean you've found a **whole new crew ...?**

Mr Wye: ... and they're all **female**?!! (starts to get excited) Corr!

Bosun: Arr, scurvin anchor-flukes 'n bilge!

Mr Hoo: I know we SAID get females, but it was a JOKE! You can't have a pirate ship run by 'females'! You'll have to take them all back!

Mr Wye: What?! But ...!

Mr Hoo: Sorry, Bosun. Tell them we can't use them.

Bosun: Scurvin rum 'n whale meat. (Goes to leave)

Mr Wye: But - but - but - STOP!! Are you all mad?! WHAT ARE YOU DOING?!

Mr Hoo: Eh?

Mr Wye: Stop. Think. ...... Feeeemales! Winnetiiiiiiimin! Remember?

Mr Hoo: Of course I remember! I've had more girlfriends than you, matey!

Mr Wye: I told you before - an old lady that helped you across the road does not count!

Mr Hoo: But even **you** can't fancy any of THESE. (Pushes list at him)

Mr Wye: (reads) (With rising hysteria) Gripper Grimes; Vicious Val Verruca, Cut-throat Enid - curse of the China Seas! Foul Belinda Blackhead ... **Gladys the Goat-strangler!** What?!!

Mr Hoo: See? Told you!

Mr Wye: But they might not be ALL terrible?

Mr Hoo: We shall see! Bosun! Summon the new crew!

Bosun: Scrimshaw 'n weevils. (Exits briefly. Returns with new crew. They are glamorous.)

Mr Hoo & Mr Hoo: speechless drooling sounds

Pirate Girl 1: This one be a'looking at us in that way again.

Pirate Girl 2: What way be that?

Pirate Girl 1: You know .... THAT way!

All: Oo - arrr. 'Ee be, right enough.

Pirate Girl 3: And what be your problem, matey?

Mr Hoo: N - n - nothing at all.

Pirate Girl 1: Be you suggestin' - by your LASCIVIOUS AND LECHEROUS LOOKING - that we're not what you might call 'proper' pirates? (Makes threatening gesture with knife)

Mr Hoo: No -no-no - not at all! I'm sure you can be whatever you want to be!

Pirate Girl 1: That is exactly the truth! My mum said I was to reach for the stars and be whatever I wanted!

Pirate Girl 4: Just so long as we all helps each other.

Pirate Girl 1: Let's show the scurvy dogs what REAL buccaneers can do!

Song – or simply cut all that bit out and upset the chorus.

Pirates exit Right. Children enter Left.

Child 1: In here! This room's empty!

Child 2: You know - I think this is a PIRATE ship!

Child 3: I think you're right!

Child 4: What Will they do if they find us?

Child 5: They make stowaways walk the plank!

Child 6 (SMALLEST): But I can't swim!

Child 1: And the sea round here is full of **sharks**!

Child 2: And octopussies!

Child 1: And sea-monsters!

Child 3: Don't be silly: there's no such thing as sea-monsters!

Child 1: There is too!

Child 3: Someone's coming!

Child 4: Quick! Hide!

Child 5: Where?

Child 6: Here! There's a hatch! (All run to hatch, front centre)

Child 1: Open it up! (They do)

Child 2: (pushing smallest child toward hole) Go down!

Child 6: Down there?! It's all dark!

Child 1: Ooh! I bet there's sea-monsters in there!

All: (huddled around hole and nervously looking in) Oooer!!

Child 2: There's no such thing as monsters! But there **are** pirates!

Sounds of pirates offstage. Children turn backs on the hole to look around. A sea monster rises from the hole. When the children turn back it has dropped out of sight.

Child 6: Do you think it's safe? (To audience) Shall I go down? Shall I?

Child 1: Go on - down you go!

Child 6: No way! (Runs upstage. Others run after him. While they are away the monster reappears; the children return and it hides again.)

Child 2: Drop 'im in the 'ole! (They go to drop smallest child in hole but after a moment the monster appears and tries to grab him/her)

All: A monster!!!!

They scatter and hide, two in the cupboard. The smallest child is left. He/she sees a cardboard box and climbs in the top. The monster gets out of the hatch. Looks around, hears a sound, opens cupboard- children run out & off screaming - then the monster hides inside.

The ladies return.

Mrs Chop: Right: any more washing to be done?

Both: No! We're going to work out where we are. (Sit on bench at back to look at large, old map)

Mrs Chop: Look - here's some more washing! (Sees a large sheet) This'll have to wait until the next load. Where shall I put it? (Sees cardboard box) I'll put it in this box.

Opens lid but suddenly turns at sound of groaning as monster opens cupboard door. Door closes before she can see it. When she turns back the box is shut again. She jumps.

This all happens twice - quite rapidly)

Mrs Chop: There is something most ODD happening here.

It happens again, but this time the monster leaves the cupboard and goes back down the hatch, unseen by Mrs Chop who, passing it back-to-back, walks to the cupboard. When she gets back the box is closed again.

This is most peculiar.

Mrs Wick: What is the matter with you now?

Mrs Chop: Look - I opened this box - went to this cupboard ... (as they go to cupboard the box is picked up, legs appear beneath it, and it walks across the stage.) ...and when I went back to the box ... Aargh! It's gone!

Loraine: You mean this box here?

Mrs Wick: Stop messing around! (They go back to the map)

Mrs Chop: But ... (she re-enacts the business, turns away from the box; the box moves again)

...and the box was ... Wah!

(She looks suspiciously at the box)

One more try ... (she turns away, - but this time instead of moving the box, the child gets out of the box, darts behind her, and exits - pausing to curtsey/bow and get a clap.)

Ooh - (thinks applause is for her) - thank you!

Now we'll see what's ... (pounces, lifts up box and peers through.)

Nothing!

Mrs Wick: When you've finished playing perhaps we can plan our next step?

Mrs Chop: But ... (drops sheet onto box) I think this ship is - rather odd!

Mrs Wick: Perhaps it's – haunted!

Mrs Chop: You what?!

Suddenly Captain Watt bursts in, carrying a small cream cake.

Captain: I heard you! You was a-talking about my family!

Mrs Chop: We weren't!

Captain: You certainly were! (Hands cakes to Mrs Chop to hold) You was a'talkin about **U. Watt** - my late Grandfather: **Unwinn** Watt.

(Looks manic) He was a USELESS pirate! (He grabs Mrs Wick)

He hated fighting! (Shakes her by throat)

He would sail this way (heaves her to left) and sail that way (to right) and he was as much use as a cream cake in a hurricane!

(Grabs cake and splats it on Mrs. Wick's forehead)

Now - never mention my family again!

Mrs Chop: Here we are sinking and he's worried about his relatives!

Mrs Wick: Is it getting rough? My head is going round and round and ...

(the monster gets out of the hole and sits next to her)

Hello. (Double take) Waah! (Jumps up.)

(Monster goes back in hole)

Lubalubaluba... (she staggers over to the others) Errr ... ummm ... ahhh ...

Mrs Chop: I'm not sitting here for the rest of my life! Look - there's a cork stuck in over there!

(Pulls cork out. Water squirts.)

Oh no! (She drops the cork)

Loraine: No! Put that cork back!

Mrs Chop: Oh no! I've dropped it!

Loraine: There's another one there! Use that!

Mrs. Chop pulls that out. More water squirts in. She puts her finger on it; Loraine does same to first one)

Mrs Wick: (standing shaking in centre) I tell you. I j...j....just saw a ...monster!

Mrs Chop: Eh? What?

Captain: (enters with cream cake) YOU'RE A'TALKIN ABOUT MY FAMILY AGAIN!

Mrs Chop: We're not!

Captain: You certainly are! (Hands plate to Mrs Chop)

You was a'talkin about **A.Watt** - my late brother: **Abraham** Watt. (manic)

He was a USELESS pirate! (grabs Mrs Wick)

He hated fighting! (Shakes her) He would sail this way (to left) and sail that way (to right) and he was as much use as a cream cake in a hurricane! (splats cake on her chin)

Now - never mention my family again! (storms off into cabin)

Mrs Chop: Don't stand there eating cream cakes! Give us a hand!

Loraine: Find us two corks! Have a look around - try in that cupboard!

Mrs Wick: (very dazed) Doh...cupboard! Two corks. (Goes to cupboard; gets two large forks)

Mrs Chop: Not two FORKS; two CORKS!

Loraine: At least things can't get any worse! (Water starts to squirt from many places. They have to stretch to block each hole) This is your fault - you started all this!

Mrs Chop: I what?

Captain: (enters) I HEARS YOU A-TALKIN' ABOUT MY **FAMILY**!

Mrs Chop: We're not!

Captain: You certainly are! (Hands **cream flan** to Mrs Chop)

You was a'talkin about **I.Watt** - my late father: **Isaac** Watt. (manic)

He was a USELESS pirate! (grabs Mrs Wick) He hated fighting! (Shakes throat) He would sail this way (to left) and sail that way (to right) and he was as much use as a cream cake in a hurricane! (splats flan on her face)

(He looks around)

In the name of Billy Bones! What be you two wenches a doin'? And where's my washing?! All I can see is this sheet! Is it washed? Let me see now! (He flaps sheet and lays it over the hole in the stage)

Not very clean! The rest had better be cleaner! Those things was very precious!

Other pirates enter and start to ask for their washing.

Wye/Hoo/Bosun: Where's my vest/shirt/pants?!

Mrs Chop: It's all under control. Your washing is still in the machine!

Captain: What machine?

Mrs Chop: That one over there! (To Mrs Wick) Don't just stand there waiting for your face-pack to work! Get the washing out of the machine!

Mrs Wick: (dreamily) ...machine ... washing ... monsters ... (opens porthole - water splashes in)

Mrs Chop: The cycle isn't finished yet!

Captain: You blistering barnacle! That ain't a washing machine! **That's a port-hole!** Have you thrown all our washing out into the ocean?! Stand up and answer me, woman!

Mrs Chop: Can't.

Captain: On yer feet NOW!

Mrs Chop: OK - if that's what you want. (Stands up, water squirts)

Captain: My ship! She's sinking my ship!! (Hoo and Wye stop the leaks)

Mrs Chop: Well, if you're all down here - who's STEERING your precious little ship? Eh?!

Captain: Never ee mind that! I want to know WHERE'S OUR WASHING?!!

The sheet starts to rise. General screaming and panic.

Mrs Chop: It's a ghost!!

Captain: I'll have no ghosts on MY ship! (Pulls sheet off hatch to reveal sea monster wearing all the clothes that had been thrown out of the porthole.) **OUR WASHING!** (Much screaming of 'Monster' etc, and panic)

Children run in.

Child 1: There's nobody steering the ship!

Child 2: There's an island straight ahead!

Mrs Chop: What on earth are all you children doing here?!

Child 3: Never mind that ... someone has to steer the ship NOW!

Loraine: Why?!

Child 4: Because the ship is going to CRASH!!

Mrs Wick: I don't think I'm really enjoying this trip.

Terrible crashing and splashing sound. Everyone lurches right, some fall over.

A mast with a sail on crashes down amongst them in a shower of wood and dust

Captain: Abandon ship! Women and children AFTER ME!! (mass exit)

Mrs Wick: (to aud) I think I'm going to write to Trip Advisor about this.

Curtain
Interval

ACT TWO: ON THE ISLAND
Scene Six: The Prison on the Secret Island.
A dark cave. Grill and door across cave mouth Up Left.

Boss strides on while Toady and Hench drag PJ through the grill door.

Boss: Stop struggling! This island is mine - and on the whole island there is not one...

Toady: ...cornetto?

Hench: ...toilet?

Boss: ... no! Not one way to escape!

PJ: Somebody Will come and rescue me!

Boss: Pah!

Toady: Pah! Pah!

Hench: Pah! Pah! Pah!

Boss: Nobody even knows you're here! This is my secret island; here I am invincible!

PJ: No you're not - I can see you!

Boss: Idiot! Now, I was saying: this is my island, where I keep all the stupid, ugly creatures before I turn them into something more useful!

PJ: (nervously) W ... what sort of ... creatures?

Boss: Ha-ha! You shall see - when I leave you in here with them! You two, over here and open the ...

Toady: ... bidding?

Hench: ... baked beans?

Boss: No ... open the door! (They open the door, go through and close it behind them, then peer out) And who can spot the ...

Toady: ... Spot the Dog?

Hench: ... spot the ball?

    Boss: No ... spot the deliberate mistake?! (they look puzzled at each other, holding the bars) (shouts)

    I am supposed to be on **that** side! Give me strength.

    (They let him out. They close the door. PJ peers out. Boss bends down to look closely)

    And THAT is where you shall stay - if the creatures in there don't get you first! Hahahahahahahaha!

    How long was that?

Toady: Not bad, about seven seconds.

Hench: But not a record.

Boss: OK ... hahahahahahahahahahahahaha. Better?

Toady: MUCH. (As they start to exit)

Hench: Nobody does the evil laugh as well as you, Boss. Exit

(PJ drifts miserably down centre)

Song (There is a castle: Les Mis?)

    PJ: I thought I heard something moving! Who's there?!

    (PJ runs to gate but it is locked. Runs back down centre.)

    Keep away!

    (Dark shapes appear around edges of stage)

    Don't come any closer!

    (Lights up slightly to show that the shapes are all cuddly toys: teddies, clowns, dolls, cowboys, animals, etc.)

Teddy: It's alright! We won't hurt you!

PJ: Who are you?

Toy 1: We're toys.

PJ: But what are you all doing in here?

Toy 1: Somebody stole us!

Toy 2: And threw us in here!

    PJ: I know them! They're wicked! (Toys shudder and look around nervously) What do they want you for?

    Teddy: They take us up to the factory. (Points up) And toys that go there - never come back again!

PJ: Is there no way out?

Toy 2: We've tried.

Toy 3: Looked everywhere.

Toy 4: To infinity and beyond.

PJ: What does that mean?

    Toy 4: No idea. One of the toys that used to be in here said it all the time.

Toy 5: Woody (cowboy): Then he buzzed off.

Teddy: To be honest we're all a bit miserable.

    Toy 1: Some of us have been in here so long we're afraid to go outside!

Toy 2: It might be even worse "out there"!

OPTIONAL EXTRA BIT (if you have a good singer)

    Doll: No - no - NO! You're all still brand new - hardly out of your wrappings yet. Not one of you knows what it's like to have ... an OWNER!

Toys: (in awe) An Owner!

Doll: Yes - an owner. I used to have an Owner!

Toys: (in more awe) Wow! Crumbs!

Toy 6: Tell us what it's like to have an Owner!

    Doll: To have an owner - why - that's our reason for being! That's why we were created. And let me tell you - there is no more wonderful thing in the whole wide world than to have an Owner that loves you!

Toy 1: Did your Owner love **you**?

Doll: She did. More than anything. (big sigh. moves aside sadly) At least, for many years she did, then something happened to her.

Toy 2: I've heard of that happening. Sometimes Owners get broken!

Toys: (in even more awe) No! How awful. Oo-er!

Doll: No - she didn't get broken. It was worse.

Toys: (in huge amounts of awe) Worse??!!

Doll: Yes - she grew up.

SONG ('When she loved me 'Toy Story 2)

Toy 1: I vote we stay in here. I couldn't cope with rejection like that. I'm too sensitive.

PJ: You can't start thinking like that. (Toys wander off morosely. PJ looks up at teddy) Are you a real teddy?

Teddy: Of course. Are you a real little boy/girl?

PJ: (nods) Yep.

Teddy: Er ... do you have many toys at home?

PJ: No; not one at all; though I used to have a piece of bone I called Derek.

Teddy: So you don't have a ... ummm ... teddy.

PJ: Not even a little one - but I have always wanted one. Er ... do you have an ... umm ... an owner?

Teddy: Not even a little one!

PJ: Well, you have now!

(They laugh and shake hands)

Toy 3: Look out! Someone's coming! (Toys huddle in corners)

Enter Mr Chop, Mr Wick & Sticky. They appear behind the bars.

Mr Chop: Let's try in here!

Mr Wick: Anywhere is better than that stupid bath tub!

Sticky: Don't you two start fighting again. Let's do what we came here to do, then get off the island as quick as we can!

Mr Chop: There! Got it open! (They tiptoe into the prison)

Sticky: This place gives me the willies!

Mr Wick: You know what I think about all this.

Mr Chop This can only end badly?

Mr Wick: My very thoughts exactly!

Sticky: Shhhh!

When they reach centre front there is a loud clang. They look at each other.

Mr Chop: Was that you?

Sticky: Not me.

Mr Wick: If you ask me, that was the sound of the door slamming behind us.

Mr Chop: Oh; right! (Calm - then it sinks in) Oops!

They run back to the door but it has locked behind them.

Mr Wick: As I thought - locked! (Looks down at Mr Chop) I just want to tell you I blame you for this.

Mr Chop: Come on; there must be another way out.

Mr Wick: Of course. (Sarcastic) Prison cells are known for their wide choice of exits.

The men tiptoe diagonally across the stage, Right, turn, then cross Left - this time with PJ, unseen, close behind, grinning. At Left they stop, bending over to listen.

Mr Chop: Shhh... Listen!

Mr Wick: What? (leans close to him)

Mr Chop: (PJ taps him on back) WAAHHH!!

Mr Wick: (banging side of head closest to Mr Chop) I think I have lost the use of this ear.

Sticky: Look who it is! We've found you!

PJ: I knew somebody would come for me!

Mr Chop: Brilliant! There - my plan worked, didn't it, Wicky.

Mr Wick: Wait until the ringing has stopped. (Pokes finger in ear and looks at it) I hope this is just wax and not part of my brain coming out.

Sticky: Now we just have to get you out of here...

Teddy: And me.

Sticky: And you. (Double take) Wow! Have you lost your razor?

PJ: He's a teddy.

Sticky: (unsure) O...K...

PJ: And he's going to be MY teddy!

Mr Chop: Look out! Someone's coming! (They all try to hide)

Enter Mr Hoo and Mr Wye and the Bosun beyond the bars.

Mr Hoo: Now where are we?

Mr Wye: No idea.

Bosun: Mizzen plankin flog the cat!

Hoo: Very. Let's try in here. (They come in. Bosun closes door behind them)

Mr Wye: (is hopping agitatedly) Ooh! I hope there's a toilet in here!

Hoo: What for?

Mr Wye: Why do you think? I want to have a w...

Hoo: (slaps hand over his mouth) You can't say that word in front of children!

Mr Wye: OK! In that case I want to have a p... (hand again)

Hoo: And you can't say that either!

Mr Wye: (getting desperate) Well what CAN I say?

Hoo: The same as the Queen. She says, "Pardon me, but I need a whisper".

Mr Wye: A whisper?!

Hoo: That's right.

Mr Wye: OK - in that case .... Pardon me, but I need a whis...

Hoo: Hush! There's someone in here!

Mr Wye: hopping) Oooooer!

Mr Chop: (reappears) I know you! You're the feather collectors!

Mr Wick: What are you doing here?

Hoo: Our ship ran aground.

Sticky: (testing door) They shut the door behind them!

Hoo: Oops.

Mr Wye: Oh no!

Bosun: (cursing) Skurving Winnetnkles, whelks and skrimshaw!

Hoo: It's no time for your jokes now, Bosun.

Teddy: There's somebody else coming!

Toy 2: What a busy day!

Mr Chop: Everyone - hide again!

Mr Wye: Oh my, oh my!!!

Mr Wick: And what's your problem?

Mr Wye: I want a ... I want a ... I want a **whisper!**

Mr Wick: Oh! Then come over here! You can whisper in my ear!

They all hide. This time it is the ladies who appear outside the door.

Mrs Chop: Well I don't think much of this place. Are you sure this is the way they came? (Go through door)

Loraine: Yes, you can see their footprints in the mud.

Mrs Wick: And where their knuckles dragged in the mud. If this trip gets any worse

SOMEBODY is going to be very, VERY sorry.

Mr Chop: Don't shut the door!

Mrs Chop: Ah-ha! (Sees men) So -there you are! (She goes back and shuts the door) Now **nobody** leaves here until we know what is going on!

Mr Chop: You wally! Now we're all stuck in here!

Mrs Wick: And where is that husband of mine?!

Mr Wick: (enters, shaking and slapping head) That's both ears! Both ears! I might never hear again!

Mrs Wick: Mr Wick! I want a word with you!

Mr Wick: Oh no! I recognise that voice! Oh ... let me go deaf! (Tries to sneak off)

Mrs Wick: Mr Wick!! Come here and tell me **what** - is going on! (they move aside for heated discussion)

PJ: I don't like it in here.

Teddy: We'll be out of here and back home before you know it!

PJ: I don't like it back there much either.

Teddy: Why's that?

PJ: I don't have a family of my own. I live with lots of other orphans.

Teddy: But you've got me now!

Song: (eg: I'll be in your heart; Phil Collins: Disney's Tarzan?)

Boss: (appearing at door with Hench and Toady) What's that appalling noise? Be silent at once ... if you know what's **good** for you!

Hench: Carrots.

Boss: What?

Hench: Carrots. Carrots is good for you.

Toady: And prunes. Prunes is good, especially if you've got a bit of bother with your ...

Boss: Be quiet!! Now - if we could just try to look wicked and dangerous? Hmm? (they try)

(Everyone moves back as they advance with drawn knives)

Mr Chop: What is it you want?

Boss: Me? I want take over all the toy shops in the world. Didn't you read **anyone's** part of the script except YOUR OWN?!

Mr Chop: (embarrassed) NO.

Sticky: And what about us?!

Boss: Oh, that bit is easy. You are all going to stay here for...

Hench: ... for a picnic?

Toady: ... for whom the bell tolls?

Boss: No ... forever! Hahahahahaha! But first - I need YOU, YOU and ... YOU! (Points to a small toy, PJ and Teddy)

Sticky: (advancing on them) Leave them alone!

Boss: How brave. Get back - or you will see my nasty ...

Hench: ... nasty boil?

Toady: ... nasty habit?

Boss: No - my nasty side! Hahahahaha. (Hench & Toady take Teddy, toy and PJ out; Boss backs after them and slams the door.) Hahahahahaha

Sticky: Where Will they take them?

Toy: Up to the factory!

Loraine: Is there no other way out of here?

Mrs Wick: I've a splendid idea! Let's pick up Mr Wick and use his head as a battering ram to knock the door down!

Mrs Chop: Would that work?

Mrs Wick: Not sure; but I know it would cheer me up to watch you try.

Mr Chop: OK then; here goes!

Mr Wick: What? Actually I think she meant that as a rather unkind joke! Hey!!(they pick him up horizontally) Put me down!!

Mrs Wick: (very quietly, without enthusiasm) Stop. (Looks at fingernails) Stop. (Checks time) Put him down.

Mr Chop: Stand clear! Here goes!

They take two practice swings then start to run.

Mr Wick: This can only end baaaa...!!!!!

As they get to the door FOUR children appear and open it. The battering ram team run straight through, screaming. Terrible crashing and yelling offstage. Cloud of dust. They reappear in disarray. Mr Wick is draped in ivy.

Child 1: Why are you hiding in here?

Mr Chop: What are **we** doing? What on earth are **you** doing here?!

Loraine: We can sort all that out later!

Sticky: She's right. Let's get after them!

Mrs Wick: Not you children! This is going to get dangerous!

Child 2: What?! After **we** rescued **you** and ...!!

Mrs Chop: She's right. You get back to the ship.

Sticky: Come on! Which way to the factory? (The toys point in every direction) Right!

(They rush out through the gate. The children hurry forward. Curtain closes behind them.)

Tab

Scene Seven: CHILDREN'S SCENE: **TABS**

Child 1: (to aud) Exciting, isn't it?

Child 2: What's going to happen next?

Child 3: I think the goodies are going to win.

Child 4: You can't be sure.

Child 1: You're right. In some of these post-modernist pantomimes they can distort the traditional positive resolutions and establish a subversive anti-heroic denouement (Pronounced: danoomont).

Child 2: What, in (name of town show is in)?

They think, then say 'Naaah', shaking heads. They turn and listen to Tab Curtain.

Child 3: How long does it take them to change the scenery?

Child 4: About ten minutes.

Child 1: If they haven't been up the bar.

Listen again

Child 2: Have they had long enough?

Child 3: Nowhere near enough.

Child 4: Is that why they want us to do this soppy song-and-dance thing now?

Child 1: Yeah; gives them loads of time to move all the heavy stuff around.

Child 2: Oh, right. And if we make loads of noise nobody can hear them crashing and swearing.

They nod then go and listen again.

Child 3: Anyone feel like singing and dancing?

Children: No. Not really. Not me.

Child 4: I want to get on and see what happens next!

Child 1: Shall we go then?

Child 2: Yeah. (All nod)

Child 3: What about the scenery movers?
Child 4: What about them?
Children: Yeah. Tee hee. (Run off giggling)
Tabs Open

Scene Eight: IN THE FACTORY

At rear centre is the Transforming Machine or an opening/doorway into which people can
   be pushed and then reappear. Above it is a large rotating cog-wheel and piston or
   similar. On each flat is a large, colour-coded lever, plus a giant hammer (hidden)that
   comes down at head height and a large boot on a stick that comes up at bottom height.
   The stage is empty, possibly filled with drifting smoke & factory sounds.
The Boss strides on, Right. Hench & Toady follow, pushing Teddy, & PJ.
     Boss: Ah! My beautiful factory! Soon my work will be finished and every toy shop in
       the world will be full of my own, wonderful toys of death and destruction! (Stops
       and looks at Hench & Toady) Is something wrong with you two? I managed a
       whole speech Without you ...
Toady: ... falling asleep?
Hench: ... poking our tongues out?
     Boss: No ... Without interrupting! Now: that toy! I want to see my Transforming
       Machine working!
     (They push forward small real toy)
     Throw it in!
     (They put it into the machine. The wheel turns - smoke spurts from the machine)
     Hahahahahahaha
     (out of the smoke marches an Action Figure type, with rifle)
     Yes! Perfect! (it stands guard to one side)
Toady: Shall we do the bear now?
PJ: Leave Teddy alone!
     Boss: Hahahaha! No - the bear is too fat! Anything that size could destroy the
       machine!
     Bring them with us. I have other, wicked things to do! Haha...
     Exits Left; others follow.
Mr Chop: (Offstage) This looks like the place! This way!
Enter Right the Chops, Wicks, Loraine & Sticky.
     Mr Wick: I think we should wait for the others. This can only end ...
ALL: BADLY!
Mr Chop: Wow! Look at these levers? What do they all do?
Mrs Chop: Let's find out!
Mrs Wick: Don't touch anything!!
     Mr Wick: All we have to do is find the kid and get out of here in one piece!
     Sticky: But this must be where they destroy the toys! If we can smash the machine
       ...
     Loraine: Sticky's right. While we're here ...
     They move **up left** to examine the machine.
Mr Wick stands by **Green Lever UR**.
     Mr Chop: Yeah! Let's play with levers!
     (He runs to **Red Lever DL**) This one first!
     (Pushes it up. **Large Green Hammer UR** falls on Mr Wick's head, unnoticed)
     Nothing happened. Try the other way.
     (Pulls **Red Lever DL** down. **Large Green Boot UR** kicks Mr Wick)
Mrs Chop: Here - let me have a go! (Goes to **Blue Lever DR**)
Mr Wick: Hold on! Hold on!! I'm moving! (Comes to **Red Lever DL**)

Mrs Chop: Blue lever up! (**Red Hammer DL** on Mr Wick)

Blue lever down! (**Red Boot DL** kicks Mr Wick)

No - nothing happening!

Mrs Wick: Stop, stop, stop! You people are useless!

(Goes to **Yellow Lever UL**)

Mr Wick - you stand over there out of harm's way!

(Sends him to stand by **Blue Lever DR**)

Let someone sensible have a go. What we need is a calm, scientific approach.

(Spits on hands; braces herself. Violently waggles **Yellow Lever UL** up and down many times like a mad thing. The **Blue Hammer and Boot DR** repeatedly knock the stuffing out of Mr Wick)

Mr Wick: Ow ow ow!!! Stop! - It's MY turn to do the lever.

(Marches over to **Green Lever UR**)

Now (to Mr Chop) you stand THERE ... (Sends him to Red Lever DL)

and YOU (Mrs Chop) THERE ... (Blue Lever DR)

and YOU (Mrs Wick) over THERE (Yellow Lever UL).

Right! (To audience) I'm going to enjoy this!

(Grabs Green Lever UR, which is enormous, and pulls it hard. A large sack falls from the sky onto his head)

Enter Left: Boss, Hench & Toady, still holding PJ and Teddy.

Boss: What on earth is the meaning of ...

Hench: ... life?

Toady: ... McDonald's Happy Meals?

Boss: ... the meaning of this invasion of my factory?!

Sticky: Ah-ha! We are here to demand the return of that child!

Boss: Nope.

Loraine: You cad!

Boss: I can!

Loraine: No, I said "You cad"!

Boss: Oh, sorry. (Waves knife) Now, all of you, move aside. Over there. (Moves them all stage Right. Boss stands under Red Hammer DL)

Loraine: (stage whisper) Look! The red hammer! If we can get it to drop down...

Sticky: Yes! But which lever was it? (To audience) Can you help? What colour lever makes the red hammer work? Is it the yellow one? The green one? (Runs to Green hammer) This one? (Runs forward) Or is it this Blue one? Who knows? ... This one? ... The Blue one? ... I hope you're right! (Pulls Blue Lever DR. Red Hammer falls on Boss)

Sticky snatches PJ to safety. Boss recovers fast and grabs Teddy.

Boss: Keep back - or the bear loses its stuffing!

(Holding the bear as a shield Boss moves upstage toward the Transforming Machine)

Nobody Will stop me! Nobody!! HahahahahahahahaAAAAAAARGH!

(Falls into Machine, taking the Teddy in too)

Explosion and smoke from machine. The wheel starts to turns rapidly. Sound of grinding machinery & destruction. Flames appear. Masonry falls from ceiling.

Hench: They're too big for the machine!

Toady: It's going to blow up! Get out!

Mrs Wick: Oh, don't be so dramatic. (explosion) Argh! Run for your lives!! (grabs Mr Wick)

Mr Wick: Come on everyone!

Hench & Toady flee Left. The Wicks exit Right.

Mr Chop: Sticky! Bring the kid! Come on! (Helps Mrs Chop run out left)

Sticky: Quick! (Tries to drag PJ to safety)

PJ: No! Teddy's in there! We must save him!

Loraine: I'll get him! (Runs to machine and jumps in)

Sticky: Loraine!

Mr Chop: (runs in) Come on!!

Sticky: Here! (Pushes PJ at him) Take him/her out!!

Mr Chop: Quick! The whole island is going up! (he rushes out with PJ)

Sticky runs to machine and jumps in. There are more explosions and smoke. Beams and debris fall. Tabs start to close slowly. Just before they close completely they open slightly again. Sticky appears, carrying Loraine through the smoke (backlit). Teddy is behind them. He lays her on the stage. Tabs close.

Scene Nine: OUTSIDE THE CAVE (community scene) TABS

Teddy: (coughing, falls to knees beside them) Is she alright?

Sticky: I don't ...

Loraine: Of course I'm alright. (Sits up & gives him a kiss on the cheek) You came to save me.

Sticky: Er - um - I was just looking for the bear, and - um...

Loraine: That's it. Enough is enough!

Sticky: What - what do you mean?

Loraine: Look - are we going to get married or not?

Sticky: Married?! I ... I ... How about tomorrow?

Loraine: Tomorrow? Hmm. Well - I **was** planning to clean out the drains, but ...

Teddy: How romantic! I must go and find the other toys and tell them! Exits

Loraine: Shall we sing something romantic?

Sticky: (sings) something the kids can join in.

Loraine: One of my favourites. Let's have a bit of a singsong.

Sticky: And I know who can help us! Let's have some words. Song

Sticky: Very nice - but we need some dancers as well. I've got a basket of sweets here for anyone who'll help us sing and dance. Come on up!

Usual business (if no volunteers go down into audience with mike)

Teddy: (enters in a panic) Oh no!! Oh no!! Oh no!!

Loraine: What is it?

Teddy: They've all gone!

Sticky: Who?!

Teddy: Everyone! They've all sailed off in a pirate ship!

Loraine: They must have thought the whole island was going to explode! How can we get back now?!

Sticky: I know - there's one way off this island! Follow me! **Main Curtain**

Scene Eleven THE MAJESTIC TOYSHOP

Inside the Majestic Toy Shop. The toyshop's shelves are empty but it is brightly decorated, ready for its grand opening.

Mr Majestic: (holds up awful toy he has made) Here we are, my dear! I think it's time for the Grand Opening!

Mrs Majestic: (sadly) I just wish we had a few more 'proper' toys.

Mr Majestic: I know - but they just never arrived. (Knock on door) That must be the first customers eager to get in! (Crosses Right)

Mr Chop: (enters Right) Hello!

Mr Majestic: Is that you, Mr Chop? You're looking very posh!

Mr Chop: Yeah! All our clothes got ruined in a fire so we found some new gear in the pirate ship that brought us back! Like it?

Mr Majestic: Very smart!

    Mr Chop: Mr Majestic (arm around shoulder); my fellow shopkeeper - are you expecting a delivery?

Mr Majestic: We were, but it hasn't arrived.

Mr Chop: Well, I think it's arrived now!!

Toys all pour in. (Not Teddy) Mrs Chop, the Wicks and PJ enter.

Mr Majestic: My word! This is incredible! How can we ever thank you?!

    Mrs Majestic: I know! We shall have a party! You're all dressed up for one!

    Mrs Chop: That would be lovely - but we have to get back to the island; rather stupidly (hits Mr Chop, who looks guilty) we left two friends there.

    Mr Chop: Alright! As soon as those feather collectors have turned their ship around!

Pirates enter with Toady and Hench.

    Captain Watt: Ahoy there, mateys! Enough of the 'feather collector' stuff. Despite all these fancy clothes, me and me mates here is in fact - pirates!

All: (mock surprise) No! Really?

Mr Chop: Does this mean you can't get me those cheap feathers?

    Captain Watt: Sadly, not - but me ship is turned around and ready to go back to find your friends!

    Mr Hoo: But what shall we do (Push Toady & Hench forward) about these ...

Toady: ... problem stains?

Hench: ... unsightly nose hairs?

Hoo: No ... these scurvy rats!

Mr Wye: Shall we make 'em walk the ...?

Toady: ...walk the dog?

Hench: ... walk the hamster?

    Hoo: No ... walk the plank until they drop into the foaming black depths of the ocean!!

    Mr Wick: Good idea!

    Mr Chop: You can't do that! Think of the environment!

    Mrs Chop: Sort this out later. Let's get back and find Loraine and Sticky!

    Mrs Wick: (to the Majestics, moving PJ forward) Can we leave this child with you until we get back? Perhaps you could take him/her back to the Orphan's Home?

    Mr Majestic: Certainly! Come on - don't look so miserable! Here; how about a new toy? Choose any one you like! (Several toys line up for selection.)

    PJ: No. (Turns away) I really wanted a Teddy, but on the island something awful happened.

Mr Majestic: Perhaps we have another one here that ...

PJ: It's alright. Doesn't matter. (Walks slightly aside)

Children: (running on) Look out! Something's coming!

    They leap aside as the bath-tub rolls onstage, seaweed all around its base. Sticky and Loraine are on board. Children sit down on front of stage, L & R.

    Sticky: Ahoy there!

    Mr Chop: My bath!

    Mrs Chop: Why are you two dressed up so smart?!

    Loraine: We've got some special news ...

    Mrs Wick: Has he popped the question at last?!

    Loraine: He has!

    Mrs Chop: Amazing! Now we've got a **real** reason for a party!!

Mr Chop: What's that then?

Mrs Chop: It's like a lot of people dancing and drinking and stuff.

Mr Chop: Oh, right.

Mrs Wick: Good grief.

    <u>**Sticky:**</u> (sees PJ) There you are! Are you alright now?!

PJ: Well.... yes, thank you, but ....

    <u>**Sticky:**</u> Loraine and I have been talking ... and we think we'd have room, if you want a new family ...

PJ: Wow! That would be really nice! (smiles, then looks sad again)

Sticky: And I think I know what Will cheer you up even more!

    Music starts quietly: You'll be in my heart. Teddy walks on.

PJ: You're safe!!

Teddy: Of course!

Mr Wick: There - I told you this would happen!

Mr Chop: You did?!

Mr Wick: Of course - all along I've been saying: This can only end ... **happily!!**
They all laugh at the silly old goat.

SONG

<u>**ALL 'EXCEPT CHORUS vanish into wings for: WALKDOWN:**</u>
Children (stand, bow, sit again)
Toys & any chorus Pirates (step forward, bow, peel back to sides)
Soloist Doll (if there was one) (step forward; go Right)
Watt/Dag/Winnet/Bosun (enter from upstage, group Left)
Boss /Hench/Toady (enter from upstage, group Right)
PJ & Teddy (enter from upstage, go Left)
Couples: (together: enter from upstage, stay centre)
Finale song

LIST OF TITLES

Click to select

1. CINDERELLA
2. ROBIN HOOD
3. DICK WHITTINGTON
4. SLEEPING BEAUTY
5. RED RIDING HOOD & THE 3 PIGS
6. THREE MEN IN A TUB
7. JACK AND THE BEANSTALK
8. HANSEL AND GRETEL
9. SNOW WHITE & 7 DWARVES

CONTACT INFORMATION
and PERFORMANCE RIGHTS here:

PANTOSCRIPTS.ME.UK

JACK AND THE BEANSTALK
© Chris Lane 2018

JACK AND THE BEANSTALK
By Chris Lane

Lines & directions in grey are optional or need adapting to local / topical needs. Feel free to delete or adapt them at will (if you want to keep them change the font colour to black before you print).

ACT ONE - SCENE ONE - THE FARMYARD

Main Curtains very slowly open on dark stage.
TIGHT SPOTLIGHT ON: SOLO: Child: perhaps: ENDLESS NIGHT (LION KING) JACK takes over singing.

Music continues over:
Lights rise to show dawn over farmyard. Thatched farm building RIGHT is a huge BOOT. Barn or sty LEFT. Gate through wall at REAR.

One by one the animals are waking up and stretching. They wear human clothes. Intro to song such as: OUR HOUSE starts.
MOTHER HUBBARD: (Comes out of front door of shoe – sees audience) So – there you all are! We were expecting you! Welcome! Welcome to our house!
SONG: perhaps: OUR HOUSE: Dame & Chorus
There are children waving out of windows. Mass movement & 'posing' but not necessarily choreographed.

MOTHER HUBBARD: (She is a loud, rather bossy, woman) That's enough! Enough! (Glares at last small child to stop singing.) Thank you! I've got a bit of a headache. (Some laugh at her & make drinking motions.) Oy! You can stop that! Give me a moment's peace to regain my natural feminine tranquillity. (kids snigger) Can't you see we have visitors? (To aud) Welcome to my farm. I'm Mother Hubbard and these are …
Chicken Little scuttles forward anxiously.
MOTHER HUBBARD: Oh no; what is it this time, Chicken Little?
CHICKEN LITTLE: (looks around nervously) Well – (gulp) – well.... ooooh... (Faints)
MOTHER HUBBARD: Good grief! Is she ill?! If she's ill, we'll have to send somebody to go and fetch the v..
ANIMALS: Nooo!
STREAKY (a pig): No – don't say that word!
MOTHER HUBBARD: Say what word?
ANIMAL 1: THAT word! You know..... the 'V' word!
MOTHER HUBBARD: The 'V' word? What <u>are</u> you talking about?
ANIMAL 2: Look – she's getting better already! It's just these tight clothes!
MOTHER HUBBARD: And don't you complain about wearing these human clothes. Remember – if anyone – ANYONE! - finds out you're really <u>animals</u> (looks around) you'll end up like every other farm-animal in the county! In a meat pie! (To aud) Did you get that – it's part of the plot!
CHICKEN LITTLE: What did she say? Where will we end up? Somewhere nice?
MOTHER HUBBARD: In a meat pie. (CL faints again)
STREAKY: We understand all that – and we're really grateful to you for finding us all these clothes, and keeping us out of (quieter) "you-know", but....
MOTHER HUBBARD: But? But what?
STREAKY: But we haven't been fed for two days!
ANIMALS: All start complaining.

MOTHER HUBBARD: Not been fed! What?! Where is that useless son of mine?! Jack! JACK! JAAAAAAACK!!!!!

ANIMALS: All call for Jack.

MOTHER HUBBARD: Nothing! Where can that idle boy be? I give up! (To audience) Look – I'll give a reward to anyone who finds him (animals get excited) He did the same thing last night – and do you know where he was – he was sitting out there (indicates audience)– doing nothing! Just sitting there, eating sweets and shouting 'Look behind you'!

3 JACKS: (in audience; all dressed identically) 'Look behind you!'

MOTHER HUBBARD: I knew it! He's out there again! (Sudden idea: to aud) I know what to do! I want all you children to look for Jack! Yes – all of you! Come on kids! Here's a bag of sweets for anyone who can find him and bring him up here! You can't mistake him for a normal person – he's got bright yellow trousers and shirt, and a straw hat! Come on now! Who can find him? (House lights up)

Three 'Jack's are brought up onto the stage – they must have at least one child with each.

MOTHER HUBBARD: Three! But I've only got one Jack! How can we tell which is the right one? (Gets microphone) I hope this works tonight – we've been having trouble with the soundman. (Makes drinking gesture) Testing – testing.
(To child) Hello – what's your name? …… Now, you have to help me. My son, Jack, knows all about farm animals. If you make a noise like a farm animal and this person here (indicates first 'Jack') guesses it – then he must be Jack and you win the sweets. Can you think of a farm animal? Yes? Right – have a go then.. (First Jack gets it horribly wrong: guesses "an emperor penguin") Was that an emperor penguin? No! Then – that's not my Jack! Here – I know you – you show people to their seats! What are you dressed like that for?

USHER: I'm from LOCAL TOWN/VILLAGE/AREA.

MOTHER HUBBARD: Fair enough. Now you can show our friend back to their seat. But, look, thank you for trying – you can have some sweets anyway. (First pair exit)

MOTHER HUBBARD: Now – two left. Let's try again (repeat: guess: "Was it a goldfish?") Is it a goldfish? No it wasn't a goldfish. Wrong! Here! You're the bloke who sells the sweets for us! What are **you** dressed like that for?

SWEETS: My wife bought me this for Christmas.

MOTHER HUBBARD: Oooh – nasty. I've been to LOCAL SHOP too. Now – one left. Let's try again (repeat of animal noise business – with help if needed so Jack gets it right) Yes! Well done! You've found my Jack! Thank you very much! Here's your reward! Give them all a clap for helping. Jack! Not you! You get back here!

JACK: (is a bit slow) It's nice down there (peers back at audience) They've got sweets! (Waves)

MOTHER HUBBARD: Very nice.

BALCONY?

JACK: And – upstairs – they have special seats!

MOTHER HUBBARD: Upstairs? We've got an upstairs?

JACK: Yes – upstairs – in the Royal Box.

MOTHER HUBBARD: The Royal Box?!

JACK: Mmmm – Royal Box. (They both bow low to the balcony)

MOTHER HUBBARD: Excuse us – your majesties. Jack! Why haven't the animals been fed?

JACK: (very fast) No food.

MOTHER HUBBARD: No food? Why not?

JACK: No money.

MOTHER HUBBARD: No money? Why not?

JACK: No idea.

MOTHER HUBBARD: No idea? Why not?

JACK: No brain.

MOTHER HUBBARD: No brain? Why not?

JACK: (slower) Genetics!

MOTHER HUBBARD: Genetics! You cheeky scrap!

JACK: Tee hee!

MOTHER HUBBARD: This is dreadful. What are we going to do? No money for food! (Secretly to Jack) Whatever happens – don't tell the animals!

JACK: Right. No money for food – don't tell the animals. (Turns to animal) No money for food – don't tell the animals. (The animals pass this as a Chinese whisper right round the stage. Suddenly the animals all twig what they have said and panic.)

MOTHER HUBBARD: All right! Calm down! (To Jack) Clot! Well – at least I've got a bone for the dog in my cupboard. Let me see! (MH runs indoors Dog gets excited. MH runs out.) Aargh! No! I went to the cupboard, to get the poor dog a bone, but when I got there, the cupboard was bare, and so the poor dog had …

DOG: Chocolate biscuits? (Salivates excitedly) The poor dog had chocolate biscuits?

MOTHER HUBBARD: No. The poor dog had none!

DOG: (gruff & angry) None! NONE! What kind of poem is that for goodness sake?! It's not even proper grammar: 'a bone' is singular and 'none' is plural! You made that up!

MOTHER HUBBARD: I didn't. It's common knowledge! Look – everyone knows it! (To audience) You all know it, don't you! (Disgusted by response) Look – I know it's not Tennyson! But you do all know it, don't you!

DOG: Prove it!

MOTHER HUBBARD: What?

DOG: If they all know this 'poem', then prove it!

MOTHER HUBBARD: Go on then! We will! You can do it! (Secretly to aud) Look – it's in your programme! On page … Have look! Give them a bit of light! Found it? (House lights up) All together. Old Mother Hubbard etc.
(The audience words in the programme end: 'chocolate biscuits' instead of 'none')(Dog could also hold up sign saying that to help)

MOTHER HUBBARD: Hey! That's not right! (To aud) And whose side are YOU on?!

CHICKEN LITTLE: (Wakes up in a panic) Aaargh! The sky's going to fall! The sky's going to fall!

MOTHER HUBBARD: Oh – not again! Chicken Little. Come here!

CHICKEN LITTLE: (breathless) But the sky's going to fall!

MOTHER HUBBARD: Chicken Little, we've been through this before. Repeat after me – the sky is not going to fall.

CHICKEN LITTLE: The sky is not going to fall? Are you sure?

MOTHER HUBBARD: Totally sure. The sky cannot fall. It will never happen!

CHICKEN LITTLE: Well … (Jack creeps up behind her and taps her on the head). Aaargh! (Shrieks then faints)

MOTHER HUBBARD: Now look what you've done! She's fainted again!

STREAKY: She might not have! It might be - bird flu! (All look worried & back away)

MOTHER HUBBARD: It's not bird flu! She's just fainted. (To aud) She does this a lot. We're have to get her some therapy.

STREAKY: If you have bird flu they give a huge INJECTION! (Panic returns)

MOTHER HUBBARD: Stop!! It's not bird flu! If one more person says that I'll send for the v…

ANIMALS: Nooo!

STREAKY: Don't say the 'V' word!

MOTHER HUBBARD: All right! Here! Jack – you started this – you sort it out! Come on, Chicken Little. Let's make you a cup of tea. Jack – I need some water. Here, take this bucket, go up the hill, and fetch a pail of water!

JACK: Up the hill – but that's dangerous. I might fall down and get hurt!

MOTHER HUBBARD: Then take someone with you!

JACK: Someone with me? Like who?

MOTHER HUBBARD: I know: take Jill, you can't BOTH come tumbling down! (Exits with CL)

JACK: Jill! That's a good idea. (To aud) You'll like Jill. I've known her since I was little – we're best mates!

STREAKY: Best mates! Oooh! Jack fancies Jill! (Animals mock) Come on, kid – deny it if you can!

JACK: (really embarrassed) Ha! Don't be silly.

CHILD: Jack – have you actually told her that you like her?

JACK: What?! What <u>are</u> you talking about?

CHILD: Well, if <u>you</u> don't tell her - someone else might!

STREAKY: The kid's right. Leave it too late and you'll lose the chance!

Animals wander off, all agreeing with Pig.

JACK: Ooh – just between you and me, I do quite like Jill, just a little bit. Perhaps I <u>should</u> say something – but I'm not very good at words. I know – I'll do it tomorrow! But what if tomorrow never comes!

SONG: IF TOMORROW NEVER COMES ? (Brief version)

Jack exits sadly

JILL: (enters down theatre) Daisy! Daisy? Where is that silly cow? Daisy! Have you seen Daisy? How about you sir? Have you seen a rather fat, old cow? ("ad lib") What was that? No – not your mother-in-law! Charming!

(Arrives on stage)

Hello – I'm Jill. I live on the next farm - but all our animals have disappeared. Mother Hubbard's is the only farm with any animals left – and that's because she disguises them to look like people! All except for one – Daisy the Cow! And now she's disappeared too! (Daisy appears behind her)

I just don't know where to look!

Business.

JILL: Daisy! There you are! What are you up to? (Listens) You've just been down to the village? What for? (Listens) Auditions?! Auditions for what? (Listens) The X Factor! (Listens) And you really liked one of the judges? Which one? (Listens) Simon Cow! Oh – you had me believing you there for a moment! What could **you** do on the X Factor? (Listens) Dance?! Go on then, Daisy – I'd love to see you dance! (Listens) Who – them? Do they want to see you dance? Let's ask them. Would you like to see Daisy dance? ...... There – now – what are you going to dance to? (Listens) <u>Moo</u>sic – very funny.

DAISY'S DANCE

JACK: (returns) There you are – we've been looking for you!

JILL: (coy but excited) Were you?! What for?

JACK: I was going to ask you ..

JILL: Out on a date?!

JACK: Don't be so silly! No – ask you to come up the hill to fetch a pail of water!

JILL: Oh. (Disappointed) My dream come true! Who could refuse an offer like that? OK. I'll come and help you! (Daisy the cow starts butting between them) Hey! Daisy – what's the matter?

JACK: Daisy – what are you up to?

STREAKY: She's jealous.

JILL: What – jealous of me?

JACK: Is this true, Daisy; are you jealous of Jill? (Daisy nods & looks shy) You silly moo! Jill's just my old mate!

(Streaky sticks head in from wings)

STREAKY: This is yer chance, kid. Tell her!

JILL: (romantic) Tell me? Tell me what?

JACK: Tell you – er – tell you - we've got a new bucket!

JILL: Oh – lovely.

MOTHER HUBBARD: (Returns) Are you still here. Ah-ha! And Jill too! Hiya! There's work do. Pop up the hill and get me a pail of water!

JACK: But it's so slippery up there– I might fall down and hurt myself!

MOTHER HUBBARD: (to aud) Is he a wimp or what? Listen – that hill is perfectly safe.

JACK: Oh no it isn't!

MOTHER HUBBARD: So – it's going to be one of them sort of pantos, is it? Right then! That hill is safe!

JACK: Oh no it isn't!

MOTHER HUBBARD: Oh yes it is!

JACK & JILL: Oh no it isn't!

MOTHER HUBBARD: Oh yes it is!

JACK & JILL & CHILDREN & ANIMALS & AUDIENCE: Oh no it isn't!
MOTHER HUBBARD: Tis – tis – tis
JACK & JILL & ANIMALS: Tisn't – tisn't – tisn't
MOTHER HUBBARD: It is – it is – it (warbles) is
JACK & JILL & ANIMALS: It isn't – it isn't – it (warbles) isn't!
MOTHER HUBBARD: (very deep) IT IS!
JACK & JILL & ANIMALS: (very deep) It isn't.
MOTHER HUBBARD: (takes very deep long breath but, before she can say anything ...)

GIANT'S VOICE: "FEE FI FO FUM – I HEAR THE SOUND OF AN ENGLISHMAN!
    BE HE LIVE OR BE HE DEAD – I'LL GRIND HIS BONES TO MAKE MY BREAD!!"
ALL: Aargh! It's the giant!! (Much panic, fainting & hiding)
JACK: Perhaps we should go back in the house?
MOTHER HUBBARD: How would that help? It's his boot! What if he comes back for it and puts
    it on! We'd end up squished in the bottom like last week's corn plasters!
JILL: I thought your house was an odd shape. You mean -?
MOTHER HUBBARD: Yes; it's one of the giant's boots!
JACK: And you were blaming **me** for the smell!
MOTHER HUBBARD: Don't interrupt. This is my dramatic bit. I remember the day it fell –
    hurtling from the sky. Right on top of your father's onion patch! Ruined his day it did.
JILL: Did it squish his onions?
MOTHER HUBBARD: Squished his everything. He was planting them at the time.
JILL: Oh dear. That's awful.
MOTHER HUBBARD: I know. I was looking forward to those onions.
JACK: I wish the giant would throw down one of his sacks of gold instead!
(They all look up into the sky & then shuffle to one side, just in case)
CHICK: Oh my ... (falls over unconscious)
ANIMAL: Did the sky fall on her head again?
STREAKY: No – she's really hungry!
MILKMAID: We're all really hungry.
MOTHER HUBBARD: That's it, Jack – you've got to get some money to buy food, or they'll all
    starve to death!
STREAKY: Food – foooooood! I must have foooood! (Collapses)
MOTHER HUBBARD: My word. Perhaps I should call for the v...
ANIMALS: Noooo! Don't say it!
MOTHER HUBBARD: Jack – you'd better go and fetch the v...
ANIMALS: Don't say it!
MOTHER HUBBARD: Don't say what?
JACK: You know – **vet**!
Thunder, darkness, lightning. Vet appears on stage. She is sexy and power-dressed in a black
    suit. She has a stethoscope and a doctor's bag with a designer logo.
VET: You called for. ...(Crosses to Jack sexily) ... the vet?
JACK: Corrrr..... Are you the vet?
VET: Depends. And what do you do around here – apart from dribble? Do you have a name?
    Mmm?
JACK: My name?? .... er .... Could you start with an easy question first? (Hisses to Jill) What's
    my name?
JILL: (angry sigh) Mr Percy Poopy Pants!
JACK: (Turns to vet, proudly) I'm Mr Percy Poopy Pants! That doesn't sound right! (Glares at
    Jill)
MOTHER HUBBARD: His name is Jack. Jack Hubbard. And he's my only son.
VET: Hmm. (sneering) Well, we can at least be thankful for that. Now – where's my... patient? I
    don't see any animals here!
MOTHER HUBBARD: Oh yes – look – they're nearly all animals! (Secretly) They're in disguise
    - so rustlers don't steal them! Look. (Starts to poke at Child)
CHILD: Oy! I'm not an animal – I'm one of your children!

MOTHER HUBBARD: Ooh. Are you sure? (To aud) I've got so many children I don't know what to do. Look – here – this one's definitely an animal!

VET: Come on now – time is money! (Looks around. Animals all try to hide behind each other.)

MOTHER HUBBARD: Time is money?? I thought gold coins were money?

VET: How unique – somebody who actually IS as daft as they look! (Walks across to MH) Time is indeed money. You already owe me one gold coin just for calling me here!

MOTHER HUBBARD: We do?!

VET: You do. And another gold coin if I open my bag – like this! (Produces enormous hypodermic. Animals scream and faint.) And another gold coin if I have to stick it in somebody!

MOTHER HUBBARD: Well in that case you'd better leave – nobody here needs an innoccu-bobulation, thank you very much.

VET: Hmmm. I'm sure I can find somebody. (Prowls round terrified animals, then looks at audience) Ah-ha! Look at this pasty-faced lot. I've never seen such a sickly-looking load of geriatrics since I walked along LOCAL PLACE seafront! It's like flicking through a medical textbook. Every disease under the sun. No wonder the St John's Ambulance (or whatever) is hovering at the back. (Shades eyes to peer at them) Like vultures circling the Serengeti.

JILL: Steady on now!

VET: Oh! It talks!

JILL: Those people have paid money to be here today!

VET: Really? Just take a look at that one. I hope he didn't pay full price – I don't think he's going to make it past the interval!

JACK: Duhhh.... Interval ....

VET: Ah - Mr Poopy Pants. Hmm. (thinks – to audience) I bet this farm is worth a few gold coins! (Louder, to Jack) You might actually look half decent - with some decent clothes, a haircut and a few hours under a pressure washer!

MOTHER HUBBARD: And she called ME stupid!

VET: I do like a nice strong man. Are you strong? (Jack nods) My word. Just the thought of those rippling muscles is making my poor little heart pound and pound! I do believe you can hear my heart pounding. Can you hear it? (Jack shakes head) Here! (Grabs his head) Listen! (Presses his head to her chest) There – can you hear it pounding? Can you?

JACK: MmmmmMMmmMMMm! (Squeaky) "And" (lower) and – and what a very unusual fragrance. May I ask where you got that perfume?

VET: Oh that! Just a little something I picked up when I was last in Paris. It's called 'Eau de Parree'. (Lets him loose)

JACK: Cor! I'll never wash that side of my face again!

JILL: Oy! (Grabs him away) My heart is pounding too!

JACK: It is?

JILL: It certainly is. Here! (Presses his head to her chest) There!

JACK: MmmmmMMmmMMMm! And – what a very unusual fragrance. May I ask where you got that perfume?

JILL: Oh that – just a little something I picked up when I was cleaning out the pigsty. It's called 'Eau de Pig Sh....

JACK: Waah! Yuck! I'm going to wash that side of my face RIGHT NOW!

MOTHER HUBBARD: Then you'll need to get that bucket of water! Off you two go! Go on! (Jack is hurried away by Jill)

VET: Now – my three gold coins.

MOTHER HUBBARD: Three? But you haven't stuck that innoccubobulation into anyone! That makes it just TWO coins!

VET: Huh. Well – which animal was ill?

ANIMALS: Chicken Little! (Push her forward)

CHICKEN LITTLE: No – I feel much better now. Honest!

MOTHER HUBBARD: And an innoccubobulation won't help – it's a mental problem. She thinks the sky is going to fall on her head!

VET: Hmm. Really? So – no need for an injection?

MOTHER HUBBARD: None at all.

VET: Oh dear, never mind. In that case..... LOOK OUT!! THE SKY'S FALLING!!
CHICKEN LITTLE: screams and faints.
MOTHER HUBBARD: (rushes to her aid) Oh my word!
VET: (As MH bends over CL the Vet jabs the needle into MH's bum) Whoops! Silly me!
Much commotion. MH straightens, looks odd, and then begins to stagger drunkenly about the
    stage. If possible she does an overhang trick using foot braces.
VET: (To aud) Now's the chance to get some money out of her! Right then, Mrs Hubbard.
    Three gold coins please! Come on! I'm standing right here until I get my money.
MOTHER HUBBARD: Right there?
VET: Yes – right here.
MOTHER HUBBARD: Well that's fine – just so long as you don't stand over there!
VET: In that case that is exactly where I shall stand! (Moves) Now what are you all doing?
    (Everyone has moved as far away as possible) What are you all up to? What's that noise?
    (Sound of rolling, bumping and yelping, getting slowly louder.) I said – what's that noise?!
MOTHER HUBBARD: Well – the thumpy bit is Jack falling down; the squeaky bit is Jill, a-
    tumbling after; and the clanging sound..... Well, I think the clanging sound is probably a pail
    of ...
Jack and Jill stagger/roll in and fling a pail of water over the Vet. They collapse. She stands
    speechless, dripping.
VET: You! You! Arrrrrr! (Stamps off to rude noises from the happy animals)
CURTAIN

SCENE 2 – ON THE PATH TO THE VILLAGE

Enter three fairies in a rush through theatre/hall: COWSLIP (a rather pompous 'chav' – East
    Londoner or similar), NUTMEG (a very dim fairy; Dressed as a fairy in a tutu, even though
    plainly male) and PEASBLOSSOM (very posh).
COWSLIP: (runs down hall/or onto stage) Run! Run more fast like! She is goin' to catch us like!
    Run, for your lifes!
NUTMEG: (a moment later) Faster! She's not far behind! We're doomed! (They stagger on
    stage, near hysterical)
COWSLIP: Where is dat Peasblossom?
NUTMEG: Eh? Who?
COWSLIP: Oh no! She 'as got Peasblossom! Peasblossom is doomed!
NUTMEG: Look – there!
PEASBLOSSOM: (runs onto stage) I can't run any more! Let her catch us! I'd rather die!
NUTMEG: No! Keep running! When I saw her coming over the last hill she had - AN AXE!!
ALL: Aargh!
COWSLIP: Flee!
NUTMEG: Fly!
PEASBLOSSOM: You flee. You fly. Me knackered. (Gasps) Go on: I'll be alright. You two
    escape. I'll hold her off as long as I can.
NUTMEG: You?! Hold her off? Wait till you see the size of the axe!
COWSLIP: Then we is goin' to run as fast as our legs is – like – possible of!
NUTMEG: We'll never outrun her! The speed of her! She's inhuman!
COWSLIP: Then we is goin' to hide! Quick – be hiding!! No – you is not hidin' behind me!
    Gerrof!
PEASBLOSSOM: Oooer! Mummy! (Gets thin branch and hides behind it very badly)
NUTMEG: Oh no! She's coming! (Hides head under cloth/curtains with bottom clearly sticking
    out)
COWSLIP: What shall we ... (looks around for other two) No! They is gone! Leavin' me here all
    on me own! (Looks around desperately; sees orchestra)
    Oy! Me bro! Emergency! Life or def! Where is I goin' to 'ide? Quick!
    (Is handed brown paper bag; looks at it for a moment)
    Thankin you!
    (Pops it over head then walks crab-like sideways across stage; turns with back to audience

and walks similarly back with arms out like roast chicken. On the back of the bag is painted a startled face.)

PRINCESS: (enters opposite; she is a cute little princess) HA!! Caught you! Stop right there!

COWSLIP: You is not seeing us. We is hidin!

PRINCESS: Don't be so silly! (She drags them into view)

NUTMEG: Don't eat us! I'm still young; in the prime of life. (To piano) Oy! I heard that!

COWSLIP: 'Ere! Is this hoo I 'as just run ten miles from?

NUTMEG: Yes – she's the one! I can't look!

PEASBLOSSOM: She's not really **that** fierce.

COWSLIP: Next time you is saayin': "Run, flee – we is goin to die", I finks I is going to make myself a cup of tea!

PEASBLOSSOM: Yeah – me too!

NUTMEG: Yeah. Suppose it WAS a bit silly. And she hasn't even got a big axe!

PRINCESS: But I have! (She has. It is huge)

FAIRIES: AAAAAARGH! (Try to hide again)

PRINCESS: Get over here. (They huddle pitifully) You have ruined my life! I want my money back!

COWSLIP: Money back?! No! Kill us now!

PEASBLOSSOM: Ah – Princess! Now let's calm down a teensy bit: OK? Lovely to see you again, ya? All going well with the Prince?

PRINCESS: Prince?! (pushes him off) You know very well the prince won't let me back in the palace again – not since YOU lot tried to help!

NUTMEG: I'm not sure I really got that one. Just run it past me again.

PRINCESS: It was a disaster!

PEASBLOSSOM: But we did a very good job! Followed the instructions to the letter!

PRINCESS: Oh yes? Really?

PEASBLOSSOM: Yah, spot on, really. The Prince's mother..

COWSLIP: Da Queen!

PEASBLOSSOM: Yah, the Queen wanted to test you out, to see if you really **were** a royal princess! So – clever this - she got a great big pile of fluffy mattresses and told us to …

NUTMEG: Ooh! Ooh! I remember now! The mattresses! (concentrates) The queen told us that when the Princess went to bed we had to make sure the Princess had **a pea on the mattress**! (all turn and stare) So – that's what happened. (proudly) But in fact - it was me!

PEASBLOSSOM: No. The princess was to have a pea UNDER the mattress. Not ON it!

NUTMEG: But – how could she….? She'd have to.. (mimes actions of peeing under a mattress)

COWSLIP: A GARDEN pea! UNDER the mattress - to see if she could feel it!

NUTMEG: Ooh! I thought it was a bit odd.

PRINCESS: Odd! ODD! I was up all night washing the sheets! (Grabs Nutmeg by scruff and glares into face) Do you know how many mattresses got ruined that night?!

NUTMEG: Quite a lot, I imagine!

PRINCESS: 27! **27**!! And as I was leaving the next day I saw them burning the bed! Embarrassing or what! Now – I want com-pen-sation!

NUTMEG: I'm not sure I really got that one. Just run it past me again.

COWSLIP: Where is dis compost-nation?

PRINCESS: It's MONEY!

PEASBLOSSOM: Money – ooh no. We don't have any of that.

COWSLIP: No – none at all. On my life!

NUTMEG: Nope none at all. Just these gold coins. (Fairies shriek & grab bag before princess can get it)

PRINCESS: Perfect! They'll do nicely. Give me the gold coins then I'll be off to the next job. There's a vacancy for a princess up a tall tower. All I have to do is wait, then a handsome prince will come along, climb up my hair and we'll be happy ever after. (They look shifty) What? **What**?!

COWSLIP: I fink yoo as missed that job. But not a bad fing really. Did not go quite as wuz planned.

PRINCESS: What?

COWSLIP: We wuz in charge of that one as well.

PEASBLOSSOM: It was only a little mistake! We did really well up until then! (Acts it out) We got the Prince past the dark forest!

COWSLIP: Past da mountains!

PEASBLOSSOM: Past the dragon!

COWSLIP: Past da swamp!

PEASBLOSSOM: Past the goblins!

NUTMEG: Pass the ketchup. (They stare at Nutmeg) No ketchup?

COWSLIP: Where wuz we? Right – we got 'im past all the dangers.

PEASBLOSSOM: Past all the dangers until finally he reached the tower. At sunset. Lovely he looked, in his silver armour.

NUTMEG: Oh! I remember him now! (Moves centre and kneels, calling upwards) Rapunzel! Rapunzel! Throw down your <u>chair</u>!

PRINCESS: Duh! Hair! Throw down your <u>hair</u>! Hair! Not your <u>chair</u>!

(Guilty looks from fairies)

COWSLIP: We knows that now.

NUTMEG: Really heavy that chair was.

PEASBLOSSOM: Antique! Solid oak!

COWSLIP: It ain't all our fault! He couldn't jump out of da way quick enuff like - wot wiv de heavy suit of armour and all.

PEASBLOSSOM: As soon as we saw it was safe – no settees or tables or anything coming down – we rushed over to see if he was alright.

COWSLIP: (shakes head) It was like opening a tin of corned beef.

PRINCESS: You – you – grrrr! Give me that money! (They back away) Look! It's Goldilocks! (While they twist round in alarm she grabs Nutmeg's wand)

COWSLIP: Idiots! It couldn't be Goldilocks – doesn't you remember, we wuz supposed to wake er up **before** the bears got 'ome like.

PEASBLOSSOM: Oh yah! (chuckles) They did say she was tastier than the cold porridge though, (all agree) so, not a disaster for everyone!

NUTMEG: Wo! She's got a whatsit!

PRINCESS: Fair swap – the gold for the magic wand.

COWSLIP: Ha! That wand ain't workin proper like anyway. Everyone: we is just walkin' away. Do not give her no gold.

PRINCESS: I'm warning you!

Fairies start to walk away.

PRINCESS: I'll count to five.

COWSLIP: Don't give her the gold.

PRINCESS: 5 – 4 – 3 – 2 - 1. (Pyro in front of fairies/OR princess chants toad spell). They spin round & hurry back.

COWSLIP: (Fast) Give her the gold. Give her the gold. Give her the gold. Give her the gold.

PRINCESS: Thank you very much. Here. You can have this back. (returns wand)

COWSLIP: Always a pleasure to be helpin' royalty, like. Er – a bit of free advice - watch out for anyone hoo gives you glass slippers. It turns out they really 'as to be made by a specialist. They is not as easy to make as one might first fink.

PEASBLOSSOM: Look nice though. Till you try to walk in them.

NUTMEG: How long was that Cinderella on crutches?

PEASBLOSSOM: Oooh – ages. She missed her mother's wedding to Prince Charming!

COWSLIP: And anuvver tip for you. If you is ever in a little cottage in da woods, what is belonging to some dwarfs, and you sees an ugly old woman who comes to the door wiv a basket of apples.

PEASBLOSSOM: Before you throw her down the well, check she's not just collecting for charity.

NUTMEG: Or delivering the Betterware catalogue.

COWSLIP: Yeah. (Thinks briefly) Who was da fird one?

PEASBLOSSOM: Selling lucky heather.
NUTMEG: Wasn't very lucky for her, not really.
COWSLIP: There was no stopping that Snow White once she got an idea in her head.
PEASBLOSSOM: But she'll be out in fifteen years, with good behaviour.
PRINCESS: You people! You are not fit to **be** fairies!
(Princess storms off)
COWSLIP: Ha! If we was avin' a gold coin for every time we is 'earin' that!
PEASBLOSSOM: Never mind. What's next on our list?
COWSLIP: OK– we is getting' this one right. Who is we here to do the good deed for?
PEASBLOSSOM: (consults order form) Name of Jack. No money. No girl.
COWSLIP: Loooser! Ha!
PEASBLOSSOM: Needs a bit of luck. Easy! All we have to do is give him the bag of gold coins!
COWSLIP: Right! Even we cannot be getting' **that** wrong! (They exit)

SCENE THREE: BACK AT THE FARM

The animals are demonstrating for food. Placards & chanting. Mother Hubbard, Jack & Jill are watching.
MOTHER HUBBARD: Make a decision! How are we going to feed the animals?
CHILD: And the children.
MOTHER HUBBARD: What?
CHILD: And the children.
MOTHER HUBBARD: Them as well? Blimey. Where will it end?
JACK: I was just thinking.
MOTHER HUBBARD: Yes – but only just!
JILL: Go on, Jack; what's your idea?!
JACK: I was just thinking – perhaps we could do some magic and get some food!
MOTHER HUBBARD: Good grief. What is it with you and magic? Listen to me – there is no such thing as magic! Magic is all made up!
JACK: It's not made up!
MOTHER HUBBARD: It is! Magic is all made up!
JACK: Oh no it isn't!
MOTHER HUBBARD: Don't start all that again! Jack – get some money to buy the food!
JACK: OK. But how?
MOTHER HUBBARD: I'm sure Jill knows what you could do. She's been to school. (Takes her to one side and whispers:) Listen. Tell him (looks round) – tell him: **he - has - to sell - one - of - the animals!**
JILL: What?
MOTHER HUBBARD: Tell him (looks round) he has to sell one of the animals!
JILL: Are you sure? You're totally sure that's what you want? (nodding) All right then!
MOTHER HUBBARD: Good girl. (Moves back)
JILL: Jack!
JACK: What?
JILL: You have to sell one of the animals!
MOTHER HUBBARD: Aaargh noooo!!! (throws herself to floor, pounding in despair) You cruel, heartless creature – how could you say such as thing? These poor, dumb creatures – why – they're like my own flesh and blood. To even think of parting with one would be like ripping out me own teeth! No – a kidney! NO! A whole leg! Jack - Jack, don't you listen to her! Noooo – nooooo!! Here take my leg and my kidneys – you'll get a good price for them at the takeaway in LOCAL TOWN/AREA!
JILL: Good grief.
JACK: No – I don't think I can do it!
JILL: You can, Jack, just be brave!
JACK: Well – OK.
MOTHER HUBBARD: terrible wailing sounds and pounding on floor continue.
JACK: Come on now, Mother. It'll be for the best. But – which one shall I choose?
All the animals stand behind him as he turns left, except for the chick who just then recovers,

stands up, sees him staring, then faints again. Jack swings back the other way – all animals shuffle round to stay behind him.

JACK: I can't choose – I need a blindfold. (One is found and the hunt begins. He puts hand on MH's bottom) Oh no – Daisy, not you!

MOTHER HUBBARD: Cheeky!

(After much business he ends up holding onto the real Daisy)

ALL: gasps of horror.

JACK: Oh no! Poor Daisy. I can't ...

JILL: Just think – it will mean saving the lives of all the other animals.

CHILD: And us kids.

JACK: I know: you're right. Just give me a few moments alone with her. Come on, old girl.

JILL: Poor Jack. I'll see you at the market. Good luck! (All exit)

JACK: Not going to be the same here without you, Daisy. I really like to be with you; you don't say rude things about me.
I remember the day we first saw you, as a little calf, at the marketplace. No, don't look shy. You're a beautiful old cow!

JACK: SONG: possibly My life is brilliant: brief /heavily adapted to 'saw your face at the market place'

They exit.

Fairies enter.

COWSLIP: Did you see dat? He is needin' the cheering up. His mum said no to da magic – but there's nothing to stop us like, <u>buying</u> dat sheep off of him!

PEASBLOSSOM: Cow.

COWSLIP: Whatever. Give us da bag of gold and we is goin' home like.

NUTMEG: I'm not sure I really got that one. Just run it past me again.

COWSLIP: Give us da bag of gold – round shiny things.

PEASBLOSSOM: Oops. Angry princess!

NUTMEG: Where?!

PEASBLOSSOM: Angry princess took gold!

COWSLIP: I is not believin' this! No gold? Well what '<u>as</u> we got to give 'im?! Look in your pockets.

PEASBLOSSOM: Don't seem to have any pockets. Are you sure I have to wear this?

COWSLIP: All fairies wear that for the first year.

NUTMEG: I didn't (is muffled by Cobweb)

COWSLIP: What 'as we got then? Nothing in my pockets.

PEASBLOSSOM: Nothing. Nutmeg?

NUTMEG: Mmm? I'm not sure I really got that one. Just run it past me again.

PEASBLOSSOM: What have you go in your pocket?

NUTMEG: (search pockets) Well – I do have something in here (fumbles inside front of skirt)

COWSLIP: (nervously) Er .. what is it?

NUTMEG: My mother called it… my magic bean.

COWSLIP: Your … 'magic bean'?

NUTMEG: Mmm. Do you want to see it? (they exchange unsure looks then nod unsurely. Nutmeg shuffles across to them with his back to the audience. Still turned away from the audience they look down at his groin-level 'magic bean') What do you think of that then?

COWSLIP: (after a good look) Well – it's a bit shrivelled.

PEASBLOSSOM: (thinks & looks closer) Aren't they all like that?

COWSLIP: (concerned look) You needs to get out a bit more.

NUTMEG: I'll show these nice people. (Turns back to face aud) There – my magic bean (it is a bean)

Jack & Daisy return.

JACK: Hello! Can I help you?

COWSLIP: (to NUTMEG) This is <u>your</u> fault – <u>you</u> sort it out!

NUTMEG: Er – hello – we are – we are – (COWSLIP prods him) we are fairies.

JACK: Opens mouth to make silly comment

COWSLIP: No. You is stoppin' right there. We as heard them all before, chum. We is fairies.

Alright?!

JACK: Fairies. Hmm. I don't think I would have guessed that one.

COWSLIP: Well we is, (Shows wings) so get over it.

JACK: If you're fairies, then what are your names?

PEASBLOSSOM: Names?

JACK: Yes. If you're fairies you'll have magical names.

PEASBLOSSOM: No. Not us.

COWSLIP: Fairies' names is a secret. Too magical for mortals to hear, like.

JACK: That's silly. All fairies have really soppy names – like – er – COWSLIP.

The other two nod & smirk & point at COWSLIP.

COWSLIP: Alright! OK! It's a family thing! Thank you – PEASBLOSSOM and NUTMEG!

JACK: So – IF you're fairies – what are you doing here?

NUTMEG: GOLD! We are here to give you some gold!

JACK: Gold! Lovely!

COWSLIP: But they is losin' it.

JACK: Oh.

NUTMEG: So you can have this instead.

PEASBLOSSOM: It's a bean!

JACK: It's a been what?

NUTMEG: It's a been in my pocket! (COWSLIP hits him)

JACK: (looks at the bean) Hmm. Well – I won't pretend that I am not a little disappointed. Never mind. What sort of bean is it? Is it a magic bean?

PEASBLOSSOM: YES! Yes it is! It is a MAGIC bean!

JACK: Oh yeah – and what am I supposed to do with this 'magic' bean?

PEASBLOSSOM: Just take the bean and stick it in the ground.

JACK: You must think I'm daft. Do I look daft? (They nod) Only a proper idiot would believe that's a magic bean.

NUTMEG: (smiles proudly) Thank you.

JACK: I can't stand here wasting time – I've got to go to market and sell my poor cow.

PEASBLOSSOM: (inspired) We'll buy the cow!

JACK: Buy her? Hmmm... How much for?

PEASBLOSSOM: Er – one magic bean???

JACK: A MAGIC BEAN?! It's a deal! I can't wait to tell mother! Hang around; I'll get her! Mother!

NUTMEG: Lovely. We're going to met his mu...

COWSLIP: We is not stayin' here! You is hearin' what his mother said about magic! She is goin' loopy when she finds out what is happenin! Quick – scarper! (They exit, taking Daisy)

JACK: Mother!

Animals enter excitedly

MOTHER HUBBARD: (Enters from shoe) What's this noise – are you back already?

JACK: Yes!

MOTHER HUBBARD: And did you sell the cow?

JACK: Yes!

MOTHER HUBBARD: And did you get a good price?

JACK: Yes!

MOTHER HUBBARD: Thank goodness. How much did you get?

JACK: This! **A magic bean!** (Sees that mother is speechless) But it IS a magic bean! I mean – they said it was a magic bean. I mean ... oh dear. Have I done a really silly thing? Oh dear. (Gives Mother bean and walks off)

MOTHER HUBBARD: One bean. One dried up bean. What good is that? Not even fit to feed to the animals.

STREAKY: Are you sure? (Looks at bean then shrugs) Oh - I'm so hungry.

MOTHER HUBBARD: Don't be cross with Jack. He's just too trusting. (Looks at bean sadly). No point keeping this. Here – get rid of it.

STREAKY: OK. (Looks around) Where's your bin?

MOTHER HUBBARD: I've been in the house. Why?

STREAKY: No! Where's your <u>wheelie</u> bin?

MOTHER HUBBARD: I've <u>really</u> been in the house. What is the matter with you?! Give it here.

She walks DL (Possibly to a small well or bush in front of stage with the coiled beanstalk in it, linked by thread to overhead bars?) She drops the bean. They walk away. Slowly a sound grows, then gets louder and louder.

MOTHER HUBBARD: What is it?!

JACK: (returns) What's going on?!

CHICK: Aargh! The sky is falling! (Faints)

Much panic.

They all turn and watch. It grows darker.

Dramatic music swells.

Suddenly the tip of the beanstalk shoots up and races up to the ceiling.

STREAKY: Wow. Cool.

MOTHER HUBBARD: (all looking up) Crikey. Where do you think it goes?

JACK: Dunno. (all look up)

GIANT: FE-FI-FO-FUM; THERE'S A BEAN-STALK UP MY BUM!

MOTHER HUBBARD: Oy! Family show! Well – at least we know where it goes!

Fairies return with Daisy

COWSLIP: Look – the lads and me is feelin' really bad about taking your sheep and – Crikey! What is dat?!

NUTMEG: I said it was a magic bean!

JILL: (enters excitedly) Jack! What **is** that? You can see it all the way from the village!

JACK: Don't <u>exactly</u> know what it is.

COWSLIP: Blimey – we 'as done somepin right at last. What is you goin' to do with it?

JACK: Dunno.

PEASBLOSSOM: Well. You'll be eating beans for quite a long time I suppose.

NUTMEG: I can't eat beans. (They all look at him) My mum says they make me far…

PEASBLOSSOM: NUTMEG!

NUTMEG: Beans make me far..

PEASBLOSSOM: NUTMEG!!

NUTMEG: I was just going to say, beans make me far too fat!

PEASBLOSSOM: Cor – for a moment I thought you were going to say 'fart'! (Cobweb hits)

JILL: No! Giant beanstalks! I've read about these in storybooks – you climb up them! And see what adventures are waiting for you!

JACK: Do you think I could have an adventure?

JILL: Of course you can! As long as you're careful. You can do it! Go on!

JACK: OK! And YOU three gave me the bean, so you can come with me! Can't they mum!

MOTHER HUBBARD: (threatening) They most certainly can!

COWSLIP: Gulp! Fair enough.

JILL: And so am I.

JACK: What?!

JILL: I'm not missing an adventure! Off we go then!

JACK: (Peers up into sky then walks off) Ah – no. Too high - Can't fly - Goodbye.

JILL: You get back here. This is your chance to be a hero. Come on – show everyone you can go the distance!

SONG: maybe HERCULES: GO THE DISTANCE (Disney): JACK, JILL & CHORUS

SCENE FOUR – THE GIANT'S KITCHEN

Maybe on a rostra, at the side of the stage, is a small version of the main stage (prosc arch & fake curtains). Set into the arch is a string of white fairy lights, <u>lit</u>. The purpose of the fairy lights is to dazzle audience enough to allow black-clothed puppeteers not to be seen. The mini curtains open, or internal lights, rise to show a bare kitchen with a pair of wooden chairs and a table. The tip of a beanstalk runs up the Right edge of the stage. The background is black. A lamp/candle burns on the table. Heavy footsteps approach. The giants are normal size actors: the others are puppets.

GIANT: Enters: Wife! Wife! I need bones to crunch! Wife! Fetch my supper!

GIANT'S WIFE: (enters) Oh, hello, dear. How was your day?

GIANT: My day?! Ha! I destroyed a whole city! I smashed their puny houses with my mighty hands; I ripped the roofs from the walls, pounded the ruins into the mud and then squished the juice from their tiny bodies. Hahahahaha!

GIANT'S WIFE: Well, I hope you've washed your hands.

GIANT: Next, I went down to their harbour, lifted their ships into the sky and threw them out into the sea, where they smashed to pieces and sank down, down to the very bottom of the dark ocean. Hahaha!

GIANT'S WIFE: That's nice dear. I saw that Mrs Ogre this morning, you know – the one from the Post Office? She was getting a nice bit of haddock for their tea so I said that we …

GIANT: Then, they sent a pathetic little army to attack **me**! Do you know what I did?!

GIANT'S WIFE: No, dear; what did you do?

GIANT: I swung my great wooden club at them and then I ..

GIANT'S WIFE: Is that the great wooden club you made out of a whole tree?

GIANT: What?

GIANT'S WIFE: I said, is that the great wooden club you made out of a whole tree?

GIANT: Er – no, the other one.

GIANT'S WIFE: The one I got you for your birthday?

GIANT: Yes. That one. Anyway – I picked up my club and I ..

GIANT'S WIFE: I'm glad you like it, dear. I always worry about you using that other one. You know – with your back and everything.

GIANT: Yes – it's very nice. Anyway – er – what was I saying?

GIANT'S WIFE: You took your great wooden club.

GIANT: Yes – I took my club and I pounded them flat - as flat as mini pizzas! Hahahaha!

GIANT'S WIFE: Very nice, dear; it's lovely to see you out playing with your little chums. Now, just you wait a moment and I'll make you your omelette.

GIANT: Omelette! But – where are the pies that I like?!

GIANT'S WIFE: Simon the Pie Man says you've eaten every animal for a hundred miles. BUT he says he's got a friend helping him find some more. Anyway, you must have a varied diet, dear. Can't eat the same for every meal. And I've made you a lovely side-salad.

GIANT: SALAD! I want bread – made with the ground-up bones of an Englishman!

GIANT'S WIFE: Ha – silly boy. Think what that would do to your cholesterol levels!

GIANT: Fetch me beer! Fetch me my flagon of beer!

GIANT'S WIFE: All ready, dear. Here you are!

GIANT: (takes a sip from huge flagon) I want music while I wait! Fetch me my magic harp!

GIANT'S WIFE: Here you are, dear. Not too loud now; think of the neighbours. (Exits)

GIANT: Harp. Harp! Play for me!

Magical music. The giant lowers the light in the lamp, puts his head on the table and goes to sleep. Jack and Jill puppets enter from beanstalk (simple marionettes dressed like actors – worked from behind by a few rods by people in black – the fairy lights dazzle the audience so they are barely seen – honest, it really works!)

JACK: Here – give me your hand.

JILL: I can manage, thank you very much. Where are the other three?

JACK: Miles behind. Wow – look at this pillar.

JILL: That's not a pillar! It's a table leg!

JACK: Crikey. And I can hear music! Listen: it's really lovely. (He sits on the Giant's boot)

JILL: Jack!

JACK: What?

JILL: Look – what – you're – sitting – on!

JACK: It's a boot!

JILL: Jack!

JACK: What?

JILL: It's the giant's boot!

JACK: Yeah?

JILL: Yeah – and the giant's foot is still in it!

JACK: What?
JILL: Look!
JACK: Whoops! The giant!
JILL: I think we should go!
JACK: OK – I just want to see where that music is coming from.
JILL: It's not safe!
JACK: I'll be careful! Come on! (They scramble up onto the seat of the empty chair/stool.)
JILL: He's asleep!
JACK: Look – that harp! That's what's making the music!
He crawls up onto the table.
JILL: Jack! Come back!
JACK: Shh! Just a moment! I think I can …
HARP: Master! Master! Wake up!
JACK: Wo! Talking harp! Cool!
Jill grabs his ankle and Jack runs back. They both hide under the empty chair as the giant
    awakes.
GIANT: What? What is it? What's the noise? Harp – play on!
HARP: But, master, there's a ..
GIANT: Play on I say! Play on, or I'll use you as firewood!
He goes back to sleep.
JILL: Come down – it's not worth the risk!
JACK: I'll be careful! (Climbs onto table)
HARP: Master! Master! Wake up! Wake up!
GIANT: What? What is it now?! I was having a lovely dream – I was on Simply Come
    Dancing/Dancing With the Stars – and I was stamping on all the dancers! Ha ha ha!
HARP: Master, there's a ..
GIANT: No more! Let me sleep! (He goes back to sleep. Repeat business.)
HARP: Master! Master! Wake up!
GIANT: What?! Not again! I warned you, Harp!
HARP: Master, there's an Englishman here!
GIANT: An Englishman!! WHERE?! (He searches for them but does not find them.)
GIANT: (to himself) This is very suspicious – very suspicious. (Louder) I just think I'll pop
    outside for – ah – for a breath of fresh air! (Still looking around exits. SFx: huge door slams.
    The little stage goes black.)

SCENE FIVE : THE GIANT'S TABLE
MAIN STAGE: Same objects as on the mini version: a burning lamp Stage Right, a huge
    tankard Stage Left, salt and pepper, wooden spoon and the magic harp (now with a person
    on it as its voice). The rest of the stage is black. It is dimly lit. Full size actors enter Right.
JACK: Come on – while he's outside!
JILL: This isn't safe – we should go!
HARP: Master! Master!
JACK: Shh! What is your problem?!
HARP: Who are you? What are you doing here?
JACK: Well that's typical – start shouting 'master – master' and THEN ask us who we are!
HARP: Well – you frightened me.
JILL: Yeah – frightened you more than a mile-high giant who's going to use you for firewood.
    Right!
HARP: I've got a very nervous nature.
Fairies arrive.
COWSLIP: This place is needin' a bit of a makeover.
PEASBLOSSOM: Yeah.
JILL: If you can't be quiet then it's **you** who'll have the makeover!
NUTMEG: I'm not sure I really got that one. Just run it past me again.
COWSLIP: She is meanin' - if the giant is catchin' us we will be turned from this shape - into
    this shape.

PEASBLOSSOM: Ooh – I don't think I'd like that.
NUTMEG: No. None of my clothes would fit.
JILL: Shhh!!!
FAIRIES: OoOOooh!
HARP: Any more coming? Is it just you, or are there more idiots on the way up here?
PEASBLOSSOM: No. Just us idiots!
HARP: Lovely. Anyway – now that you're here. I do requests you know!
COWSLIP: A pint of beer would be nice, cheers.
HARP: No – not drinks. I do music!
JACK: That would be lovely. (Jill nudges him) But really – what we're after – is a bag of gold.
PEASBLOSSOM: Or two.
COWSLIP: Or three!
NUTMEG: Or one!
JACK: Yes – does the giant keep any bags of gold about?
HARP: <u>Mountains</u> of gold.
JACK: Great! (General excitement)
HARP: But – a song first, I think.
JACK: We haven't got time to ..
HARP: No song. Right then. MASTER....!
JILL: ALRIGHT! Just one song. But it will have to be a quiet one!
HARP: I know just the thing:
SONG: 'Carefully on tiptoe stealing': HMS PINAFORE.
JILL: Very nice. Now – where - is - the – gold?
HARP: Over there – in that bag. (Points offstage)
JILL: Jack – you come with me. You three! Yes – you. You stay here and keep a sharp look
    out.
NUTMEG: I'm not sure I really got that one. Just run it past me again.
COWSLIP: Keep your eyes peeled.
NUTMEG: Sounds horrid.
JACK: Just stay here and look for trouble.
NUTMEG: What sort of trouble?
JILL: For the giant! Twerp!
NUTMEG: Right - keep a look out for the giant twerp!
JILL: No – just the giant.
NUTMEG: OK. What about the giant twerp?
JILL: Good grief. Look – if you see the giant - make a signal.
NUTMEG: Like this? (Makes series of strange oriental hand signals)
JACK: Very nice.
JILL: No – make a noise – like a bird!
PEASBLOSSOM: I can do that. (makes the noise the first child made in Scene One).
JACK: That's not a bird.
PEASBLOSSOM: It is! It's the emperor penguin! I heard that kid at the beginning say …
JILL: Oh – come on, Jack. We don't have much time. (They exit)
The fairies look around, bored.
COWSLIP: I'm thirsty.
NUTMEG: No, I think it's Wednesday. (They look at him)
COWSLIP: I'm going to find something to drink. (Walks over to flagon & taps on it.) Full! Here –
    give me a hand. (scrambles onto the rim of the flagon.)
PEASBLOSSOM: What can you see?
COWSLIP: It's full up! Not sure what it is! I'll get a taste!
HARP: He'll fall in.
NUTMEG: You be careful – we don't want you to fall in!
COWSLIP: I'm not going to fall in!
HARP: He'll fall in.
PEASBLOSSOM: Be careful! You'll fall in!
COWSLIP: (loud) I'm not going to fall in!

HARP: He'll fall in.

NUTMEG: (grabs big wooden spoon) I know! Here, hold this, it'll stop you falling.. (Knocks C. in tankard. SPLASH)

HARP: Told you.

PEASBLOSSOM: What shall we do? What shall we do?! How can we help her?!

NUTMEG: Well – if I was her right now, I think I'd like … some peanuts … or some crisps… and later a kebab or perhaps an Indian ta….

PEASBLOSSOM: Twerp!

NUTMEG: No. Never had an Indian twerp. Is that like a giant twerp, only smaller?

PEASBLOSSOM: Let's get him out. Come on.

COWSLIP: (Appears wet and singing) Come on in!

PEASBLOSSOM: Hold on! We're coming to rescue you!

COWSLIP: Not bloomin likely! You could bring up some peanuts though!

NUTMEG: See. Told you.

PEASBLOSSOM: You get down here before the others get back!

COWSLIP: Not likely – this is de world's bestest swimming pool. Wheee! **Wheee!**

PEASBLOSSOM: You're not supposed to go 'Wee' in a swimming pool! Snigger (To aud.) But **I** do.

NUTMEG: Oh no! Too late!

Jack & Jill return with 2 large gold coins.

JACK: Look! There's a great pile of them back there, but these are all we could carry!

HARP: Oy! They're not yours! Master! Master! (They gag the harp)

JILL: Now – let's get out of here as quick as … where's the other one?

NUTMEG: Having a 'Whee'.

JILL: I told you all to go before we came! Where? (They point) In there?
(COWSLIP appears soaked and splashing.)

JACK: (tasting) It's beer! Come on everyone! Lets all go for a swi… (Sees Jill, slowly changes tack) go for a swiiiii- swift rescue mission and save the fairy! (gets Cowslip out at 3rd attempt)

JILL: Quick! The giant could be back any…

GIANT: (quiet) FEE FI FO FUM. I SMELL THE BLOOD OF AN ENGLISHMAN.

HARP: Master! Come quick! General alarm.

JACK: Here – you can take these coins! I'll go and get some more!

JILL: No – it's not worth the ….

GIANT: (louder) FEE FI FO FUM. I SMELL THE BLOOD OF AN ENGLISHMAN.

HARP: Master! Get in here now and you can smell Englishman's armpits as well!

JILL: Quick! You three go! Go!

Fairies run off.

Jack returns with coins. He struggle to carry them; centre stage.

HARP: <u>Master!</u>

GIANT: (loudest) FEE FI FO FUM. I SMELL THE BLOOD OF AN ENGLISHMAN.
       BE HE LIVE OR BE HE DEAD- I'LL GRIND HIS BONES TO MAKE MY BREAD!

JILL: Leave them!

JACK: Just take the one!

JILL: It's not worth it! Come on! Hurry!

HARP: Master!

JACK: It's on my foot! I can't..

JILL: Try to wiggle it … oh no!

HARP: Master!

They both freeze and look upstage. Two sets of giant fingertips appear between the black backcloths and slowly pull them apart. Revealed behind is the huge face of the giant, staring down at them.

GIANT: FEE FI FO FUM! HAHAHAHAHAHAHAHAHAH!!!
                    Jack & Jill flee.

CURTAIN
INTERVAL

ACT TWO: SCENE SIX: BACK ON THE FARM, A BIT LATER

SONG: EVERYONE: WE'RE IN THE MONEY: DANCING ANIMALS & MILKMAIDS

VET ENTERS

VET: Money? Did I hear my favourite word? Who's got money?

JILL: Nobody you know!

MOTHER HUBBARD: Jack has! He's LOADED! He's even got enough to set me up in business!

VET: Very interesting. Is this true? Are you ...... 'loaded'?

JACK: Er...

MOTHER HUBBARD: Yes – he's loaded! He's bought me my own business! Something I've always wanted; it's ...

VET: Yes, yes, yes. Thank you, Mother Hubbard; I could listen to you talk for seconds, but 'what's-his-name' and I have things of our own to talk about. Don't we, my little Scrummy-Poohs?

JACK: We do?

VET: Mmmm. We do.

JILL: Like what?

VET: Oh; are you still here? Have you no pigs to clean out today?

JILL: Yes – I am still here, and what have you and Jack got to talk about?

VET: Oooh – oodles of stuff. Like setting a date for our .... wedding.

JILL: What?!

MOTHER HUBBARD: Ooh – it's a dream come true! My only boy – married at last. And to a vet, too! Think of the savings when the animals are ill!

JILL: Wedding?! What wedding?!

VET: Why – I thought you knew. Didn't you tell her, Jed?

JILL: Jack!

JACK: Er ...

VET: Bad boy. I think you're going to need a little – 'discipline' later. Hmmm?

JACK: Ooer.

JILL: Jack Hubbard. You come here right now and tell me you're not seriously thinking of marrying this ... this ... 'person'!

JACK: Well ... er ....

VET: Come on now, James. Don't stand around talking to the - (looks at Jill) - farm workers. I want you to meet my family. They'll be so 'amused' to meet you. They'll want to know all about you, and – exactly how much money you have.

MOTHER HUBBARD: Off you go then, Jack. Meet the in-laws!

VET: Yes indeed. Come on, Jock; keep up now! (Vet & Jack exit)

MOTHER HUBBARD: How very exciting. Jack engaged, and me starting my new business, both on the same day. How wonderful, don't you think, Jill?

JILL: Wonderful. (She walks off miserably)

CHILDREN: Poor Jill.

MOTHER HUBBARD: What?

STREAKY: What do you mean – 'what'? You know she really liked Jack! No wonder she's miserable.

MOTHER HUBBARD: Nonsense. She's just worn out by all the excitement.

CHILD: I think SHE wanted Jack to marry HER!

MOTHER HUBBARD: Jill? Really? Never mind – she'll soon get over it.

STREAKY: Hah! And wait until Jack finds out what you've done with all the money!

MOTHER HUBBARD: Money? Me? I've no idea what you mean!

STREAKY: You know – the gold that you spent on your new business!
MOTHER HUBBARD: There's still some left!
STREAKY: Really? How much?
MOTHER HUBBARD: mumbles....
STREAKY: Sorry – missed that. How much is left?
MOTHER HUBBARD: All right! One gold coin! (holds up normal size coin) But as soon as my business starts making money everything will be OK!
STREAKY: Hah! Wait till he finds out it's all gone!
CHICKEN LITTLE: (enters) Wait till who finds out what's all gone?
ANIMAL: Mother Hubbard has spent all of Jack's money!
CHICKEN LITTLE: Ooer.
MOTHER HUBBARD: Don't make such a fuss. It's not like the sky's falling down or anything.
CHICKEN LITTLE: Not like what?
MOTHER HUBBARD: The sky's falling down or ....
CHICKEN LITTLE: faints
STREAKY: NOW look at what you've done!
CHILD: That chick needs some treatment.
ANIMAL: Some therapy.
MOTHER HUBBARD: I know – but it costs money!
STREAKY: But you've got some money now!
MOTHER HUBBARD: Well – I suppose so. Here you are – our last gold coin. You take Chicken Little to get some treatment.
STREAKY: Right – about time. And she won't be back until she's all better! Come on everyone!
(They all wander off except Daisy)
MOTHER HUBBARD: Just you and me left, Daisy. I'm so glad those Fairies sold you back to me!
Enter fairies wearing painting overalls & caps and carrying a large board.
COWSLIP: Yo! Be a-holdin your end up – don't let it go draggin in da dirt.
MOTHER HUBBARD: What've you fellows got there?
PEASBLOSSOM: It's the sign you asked us to make.
NUTMEG: For your new shop!
MOTHER HUBBARD: My sign! Splendid! (To audience) I've got to tell you all about it. It's something I've always wanted to do. Pay attention now.
Daisy here gives the richest, creamiest milk, and I've always wanted to sell homemade ice cream in a little shop. Isn't that right, Daisy? Yes.
And I've even thought of a perfect name for it. "Daisy's Dairy"! Isn't that good?! Daisy's Dairy. Here – take a look.
She goes across the stage to the rostrum set (Right) and pulls back/down the curtain that has been hiding the dairy. OR a handcart is wheeled on.
PEASBLOSSOM: Daisy's Dairy. Perfect.
MOTHER HUBBARD: I even thought up a sign to go over the shop. Shall I tell you what it says? It says – you'll like this – 'Enjoy Daisy's Dairy - Here Today'. Do you like it? 'Enjoy Daisy's Dairy Here Today'. And these fellows have painted that onto a sign for me, haven't you chaps?
COWSLIP: Indeed we has.
MOTHER HUBBARD: Go on then – let's have a look. They turn the sign round and hold it up.

ENJOY
DAISY'S DIARYHERE
TODAY

MOTHER HUBBARD: What?! WHAT?! I can't have that over my shop?!
PEASBLOSSOM: Eh? Why not?
MOTHER HUBBARD: Why not?! Because it says 'ENJOY DAISY'S DIARRHOEA TODAY'!!
(Daisy panics and runs off madly)
NUTMEG: Is that wrong?
MOTHER HUBBARD: Of course it's wrong! Who on Earth is going to enjoy having diarrhoea?!

PEASBLOSSOM: Well – if you were really bored!

NUTMEG: Yeah, like on holiday in NAME OF BORING PLACE!

MOTHER HUBBARD: Grr! You're not going to spoil my special day. I will stay calm, and serene and ladylike.

COWSLIP: Huh! I is believin' that when I is seein' it!

MOTHER HUBBARD: I will stay calm, and serene and ladylike, and just tell you three that you are THE STUPIDEST, DOPIEST, DAFTEST, MOST MORONIC IDIOTS THAT HAVE EVER WALKED THE PLANET!!

NUTMEG: (Nicely) You remind me of my mum.

PEASBLOSSOM: We don't have to stay here to be insulted!

COWSLIP: No! Us can be insulted ANYWHERE! We is sayin' good day to you, madam. Come, fellow fairies, let us be departin'.

NUTMEG: (closer to Dame) My mum had to shave as well. (He is dragged away)

(They exit)

MOTHER HUBBARD: I will not be upset. This is my special day. I know what'll cheer me up. I'll show you all my new shop!

OPTIONAL: SCENE SEVEN: DAISY'S DAIRY (Rostrum set)
This CAN be simplified using a market-style structure on-stage. Adapt to resources! If you have the resources here is the full scene. If you can just do slapstick then that's fine.

ROSTRUM: There are 2 walls and a waterproof floor. In the back corner is a counter with a rotating arm rising from it. This arm can swing toward either wall of the shop, at above head level. When rotated to Stage Right of the shop its end fits into the 'Ice Cream Collection Funnel'. When rotated to Stage Left it points down at the phone.

On the rear wall is a large clock or timer with a rotating hand (like Countdown).

On the Stage Left wall is an old fashioned wall-mounted phone with earpiece on a wire and mouthpiece fixed to the wall.

There is an identical phone the other side of the stage, fixed where the audience can see it

MOTHER HUBBARD: Isn't it wonderful! And how about this – this is where the ice cream comes straight from the fridge. I'll show you! First I have to set the timer.

(Turns hand of clock to zero and hits a large red button. Clock lights up, ticking starts and hand starts to move OR press a button and hear recorded countdown)

MOTHER HUBBARD: Next I have to make sure this tube is over the bowl. Like – this. Now all I have to do is wait!

(When the clock reaches the top there is a loud 'ding' and ice cream comes out of the tube into the bowl – there is a rude sound).

MOTHER HUBBARD: Ooh! Have to sort that out! Let's have a look. Perfect! Now all I've got to do is wait for my first order. (Picks up 'Goodbye' magazine)

The Fairies appear from Stage Left and go to the other phone.

COWSLIP: Here it is – now we can be havin' us a bit of fun!

NUTMEG: I'm not sure I really got that one. Just run it past me again.

COWSLIP: I is already tellin' you – we is going to pretend we is customers for Mother Hubbard's ice cream shop! (Starts dialling)

NUTMEG: Mother Hubbard? She reminds me of my father.

PEASBLOSSOM: I thought you said she reminded you of your mother.

NUTMEG: Yeah. (Thinks) I never could tell 'em apart.

COWSLIP: Shh! It's ringing! Phone rings.

MOTHER HUBBARD: How exciting! My first customer! Hello – Daisy's Dairy – home of delightful delicacies and delicious dainties, direct from under the cow! How may I be of assistance?

COWSLIP: (in odd voice) Hello – this is Lady Egg from the Manor House. I would like a large vanilla ice cream please. How soon can you have it ready?

MOTHER HUBBARD: A large vanilla ice cream? In about half a minute!

COWSLIP: Perfect. I will be there straight away! (Hangs up and laughs)

MOTHER HUBBARD: (singing) OK. First I set the timer. Right. Next – I put the cone in the cone holder. Now – just wait for the ice cream.

Phone rings again. She answers it.

MOTHER HUBBARD: Another customer! Hello – Daisy's Dairy – home of delightful delicacies and delicious dainties, direct from under the cow! How may I be of assistance?

COWSLIP: This is Lady Egg again. I'm not sure I want vanilla now. Do you have other flavours?

MOTHER HUBBARD: Do we have other flavours? (Laughs) Do we have other flavours! I should say so; I have invented these all myself; listen carefully now - we have: (NB: she can read this off a menu!)

Bottled wine

Chocolate and best plums

Two sprinkle toppings

Baby strawberries and apple pie

Cold pear; vodka on the rocks

And Freshly picked rose petals

While reciting this, the ice cream arm has rotated so that now it is over her head.

COWSLIP: Well – I'm not sure. I'll call you back.

MOTHER HUBBARD: Certainly. (Hangs up) Right. (Looks up: 'Ding!' Gets face full of cream.)

Resets arm. Phone rings

MOTHER HUBBARD: Another customer! Hello – Daisy's Dairy – home of delightful delicacies and delicious dainties, direct from under the cow! How may I be of assistance?

COWSLIP: Lady Egg again. I have made my mind up: I will just have the vanilla after all.

MOTHER HUBBARD: Vanilla. Right away. (Resets arm over new cone)

Phone rings

MOTHER HUBBARD: Hello – Daisy's Dairy – home of dormice and doorbells, straight from moo-cow to you-cow! How may I be of assistance?

COWSLIP: This is Lady Egg again. Sorry to be a nuisance. What were the flavours again?

MOTHER HUBBARD: Flavours again? Certainly, madam.

Bottled wine

Chocolate and best plums

Two sprinkle toppings

Baby strawberries and apple pie

Cold pear; vodka on the rocks

And Freshly picked rose petals

COWSLIP: Well .... they all sound so delicious. It's hard to decide .... I think I'll stick to the plain vanilla.

MOTHER HUBBARD: Certainly. (Hangs up) (Tries to grab tube but too late: 'Ding!' Gets face full of cream.) Seems to be a bit of a design fault here. (Resets it all) OK – one plain vanilla, coming up! (Starts clock again)

Phone rings

MOTHER HUBBARD: Hello – Daisy's Dairy – home of this and that! How may I be a cow?

COWSLIP: This is ...

MOTHER HUBBARD: Flavours again? Certainly, madam. (Very fast)

Bottled wind

Chocolate and pest bums

Two little sprinkles

Baby and apple

Pear and cold rocks

And fresh picked roses.

COWSLIP: Well .... they all ...

MOTHER HUBBARD: Vanilla! YES! (Rushes to get the tube back to the start)

Phone rings

MOTHER HUBBARD: Madman, again? Certainly, flavours. (Very fast)

Bottle of wind

Chocolate bums

Two ladies sprinkles

Baby and apple

Pair of cold rocks

And fresh picked roses.

BUT YOU JUST WANT VANILLA! (Hangs up)

Phone rings

MOTHER HUBBARD: (fast) We do ....

Bottom wind

Chopped bum

Toilet sprinkles

Baby's nappy

Pair of old socks

And fresh nose pickings.

 (But she is too slow and gets another face full)

Phone rings

MOTHER HUBBARD: YES! What d'ya want?!

NUTMEG: Here – let me have a go ...

PEASBLOSSOM: Shh – she'll hear you!

MOTHER HUBBARD: Hmmm...

COWSLIP: This is Lady Egg again. Sorry to be SUCH a nuisance. Perhaps you could just remind me of the flavours just one more time?

MOTHER HUBBARD: Certainly – 'madam'. But I'm afraid we've only got the one flavour left at the moment (she gets a big can of spray cream)

COWSLIP: Really? And what flavour would that be?

MOTHER HUBBARD: **VANILLA!!!!** (She squirts the cream into the mouthpiece. Cream flies out of the other phone and covers the fairies.)

She cleans herself up then looks at the mess.

MOTHER HUBBARD: Look at this place. What a mess! But I have a plan for this! Not only does this arm deliver the ice cream – it is also designed to clean the dairy. If I pull this blue lever – there – a gentle spray of water comes out. (Carefully cleans the mess by the phone) Perfect. Now – turn the water off again. Perfect.

The fairies appear crossing the stage.

MOTHER HUBBARD: Ha – ha! Look at you!

COWSLIP: Yes – you is getting us good and proper. Like. Very amusing. Now we is goin 'ome to get cleaned up.

MOTHER HUBBARD: No hard feelings. Only a bit of fun, after all. You can come in here and get cleaned up.

PEASBLOSSOM: That's very kind.

MOTHER HUBBARD: All you have to do is pull the blue lever, over there, and have a bit of a spray. Look – I'll show you.

NUTMEG goes first. Mother Hubbard pulls the lever for a second and Nutmeg gets a small squirt to wash face & hands.

COWSLIP: That is lookin' easy enough. My turn. Nutmeg – you do the lever. (Nutmeg does lever. Small spray) This is very nice – you can turn it off now.

NUTMEG: I'm not sure I really got that one. Just run it past me again.

COWSLIP: I said – get the blue lever for me now!

NUTMEG: Oh – right. Get the blue lever. (Rips it off the wall and carries it over) Here it is!

Water sprays out over COWSLIP.

COWSLIP: Aarrrr!! Turn it off!

She pushes it aside all over PEASBLOSSOM.

PEASBLOSSOM: Aaarrr! Ooooh! Cold! Cold! Cold!

She pushes it aside all over NUTMEG.

NUTMEG: Aieeee!!

NUTMEG pushes it aside toward Dame, but it stops. They all freeze, dripping, & look up at it. Slowly the arm swings back over their heads. It squirts again. They all scuttle to the side. Slowly the arm follows them. They scuttle back to the other side. Arm follows. Repeat twice. The arm stops overhead. They quake, look up: nothing has happened.

MOTHER HUBBARD: I think it's alright. I think it's out of water.

Massive spray over all of them, continuing wildly and chasing them around Dairy through:

COWSLIP: Aaaarrr!! Stop it someone! Stop it!

MOTHER HUBBARD: Put the lever back on!

NUTMEG: I can't. I CAN'T!!

PEASBLOSSOM: I can't swim!!

COWSLIP: We is all goin to die!!

MOTHER HUBBARD: Put a finger in the hole!

COWSLIP: (Waving arms) I can't – I is usin them all to panic wiv!

PEASBLOSSOM: Look! A cork!

MOTHER HUBBARD: Quick! (She jams cork up end of arm. Water stops)

They all stand and drip.

COWSLIP: I is thankin' you for your kind offer of getting us clean.

NUTMEG: Yeah – I don't think I have ever been so clean before!

PEASBLOSSOM: (thoughtful) Do you think it is safe to have the electric on?

MOTHER HUBBARD: How do you mean|?

PEASBLOSSOM: With all this water – electricity –all together – is it safe?

COWSLIP: Ee is totally right. Water and 'lectricky is not good togever. Someone should turn the 'lectricky off.

They all stare at the big red wall switch

MOTHER HUBBARD: Off you go then.

COWSLIP: Me? Er … me 'ands is wet! Dangerous! It was your idea - you do it PEASBLOSSOM, my 'ands is too wet.

PEASBLOSSOM: Me?! No - my everything is too wet! NUTMEG — you do it!

NUTMEG: I'm not sure I really got one. Just run it past me again.

COWSLIP: Just go and flip that red handle over there.

NUTMEG: OK then.

NUTMEG crosses to switch while others huddle back, but there is a loud buzzing and Nutmeg jumps back. They push Nutmeg forward with encouraging comments. Repeat: push- buzz – jump ; Repeat: push - buzz – jump .

NUTMEG: It keeps buzzing at me!

MOTHER HUBBARD: Oh – for goodness sake – just do it! (She strides forward and yanks lever. SPARKS. Loud sound of electricity and hysterical scream. Blackout.)

SCENE EIGHT: BACK ON THE FARM
Can be a TAB SCENE

VET: (Enters shiftily) Sss. Come on – there's nobody here!

SIMPLE SIMON THE PIE MAN: (He is an appalling character, very ugly, very messily dressed, in a long apron with red and brown stains. He is very dim) Where's all the wotsits?

VET: Wotsits?

SIMON: Yer – you knows – haminals.

VET: Haminals? I'm at a loss ...

SIMON: Blimey – youm a bit thick like, inn yer? You knows – haminals – furry fings wiv ears 'n tails and wot like. What we'm 'ere for!

VET: Oh! Animals! Well – they're usually around. I'm sure they can't be far away.

SIMON: Well I'm opin you'm right – cos I needs all the haminals I can get me 'ands on! I 'as a very 'ungry customer and a lot of empty pies a'waiting!

VET: Don't you worry about that. When I marry Jack and this farm is all mine you can have every single one of the stinky animals!

SIMON: Lovely! (IF you did Scene 7:) And let me tell you one important thing ...(Fairies & dame stagger across stage: They are twitching and gibbering robotically. The vet and Simon watch in confused silence)

SIMON: No - I won't waste one little bit of 'em! Every last bit will be goin' inta Simple Simon's Luxury Pies!

VET: Every bit?

SIMON: Yeah I eat wart-hogs' <u>nose holes</u>, walruses' <u>fat rolls</u>, centipedes' <u>ear 'oles</u>, and even camels' <u>ar</u> ...

VET: Steady!

SIMON: Armpits!

SONG: (to tune of Alouette)

Horses ear-holes, lovely horses ear holes.Donkey's dentures, lovely donkey's teeth. <u>I puts everything in pies.</u><u>I puts everything in pies.</u>All the feet! And the nose!All the fur! And the bones!   O-o-o-o-ohPiglets eyeballs, lovely piglet eyeballs.Chicken giblets. I use everything!

Rabbit-droppings, lovely rabbit droppingsHamster nostrils, lovely hamster snout.<u>Even all the squidjy bits.</u><u>Especially all the squidjy bits.</u>All the joints! And the tongue!And the brain! And the bum!   O-o-o-o-ohChicken feathers, crunchy chicken feathersKitten kidneys. I use everything!

Hairy outsides, lovely hairy outsides.

Slimy insides, lovely wriggly tubes.<u>Even all the dangly bits.</u><u>Especially all the dangly bits.</u>Mince it up! Add some salt!Cook it fast! Sell it cheap!   O-o-o-o-ohPuppy pasties, lovely puppy pastiesKitten ke-babs - <u>I use everything!</u>

SIMON: Here do you want to try a bite?

VET: Perhaps another day? Do people actually BUY your pies?

SIMON: Cor yeah – loads! (Pause) Well – one person, anyway.

VET: One person? Just <u>one</u> person eats <u>all</u> your pies?! Who on earth is it?

SIMON: Er .. can't say. Secret, like. But – let me just say this – it aint necessarily someone 'on earth' (looks skywards) Get me drift?

VET: No – not really.

SIMON: And – let me tell you – they aint had a decent pie in weeks – and they'm getting' mighty hungry! So – to business – where is all me ingredients then?

VET: Look - I told you! Here they come now! (Animals enter.)

IF USING TABS YOU COULD OPEN ONTO MAIN STAGE HERE

SIMON: (Takes vet aside) No! Look – I told you, I needs <u>'animals'</u> – I can't put <u>people</u> in me pies. Well, not officially anyhow; not since I sold the kebab shop. (Sniggers unpleasantly)

VET: Ahah! Look closely. They're not really people – they're animals dressed up! Watch out – here comes that nosey girl!

JILL: (enters) So Chicken Little has gone off to be cured, eh? That's really good news! Let's hope that …Oh, you again!

VET: Mmmm. I can see you're overjoyed.

JILL: (Looks at Simon) And who's this – your grandson?

VET: Very good, almost witty. No this is – ah – this is a friend, another vet. Mr Druff.

SIMON: But you can call me Dan. (Holds out grubby hand but is ignored)

JILL: Dan Druff. How appropriate.

VET: Mr Druff is here just to look at the animals and check they are all healthy.

SIMON: That's right – but I must say they'm a poor lot; they's nuffink but skin and bone! (To vet) It'll take a lot of them to make a decent pi...

VET: Coughs and hits. Perhaps you'd better take a closer look. Run a few tests?

SIMON: Good idea. (Opens pocket in apron) First – you. Yes, you. You hold these – er – test thingies here – like this. (Places two big slices of bread either side of animal's head) Good – that's very good.
And you, you just stand perfectly still – that's it. (Sprinkles salt & pepper. Pig sneezes) Got a cold? Don't worry; you'll be a lot better when you're 'cured' - teehee. Now you....
(Gets out gravy boat and goes to pour it over animal)

JILL: Hey! What kind of tests are these? You're pouring gravy over her!

VET: Oh – suddenly she's medically qualified! I don't think your efforts here are appreciated; off you go. But be back first thing tomorrow morning, Simon!

SIMON: Dan!

VET: That's what I said; off you go, Dan, leave these 'peasants' and their sickly animals!

SIMON: Very nice eating you all.

JILL: Don't you mean 'meeting' us all?

SIMON: Maybe, maybe. (Exits, chuckling)

JILL: Something very odd going on here.

MOTHER HUBBARD: (enters) Ooh – it's Jack's fiancée! Perhaps she's here about the wedding arrangements?!

VET: Ah – Mrs Cupboard.

JILL: Hubbard.

MOTHER HUBBARD: No – Cupboard's fine, dear.

VET: Whatever. I've brought you the details for the wedding (unrolls huge list) – and the list of wedding presents (Unrolls another). It looks like a lot – that's because it is. But you can afford it – with all those gold coins 'thingy' got from the Giant.

MOTHER HUBBARD: (nervous laugh. Reads list.) Right.... champagne; orchestra; fireworks; gold coach for bride, gold coaches for bridesmaids, er .. What's this say?.... Westminster Abbey?

VET: For the wedding service.

MOTHER HUBBARD: Robbie Williams & Elton John?

VET: For the party.

MOTHER HUBBARD: Two pairs of handcuffs, a rubber chicken and a large jar of peanut butter?

VET: For the honeymoon.

MOTHER HUBBARD: Oh my – it does seem rather a...

VET: Is there a problem? I don't have to marry – what's-his-name - you know!

JILL: Jack.

VET: Whatever.

MOTHER HUBBARD: (nervous laugh again) No! No problem at all!

VET: Good: then I will leave you to whatever it is that peasants do. Farewell. (Exits)

MOTHER HUBBARD: Oh my – what shall we do?

JILL: We could hit her with a shovel.

MOTHER HUBBARD: Now concentrate! The last gold coin went on getting Chicken Little cured! What can I do?

STREAKY: I've got it! All you have to do is get Jack back up the beanstalk to get more gold coins!

JILL: Oh no! You can't! I thought it was a good idea once, but in fact it's much too dangerous. And it'll be night time soon!

MOTHER HUBBARD: Of course! Gold coins! Yes! That's it! Now – where is he?

JILL: But it's not safe...

MOTHER HUBBARD: Jack! JACK!! Cooee!! Mumsy wants a little word with you!!

JACK: (Enters) Helloo! What's all the fuss?

MOTHER HUBBARD: Ah – come closer, my special little feller. My word – you look a bit ill!

JACK: I do?

MOTHER HUBBARD: My word yes. I think you need some exercise and fresh air!

JACK: I'm fine! (Tries to walk way but she is holding him back)

MOTHER HUBBARD: Look – you can hardly walk! And listen to your breathing! You're all wheezy!

JACK: I do?

MOTHER HUBBARD: Listen! Put this on! (Puts stethoscope on him)

JACK: Sounds fine to me ... (she makes strange noises into it) – Aargh!

MOTHER HUBBARD: My word – you'd better listen to your heart!

JACK: Ah – well at least that sounds to be .... (Clothes peg on it) – Oh no! It's stopped!

MOTHER HUBBARD: It's worse than we thought! No time to lose! Quick! Get some exercise!

JACK: But..! (Starts him running on spot)

MOTHER HUBBARD: I know!

JACK: What?!

MOTHER HUBBARD: Exercise and fresh air!

JACK: How?

MOTHER HUBBARD: Up the beanstalk!

JACK: Up the beanstalk?

MOTHER HUBBARD: Up the beanstalk!

JACK: Up the beanstalk!!

JILL: Duh – are you so stupid that you're going to fall for that old trick?

JACK: Duh – obviously! (Is led – jogging - toward beanstalk – now possibly offstage)

CHILD: (To Jill) But you can't let him go up there again!

JILL: And why not? If he's so stupid that..

CHILD 2: But it's so dangerous up there!

JILL: Huh – what do I care? (Looks cross then suddenly changes mind) Jack!

JACK: Mmm?

JILL: If you have any trouble....

JACK: What?

JILL: If you have any trouble. Just shout and.....

JACK: What?

JILL: If you have any trouble. Just shout and..... I'll come and help!

JACK: Trouble?

MOTHER HUBBARD: He won't have any trouble. Come on now! And of course – while you're up there – get some exercise – I know – carry some of those big round heavy things!

JACK: Gold coins?! (Dame nods) Right! Byee! (Is jogged off stage – all others except Jill follow)

JILL: This is awful. I shouldn't have let him go. What shall I do? Perhaps I should go and stop him? No – he'll be alright. (Thinks) No he won't! Oh dear! What to do? What do you think? Shall I go and stop him? What? Do you think I should go after Jack and stop him climbing up the beanstalk again? ... Right – then that settles it! I'm going to stop him! Wish me luck!

VET: (Enters in front of her) Luck? It'll take more than luck.

JILL: Let me get past! I've got to stop Jack!

VET: Jack? He's none of your business now, 'farm-girl'. He's mine!

JILL: Oh no he isn't! And he never will be!

VET: Really. And what – exactly – are you going to do to stop me?

JILL: Well first I'll stop him going up the beanstalk to get more gold coins!

VET: More gold coins? For me? How lovely. I definitely don't think I can let you do that.
JILL: Ha! And how are you going to stop me?!
VET: Easy. I'll just give you the sack.
Simon the Pie Man enters behind Jill carrying a sack.
JILL: Give me the sack? How can you do that? I don't even work for you!
VET: (Leans closer and smiles nastily) Wrong sort of sack.
Simon the Pie Man puts big sack over Jill.
SIMON: Cor – she'd make a lovely steak and kidney pi...
VET: My good man – have you no sense of decency?
SIMON: (thinks briefly) No.
VET: Just lock her in the pigsty. We can't hang around. We'll have the wedding tonight and
    then, first thing tomorrow morning, the animals will be yours. You will have more pies than
    you ever dreamed of! (Laugh at audience)
They exit quickly Left
Enter fairies from Right.
PEASBLOSSOM: Everything seems to be working out alright this time.
COWSLIP: Perhaps we 'as got something right at last.
NUTMEG: It's a bit quiet round here.
COWSLIP: Never mind. We 'as uvver jobs to do. What is next on da list?
PEASBLOSSOM: (Checks sheet) Er .. it's from a B. B. Wolf.
COWSLIP: Sounds like a rapper. And what special magic is we doin' for this Mr Wolf?
PEASBLOSSOM: Couple of things. He seems to have lost the keys to all of his cottages and
    wants us to let him in.
COWSLIP: 'All' of 'is cottages?
PEASBLOSSOM: Yeah – it seems some old granny is hiding in bed in one of them – and some
    pigs is using the land for a D.I.Y. eco-project! Building houses out of recycled bricks, twigs,
    organic straw...
COWSLIP: Probably designed by dat Prince Charles.
PEASBLOSSOM: Right. Soon we'll have Mr Wolf back in his cottages!
NUTMEG: (Looks round) It is a bit quiet round here.
COWSLIP: It is a bit! Let's be askin' dis lot what is a-goin' on. Oy! Bros! Where is Jack and Jill?
    What? It is no good – I is not makin' out what they is saying. One at a time now! You two –
    go down and find one person who can come up here and tell us where Jack and Jill are. Off
    you go. We need just ONE small person to come up here and tell us what has been going
    on!
They return with child of the correct size.
COWSLIP: Hello. What is your name? ___ I is pleased to meet you. Is you enjoying da show?
    Now then. Do you know where Jack is? ____
NUTMEG: I'm not sure I really got that one. Just run it past me again. Where's Jack? ____
COWSLIP: Gone up da beanstalk?! And where is Jill? 'as Jill been an gone wiv im? ____
NUTMEG: Oh no! We must save them!
PEASBLOSSOM: (To child.) What do you think? Should we go and save Jack and Jill?
COWSLIP: Right. That's agreed then. Peasblossom, Nutmeg, you come with me and we'll go
    and rescue Jack. You – do you want to help us save Jack and Jill? Right then. You go into
    the pigsty and rescue Jill.
PEASBLOSSOM: Woah! Pigsty! Not in those clothes! Here! Put these on.
(Child puts on very bright overalls and hat)
COWSLIP: Right – we is gonna climb up da beanstalk, fight da giant....
PEASBLOSSOM: Woah – I'm not sure I really got that one. Just run it past me again.
NUTMEG: Here – I says that!
COWSLIP: I is sayin - we is gonna climb up da beanstalk, **fight da giant**.... Ah – slight change
    of plan here. (Takes child aside). My friends and I have thought this through, and we think it
    might be better if we go and rescue Jill from the pigsty ...
PEASBLOSSOM: ...and you go up the beanstalk and rescue Jack. Is that alright with you?
    Jolly good. (Arm appears from wings with long sheet of paper and quill) What's that?
COWSLIP: (reads it) Ah – right. (To child) Is you here wiv a grown up today? (To grown up.

NUTMEG runs into audience to get it signed.) You need to put your mark on dis – it is sayin', basically dat if dis child is ground up to make the giant's bread, ...

PEASBLOSSOM: ...or is eaten by da giant in any form of pie, roast, casserole, pasty, curry, or uvver dish, ...

COWSLIP: ... it isn't not, like, de fault of NAME Drama Club, de THEATRE Management, or AREA Council. OK?

PEASBLOSSOM: That's it. To the rescue! (To child) You have to say that bit too. "To the rescue!" Brilliant! Byee!

(All exit. The child is escorted to a microphone – possibly at back of hall?)

SCENE NINE: THE GIANT'S KITCHEN (same again: with lights on)

GIANT: FEE FI FO FUM; I SMELL THE BLOOD OF AN ENGLISHMAN!

GIANT'S WIFE: No you don't, dear.

GIANT: FEE FI FO FUM; I SMELL THE BLOOD OF AN ENGLISHMAN!!

GIANT'S WIFE: No you don't, dear.

GIANT: FEE FI FO ... (Sees her shaking her head) Well what can I smell then?

GIANT'S WIFE: It's the new perfume you gave me for Christmas.

GIANT: Perfume? I didn't give you any perfume!

GIANT'S WIFE: Don't try and pretend, you big softie. It was the first time you've ever given me anything really nice.

GIANT: I gave you that lovely necklace for your birthday!

GIANT'S WIFE: Made of sheep skulls. Same as last year.

GIANT: Last year it was made of goat skulls.

GIANT'S WIFE: Anyway – the perfume was really lovely. I've worn it every day since and loads of people have commented on it! And in such an unusual bottle too! It didn't even matter that you hadn't wrapped it up.

GIANT: Hadn't wrapped it up? (Suspiciously) What did you find this – er - bottle of "perfume"?

GIANT'S WIFE: Where you left it. On the little shelf in the bathroom. Here! (Holds up big ornate bottle)

GIANT: You silly woman – that isn't perfume! That's the sample of pee I had to take to the doctor!

GIANT'S WIFE: Oh. (Looks at bottle) Well – it's still lovely. (Dabs more on)

GIANT: You stinky old woman. Fetch me my food!

GIANT'S WIFE: Food? There isn't any food.

GIANT: NO FOOD!!

GIANT'S WIFE: No – nothing at all. But I phoned Simon the Pieman, and he says he's expecting new supplies tomorrow morning.

GIANT: I can't wait until tomorrow!

GIANT'S WIFE: I could do you a nice toasted cheese sandwich?

GIANT: No!

GIANT'S WIFE: You could always have another one of these. (Holds up giant bean) There are loads of them on that beanstalk!

GIANT: No more beans! You know what happened last time!

GIANT'S WIFE: Hurricane/Cyclone (topical name).

GIANT: Graah! I'm going out! I'll see you later!

GIANT'S WIFE: Kiss?

GIANT: Huh. (Gives her kiss on cheek) Hmm. It is rather nice that perfume!

(Exits) Giant's wife tidies table. She has a nibble at the giant bean, then exits to string of genteel farting sounds. She giggles at each one. Puppet Jack appears up the beanstalk.

JACK: Nobody here. Good. Next – bag of gold! (He climbs up onto the table.) Here they are! How many can I carry? (Return of farting sound) What's that noise? I'd better hide. (Rushes about but is too slow)

GIANT'S WIFE: Aaargh! A mouse!

JACK: I am NOT a mouse! I am an Englishman!

GIANT'S WIFE: Oooh! An Englishman, eh? And do you have any bones?

JACK: Of <u>course</u> I have bones! Why?

GIANT'S WIFE: No reason. Are you allergic to onions, garlic or parsley?

JACK: Don't think so.

GIANT'S WIFE: Good. In you go then. (Puts him into big pot and puts lid on)

JACK: (echoing) Let me out!

GIANT'S WIFE: Now – what can I use for gravy? (Thinks) I know! (Lifts lid and pours 'perfume' in)

JACK: Urgh! What was that?

GIANT'S WIFE: Perfume. Just off to get the onions! (Exits)

JACK: Bleugh – that perfume smells like something the cat did. It must be that new one by CELEBRITY. Hello? Hello? Hey! Let me out! (Pushes lid off but can't climb out) Oh no! It's too slippery. What shall I do? I know – I'll call for Jill. Jill! Jill!

GIANT'S WIFE: (Returns) You're a noisy little casserole, I must say. Here are the onions. Now to pick some parsley for your stuffing! (Exits)

JACK: Stuffing! Oh dear! JILL!! Why aren't you here?

SONG: ENDLESS NIGHT (LION KING) first half

Child puppet appears and climbs onto table.

JACK: Hey. Who are you?

CHILD: My name is _____.

JACK: Hello, _____. What are you doing here in the Giant's castle?

CHILD: I'm here to help you get out!

JACK: Great! Come over here and hold onto my hands. That's it. (Farting sounds) Look out! The giant's wife is coming back!

CHILD: What shall I do?

JACK: Do what I usually do – scream and run around!

CHILD: OK. Yells loudly. Hides.

GIANT'S WIFE: Here's the parsley. Now – what was the other thing?

JACK: Garlic.

GIANT'S WIFE: So it was! Right then. (Exits)

JACK: Quick, _____, try again! That's it. Hold tight! Heave! (Pops out of pot) Super – you've saved me, _____, now lets get out of here! Look! Gold coins! Grab one!

GIANT'S WIFE: Here's the gaAARGH! Two mice!!

CHILD: I'm not a mouse! My name is _____. Pleased to meet you.

JACK: Not now, _____. RUN!!!!

The giant returns

GIANT: FEE FI FO FUM! I CAN SEE <u>TWO</u> ENGLISHMEN!!!

Chase. They escape down the beanstalk.

GIANT'S WIFE: Get them! That's your tea running away!

GIANT: Get them – but how?

GIANT'S WIFE: Climb down the beanstalk after them!

GIANT: But.. it's not safe!

GIANT'S WIFE: They've taken your gold coins!

GIANT: Graah! Here I come!

Blackout.

SCENE TEN: BACK ON THE FARM: EVENING

All animals on stage plus Mother Hubbard. Jack and Child come running on.
BOTTOM, OF BEANSTALK ON STAGE

MOTHER HUBBARD: Jack! Who's this?!

JACK: This is _____. He/She rescued me from the giant! Not like Jill – she didn't even turn up to help! I want to say thank you very much for saving me from the giant, and to give you some of the gold coins as a little present. (bag of chocolate coins) Mr Streaky - you can just take _____ back to his/her seat. Everyone give _____ a huge clap for being so brave.

GIANT: GRAHHHH!!!!! **General panic.**

MOTHER HUBBARD: It's the giant. It's the giant! (Looks around) I can't see him – where is he? All pause.

JACK: (points up) **There! Coming down the beanstalk!**

MOTHER HUBBARD: **We're all going to die! We're all going to die!** General panic.

Fairies return with Jill – looking very disgusting. All pause.

JACK: Where've you been?!

JILL: Me? Where have I been? I've been in the – hang on, what's going on? (They all point upwards) General panic. Don't just stand there! Do something!

JACK: Me? What?

JILL: (rushes to wings & returns with big axe) What do you think?

JACK: Don't know!

GIANT: GRAHHHH!!!!!

JACK: What shall I do? (To audience) You tell me! What should I do?

GIANT: GRAHHHH!!!!!

JACK: What? I can't hear!

GIANT: GRAHHHH!!!!!

JACK: Louder! I can't hear! ... Chop down the beanstalk?

(Chops down beanstalk) Sound of falling beanstalk.

ALL: Hooray! Well done, Jack! Etc

STREAKY: (looking up) Hang on a minute – what's that up there – in the sky – getting bigger and bigger?

They all peer up.

ANIMAL: Is it a bird?

STREAKY: No – it's got arms and legs.

MOTHER HUBBARD: I know! It's just the giant falling out of the sky!

ALL: general amusement and relief.

MOTHER HUBBARD: **We're all going to die! We're all going to die!** General panic. They look up and all rush Left. They look up again and all rush Right.

CHICKEN LITTLE: (enters Left with small suitcase. ALL FREEZE.) Hello everybody! It's me! Chicken Little! I'm back – and - I'm all cured!

MOTHER HUBBARD: What?!

CHICKEN LITTLE: I said – I'm all cured! I don't think the sky is going to fall on me any more! (Looks around) I say – what <u>are</u> you all doing? (Mother Hubbard points upwards) What? (Looks up) AaaAAaaaaaRgh! I told you! (Hysterical) <u>I TOLD YOU</u>! The sky's falling! The sky's falling!

They all look up. Terrible panic as before.

Dark shadow passes.

Earth-shaking crash.

Bottom of huge boot appears at edge of stage.

JILL: Is everyone alright? (Helps people up off ground)

MOTHER HUBBARD: It looks like it.

JACK: That was close!

MOTHER HUBBARD: Oh no! Look! Someone was squished under the giant!

JILL: Who? Who was it?

MOTHER HUBBARD: Don't know. All that's left is his hat. (Produces Simple Simon's hat) It says – Simple Simon the Pieman.

VET: (Has entered at other side in black suit) What? (To audience) The pie man has been squished?! <u>Now</u> what will I do with all these animals? I know ... when I run this farm I shall start my <u>own</u> pie company! (To Jack) Oh! I see you've more gold coins, Jim.

JILL: Jack.

VET: Whatever. (To Jill) Hmm, I must say you're looking lovely today.

JILL: Hmm – I must say you're looking – here, why <u>are</u> you dressed up like that?

VET: Oh dear – didn't you get an invite? Why, tonight is our wedding; isn't it Jack!

JACK: It is?

VET: It is! In about two minutes! Come on, Geoff. Let's <u>try</u> to make you look decent. (Exits with Jack)

Fairies, Jill & Mr Streaky walk forwards as **TABS CLOSE.**

SCENE ELEVEN: THE FARM – COMMUNITY SONG
TABS / curtain

PEASBLOSSOM: Another wedding! I do love a happy ending. Come on, fairies, let's get ready! (As they leave they notice Jill)

COWSLIP: Now what? We is rescuin' you from da pigsty, what more is you wantin?

STREAKY: I think she wanted to marry Jack.

PEASBLOSSOM: Like – that's going to happen! Ha! This is real life – not some lovely-dovey, happy-ever-after panto!

COWSLIP: I knows what is cheerin' you up! We is at least goin' to make you look nice for the party!

JILL: I don't think I really want to go to the party.

NUTMEG: You're right. When I don't get what I want I go into the woods and put my head in a bucket of jelly. That shows people! Ha!

COWSLIP: Dopey here is making a good point, like.

JILL: I'm not putting my head in ..

PEASBLOSSOM: No. If you hide they'll think you're sulking. Go to the wedding and show you're not bothered!

JILL: Hmm. Maybe. But – dressed like this?

PEASBLOSSOM: I reckon we could knock up a decent frock.

JILL: We haven't got time! It'll take...

COWSLIP: Ten seconds! (Maybe 5?)

JILL: Don't be daft – look at me!

COWSLIP: Trust me! Ten seconds! These people can help me count!

JILL: I don't think...

COWSLIP: We don't have time for thinking! Get in there! (Pushes her behind screen or into wings.)

JILL: Now what?

PEASBLOSSOM: Ten-second countdown. EVERYBODY!! TEN!! NINE!! Etc

Jill reappears in BLACK gown.

JILL: That is super! Right – now to do something with this face. See you in two ticks! (exits)

COWSLIP: Two ticks. If she is anyfin like mY girlfriend she is meaning two hours!

PEASBLOSSOM: What shall we do now?

NUTMEG: I can show you my jumping song.

COWSLIP: What 'jumping song'?

NUTMEG: I'll show you. (Strides into space) Ready?
   Oh – Old MacDonald had a JUMP (jumps) Ee-aye-ee-aye-oooooooooh!
   And on that farm he had a JUMP! (jumps) Ee-aye-ee-aye-oooooooooh!

COWSLIP: That is madness. That is not being even the right song, like.
BUSINESS WITH KIDS. COMMUNITY SONG.

SCENE TWELVE: THE FARM AT NIGHT
Curtains open to show Jill in beautiful BLACK gown, with smart hair and clean face. There are small lights scattered about. All company are present (not Simon)
The fairies take Jill to one side. Formal line-up.

JACK: Another story has been told,

VET: And I have got my bags of gold.

NUTMEG: It didn't go just how we planned

COWSLIP: But our brave Jack has saved the land.

PEASBLOSSOM: The giant's gone; no big surprise.

VET: (to aud) And soon they'll all be tasty pies!
FINALE SONG music starts
Jill runs off the stage, down the hall. Everything stops gracelessly.

VET: Ha! That's it: <u>run away</u>! Good! Because if you <u>stay</u> here – I'll throw you back in the pigsty and lock you in again! (Mimics) "Ooh, let me out – I must go and save Jack". Ha-ha! And if you <u>ever</u> show your ugly mug back here again - I'll have <u>you</u> in a meat pie with all these <u>other</u> animals! Ha! That's it – run! Hah-ha-hah... What? What are <u>you</u> all staring at?
JACK: So Jill <u>was</u> coming to save me!
STREAKY: You're going to make us into – <u>meat pies</u>?!
VET: Oh – get over it! Where were we? (Carries on with song.) All together now!
The others look at her in horror and move to the sides.
There is a sudden roar from Jill who runs down the hall (or from wings) with the pail of water, up onto the stage and throws it over the Vet. Moment of stunned silence then everyone cheers.
VET: Oh! Oh! Arrr! (She turns and stamps away while others jeer)
JACK: Crikey. I think I've done something a bit silly.
JILL: Right, well – as the wedding seems to have been cancelled, I'm off.
JACK: No. Stay!
JILL: No? Just give me <u>one</u> reason why not.
JACK: I think the wedding should carry on!
JILL: But: hell-o! The bride has gone!
JACK: No she hasn't – I'm looking straight at her.
JILL: Me?! And give me <u>one</u> reason why I should marry <u>you</u>!
SONG: JACK: something like YOU RAISE ME UP
JILL: (interrupts) Stop! I am <u>not</u> going to marry you…!
JACK: OK – I understand; I've been really stupid.
JILL: True. I am <u>not</u> going to marry you…!
JACK: That's fair enough. I'm sure you can do better than me!
JILL: For goodness sake – let me finish! I am <u>not</u> going to marry you …wearing black!
JACK: You mean..?
JILL: Of course. (To fairies) Here. Do something useful. How about a bit of <u>real</u> magic?! Does that wand of yours actually work?
NUTMEG: Well – sort of, but it needs lots of help.(To audience) I need you all to help. Will you do that? Will you? Great – I want everyone to count "5, 4, 3, 2, 1 - NOW!" (LIGHTS DIM)
FAIRIES: Are you ready? Here we go! 5, 4, 3, 2, 1 - NOW!" (THUNDERFLASH)
They quickly turn together and part to reveal Jill in sparkling white gown with lights.
JILL: That's better. Now – what were you saying?

SONG: JACK: something like YOU RAISE ME UP
Mix of solos duets and chorus**Big hugs. Blackout.**
Walk down to reprise: OUR HOUSE?
Children, Animals,
Princess, Streaky & Chicken Little,
Vet & Simon,
Fairies,
Dame,
Jack & Jill.
Orchestra bow.
Main stage dims & Mini stage lights up for GIANTS' & PUPPETEERS' bows.
ENCORE IN DAWN LIGHTING.
SUN RISES BEHIND SHOE HOUSE.

Something like "Endless Night"?

LIST OF TITLES

Click to select

1. <u>CINDERELLA</u>
2. <u>ROBIN HOOD</u>
3. <u>DICK WHITTINGTON</u>
4. <u>SLEEPING BEAUTY</u>
5. <u>RED RIDING HOOD & THE 3 PIGS</u>
6. <u>THREE MEN IN A TUB</u>
7. <u>JACK AND THE BEANSTALK</u>
8. <u>HANSEL AND GRETEL</u>
9. <u>SNOW WHITE & 7 DWARVES</u>

CONTACT INFORMATION
and PERFORMANCE RIGHTS here:

<u>PANTOSCRIPTS.ME.UK</u>

Hansel and Gretel
© Chris Lane 2018
Originally performed by Axminster Drama Club 2002

ACT ONE SCENE ONE
Front of magnificent Hotel Western (Cloth or cut-out)
Tripod camera stands to the side.

CAMERAMAN: Shake a leg you guys! This is only an ad for some hotel in the middle of Germany! It aint Gone With The Wind! (**All** appear and form lines)

CLAPPERBOY: Western Hotel - TAKE ONE!

CAMERAMAN: Right! Lights! Music! Action!

CHORUS NUMBER: (Possibly: Go West -Village People)

CAMERAMAN: That's a wrap! Strike the scenery! (Cloth/cut-out off) Get your costumes back to wardrobe! (All exit except for Herr Inmeizoop & Gretah)

SCENE TWO
Lobby of a very run-down German hotel. Stage Left: reception desk with secret panels in front. Main door DR. Upstage: centre: stairs up to rooms; left centre boiler room door. Kitchen door UL. Someone is sat reading a paper.

Herr Inmeizoop: (grey-haired German with mild accent) Sssplediden! Das iss just der zing zat vill bring inn ze tooooriztz! Soon ze name of der Hotel Vestern will be ont zer lips offf peoples all over ze vorrrrrld!

Gretah Chewitt: (orange mop of hair, red cheeks & glasses, bright clothes. Very dim) Ooh, Her Inmeizoop - I think I like the old name better.

Herr Inmeizoop: Nonsense, Gretah! Nobody can remember the long name: Hotel Vestenpantzen-socksen! Hotel Vesten is much snappier!

Gretah Chewitt: Oooh, Herr Inmiezoop, I hope so! The last tourist we had here was...... Ooooh .... It must have been that nice old gentleman from Sniffencoffen!

Herr Inmeizoop: Zat scoundrel! He nefer paid hisss bill!

Gretah Chewitt: Oooh, well - he **was** dead.

Herr Inmeizoop: Zat is no excuse!

Gretah Chewitt: Oooh... But it **was** your fault.

Herr Inmeizoop: **MY** FAULT! Mein goot voman - it vas not I who killed him - it vas you! Vit your terrible **cooking**!

Gretah Chewitt: Oooh, Herr Inmeizoop - how can you say that? You put him in the East Wing! You know very well he died of fright. It was **the ghost**!

Herr Inmeizoop: Be qviet, voman! (Looks around) You know what walls have!

Gretah Chewitt: Ooh - yah! Ice cream! (or, if not sold where you live, change it to 'wallpaper' or similar)

Herr Inmeizoop: Not Valls ice cream! Valls haf EARS! Now listen to me! Ze East Ving isss <u>not</u> haunted! Zer are no ghosts in zis hotel! (To aud) You goot people! You can see! Is there a ghost in zis hotel?! (The ghost – maybe headless? - puts down newspaper, gets out of chair, wanders around a bit and exits) Oh no zer isn't! (etc) Pah! I vill not haf zis talk! Zer iss no ghost! Now - (lights dim) iffen you had said zat there vasss a terrible, vicked, ugly vitch who liffed in ze forest!

Gretah Chewitt: Oooh... a witch!?

Herr Inmeizoop: Yah - a vitch mit ze long nose - unt ze green skin - who lives in ze darkest depths of ze forest - and who catches little children - and turns zem into gingerbread! (Flash & thunder; lights back up) Nein - ve shall not talk of zeze thinks - zis talk iss vot sent all ze tourists avay in ze first place! Now get back to your kitchen, you saggenbaggen-mitder-grossenrumpenbotzen!

Gretah Chewitt: Oooh! I don't think I have ever been so insulted!

Herr Inmeizoop: Ha! You should get out more! So - vy are you sstill sstadnink here viz zat face like der back of der tram?

Gretah Chewitt: Oooh - don't know really. Ooh yes! I have **two** messages for you.

Herr Inmeizoop: Vell?

Gretah Chewitt: First - the sewer is blocked so none of the toilets can be used. OK then? (Turns to go)

Herr Inmeizoop: Vait! Vot is der SECONT vun?!

Gretah Chewitt: Oooh? Second one what?

Herr Inmeizoop: Der secont MESSAGE, you stroodlekopf!

Gretah Chewitt: Ooh arr.... ooh - I know! Second - there is no heating in any of the rooms - because there is a gas leak - and the hotel could explode at any moment.

Herr Inmeizoop: Pah! I know zat! You told me about ze gas last veek!

Gretah Chewitt: Ooh - did I?

Herr Inmeizoop: Yah – unt I haff it under **total** control!

Gretah Chewitt: Oooh! Have you?

Herr Inmeizoop: Yes. I haf put ze advertisement in ze vindow of ze post office - it says 'Vanted! Somevun who knows about gas leaks!'

Lady Aigz: (appears at top of stairs) Herr Inmeizoop! Herr Inmeizoop!!

Herr Inmeizoop: Ach no! Lady Aigs – our only guest! (Turns to her) Vot is it, my dear Lady Aigz?!

Lady Aigz: It is my poor cat - Mr Snookums! He is not in his basket and it is nearly time for his manicure! I insist that you find him!

Herr Inmeizoop: My good Lady Aigz - ve haf not seen Mr 'Snookums'!

Lady Aigz: I shall be VERY cross if I find that you have put him in the freezer again!

Herr Inmeizoop: Ve haf not seen your fluffy little pink pussycat.... not since yesterday ven ze armoured police brought him home!

Lady Aigz: Very well - but if you see the poor little creature do tell him his mumsy-wumsy is looking for him! (Exits)

Lotta Bottle: (enters excitedly DR) Herr Inmeizoop! Herr Inmeizoop!

Herr Inmeizoop: Vat is it Lotta? Haf you found a boyfriend at last?

Lotta Bottle: No, Herr Inmeizoop.

Herr Inmeizoop: I tell you - you should try ze blind school! Give zeir dog a biscuit and you vill haf a friend for life!

Lotta Bottle: Her Inmeizoop – you are always taking my leg and pulling the mickey! No - it is your grandchildren! Hansel and Gretel!

Herr Inmeizoop: (happy & excited) Vat - zey are here at last?!

Lotta Bottle: Yes - I have just seen them walking up the track! As bold as daylight and in broad brass!

Herr Inmeizoop: Quick! Quick! Get zem in off ze track before they are seen by the vi....

Gretah Chewitt: Oooh! By the witch?!

Lotta Bottle: A witch?! Don't tell me YOU believe that! It's a load of old tale and nothing but an old wife's cobblers! (Exits to get children)

Herr Inmeizoop: Nein - nein - laughs - of course not.

Lotta Bottle: (Lotta + H & G enter with small bags)

Herr Inmeizoop: Come in children! Come in! Velcome back to the Hotel Vestenpantzensocksen! (Hugs)

Hansel: Thank you, grandfather.

Gretal: It's lovely to see you again, grandfather!

Herr Inmeizoop: You remember our cook, Fraulein Chewitt.

Hansel: Of course. How are you, Fraulein Chewitt?

Gretah Chewitt: Ooh - oy don't know!

Herr Inmeizoop: Unt ze chambermaid, Lotta Bottle?

Gretal: Hello Lotta. How are you putting up with these two?

Lotta Bottle: Drive me round the planks – theyre both as daft as two short bends! Did you have a nice journey?

Herr Inmeizoop: Pah - talk of these things later! Let us get you into your room!

Hansel: And can we play with the other children in the village later?

Sudden silence and funny looks.

Herr Inmeizoop: (trying to be jolly again) Ve shall see! Lotta - vich rrrroom shall ve put zem in?

Lotta Bottle: There's only one guest - Lady Aigz - in the West Wing.

Gretal: Does she still have that awful pink cat?

Lotta Bottle: Mr Snookems? I'm afraid she does.

Gretah Chewitt: Oooh.... the East Wing is empty!

Herr Inmeizoop: Are you totally mad, voman?! You cannot put zem in zer met der gho.... der gho.... gho.... (Looks around)

Gretah Chewitt: Ooh. The goldfish in the bed?

Herr Inmeizoop: No! You know! The gho - gho -

Gretah Chewitt: Oooh. The go-faster-stripes on the toilet?

Herr Inmeizoop: No! Shhh! You children can come upstairs and sleep int ze North Ving! Off you go!

Gretah and children exit up stairs

Hans 1: (enters DR with Hans 2 & Hans 3) Excuse me - my jolly landlord!

Herr Inmeizoop: Vot?

Hans 1: You put this advertisement in post-office window I believe? (Reads card) 'Lonely hearts: One-eyed goblin with wooden leg wishes to meet similar, with view to marriage'

Hans 2: (snatches it back) Not that one! Have you got it, Hans?

Hans 3: (reads a card) 'Embarrassing itching - cured by acupuncture - in the comfort of your own home, by former British Darts Champion'?

Hans 2: (snatches it back) Not that one! Hans?

Hans 1: (next one: bright red & tassles) 'Naughty Nanny Natasha offers....' (Tries to snatch it back but Herr Inmeizoop snatches it and puts it in pocket)

Hans 3: You wanted expert gas engineers!

Herr Inmeizoop: Yah!

Hans 1: Well - we are your men! We are the Twitzen Twins.

Lotta Bottle: Twins?

Hans 2: I know - identical!

Hans 3: Nobody can tell us apart!

Hans 1: I am Hans Twitzen, and this is Hans, and this is - Hans. (They bow)

Lotta Bottle: Hans, Hans and Hans. Your mother was a simple woman, was she?

Hans 2: It was our father who brought us up.

Hans 3: Sadly - we never knew our mother.

Hans 1: She left before we were born.

Lotta Bottle: How sad.

Herr Inmeizoop: But now - you men must find ze leaking gas pipe unt mend it!

Hans 1: Certainly sir! Where is this gas leak?

Herr Inmeizoop: If I knew zat vy vould I haf to pay YOU?! Unt also - der sewer is now blocked as vell - if you will unbung it vile you are here? Come - Lotta - let us prepare lunch! (They exit to kitchen UL)

Hans 1: (pompous) Don't you worry, Sir! Rely on the Twitzen Twins! To work! Let us look around for the gas leak.

Hans 3: (not too bright) And the blocked sewer!

Hans 2: (very enthusiastic) We shall use our noses!

Hans 3: There's a man-hole over 'ere! .... It's got them **things** on it!

Hans 1: What things would that be, Hans?

Hans 3: You know - **them** things.

Hans 2: He's right. It's got **them things** on it.

Hans 1: So it has. It's those .... what-do-you-call-ems.

Hans 3: .... Words?

Hans 1: That's it! Words! Stand aside. I shall read out the letters for you!

Hans 2: Showin' off yer educations again, Hans!

Hans 1: S - E - W - E – R (much thinking)

Hans 3: ....GAS!!

Hans 1: Well done! Just waiting to see which of you got it first!

Hans 2: Let's open 'er up and have a look!

They lift the hatch and stick their heads down. They come up looking really ill.

Hans 3: What sort of gas do they have up here?

Hans 2: I dunno - but I wouldn't want to cook on it.

Hans 1: I don't think this IS the gas. I think someone unable to read has put the wrong label on it and that - in fact - in my opinion - this is .... the SEWER! Check it out with another inspection.

Hans 2: I think you're right!

Hans 3: These people - (shakes head) they don't have enough roughage.

Hans 1: Well, brother Hans (2)! Down you go then! Find that blockage!

Hans 2: Great! Right you are! (Gets snorkel out of bag/pocket, puts it on, grabs a child's beach-spade and slithers down into sewer. Splashing)

Hans 1: Hans?! Are you alright?!

Hans 2: (echoing voice) A bit dark down here. (Big splash - up into their faces)

Hans 3: Are you still alive, Hans?

Hans 2: Never better, Hans! (Sound of echoing splashing and topical singing.)

They replace cover and look about.

Hans 3: What was the other thing?

Hans 1: Gas leak! Come on! Let's follow our noses again.

Lady Aigz: Enters on landing. Mr Snookems! Coochie coo! Mr Snookems? I say! You men! Have you seen Mr Snookems?

Hans 2: What?

Lady Aigz: (tersely) I said - **have you seen Mr Snookums**?!

Hans 1: Mr Snookems? (To brother) Hans - have you seen anyone?

Hans 3: No. I haven't seen anyone at all! (Louder) What does he look like?

Lady Aigz: You can't mistake him: he is pale pink.

Hans 1: Well that's not much to go on. We're all pale pink, are we not, my good woman! Hans - even you're pale pink!

Hans 3: I am?

Hans 1: The bits you wash - aren't they pale pink?

Hans 3: Can't properly remember - been so long now.

Hans 1: Give us another clue - what was he wearing?

Lady Aigz: Wearing? Why - nothing of course!

Hans 3: Nothing?! Ooh!

Lady Aigz: Nothing except a small, diamond covered chain around his neck.

Hans 1: Have you seen anyone round here like that, Hans? Pale pink and wearing nothing but a small chain round his neck.

Hans 3: Hmmm **......** there's Old Dan in the village of course - he likes that sort of thing - airing his differences as it were. But he don't have no chain round his neck; though I did hear last Halloween he tied a pumpkin to the end of his...

Lady Aigz: Bah!! You are both perfect examples of rampant lunacy!!

Hans 1: Why, thank you kindly, Madam. (Bows)

Hans 3: Very nice of you to say so. Come on, Hans. Let's look for the gas leak in here. (Exit into Boiler Room).

Lady Aigz:(To audience) I say - you 'peasant folk'. Have you seen a pink cat anywhere? Don't mumble - speak up for goodness sake. **Have you seen my cat?!** What? No? Oh drat. Where **can** he be? I don't know why I stay in this place! I do have my own property, you know. A lovely little cottage in the country.

Phil de'Pottie: (enters rapidly DR carrying cases) Quick! **Customers**! I've found some **customers**!!

Lady Aigz: My dear Mr Whatever-you're-called, do I look like somebody who cares?

Phil de'Pottie: They just arrived at the station! They were asking for the 'Hotel Happy Rest' so I said I'd show them the way!

Lady Aigz: This certainly is **NOT** the 'Hotel Happy Rest'! Far from it!

Phil de'Pottie: Well - I didn't exactly say that it **WAS** the Hotel Happy Rest.... but we do need some customers!

Herr Inmeizoop: (appears UL followed by Lotta. H & G also appear) Cuzzzztomers!! My dear nephew - where did you find cuzztomers?! Vere are they?!

Phil de'Pottie: Look - they think this is a **different hotel**! They'll never find out - and it won't do any harm!

Herr Inmeizoop: A different hotel? But vich hotel do they think**....**?

Phil de'Pottie: Shh! Here they are!

Trifle Family ENTER and look around confusedly.

Mr Trifle: (very English: very prim & bossy) Oh, I say! What a rush!

Mrs Trifle: That hill **was** rather steep! Someone should do something about that!

For goodness sake, just remember to breathe, George. George!

Mr Trifle: Yes dear?

Mrs Trifle: Breathe, George!

Mr Trifle: Right dear; breathing dear.

Mrs Trifle: And – George.

Mr Trifle: Yes dear?

Mrs Trifle: Don't trail your new coat in the **dirt** in here.

Mr Trifle: Sorry dear. New coat being picked up, dear.

Mrs Trifle: (Looks around) I say! It's not like in the brochure!

Cherie Trifle: (To Phil; she is very 'Public School') Golly! I don't know about you folks, but I really don't think that name outside is German for 'HAPPY REST'!

Phil de'Pottie: (to Cherie) You speak German?

Cherie Trifle: Mmm. A little.

Phil de'Pottie: How clever of you.

Lotta Bottle: I speak German too!

Phil de'Pottie: But you ARE German, Lotta.

Lotta Bottle: Hmm. (Glares at Cherie)

Herr Inmeizoop: Welcome dear people! Velcomen to the Hotel....... Hotel ... er.... Vot vas it?

Phil de'Pottie: (stage whisper) Happy Rest!

Herr Inmeizoop: Vot?

Phil de'Pottie: Doh! (Starts to act out name - smiles happily)

Herr Inmeizoop: (trying hard to guess) Hotel False Teeth!

Mr Trifle: Hotel False Teeth?!

Herr Inmeizoop: No? Err - Hotel Loony? Hotel Completely Bonkers! No? .... Cheerful? Happy? Yes!! Yes!! Welcome to the Hotel Happy ...... er......

Mrs Trifle: Don't you know the name of your own hotel?

Herr Inmeizoop: Of course - it is the Hotel Happy.... Happy....

Phil de'Pottie: (crouches as if sitting and points behind him)

Herr Inmeizoop: Right! Of course! Velcomen to the Hotel 'Happy Bottom'!

Mr Trifle: Hotel Happy Bottom?!

Phil de'Pottie: No! (Crouches lower and smiles, as if resting)

Herr Inmeizoop: Ah! The Hotel 'Happy Visit To The Toilet'!!

Mrs Trifle: George, I don't think I want to stay at a Hotel called the Hotel 'Happy Visit To The Toilet'. I mean - what would we put on the postcards?

Lotta Bottle: Welcome to the Hotel HAPPY REST!

Herr Inmeizoop: Yah! Velcome!

Mrs Trifle: George - where is your Mother?

Mr Trifle: Oh lor - I thought she was with us!

Lotta Bottle: Is this her?

Granny Trifle: (enters dancing and scattering petals) Ah - the Black Forest of Germany! Wild flowers, bubbling mountain streams, gateau, cuckoo clocks, - what romance! What freedom! Are you the manager? Do you have a cuckoo clock? I was promised you would have a cuckoo clock!

Herr Inmeizoop: Er – not vun cockoo clock!

Granny Trifle: Then how can you tell the time? This is disgraceful! How can this be the Black Forest if there is no cuckoo clock? It's like being in Italy and not having

spaghetti! Or France and not having frogs' legs! Or Belgium and not having a....
what do they have in Belgium? Never mind - the point is this! I insist on a cuckoo
clock. It must cook on the quarter hours and oo on the half hours and cuckoo on
the full hours. Am I quite clear? CUCKOO! Don't you love that sound? CUCKOO!
CUCKOO! (Exits dancing up stairs, cuckooing and laughing)

Mrs Trifle: She's HIS mother!

Mr Trifle: Perhaps I was adopted.

Mrs Trifle: Don't be silly, George. Who'd want you?

Herr Inmeizoop: Well - now zat ve are all here, let me introduce you - this is Lady
Aigz - one of our valued residents! Lotta Bottle - our chambermaid. And you have
met my nephew from France, Phil de'Pottie.

Cherie Trifle: Phil de'Pottie? I suppose you're a CHAMBER maid?

Phil de'Pottie: Ah – one of your famous English jokes! .... I don't get it.

Mrs Trifle: Is this a QUIET hotel? We really want somewhere quiet. You see -
(takes them aside) Mr Trifle suffers from .... his nerves.

Herr Inmeizoop: Hizz nerfs?

Mrs Trifle: Yes.... he needs total peace and calm! (Confidentially) He's on
medication!

Herr Inmeizoop: Vas is dis 'metrication'?

Mrs Trifle: Look - you've seen his mother. On his side of the family, she's the
normal one. (Louder) Anyway - it seems quiet enough here.

Phil de'Pottie: I can assure you this place is so quiet you won't be disturbed by
anything!

Hans 2: (rises from sewer and blows water out of snorkel)

Mr Trifle: Aargh!

Mrs Trifle: What in the name of Heaven is THAT?!

Hans 2: (goes back down)

Herr Inmeizoop: That is just Hans!

Hans 1: (enters from boiler room) I've found the gas leak.

Herr Inmeizoop: Well done, Hans!

Mr Trifle: Hans? But....? (Stares at sewer in confusion)

Hans 3: (appears from boiler room) Good news!

Herr Inmeizoop: Vot iss zat, Hans?

Mr Trifle: Hans??!! Ooooo.........

Hans 3: You're lucky this place hasn't been blown clear off the mountain! Ha-Ha!

Mr Trifle: OooooOOoooOOOO.......... (Starts to twitch)

Mrs Trifle: Have one of your tablets, George. (Pops it into his mouth & he calms)

Mr Trifle: Tablet taken dear.

Hans 1: Hans - are you still down there?

Hans 2: Yes! I am still down here in the sewer!

Hans 1: Have you found out why none of the toilets will work?

Mr Trifle: None of the toilets work?! OoooOOOooooo (receives another tablet)

Hans 2: Yes – I think I've found the blockage!

Hans 1: So why are you still down there?

Hans 2: (pops up eating sandwich) I've been having my lunch! (All cringe)

Hans 1: That is awful! .... While we are up here **working**....!

Hans 2: Hang on!

Hans 1: What?

Hans 2: I've dropped my pickled onion. (Bends down into hole to pick it up) Here it is! (All cringe again - but more) (Hans licks pickled onion) (All cringe again - but even more) No - that's not it. (Gasps of horror from all) (Picks up new object) This is it! (Goes to eat it)

Hans 3: Hans! How could you?! Are you not civilised?!!

Hans 2: (stops, thinks, looks at onion) You're right, Hans. What am I thinking of. You have it! (Pops it into Hans' mouth.) Much screaming, fainting, tablets, etc.

Hans 1: Now, you finish up in there, then come and help mend this gas leak! And give me your torch - its dark in there!

Hans 2: I do not have my torch (proud grin) but I have these matches!!

Hans 3: Perfect! (Hans 1 & 3 go back into boiler room rattling matches)

Mrs Trifle: You said this was a QUIET hotel!

Herr Inmeizoop: And so it iz - my good lady! Ah – can this be MORE guests?

Bandleader: (This could as easily be 'The Von Something Family Singers' if you have many children, though with a local name.) (Enters DR wearing coat over uniform) Hello - have you got a family room for a couple of nights?

Herr Inmeizoop: Yes - yes - we haf a LOVELY family room!

Bandleader: Brill! Come in guys! (Others enter - all with coats over uniforms/instruments) I can't tell you how relieved we are! Aren't we chaps! (They agree) We must have tried a dozen hotels round here but **not one** said they had room for us!

Lady Aigz: You have an awfully large family!

Bandleader: Well - we're not just an ordinary family.

Lotta Bottle: Then what are you?

Bandleader: We are the Von (local name) Family Equal Opportunity Marching Band/Singers

Cherie Trifle: Equal Opportunity?

Bandleader: Indeed - and proud of it! Everyone is treated the same - no matter who you are! Show them, lads! (Take off coats to show that they are ALL wearing vivid majorettes skirts, even the boys & men.)

Loud and appalling music and even worse marching, with very dangerous baton twirling. GrannyTrifle appears and joins in with loud cuckoo noises & marching.

Herr Inmeizoop: Shtoppen! Shtoppen!

Granny Trifle: Cuckoo! Cuckoo!

Herr Inmeizoop: Sshhtop!!

Granny Trifle: CUCKOOooooooo ooo oo. ....

Bandleader: Hang on - wait for Klaus to do his twirl! You'll like this! Klaus throws the largest baton in the world!

Klaus has gigantic gold & red baton. Dramatic twirl then up into the air. Terrible crash; dust & plaster rains onto them. All look up, no baton. The Trifles attempt to leave but are blocked.

Herr Inmeizoop: So - mein guests! I can guarantee it vill be VERY qviet from now on! Allow me to proudly velcome you all to......

Hans 2: Look! (Pops out of sewer) I've found the blockage! **It's a cat**!! (Holds up very bedraggled pink cat)

Lady Aigz: Terrible blood-curdling scream. **Mr Snookums!!!!**

Mr Trifle: Aaargh!!! .... What ......?!

Lady Aigz: What have you people done to him?! (Goes to take him but recoils at smell) Here - you - give me that! (Takes new coat from arm of Mr Trifle)

Mr Trifle: My new coat!

Lady Aigz: Poor Snooky-wookums! (Wraps cat in coat)

Mr Trifle: My new coat!!

Herr Inmeizoop: Goot - a happy ending!! So - mein guests! Velcome to......

PYRO. Explosion. Boiler Room door flies off and falls flat. Smoke from doorway. Hans 3 appears. Face is black, clothes blown to shreds. Hair is on end. He staggers aside. Hans 1 appears wearing the remains of trousers legs about his ankles, large burnt pants and top half of a burnt string vest. He is also rather black.

Herr Inmeizoop: Velcome to the Hotel...

Phil de'Pottie / Lotta Bottle: Happy Rest!

The band strikes up a rousing march.

Mrs Trifle: Grabs bottle of tablets and empties them down her throat while using other hand to stop MrTrifle running away. BLACKOUT. ALL EXIT

SCENE THREE
same set: LOBBY AT MIDNIGHT

Dramatic, evil music. Slowly, one by one, ugly goblins appear from holes in the reception desk, down the stairs, etc etc. With crouched and evil movements they hiss and cackle and giggle until they are all gathered wickedly in one ghastly green light centre stage.

Goblin 1: The weather's been nice again.

Goblin 2: Very nice.

Goblin 3: You're right, can't complain about the weather.

Goblin 4: Bringing the flowers on lovely it is.

Goblin 5: Forecast is good for the rest of the week too!

Goblin 6: That's nice.

Goblin 7: Nice for people on holiday. I always think.

ALL: Yes**.......**

Unseen the witch appears – a very evil, menacing character

Goblin 1: Going anywhere for your holiday this year?

Goblin 2: Not really. Staying at home. Do a bit of decorating.

Goblin 3: That's nice.

Goblin 4: I've just done my sitting room - Misty Pink the colour is.

Goblin 5: I like that. Or magnolia.

Goblin 6: You can't beat magnolia.

Goblin 7: Peach is nice, too. My spare room is peach.

ALL: Lovely.

During all this the witch has (unseen) crept up right behind them.

Witch: (rising dramatically. Lightening & thunder) HAAAAA!!!!! (The goblins throw themselves to the ground at her feet and grovel) You are supposed to be GOBLINS!! You are supposed to be demons from the darkest depths of the underworld, sent to the surface to torment mankind!! And what are you doing?! TALKING ABOUT … DECORATING!!!

Goblin 1: Forgive us, oh mistress of foul smells!

Goblin 2: Do not be angry with us, oh really rather ugly one!

Witch: It is bad enough that I have to hide here **in disguise** - in this foul hotel -

away from my beloved gingerbread house in the forest - but I have the most useless helpers in the history of wickedness! For badness sake - do something nasty!

Goblin 7: Certainly oh stinking one! You breath is like the rear of a camel and your armpits like the scrapings from the bottom of a fishpond!

Witch: Flatterer! Giggles Anyway - you are lucky that tonight I am in a good mood. (Sneers) Tonight is a special night!

Goblin 3; (to G4) It's not tonight you're on (name of TV show like Weakest Link)?

Goblin 4: No - that's next week.

Goblin 5: Are you excited?

Goblin 4: Mmm - a bit!

Witch: Be silent! Tonight I can smell............. CHILDREN!! (Flash & crash)

Goblin 6: Children?! Where?!

Witch: Somewhere - **in this very building** - there are ....CHILDREN! And I am going to **catch them** - turn them into **GINGERBREAD and EAT THEM**!! HAHAHAHAHAH!!! (Starts to search)

Goblin 1: What about down **there,** (to audience) oh wicked one?

Goblin 2: I think I can see some **children** down there.

Witch: Yes - I think there may be one or two......

Goblin 3: You wait until the matinee!

OR   You should have been here this afternoon!

OR (if it IS the matinee) One or two hundred!

Menacing advance on audience.

Cherie Trifle: (offstage) Yes – I can hear it too! I'll go and see if anyone is downstairs!

Witch: Quick! Hide! (Witch behind desk, goblins onto stage extension R or off)

Cherie Trifle: Nobody here! I'll get you a drink myself! (Comes down stairs) Now - where is the kitchen? (Exit into kitchen) Hellooo?

Gretel: (offstage) Hansel! Wait for me!

Hansel: (enters at top of stairs) Come on, Gretel. I'm hungry!

Gretel: But Grandfather told us to stay in our room until daylight!

Hansel: I've got some chocolate in my bag. (Finds bag on chair) Let's have a look.

Gretel: Anything?

Hansel: Just the wrapper. Someone has eaten it! Burp from Goblin 1. And I'm still hungry.

Witch: There are wild strawberries growing in the forest.

Hansel: How do you know that?

Gretel: What?

Hansel: That there are wild strawberries in the forest.

Gretel: Are there?

Hansel: Girls! Let's see if there's anything left in here.

While they look in the bag the Witch tries to creep up behind them but retreats when a floorboard creaks or if there is shouting!

Gretal: What was that? Did you hear something?

Hansel: This place is full of noises. Repeat action.

Gretal: Hansel! I heard it again!

Hansel: Hang on - I think there are toffees in the side pocket! Repeat action.

This time she is about to grab them when Hansel finds the toffees. With a cry of delight he throws the bag over his shoulder and hits the witch, who shrieks.

Hansel: I heard it that time!

They slowly turn and the witch circles to stay behind them. She rises to grab them but Cherie appears from the kitchen with a glass of water. Witch dives off into wings.

Cherie Trifle: Oh hello there! Just getting a little drinky for mumsy!

Phil de'Pottie: (on stairs) What is all the noise down here? Oh - it's you!

Cherie Trifle: Just getting a drink for mumsy!

Phil de'Pottie: Water. Yummy.

Gretal: Come on Hansel - let's have a look in the kitchen.

Hansel: Goodnight!

Phil de'Pottie: Bonne soir! (H & G exit UL)

Cherie Trifle: So - you work here do you?

Phil de'Pottie: Just for the Summer - then back home - to Paris.

Cherie Trifle: Paris! Golly-gosh! How jolly romantic!

Phil de'Pottie: And you - where are you from? London? (Or other capital city)

Cherie Trifle: Almost – LOCAL TOWN.

Phil de'Pottie: Is that near London? (Or other capital city)

Cherie Trifle: Pretty close actually! (To audience if it's not close) Shhhh!

Phil de'Pottie: Is LOCAL TOWN the home of romance and .... love?

Cherie Trifle: Oh - well - sort of. Actually ...... it's the home of SOMETHING SUITABLY BORING

Witch: (to audience) Bah! I can't stand listening to any more of this drivel! I'll scare them away! (Creeps up to the couple and tries to scare them but they just look into each other's eyes.) OK - that's it - into gingerbread for you two!

Granny Trifle: (appears in nightgown & cap) Cuckoo!! Cuckoo!! Midnight! Cuckoo!

Witch curses and hides again.

Cherie Trifle: Granny - get back to bed! Stop that noise!

Granny Trifle: I can't! It's midnight, dear! Nine more to go! Cuckoo! Etc

Lotta Bottle: (enters DL) Is there a bird in here? Oh - I can see two **LOVE**birds! (Walks up to Philip) So –THIS is what goes on under my back, the minute I turn my nose!

Cherie Trifle: I'm sorry - this is my fault. I must take mother her drink. Come on, Gran.

Granny Trifle: Now I've lost count - I shall just have to start again. Cuckoo etc. (exits)

Phil de'Pottie: I wasn't doing anything!

Lotta Bottle: I'll find out what's been going on here – I'll get to the **nose** of this – and in the meantime you keep your **bottom** clean! (They exit)

 Hansel & Gretel reappear from kitchen.

Gretel: Nothing! Now what?

Hansel: Wild strawberries. There are some growing not far off!

Gretel: What - in the dark forest?

Hansel: Don't be a sissy - it's a full moon tonight. It won't be dark!

Gretel: Well - I **am** hungry.

Hansel: And we'll pick enough for Grandfather's breakfast! He'll be so surprised!

Gretel: I'm still not sure.

Hansel: (to audience) What do you think? Shall Gretel and I go into the dark, evil forest all alone tonight to pick strawberries? What? Shall we go?

Gretel: What did they say?

Hansel: Didn't you hear? They were shouting - GO! GO! Thanks! See you!

They exit. The witch cackles evilly then follows them off.

Herr Inmeizoop: (enters at top of stairs) All zis shouting! So much noise! (To audience) Please! Not wiz the shouting so much! You vill wake ze Trifles! Now - I am looking for Hansel and Gretel - zey are not in zeir room. (To aud) Are zey down here? Are zey in the kitchen? So vere **ARE** zey zen? Vere? VERE?? ZE FOREST?! (Look of horror) No - not ZE FOREST! Ach! Gottensihimmel! ZE FOREST!! (Runs out of door) HANSEL!! GRETEL!!

BLACKOUT

If time is needed add: GOBLIN SONG, possibly: Blue Moon

SCENE FOUR
THE DARK FOREST
FRONT CLOTH/GAUZE: On stage: large, black rock; witch is next to it, curled in ball, facing away from audience - very still!

Hansel: (Enters DR.) I'm sure this is the way. (He takes a stone from his pocket and places it carefully on the ground.)

Gretel: I see what you're doing!

Hansel: What then?

Gretel: You're leaving a trail of stones so we can find our way back!

Hansel: Clever, eh?

Gretel: But how will you know which stones are which? There are loads of stones all over the place!

Hansel: Look - these are all **white** stones - I picked them up outside the hotel.

Gretel: You are just too clever.

Hansel: You said it! Look! Over here! Strawberries!

They run level with the witch and start to pick and eat strawberries.

Gretel: Delicious!

Hansel: Mmmmm!

Gretel: Can we go back now? It's a bit cold out here.

Hansel: Just a few more.

The witch slowly rises behind them and turns to loom over them.

Gretel: Urgh – this one's mouldy! (Throws over shoulder into witch's face)

Hansel: They're all a bit manky! (Same business) Let's look over there! They exit SL

Herr Inmeizoop: (offstage) Hansel! HANSEL!! (Enters SR. Witch curls up again) They haf come zis vay - zere are more of ze vite stones from ze hotel. He is a smart boy zis Hansel - but ven I find him I vill take my slipper to his bumbenbotzen!

Phil de'Pottie: (enters DR) Her Inmeizoop!

Herr Inmeizoop: Philip! What....?

Phil de'Pottie: I saw you leave the hotel - in your nightclothes! Something's wrong!

Herr Inmeizoop: Ze children! Hansel und Gretel - are out here somevere!

Phil de'Pottie: In the forest!

Herr Inmeizoop: Ya!

Phil de'Pottie: Oh no!

Herr Inmeizoop: The stones go zis vay! Quickly! (They exit DL)

Witch: Drat and double drat! These meddlers will – ooo! (Curls up again)

Cherie Trifle: (enters DR) I know I saw that rather nice boy - Phillip - run out into the forest! There must be a bit of a problem! Oh my - I hope it isn't serious! Golly gosh!

Phil de'Pottie: (reappears, listening) What does that mean – Golly gosh? How very English!

Cherie Trifle: Thanks! And you're French, are you? You don't SOUND French.

Phil de'Pottie: My dad is – zat is why I haf ze French name - Phillippe Francois Louis de'Pottie.

Cherie Trifle: So - you're called....... Phil de'Pottie. Giggles

Phil de'Pottie: Yes – what's funny about that?

Cherie Trifle: You're not related to the rap singer - M.T. de'Pottie? Giggles

Phil de'Pottie: I don't think so. Why are you still giggling at my name?

Cherie Trifle: I think it's a lovely name.

Phil de'Pottie: I think Cherie Trifle is a lovely name. But - we can't stay here: I'm following my uncle! Come on! This way!

Cherie Trifle: An adventure! How jolly! (Both exit SL)

Witch: This place is getting so busy that -

Lotta Bottle: (enters SR) I saw that girl running after **my Phillip**! That girl is under her mind if she thinks she's going to steal him from out of my nose! Oooh! (Exits DL)

Witch: I don't believe these people! Whose forest do they think this is?! Oh no!

Granny Trifle: Toowit-toowoo! (Enters DR) Toowit-toowoo! Toowit-toowoo! Whooooo! Whoooooo! Where are you, my beloved feathered friends of the night?! Speak to me! Toowit-toowoo! Toowit-toowoo!! Nothing! Silence! Why do my little friends of the starry sky not talk to me? I must sit, alone - in the moonlight - and be sad. (She sits on real rock.) OOOOh – that's bloomin' cold! (Sits on witch.) That's much better! Towoo – towooo!

Witch: Owoooo!

Granny Trifle: Toowoo-toowoo!

Witch: Owoooo!

Granny Trifle: At last! They speak to me! Toowoo! Toowoo!

Witch: Owoooo!

Granny Trifle: (excited) Again! Speak little owlies! Toowoo-toowoo!

Witch: Owoooo!

Granny Trifle: Oh – If only I could understand what you are trying to say to me! If only you could **talk** to me! I beg you - speak to me NOW!

Mrs Trifle: (standing DR) What on Earth are you doing here in the forest?!

Granny Trifle: Yes! That's it - little birdies - I can understand you! Speak to me! Speak to me!!

Mrs Trifle: Why are you out here in the cold?

Granny Trifle: Birdies - I am out here to find you! Oh joy - oh rapture - to at last speak to my little, feathered friends! Talk on, oh beaky ones – reveal to me some great and wonderful and magical secret of nature!

Mrs Trifle: You'll get piles if you sit on cold rocks!

Granny Trifle: Oh! Is that it? Never mind! Speak on, my little twittering cousins!

What else?

Mrs Trifle: You get back to hotel at once - you dopey old bat!

Granny Trifle: Well - that's not very polite for a little birdy!

Mrs Trifle: When you've got a sore bottom in the morning, don't say I didn't warn you!

Granny Trifle: Very well - but I shall never forget this magic moment. Farewell little birdies - farewell!! (Exits DL)

Mrs Trifle: Oh no – now where has she gone? Come back, you silly old coot! (Exits DL)

Witch: That's it. My bones aren't up to this. (To audience) Look - I'm going back to the hotel for a bath. I'm too tired for all this - if you want to boo that's fine! (Exits DR)

Hansel & Gretel enter DL

Gretel: Here's another stone! Soon be back now!

Hansel: And look at all these strawberries! Grandfather will be so pleased!

Herr Inmeizoop: (enters DL) Oh no he von't! Vat are you doink out here? I haf looked eferyvere!

Hansel: But look at these strawberries!

Herr Inmeizoop: Don't you know zat in zis forest lives a vicked, ugly, spiteful old...

Mrs Trifle: (enters DL) My word - is everyone out here?

Gretel: What were you saying, Grandfather?

Herr Inmeizoop: (looks nervously at Mrs T) Nothing, children. These voods are perfectly safe!

Phil de'Pottie: (enters DL) There they are!

Cherie Trifle:(enters DL) I say – is this a party game?

Lotta Bottle: (enters DL) Here you all are! And WHAT is going on?!

Mrs Trifle: I don't know about you - but I find these woods rather CREEPY!
(All look round nervously)

Herr Inmeizoop: (not really convinced) Nonsense! Zere is nothing here to be......
Terrible evil laughter. All flee off stage in panic

Granny Trifle: (enter DL laughing madly) Oh I say - I seem to have sat on an ants' nest! (Terrible screams and laughing. Exits SR) BLACKOUT

Or you could have the GOBLIN SONG here

SCENE FIVE
THE HOTEL DINING ROOM
There is an open window UL. A table with a large cloth runs across the edge of the stage DR, touching the flat. A low bench or box runs across the stage DL, with an old cloth over it. There is a stepladder, rolls of odd wallpaper and on the table buckets of paste/water. There is a compressor near the bench and rolls of tubing. One roll of paper has already been applied, very badly, to the wall, DL. There is the clear shape of a cat pasted beneath it. Hans 3 is busy up the ladder, fixing the sagging, creased top of the wallpaper with a staple gun. Hans 2 is mixing paste in a bucket on table so audience can see it is real.

Hans 3: There - finished!

Hans 2: Hans - you are a perfectionist! (Takes bucket of paste across and places at bottom of ladder)

Hans 3: I like to think so. Right - next roll! (Jumps down ladder but puts feet either side of bucket)

Hans 2: Look at the lovely colours on this roll! Don't you think it will look wonderful!

Hans 1: (enters DR carrying more paper) Right then you two! Let's show we can do a good job and get this finished today! (Looks at the hanging paper) Is it straight at the top?

Hans 2: Let me see! (Runs up ladder) Yeah - perfect! (Jumps down & again misses bucket)

Hans 1: Hmm - I'm not so sure. Stand aside - let **ME** have a look! (Climbs ladder, adjusts paper, jumps down - one foot in bucket)

Hans 3: Oooh - Hans: you shouldn't have done that!

Hans 2: No - Hans; I don't think I'd have done that.

Hans 1: (slowly removes foot and lets paste drip off) Aah – I meant to do that. Just to test it. Yes – perfect – well-mixed, you two!

Hans 2: We've mixed plenty of paste! (Gets bucket 2 – just water)

Hans 3: Right - next roll!

He tries to paste roll of paper but it keeps rolling up. Three attempts.

Hans 2: Let me try! (Repeat)

Hans 1: No-no-no! You two! Look, let me show you! All you have to do is get someone to hold it down!

He stretches across table, lying flat to hold both ends. The other Hanses start to paste (only water) at his finger tips, work up his arms and meet at his face. He stands and wipes paste off.

Hans 3: Oooh - Hans: you shouldn't have done that!

Hans 2: No - Hans; I don't think I'd have done that.

Hans 1: Stand aside! (He goes to hold one end of the roll. Hans 2 pastes and slaps brush up into Hans 1's face.) No! (Changes ends) Let HANS do the pasting! (Repeat, other way round)

Hand 3 & 2 cower as he wipes face. He gets two paste brushes, dunks them slowly wipes them up the others from chest to forehead

Hans 1: Now get on with it!

Hans 3: Do you think there is enough paste on the paper now, Hans?

Hans 2: I think so, Hans.

Hans 3 picks up paper, carries in front of him toward ladder, lays paper on steps of ladder and walks up it, wrecking it. At the top he is surprised to see only a tiny piece left in his hand.

Hans 3: Did you measure this properly, Hans? I think it might be a bit short.

Mrs Trifle: (enters DR) Come along, George. You must have something to eat before your next tablet.

Mr Trifle: But I'm not really very hungry, dear.

Mrs Trifle: Nonsense. I have ordered you a large bowl of very thin, vegetable soup. Now sit here. (He sits) Oh - I say. What IS going on in here?

Hans 1: Don't you mind us, madam. I assure you we will be as quiet as little mices!

Lotta Bottle: (enters DL) Here is your soup, Sir.

Mr Trifle: Thank you. (The soup is placed before him, next to a paste bucket)

Lotta Bottle: Is the soup all right, sir?

Mr Trifle: Lovely – thank you. Are these locally grown vegetables?

Lotta Bottle: Yes, sir – one of every sort goes into it! The cook puts in a carrot and an onion and a potato! But the special flavour comes from her having a leek in the pot! (He looks into the soup in horror) Will there be anything else?

Mrs Trifle: I will have a full, **English** breakfast please! (Lotta exits DL) Do you think she knows what that means, George - I don't want any of that flaky bread and hot chocolate nonsense! I'd better go and make sure. (Exits after Lotta)

While they are away, Hans 2 dips his paste brush in the soup, & looks down at his mistake in horror! George Trifle is reading paper.

Hans 2: What's the matter, Hans?

Hans 3: The soup - I put the glue brush in the SOUP!

They look in horror as Mr T spoons up his wooden soup. This horror grows, as Mr T is unable to remove the spoon from his mouth.

Hans 1: What's going on?

Hans 2: Hans put wallpaper glue in the soup - now he's stuck!

Hans 1: Let me deal with this. (He holds spoon and tries to pull it out. He puts one hand to Mr T's forehead and tries again; then he puts a foot on his chest. No luck. Hans 3 goes round the back and holds Mr T's ears, Hans 2 pulls on the waist of Hans 1. No luck.)

Hans 1: Look out! (Mrs T returns DL. Quickly they put a dustsheet over Mr T's head.

Mrs Trifle: Hello? Where has Mr Trifle gone?

Hans 1: He just left! Something about **...** er...

Hans 2: His pants were on fire!

Hans 1: What? That's right - his pants had caught fire! Smoke everywhere!

Mrs Trifle: His pants were on fire! My word!! (She exits rapidly DR)

Lotta Bottle: (enters DL) Here we are - full English breakfast! (Exits)

Hans 1: Smashing!

Hans 2: Lovely. (They eat it, forgetting about Mr T under the cloth)

Lady Aigz: (enters DR) Mr Snookums! Cooee! Coochecoo! (Sound of distant cat) Mumsy can hear you! Where are you hiding?! (She looks around, looks under the dustcloth) Good morning Mr Trifle! Lovely morning! (He nods back, still with spoon in mouth. She replaces the cloth) Where are - you naughty cat - have you been begging for tit-bits again? (Suddenly sees cat-shaped lump under wallpaper) Aaargh! Mr Snookums!! Is that you?! (She carefully pokes it and it wails) You fiends! You monsters!! How could you do such a thing?!

Hans 3: What?

Lady Aigz: What?!! Just look at THIS!!

Hans 3: Oh yeah - Hans, look!

Hans 1: What?

Hans 3: You've got a bubble under the paper!

Hans 1: Not me – I don't get bubbles! But - I can get rid of it! Here! (Goes to flatten it with large wooden mallet)

Lady Aigz: Stop! How DARE you?! (She rips off the paper and releases the cat) Poor Mr Snookums. Look at him - he can hardly breathe! I must fetch a vet! Here - you workers! Yes - you! I will leave him in your care until the vet arrives! Make sure that NOTHING happens to him, do you hear me? (She places him on the bench, on top of the compressed air tubing, then exits DR)

Mrs Trifle: (enters DR) I couldn't find George anywhere! He'll have to sort himself out - I'm starving! Oh! (Holds up empty plate)

Lotta Bottle: (enters DR) Everything alright?

Mrs Trifle: I want a FULL ENGLISH BREAKFAST!

Lotta Bottle: Wow - you've got an appetite! (Exits)

Hans 1: Back to work! Tell you what we need - we need a plank to work on! Get that one over there!

   Hans 3 gets plank, swings it just as Mrs Trifle sits down, but catches Hans 1 with it.

Hans 1: (bangs Hans 3 on head with mallet) Just put it down! (They lay it on the table in front of Mrs T) Don't worry, madam - it is but for a moment!

Gretah Chewitt: (or LB) (enters DL) Oooh ordered this? A FULL ENGLISH BREAKFAST! (She places it on the plank)

Mrs Trifle: Oh - and I want a pot of tea and three slices of toast and some strawberry jam please etc...... (While she is turning to give her order the men put the free end of the plank on the edge of a paste bucket. The plate slides down it into the bucket. They stare down at it then quickly wipe it off and return it, empty.) Now then - I'm ready for this......... (She looks around for the food but the others are all looking very innocent)

Gretah Chewitt: Anything else?

Mrs Trifle: Yes - I WANT A FULL ENGLISH BREAKFAST!!

Gretah Chewitt: Ooh! My word alive – they warned me you was a big eater! (Exits)

Hans 1: Now bring the plank over here! Hang on! I'm getting out of the way! (He moves back and sits on window sill)

As soon as Hans 1 picks up plank again the Marching Band/Singers enter, in full costume, marching & playing. They duck and weave around the room and all avoid being hit by the swinging plank. They remain.

Hans 3: Phew!

Hans 2: Hans - you are a master of the plank!

Hans 3: You're right there, Hans! (Lays plank on ground, one end by Hans 1's feet. Hans 3 lifts plank upright on end against window, knocking Hans 1 out of it.) Don't you think I'm the master of the plank, Hans? Hans? Now where is he hiding? Hans!?

Hans 2: Come on now, brother! Stop messing about - there's work to do!

Hans 3: We don't need him! Let's get one more roll of paper up on the wall!

They unroll a length of paper along the chests of the standing band-members, who hold it for them. The twins get two brushes and madly paste the paper with water, slapping faces as they go along. Band throws down roll angry and wet & exits.

Hans 2: Perfect! Pass it up! (He climbs up the ladder, now by the window.)

Hans 1: (leaning in through window) Grrrrrr!

Hans 3: What was that?

Hans 2: It sounded like Hans!

Hans 1: Grrrrrr!!

Hans 3: No - nothing like him. Come on! (They lift the paper right over the window, straight across the opening and Hans' face. The lump of his face is visible - in fact it is a wooden replica held in place)

Hans 2: How is that?

Hans 3: You have a large bubble in the paper! (Presses it around face)

Hans 1: Grrrrrr

Hans 3: It's that noise again!

Hans 2: Never mind that - let's get rid of the bubble. (Gets mallet, swings and hits lump)

Hans 1: OwooOOO!!!!

Hans 3: Did you hear that?

Hans 2: What was it?

Hans 3: Don't know.

Hans 2: One more try...... (Hits lump)

Hans 1: OwooOOO!!!!

Hans 3: This is spooky! It sounded like the bubble was talking!

Hans 2: Here - let me have a go. (Hits lump)

Hans 1: OwooOOO!!!!

Hans 2: You're right!

Hans 3: Give it a really hard bash!

Hans 2: OK! (Takes a run at it, swinging like mad. Hans 1 rips paper and pushes face through. At last moment the mallet is stopped)

Hans 3: Oooh - Hans: you shouldn't have done that!

Hans 2: No - Hans; I don't think I'd have done that.

Hans 1: You idiots! (They help him climb in. He taps both of them on the head with the mallet. There is a hollow echo) Now, get another bit of wallpaper and do it properly!

Greta Chewitt: (enters with plate) Oooh – another full English breakfast, madam! (Puts it down)

Mrs Trifle: About time! Oh no - now I've dropped my fork! (While she reaches down for it, helped by Lotta, the twins lay a length of wallpaper over the table, covering the food) I'm certainly ready for this .... arrgh!! Gone!

Gretah Chewitt: Oooh! Whatever is the matter, Madam?

Mrs Trifle: Just get me a FULL ENGLISH BREAKFAST!!

Gretah Chewitt: Oooh – ow **do** you stay so thin?! (Exits DL)

Hans 1: While you finish the papering, I'm going to use the paint sprayer!

Hans 2: What paint sprayer?

Hans 1: This thing! (Shows them machine) Look - this pumps air down this tube and into the paint sprayer! I'll show you!

Hans 2: Hang on, Hans! That cat is asleep on the tubing!

Hans 1: Then move it!

Hans 2: Ooh no! Hans - **you** move the cat!

Hans 1: Hans (3) YOU move the cat!

Hans 3: But - but - I............. (They push him forward)

Lotta Bottle: (DL) Another FULL ENGLISH BREAKFAST! I hope you enjoy it!

Mrs Trifle: I hope I EAT IT! Oh - there's no fried egg! I knew they'd get it wrong! Excuse me - Miss? Miss! (Turns to talk to Lotta)

Hans 1: That's it - now put the cat somewhere else!

Hans 2: Over on that table should do.

  (Hans 3 puts the sleeping cat on the plate of food) Lotta exits DL

Mrs Trifle: Oh – and Miss?! Oh never mind - I'm too hungry to wai.... eEEEE!!!

Hans 1: What appears to be the trouble, Madame?

Mrs Trifle: This is NOT what we eat for breakfast in England! Take it away!

Hans 1: So sorry, Madame! Hans - put it over there by the bench. That's right.

Hans 3: What, on the tube for your paint machine again?

Hans 1: Yes - that'll do. Now put a cloth over it, so it stays asleep. Perfect!

Hans 2: (eying up cat-sat-on plate) Do you want that?

Mrs Trifle: I certainly do NOT!

Hans 2: You don't mind if...... (He takes it & eats it)

Lotta Bottle: (enters with Gretah and Herr I plus Hansel & Gretel) This lady here!

Herr Inmeizoop: Oh yes! Mrs Trifle! I am afraid zat you haf eaten nearly all ze food in ze kitchen! There is nothing left for these poor children!

Mrs Trifle: But I haven't eaten **anything** yet!

Herr Inmeizoop: It iss all gone - except for **one bowl of soup**!

Mrs Trifle: Right! If soup it is - soup it will be! Stand aside!! (Exits angrily to get soup)

Hans 1: Ah! Herr Inmeizoop! Just in time. Let me show you our new paint sprayer!

Herr Inmeizoop: Vas is das?

Hans 1: You watch! Turn her on! (Compressor starts) Nothing is coming out! (The four examine the nozzle. While they do this the cloth by the bench starts to rise.) Nothing - turn her off. (The shape goes down.) Try again! (Repeat) Still not working. See if that's any better. Turn her on again. (Repeat - this time Hans 3 sees the shape and gets afraid. He tugs at nearest sleeve)

Hans 3: G - g - g - g...... (Twins turn and see rising white shape) GHOST!!

Herr Inmeizoop: Zer is no ghost in my hote ....AAHHH GHOST!!

Hans 1: Wait a moment! Look! (He adjusts compressor down and up twice - the objects falls and rises accordingly) It's not a ghost - it's something on the air hose!

Hans 2: But what? What can it be?

Lady Aigz: (enters DR) Mr Snookums! Ooee! Mr Snookums! I say you workmen - what have you done with my little pussycat?

Hans 1: Your pussycat ...... ooooh no!

Lady Aigz: What do you mean 'Oh no'? Where is Mr Snookums?

Hansel & Gretel: There!

Hans 1: (cautiously approaches inflated shape and pulls cloth off. It is a very large, round, pink cat with a bulging, startled expression.) All scream.

Lady Aigz: Mr Snookums!!

Hans 1: Oh no - he was sitting on the end of the air hose!!

Lady Aigz: (distressed cat sound) Well - do something!

Hans 1: (he carefully reaches cat and turns it to show tube stuck in rear) Oh dear!

Hans 3: This is a cat-as....

Hans 2: Hans!

Hans 3: But it's a cat-as....!

Hans 1: We know what it is, Hans! Shh! This is a children's show!!

Hans 3: No - it's a **catas-trophe!**

Hans 1: I'll have to pull it out! Here goes! (He quickly pulls out the tube. Sound of escaping air and wailing cat. The cat flies off with Hans 1 holding on [really he is guiding it with a broom handle as its tail] and it crosses the room . Everyone ducks. It circles back, past the window)

Mrs Trifle: (enters DL with bowl of soup) Now - I have my soup and nobody is going to ... (they all duck, except her, as the cat flies back. It rises under the soup and tips it into her face.) Waah!!

The cat now soars back across the room with them all in pursuit. At the window it suddenly flies out. The watchers look up higher and higher into the sky through the window. Sound of wailing cat gets dimmer. Escaping gas stops. Sound of wailing cat gets louder, with whistling sound of rapid falling. All heads move downwards. Terrible serious of cat-screeches, crashes, breaking glass, twangs, ending with slow and dwindling tinkle as of hub-cap coming to rest. Silence.

Lady Aigz: Mr Snookums! (Exits rapidly DL)

Mrs Trifle: This is the worst hotel I have EVER been in! AND WHERE IS MY HUSBAND?!

Hans 1: Ah - I think we can help you there, madam! (Points to cloth at table)

Mrs Trifle: George?! George - what on Earth are you playing at?

Mr Trifle: (appears at window covered in wreckage) Yes dear. Did you call? (All heads turn to him - he has the cat on his head.) I was just taking a quiet walk in the garden when this came crashing down out of the sky!

Herr Inmeizoop: Iffen you are int ze garden - zen who is under.... (All heads slowly turn back. Removes cloth but it is not George - it is now the the ghost)

Much screaming - Ghost!!! They fight to get out of door leaving Hans 1. He is frozen until the ghost waves at him, then he runs shrieking straight through the wall, centre left (or down the theatre or out the window) Crash! BLACKOUT

SCENE SIX

THE FOREST – front GAUZE / CLOTH again

Hansel: Yes - I **have** got some white stones!

Gretel: But it's so muddy here. Will they still show?

Hansel: Of course! I don't know – you girls worry about everything!

Gretel: Hmm. AND - we promised not to come into the forest again.

Hansel: We promised not to go into the forest again AT NIGHT! Remember? It's not night - it's the middle of the morning! What can happen in broad daylight?! And we're both really hungry after that stupid woman ate all the food!

Witch: (offstage) Cackle!

Hansel: What was that?

Gretel: Don't start that - trying to frighten me! Let's find these strawberries!

They exit DL

Phil de'Pottie: (enters DR) It's alright - I'm following the children - they can't get into any trouble!

Goblins: Giggle

Phil de'Pottie: Who was that?

Goblin 1: It was me!

Phil de'Pottie: Wow! Someone's been busy with the ugly stick!

Goblin 2: We're goblins.

Phil de'Pottie: I would never have guessed.

Goblin 3: Aren't you afraid? WooOOOoooOOOoo!!

Phil de'Pottie: Not really.

Goblin 4: We work for the witch!

Phil de'Pottie: That's nice!

Witch: (enters and stands behind him)

Goblin 5: Are you afraid of the witch?

Phil de'Pottie: Don't really know - never met her before.

Goblin 6: Before now.

Phil de'Pottie: What do you mean - before now? Silly little people! (To audience) Can you see a witch? Really? Where? This way? That way? Where is she? Where?

Witch: Here!

Goblin 7: Well - frightened now?

Phil de'Pottie: Mildly hysterical.

Witch: What are you doing here in my forest, Mr de'Pottie?

Phil de'Pottie: I - er - I .... oh dear!

Witch: Well - ?

Phil de'Pottie: Well what?

Witch: Shouldn't you be doing this? (Runs, flapping arms and shrieking)

Phil de'Pottie: I think that is my very next step. (Does it - exits DL)

Witch: Now - to find those children! (Exits DL laughing)

Lotta Bottle: (enters DR) Phillip! Phillip!! I don't know why I'm worried about him – he's always as cool as a lion and as brave as a cucumber! Now where is he?

Goblin 1: We know here he is!

Lotta Bottle: Urgh! Goblins! Get away!

Goblin 2: Your boyfriend has run away with a beautiful girl - to get married!

Lotta Bottle: Married? Beautiful girl ...... but that's......... Grrrr! Is it that English girl?! I bet it is!

Goblin 3: That's right - English!

Lotta Bottle: We'll see about THAT! (Moves off DL. Lights dim on her)

Cherie Trifle: (enters DR) Phillip! Phillip? I'm pretty certain he came this way!

Goblin 4: He's run off with that other girl!

Goblin 5: To get married! (They giggle)

Cherie Trifle: Urgh – I say! Who are you horrid little people? Are you from UNPOPULAR LOCAL PLACE?

Goblin 6: Stick to the plot! Your boyfriend has gone to get married!

Cherie Trifle: Married?! You mean to Lotta Bottle!! The girl from the hotel?

Goblin 7: Yeah - that's the one! Giggling exit onto rostra R

Cherie Trifle: OPTION for song with whoever can sing (goblins OR Phil OR Lotta) They all exit at opposite sides.

Hansel: (enter from auditorium & up steps) I'm sure this IS the way back!

Gretel: But what about the trail? Where are the stones?

Hansel: I - er - I can't see them!

Gretel: I knew it was a bad idea.

Hansel: Never mind - it can't be much farther.

Evil cackle

Gretel: I told you to stop doing that!

Hansel: But it's not....!

Gretel: Listen! (Music starts softly) Beautiful music! There must be a house nearby!

Hansel: I hear it! It's coming from this way!

Gretel: No - this way!

They split either side of stage. Front curtains open (or gauze backlit) to show Gingerbread House. Music grows. Rest of stage is black.

Gretel: Oh – Hansel! Look! A beautiful little house!

Hansel: Whoever can live in such a funny place!

Children start to walk toward it. Music becomes more threatening.

Gretel: Look - it's made of sweets! And I'm so hungry.

Hansel: No - Gretel - there's something wrong about this.

Gretel: But aren't you hungry?

Hansel: Well - yes - but -

Gretel: Come on then - it can't possibly hurt!

Hansel: Oh - alright - just one tiny nibble.

They inch toward house as music gets louder. Evil laughing

Hansel: Gretel! Look at all those sweets!

Gretel: But – they're not ours!

Hansel: Don't be such a girl! Here - have a bit of chocolate. Mmmm - this is delicious.

Witch: (unseen) Nibble, nibble, mousekin; who's nibbling at my housekin? (for added drama, each time this is said a 'double' witch briefly enters from a wing, unseen by twins, just to alarm the audience, then retreats)

Gretel: Did you hear that?

Hansel: What?

Gretel: I don't know.

Hansel: Come on - try some of this strawberry sugar icing!

Witch: (unseen) Nibble, nibble, mousekin; who's nibbling at my housekin?

Gretel: There it is again!

Hansel: What?

Gretel: It's like a voice.

Hansel: A voice? Saying what?

Gretel: I can't really hear. Perhaps it's just the wind. Pass me down a bit of that barley sugar, will you?

Witch: (unseen) Nibble, nibble, mousekin; who's nibbling at my housekin?

Hansel: I heard it that time!

Gretel: Ooer! What is it?

Hansel: I don't know.... where did it come from ... (as they look back toward the audience the house behind them splits open down the centre to show Witch, raised on low block looming horribly over them as they back toward her)

Dramatic music. BLACKOUT / CURTAIN

INTERVAL

ACT TWO

SCENE SEVEN in the Forest

HALF TABS

Witch: Ah-ha! So - two horrible little children eating my house?! I'll show you what I do to children like you! **Bring me the cage!** (Goblins wheel on the cage) In you go! (Pushes Hansel in & locks it. She and the goblins wheel the cage across the rostra and leave it R.)

Gretel: Let us go!

Witch: I don't THINK so!

Hansel: What will you do with us?!

Witch: I'm so very glad that you asked me that. **This** is what I am going to do to you - normally I turn naughty little brats like you into gingerbread then EAT

THEM! But I am sick of gingerbread. I can't even finish all the ones I have! So - I am going to fatten up this horrible little boy - and when he is nice, and plump, and juicy - I am going to put him in my oven - and cook him! Hahahahahaha!!!!!! (She drags Gretel away. More laughing.)

GOBLIN SONG Always look on the bright side, or similar. BLACKOUT

SCENE EIGHT
The Haunted Bedroom

There is a four-poster bed central upstage and two doors either side of it, marked as 2 toilets & 2 bathrooms. There is a cupboard door by the bed, rear L, and the main door to the room is DR. DL is a chest of drawers with a small, wooden box standing on top of it.

Herr Inmeizoop: Zis way! Come in dear guests! Come in.

Mrs Trifle: Well - this room certainly looks a lot better than the last one - but is it quieter?!

Lotta Bottle: (carrying cases) You can't put people in HERE! What about the - you-know-what?! You've seen it yourself now, so don't say it's not real!

Herr Inmeizoop: SSHHH!! Lotta – don't say it out loud! (To Trifles) My dear Frau Trifle - I am sure zat you vill not hear that dreadful marching band up here int ze North Ving!

Lotta Bottle: Are you going to tell them about it?

Mr Trifle: About what? (Gets worries & searches) It's not that cat again - is it?!

Herr Inmeizoop: Nein, nein, nein! (Ushers Lotta out DR)

Mr Trifle: Nine-nine-nine! What is it - Police? Fire?! Ambulance?!!

Mrs Trifle: Get a grip, Gerald. This is my holiday and I'm not having you spoil it. Now - what are all these doors? There seem an awful lot of them?

Herr Inmeizoop: Zis side is for ze lady, zat fur ze gentleman.

Mrs Trifle: What is this sign: is it in German?

Herr Inmeizoop: Ya - it is German for 'lady's bathink room'.

Mrs Trifle: What does it say?

Herr Inmeizoop: It says: 'splash-unt-spray-und-get-ze-move-on-or-ve'll-be-laten'

Mrs Trifle: And this door?

Herr Inmeizoop: The lady's vater-closet? In German it is the 'tinklen-sprinklen-hausen' which in English is....

Mrs Trifle: Thank you very much. I can work it out for myself.

Mr Trifle: How wonderful to learn another language! How about the men's rooms?

Herr Inmeizoop: For ze washing - it iss ze: 'scratch-unt-sniff-und-spray-ze-pitzen' and ze toilet, in German, is ze: 'grossen-tinklen-und-shake-zer-drippzenoffen'.

Mrs Trifle: Lovely. And a four-poster bed too! How romantic, George. Hmm. Smells a bit - but as long as it's quiet in here.

Herr Inmeizoop: Guaranteed, my dear lady! Guten-nacht to you! (Exits DR)

Mr Trifle: Seems very nice, dear.

Mrs Trifle: We shall see, Gerald. Time to brush your teeth; off you go. (They go into their bathrooms)

 (Twitzen Twins enter DR)

Hans 3: And you're sure that we can stay here tonight?

Hans 1: I'm not going home in the dark! I'm staying here where it's safe!

Hans 2: Me Too!

Hans 3: Perhaps we should check with Herr Inmeizoop first?

Hans 1: No - no - no – they said he NEVER uses this room. It'll be fine! Right - busy day tomorrow! Let's get sorted!

Hans 3: But - there's only one bed! And it's a funny looking one at that!

Hans 2: You're right there, Hans! What sort of bed do you think that is?

Hans 1: You two are so stupid! The daftest idiot in the world knows what sort of bed that is!

Hans 2: You do?

Hans 1: Yes - I do! It's called - a BUNK bed! One of you sleeps on the top!

Hans 2: Ooh - can I sleep on the top?

Hans 3: Fine by me!

Hans 1: Here - I'll give you a leg up. (He cups his hands and Hans 2 puts foot in them, but presses them down onto the floor and stands on them) Hnnnn!

Hans 2: No - still can't reach!

Hans 1: Gdddffffff...!!!

Hans 2: What?

Hans 1: Getoffmefingers!

Hans 3: Come on - I'll help. (Between then they get him onto the top of the bed)

Hans 2: This is very nice! (He settles down so the soles of his boots are seen)

Hans 1: Right then - first things first (goes DL)

Hans 3: But - this is the ladies'! (DR)

Hans 1: Get in there - nobody's going to know! (He goes in: Hans 1 goes DL)

Mr Trifle: (reappears in pyjamas and dressing gown) Teeth cleaned dear! Now - where can I hang these clothes? (Looks around, sees cupboard; opens door. The ghost is standing there. Hands clothes to ghost who takes them. He shuts the door. Stops. Thinks. Creeps back to door but cupboard is now empty. He looks inside.)

Hans 1: (enters DL. He goes to door UL, closing cupboard door on Mr T. Exits UL)

Mrs Trifle: (enters UR, goes to put clothes in cupboard) Aaah!! George! What on Earth are you doing in there? Stop playing silly fellows! Come out at once!

Cherie Trifle: (enters DR) All comfy in here? My room's rather grotty I'm afraid.

Mrs Trifle: It'll have to do! And do put on a brave face, dear, we **are** supposed to be on holiday. (Mr T goes DL into the men's loo. Mrs T sits in the bed.) I am exhausted! (Then flops back)

Cherie Trifle: I'll hang these up for you. (Puts clothes in cupboard)

Hans 1: (enters UL. Closes cupboard door again, locking CT inside. Walks past Mrs T without them seeing each other and tries loo door DL. Locked. Puzzled he crosses and sits on bottom of the bed.)

Mrs Trifle: (without looking) Be a dear and put the main light out for me.

Hans 1: Without thinking goes across to light switch by door, turns it off, then freezes. In this time Mrs T gets up and goes into the bathroom UL. Hans 1 slowly turns and creeps back to the bed, pounces at it. Nobody. He searches then lies down. Starts to snore.

Cherie Trifle: (Opens cupboard door and comes out. Sees boots sticking out of end of bed.) Oh, father - shoes on in bed! What will mother say? (Pulls boots off) Good night! (She exits through door.)

Ghost comes out of cupboard and lies on bed by Hans.

Hans 3 appears DR, struggling to get shirt over his head. Mr T appears UL with soap suds over eyes, by the foot of the bed they turn back to back, almost bump but don't; revolve round each other then cross room. Hans 3 goes round bed and into L side (ghost still in middle); Mr T into UR bathroom.

Hans 1: Here – who took my shoes off?!

Hans 3: Not me, Hans!

Hans 1: Well who else is in the room?! You twerp! You know I can't sleep with my shoes off!

Goes to put boots on. Gets right foot on but ghost has swung leg over his. Puts other boot on ghost's leg. Looks at spare leg. Confused.

Hans 1: Hans?

Hans 3: What?

Hans 1: How many legs do people have?

Hans 3: Er .... TWO – two legs! Why?

Hans 1: Nothing. (Thinks) Hans?

Hans 3: What now?

Hans 1: You're good at Maths: what is – one – and one – and one?

Hans 3: Er .... One and one and one is .... TWO!

Hans 1: Two eh? That's a relief. (Thinks) Bother and drat!

Hans 3: What's the matter?

Hans 1: I think I've lost a boot! (Sighs) Ah well - Goodnight, Hans!

Hans 3: Goodnight, Hans!

Ghost: Sits up and moans. Lies down

Hans 3: Sits up. Now what's wrong with you?

Hans 1: Sits up. Me? Nothing!

Hans 3: So get to sleep! (Both lie down)

Ghost: Sits up and moans. Lies down

Hans 1: Stop doing that!

Hans 3: It's not me!

Hans 1: Well - don't do it again!

Ghost: Sits up and moans. Stays up

Hans 1 & Hans 3: I told you.... (See ghost sitting up between them)
        Waaahhhh!!! (Run off - Hans1 DL loo, Hans 3 DR loo)

Mrs Trifle: (enters from UL bath)

Mr Trifle: (enters from UR bath) (They go to the bed and get in.) Good night!

Ghost: Sits up and moans.

Mrs Trifle: Not tonight, George - I've had a very stressful day.

Ghost: Sits up and moans.

Mrs Trifle: I told you, George! I'm not in the mood! Have one of your tablets - but NOT one of those dreadful blue ones you got off the Internet!

Ghost: Sits up and moans.

Mrs Trifle: That is quite enough! I'll take a wet flannel to you again if....
    Waaaahhh!! (Runs to UL bath)

Mr Trifle: What on earth is going on now? What **is** the matter with ... Wah! (Exits UR bathroom)

Ghost: Sits up and exits to cupboard, clomping single boot.

Hans 3: (enters DR and tiptoes into room, holding loo brush for defence) Hans - where are you?! Where are you hiding?

Hans 1: (after a moment he appears from DL loo - closely followed by the ghost. In silence they creep up behind Hans 3 and tap him on shoulder)

Hans 3: Waahh! (Runs and dives into bed, hiding under cover)

Hans 1: You big softy! Afraid of some silly ghost! (Turns and laughs at ghost) What a wimp, eh? (Double take) Waah!! (Dives into bed) Ghost exits into cupboard)

OPTIONAL BIT: The next section is completely unnecessary.

Cherie Trifle: (enters DR door) What are you people up to?! I'm trying to get some sleep! Nobody here! (Goes to box on chest of drawers)

Ghost: (head in box) Hello!

Cherie Trifle: Who said that?

Ghost: (head in box) Hello!

Cherie Trifle: It's this box! (Opens front door of box)

Ghost: (head in box) Hello!

Cherie Trifle: Wow! Spooky! (She pulls box back to reveal head sitting on cupboard)

Ghost: Ah – a beauteous young maiden! I pray thee – couldest thou scratcheth my head for me? Forsooth – that is most agreeable!

Cherie Trifle: You seem very polite for a ghost!

Ghost: And thou seemest most calm for a mortal-human. It is the custom for any knave or varlet who seest me to run about, hither and thither, wailing in a most unseemlyfashion, thusly: WAHHH!!

Cherie Trifle: Have you been in that box very long?

Ghost: Odds bodkins, I truly have! Verily hundreds of years! It is my curse to remain in this lamentable condition until once more I am reunited with my body!

Cherie Trifle: How sad. And where is your body?

Ghost: That – my dear maiden – is a question of which I know not the answer!

Cherie Trifle: (to audience) Have you seen the ghost's body? Where? In here? In the cupboard? (Looks inside - there it is! It starts to come out)

Mrs Trifle: (enters UL) Hello dear, not asleep yet?

Cherie Trifle: (rushes to hide head with box, despite it protesting) Sssh! No - not yet!

Mrs Trifle: Oh well - I'll not be long before I'm asleep - I'll just hang this in the cupboard.

Cherie Trifle: Let me do that! (Takes dress and throws it on the floor)

Mrs Trifle: I say! (While she gets it Cherie pushes ghost back into cupboard) Now it's dirty - I'll just give it a rinse! (Back into UL bathroom)

Cherie Trifle: (checks head is still in box) We'll have to be quick! (Shuts box) Hold on tight! (She carries box to body and places it on top, where ghost holds it)

Mr Trifle: (enters UR with toothpaste) Oh hello, dear! Where's your mother?

Cherie Trifle: (closing cupboard door quickly) Ah! Not sure! In the bathroom I think! Oh dear!

Mr Trifle: What is it?

Cherie Trifle: You've got some toothpaste down your front! (Squirts loads over him) Better go and wash it off!

Mr Trifle: Oh, have I dear? Right then. (Exits UR)

Cherie Trifle: (opens cupboard. Ghost walks out with box still on head. She removes it - ghost is now whole) That looks better!

Ghost: I'm so terribly grateful!
Cherie Trifle: Nothing to it! Now I must get some sleep! (Room door slowly opens)
 Look out - someone's coming! (Rushes both of them into DL loo)
END OF OPTIONAL BIT

Bandleader: Shhhh! This is it! This is the haunted bedroom!
Musician: Will we see the ghost?
Bandleader: If we're very quiet! (All band/singers enter – plus Gran Trifle - and
 tiptoe round room. At the UR bathroom Mr T comes out. Silently they all tiptoe
 close after him. He stops when Gran Trifle goes CUCKOO. They try to gag her.)
Mr Trifle: turns & sees them. Shrieks and dives into centre of bed.
The twins sit up, look at the surrounding band, and scream. Mr T sits up looks at
 the Twins and screams. Mrs T comes in - sees Mr T in bed with the Twins &
 screams. The ghost enters and tries to tiptoe across the front of the stage to
 escape. They all see it and scream. The ghost screams.
Mrs Trifle: OUT-OUT-OUT-OUT!!!!! EVERYBODY OUT!! (They all leave anyway
 they can as she shrieks at them) (To ghost) And you. Out! (Get sympathy from
 audience) OUT! There! The door is now LOCKED! Now stop dribbling, George.
 Have another tablet and get to sleep. I want total peace and quiet! Not one more
 disturbance! (She gets in and they settle to sleep)
Hans 2: (sits up on top of bed and yawns and stretches) What's all the noise?
 What's going on? (He rolls to centre of bed and falls through canopy to land
 between Mr & Mrs T.   False front of bed collapses and they both fall out.

BLACKOUT

SCENE NINE

THE FOREST – front cloth
Hansel is still in the cage on the rostra and Gretel enters DL carrying armfuls of
 giant sweets.
Gretel: Hansel - are you alright? (Turns cage toward audience)
Hansel: Yes - quick! Can you open this cage?!
Gretel: (tries) No – she's locked it! Stand back. (She tries to smash it with a big
 walking stick of striped candy) It's too strong.
Witch: Enters DL. What is this noise? Hmm- playing with your food? Give him the
 sweets, girl - I want him plump and tender! (To audience) I'm getting hungry -
 perhaps he is fat enough already? Boy! Stick out your finger so I can see how
 succulent you are!
Gretel: Hansel! Here - use this thin stick - pretend it's your finger!
Hansel: Right!
Witch: Out of my way, girl! Stand aside! Well, boy - hold out your finger! Hmmm -
 you are nothing but skin and bone! Your finger has no more meat on it than a dry
 twig! EAT MORE SWEETS! (To audience) And that goes for ALL of you!! Eat
 more sweets! Get fat - and spotty! Oh - I see many of have started already!
 Hahahahaha!!!! (Exits DL)
Hansel: Gretel - you must get back to the hotel and get help!
Gretel: I already tried! But there are no stones for me to follow! They've sunk in the
 mud and I don't know the way! And there are goblins everywhere - spying on me!
Hansel: I really hate goblins! Ugly little things!

Goblin 1: Well - that's nice!

Goblin 2: Charming!

Goblin 3:. And look at him - with his **little** stubby nose.

Goblin 4: And his disgusting **pink** skin.

Goblin 5: And revolting **brown** hair!

Goblin 6: Yuck - yuck – yucky-yuck-YUCK!

Goblin 7: I think he's quite cute!

Goblin 1: Pah!

Goblin 2: Why is he in the cage?

Goblin 3: He's waiting for the witch to eat him.

Goblin 4: What's he doing that for?

Goblin 5: Seems an odd sort of hobby, if you ask me.

Gretel: He's not doing it for fun!

Goblin 1: He's not?!

Goblin 2: Well what's he doing in there then?

Hansel: I'm trapped!! I cannot get OUT!

Goblins: OoooOOOHH!!

Gretel: Can you get him out?

Goblin 3: Oooh no!

Goblin 4: Union rules!

Goblin 5: Can't do anything NICE!

Goblin 6: No - if we do something nice....

Goblin 7: .... then we can't work for the Great Witch anymore!

Goblin 1: (thinking) and ...... we wouldn't have to do what she says.

Goblin 2: We could go where we like! We would be FREE!

Gretel: So - if you want to be free of the witch - do a good deed! Open the cage!

Goblin 3: Can't do that!

Gretel: Why?!

Goblin 4: Cos we've not got the KEY!

Goblins: OoooOOH!

Goblin 5: Ooh - I wish I knew how it feels to be FREE!

Goblins: FREE!!

Hansel: Excuse me - I wish **I** knew how it feels to be free to!

Goblin 6: Don't interrupt!

Goblin 7: Cos we're going to SING now!

SONG: possibly: I WISH I KNEW HOW IT FEELS TO BE FREE (LIGHTHOUSE FAMILY) If not adapt last few lines to fit.

SCENE TEN

Somewhere in the hotel: possibly the bedroom again, or the dining room, or a tab scene if practical. **Phil de'Pottie and Lotta Bottle** are there.

Lotta Bottle: See – I always said there was a ghost in this place!

Phil de'Pottie: That's nothing – I've seen a witch in the forest! I've seen her! Why won't anyone believe me?!

Lotta Bottle: Witch! Don't try that silly story on me! I know why you were out in the woods – it was with that 'girl'! You're not pulling my eyes on me – you're not pulling the wool over a fast one! (Exits DR)

Phil de'Pottie: Brr - that terrible witch. And nobody believes me! What about you; did you see the witch? Did you? So - I'm right. I'm not imagining things. And people round here says that she eats horrible things - like worms and bats! I wonder if that's true. (To aud) Do you know what she eats? What is it she eats? What? She eats CHILDREN?! Why - that's TERRIBLE! You can't eat children - not one of them washes! At least I'm glad that Hansel and Gretel are safe in the hotel! They are safe in the hotel, aren't they?! What?! Where are they?! The witch has got them?! NO! That's awful! We must go and get them!

Goblin 1: (from suitable secret opening) Pssst!

Phil de'Pottie: (looks around) What was that? Did you hear that? (To aud member) Was it you?! What was it then? A what? A goblin! No! So - where is it now? (Goes to look but another goblin appears at another place) Well make your minds up. Where is it now? (Goes to look but another appears elsewhere) What? Over here? (Goblin appears and follows close behind him as he searches; other 2 join in.) What? Where is this goblin now? Down here? (Looks under bed/table. Goblins look with him. He kneels up, so do they, he looks at them –double take) Waah!

Goblin 1: Chill out, dude!

Goblin 2: Yeah - like, we're doing a 'Good Deed'.

Phil de'Pottie: A good deed?

Goblin 3: We are born-again goblins, here to do a good deed.

Goblin 1: We have come to tell you that Hansel and Gretel are being held captive - in the forest - by the witch. There - that's that done.

Goblin 2: Not so hard, was it!

Goblin 3: Piece of cake! OK – that's it then. We're off!

Phil de'Pottie: No! We must go to the forest and rescue them!

Goblin 1: Who?

Phil de'Pottie: Hansel & Gretel!!

Goblin 2: Don't need to go to the forest!

Phil de'Pottie: Why not?

Goblin 3: Because - the witch actually lives **here** - in this hotel - in disguise as an ordinary person!

Phil de'Pottie: But who IS she? Which person?!

Goblin 3: Oh - I don't know that! Ha! - It might even be YOU! Hahah**....**

Goblins: Realise what he has just said. Scream & flee.

Phil de'Pottie: So - the witch lives HERE - in disguise! If only we knew who it was? Hey - you know a lot! Who do you think is the witch? Who? Well, I don't know. What if we're wrong?! Shh shh – someone's coming!

Lotta Bottle: (enters with a 'witch's' broom & starts to sweep)

Phil de'Pottie: Look! She's got a broom! Do you think Lotta is the witch?!

Gretah Chewitt: (enters with a small cauldron) Ooooh! My cooker's packed up again. I'll just put this by the fire!

Phil de'Pottie: Look! She's got a cauldron! All witches have pots like that for mixing spells! Do you think Gretah is the witch?

Mrs Trifle: (enters with a toad & husband) Look what I found in the forest - a poor old toad!

Phil de'Pottie: A toad! All witches have pets like toads! Do you think that Mrs Trifle is the witch?!

Cherie Trifle: (enters with bunch of herbs) I picked these lovely herb in the forest! We can use then in our cooking!

Phil de'Pottie: Look! HERBS! All witches use herbs for magic spells! Do you think Cherie is the witch? No?

Granny Trifle: (enters making bird noises) Where are you, my feathered friends? Speak to your earth mother!

Phil de'Pottie: Of course! She can speak to animals. Witches can do that! Do you think its Grandma Trifle? Are you sure? Who else is there?

Lady Aigz: (enters angrily) Where is that cat - he has got himself lost again!

Phil de'Pottie: Aaaahh!! A cat! All witches have cats! Do you think that Lady Aigz is the witch?! .... But if we get this wrong - what will happen to Hansel and Gretel?!

Rest of hotel staff & guests arrive chattering.

Phil de'Pottie: STOP!!

Herr Inmeizoop: Vas is dis Shhtoppp?!

Mr Trifle: Does he **have** to shout like that?

Lady Aigz: Get on with it, young man!

Phil de'Pottie: Well - I must tell you that - that.... one of you is.... the Great Witch!

Gasps and denials.

Herr Inmeizoop: Ze vitch?! But WHO?!

Phil de'Pottie: It is...... It is .... the cook! Gretah Chewitt!

More gasps and denials

Gretah Chewitt: Oooh?

Phil de'Pottie: Yes! You had us all fooled into thinking it was Lady Aigz, but in the forest the Witch called me Mr DePottie – Lady Aixz doesn't even know my name! AND ...... if you mix around the letters of her name: L-A-D-Y-A-I-G-Z ...... you just get ZGATLYAD

Mrs Trifle: What on earth does ZGATLYAD mean?

Phil de'Pottie: Nothing! Exactly. But if you mix around the letters of Gretah Chewitt: G-R-E-T-A-H-C-H-E-W-I-T-T ...... what do you get?!

Much thinking and doodling

Mr Trifle: topical or local name

Lotta Bottle: No - you get...... Hatgr-wi-teech

Gretah Chewitt: You simpletons - you don't get **Hatgr-wi-teech,** you get....

Pyro in front of her. Quick swap. Real witch or double leaps forward:

Witch: .... THE GREAT WITCH!!!! Hahahahahahahahah!! (Exits dramatically)

Phil de'Pottie: Quick - everybody - after her!

Herr Inmeizoop: But – ze foerest is enormous – who knows the way?!

Goblins: Here! We know the way! (General discomfort) Come on! Follow us! (Exit DR)

Cherie Trifle: Come on then – don't just stand there! Follow them!

(All exit leaving Mr Trifle gibbering)

Mrs Trifle: (return to get him) Come on, Gerald, the fresh air will be good for you!

BLACKOUT

SCENE ELEVEN
FOREST front cloth or black curtains with gap in centre.
The witch rushes across to side opposite the cage. While she speaks she is in

spotlight. In the darkness the cage could be wheeled on stage.

Witch: Oh - boo - yourselves! I hope all your teeth fall out! Don't think they will be able to defeat me! I am the GREAT witch! And when I have finished all the little children here - I think I might pay a visit to YOUR TOWN/VILLAGE! (Advances menacingly, laughing) But first - GOBLINS! Come to me! GOBLINS! Here NOW!! Where are those filthy little creatures? Are they down there in the darkness with you? Shall I come down and find out?!! It can wait! First - I think I am getting...... HUNGRY!! (She looks across stage wickedly then crosses to the cage. Spotlight follows

Gretel: Quick Hansel - the stick!

Hansel: I can't find it - I think I've dropped it!

Gretel: Leave him alone - he's not fat enough yet!

Witch: Well I can't wait any longer! (She opens the cage and drags him out)

Gretel: What are you going to do to him?

Witch: Do? Why, child, I told you what I'm going to do! I'm going to cook him in my magic FIRE!

(At this the witch's fire roars into life behind the gauze. It is a lighting, fan & silk effect, with a hint of smoke, in an evil rocky surround amongst black drapes. Standing beside the fire COULD BE the cut-out, life-size gingerbread shapes of children)

Gretel: Let him go!

Witch: That, I will NOT do!

Gretel: But.... but...... (Gauze opens if possible; witch drags them closer to fire) ... but ... you have to preheat the oven!

Witch: What? What are you talking about?

Gretel: Yes - you have to get the oven really hot before you put anything in it!

Witch: Really?

Gretel: Really - and if you ask me, that oven doesn't look nearly hot enough!

Witch: Hmm. (She approaches the fire. She bends to look and Gretel creeps up behind her to push, but ...... suddenly turns back.) No! This is hot enough!

Gretel: No - no! Really - if it's not hot - it will spoil the cooking!

Witch: Who told you about this hot oven business?

Gretel: Er....

Hansel: CURRENT COOKING STAR

Witch: CURRENT COOKING STAR?

Gretel: Yes! In his/her book 'How to Cook ...'

Hansel: .... for witches'!

Witch: 'How to cook for witches', eh? I haven't got that one! Perhaps, one last check. (She approaches the fire again. She bends to look and Gretel creeps up behind her to push, but ...) Bah! That is as hot as I usually have it! Now – where is the boy?!

Hansel: I think the fire is going out! You haven't put enough wood on!

Witch: Nonsense - (goes to check) There looks to be plenty of wood. (She bends to look and Gretel creeps up behind her to push - and this time in she goes, with a scream and a puff of smoke. PYRO?)

The gingerbread figures could change into children (or they could just enter) who look dazed and surprised.

Hansel: Gretel! Look! The spell is broken!

Child 1: What happened to us?

Child 2: Where are we?

Gretel: Not now - we must get you all back to the village - to your families!

Herr Inmeizoop: (enters in posh clothes under a cloak) Hansel! Gretel! You are safe! But - I know zese odder children! Zey - zey are from the village!

Child 3: I don't like it here. It's dark & frightening!

Herr Inmeizoop: Do not vorry! As ve march through ze forest ve vill all sing a jolly marching-through-ze-forest song! Look - here is.... (Suitable actor) **...** zey vill help us sing!

BUSINESS WITH CHILDREN / COMMUNITY SONG

SCENE TWELVE - FINALE
The Ball Room of the Hotel (or lobby), looking splendid

Herr Inmeizoop: Great news everybody!

Lady Aigz: (carrying cat) Oh – don't tell me – I've been to these things before "there is going to be a wedding and some prince or other and some scullery maid will live happily ever after"!

Herr Inmeizoop: Vell – I don't think so. (Looks round) Phillip? Are you going to marry anyone? Mm?

Phil de'Pottie: Well … (looks at the two girls who glare at each other)

Mrs Trifle: Oh I say! Good idea! Which one of you is going to be known as – Mrs de'Pottie?

Cherie Trifle: MISSES de Potty?! Oh no! You're welcome! No thanks – after you!

Lotta Bottle: Cheers! (Grabs his arm)

Herr Inmeizoop: No – zat iss not my goot news! Now zat the vicked vitch is gone - I have filled ze hotel with guests!

Lotta Bottle: So how did you get all these new guests?

Herr Inmeizoop: Vell, it is no longer going to be a hotel! It is going to be something new!

Mrs Trifle: So what will it be now?

Herr Inmeizoop: It is going to become a school for training young mice!

Cherie Trifle: Training young mice? Training them to do what?

Herr Inmeizoop: Training zem to paddle tiny little canoes! It vill be an ACADEMY!

Lady Aigz: An academy for training young mice to paddle canoes?

Herr Inmeizoop: Yah! It vill be called ze Young Mouse Canoeing Academy!

Phil de'Pottie: The Y.M.C.A.

Herr Inmeizoop: Yah! Zat is right! So ve must make ANOTHER advertisement for ze television! If only ve had a good song!

Mr Trifle: What sort of song?

Herr Inmeizoop: I don't know - a song zat vill tell people zat it is fun to stay at ze Vy-M-C-A!

(All look thoughtful)

Phil de'Pottie: How about this? Song: YMCA: "YOUNG **MOUSE ......**

During which large mouse wearing lifejacket and carrying paddle enters & joins in

BLACKOUT
WALKDOWN
FINALE NUMBER

LIST OF TITLES

Click to select

1. CINDERELLA
2. ROBIN HOOD
3. DICK WHITTINGTON
4. SLEEPING BEAUTY
5. RED RIDING HOOD & THE 3 PIGS
6. THREE MEN IN A TUB
7. JACK AND THE BEANSTALK
8. HANSEL AND GRETEL
9. SNOW WHITE & 7 DWARVES

CONTACT INFORMATION
and PERFORMANCE RIGHTS here:

PANTOSCRIPTS.ME.UK

SNOW WHITE
& THE SEVEN DWARFS
© Chris Lane 2018
OVERTURE
ACT ONE
INTRODUCTION

Dramatic music rises then fades mystically; low light goes up behind Magic Mirror (front of tabs or side stage: box with 'cling film'/'glad wrap' over front. Internal light on floor and/or top.

SPIRIT OF THE MAGIC MIRROR: (a microphone might help, with a bit of echo; or just a very miserable actor)

Once upon a time – in a land far, far away, lived a wise and happy King and a beautiful and graceful Queen. They were loved by all the people in their kingdom and, in time, they had a baby daughter who was so fair of face, and whose skin was so delicate and pale, that they called her - Snow White.

But the Queen never recovered her strength. The wisest doctors in the whole Kingdom tended her, but the Queen grew weaker and weaker until – sadly - she died.

The King was filled with grief but his sadness was reduced by the lovely baby and in time he became happy just to watch Snow White grow up into a beautiful young woman.

Then - one day – a mysterious woman appeared at the palace. The King seemed unable to take his eyes off her – almost as if he were under a magical spell - and in a short time the King took her to be his new Queen!

SCENE ONE: THE THRONE ROOM OF THE CASTLE

A colourful scene with drapes & shields. Two thrones raised on a platform at rear.

FANFARE: Curtains open to show most of chorus in medieval, colourful clothes. Bishop carrying the crown. Two large flags enter down the theatre carried by pages, leading the King and future Queen plus attendants, small pages, flower girls etc. They mount onto the stage. The music changes to a lively medieval DANCE.

CHORUS DANCE

KING: People of Pimplevania! Kneel and greet your future Queen!

QUEEN: (Smiling graciously) No – no – no! Please get up! Really – there is no need for such a fuss. It is so kind of you all to be here today! And some of you have even tried to put on decent clothes! (looks at audience) Well – most of you.   (looks around impatiently) So – is it time to begin?

KING: Begin? Begin what?

QUEEN: To begin the coronation.

KING: But I've already had one of those, thank you.

QUEEN: No – my little Kingy-poos; this one is for me.

KING: (Confused) For you?

QUEEN: Yes – you want to crown me as your QUEEN.

KING: I do?

QUEEN: Yes – (Makes magical pass in front of his face) - you do!

KING: Oh yes – (in trance) – "I want you to be my Queen."

QUEEN: That's right.

KING: "I want you to be my Queen."

QUEEN: All right – that's enough! Now - if we're all here, can we start the ceremony?

KING: "If we're all here..." (Wakes up) Yes. Perhaps we had better just check the guest list?

QUEEN: I'm sure we're all here; let's get on with it.

KING: Who has the guest list? (louder) Who has the guest list?

QUEEN: Those two useless 'spies' of yours!

KING: Sniff and Dribble! Where are the spies, Sniff and Dribble?

SNIFF: (In disguise) We are here, your majesty! (To suitable music Sniff pulls off the dress & wig - revealing James Bond type DJ & bow tie) At your service: Agent Sniff!

DRIBBLE: And - Agent Dribble! (Repeat, but to show vivid disc-jockey outfit)

SNIFF: Dribble! What are you wearing?!

DRIBBLE: What you said – my Disc Jockey clothes! (makes DJ moves and sounds)

SNIFF: No, Dribble, – I said wear your DJ – your DINNER JACKET!

KING: Ah – Sniff and Dribble – very good disguises. Now – can you tell us, are we all here?

SNIFF: Let me see – (consults long list) – ooh no, a few missing! Prince Charles of England?

DRIBBLE: His wife won't let him out by himself.

SNIFF: ***********? TOPICAL OR LOCAL

DRIBBLE: Reason they are not there

SNIFF: Snow White!

DRIBBLE: Snow White isn't here yet!

KING: Good heavens – how could we have forgotten?!

QUEEN: (sarcastic) How indeed.

KING: Somebody fetch my daughter!

SNIFF: Look – here she comes now!

(Music.) She appears running down centre of hall in traditional Snow White costume. She runs up the ramp daintily and dances lightly around her father. **SONG with CHORUS??**

SNOW WHITE: I'm so sorry I'm late.

SNIFF: Were you cleaning out the fire-places and scrubbing the floors?

DRIBBLE: Don't be daft – that's Cinderella! This is real life, not a fairy story!

KING: Not to worry; you're here now!

QUEEN: Mmm – indeed. So: can we perhaps make a start? Mmm?

SNIFF: One more person to arrive: Snow White's old Nanny. (To QUEEN:) Nanny Goat.

QUEEN: What did you call me?!

DRIBBLE: Not you! Snow White's old nanny. Nanny Goat. She's not here yet.

SNOW WHITE: Nanny was right behind me. Yes – here she comes!

Comedy music. NANNY GOTÉ appears at back of theatre with a crown, runs noisily down centre of hall in army boots & outrageous costume. She stumbles onto stage, crashes through royal party and collapses onto throne steps, with crown.

NANNY GOTÉ: Whoops! (Hands crown to QUEEN.) Here you are, Mrs Q.

QUEEN: (angrily) "Mrs Q"?! (snatches crown)

NANNY GOTÉ: Sorry I was bit late. I've been down to the fair. (To QUEEN:) Have you been yet? Ooh – you should. I won a prize!

SNOW WHITE: Well done, Nanny! What did you win?

NANNY GOTÉ: I won a goldfish!

SNOW WHITE: How super! Where are you going to keep it? In a bowl?

NANNY GOTÉ: No. Something bigger!

SNOW WHITE: In a tank?

NANNY GOTÉ: Bigger! I've put it in the bath!

KING: In the bath! But - what will you do – ah (embarrassed) when you want to – ah - use the bath?

NANNY GOTÉ: Oh, I've thought of that! (produces tiny strip of black cloth). I've made it a blindfold!

SNOW WHITE: You're always so thoughtful to protect poor, little creatures, Nanny.

QUEEN: Yes – alright – now that you're here, Nanny Goat.

NANNY GOTÉ: Nanny Go-tay; it's pronounced Go-tay! (Sniff & Dribble drag her aside.)

QUEEN: Can we PLEASE get on with this?!

NANNY GOTÉ: Hold your horses. Let's just check everyone's here. (Takes list and looks at audience) Right – are the *** party here? Give us a cheer! (Goes through list of known or imaginary members of the audience) And I have a note here from the box-office: name of your town's oldest resident, Arthur Rackman, was hoping to be here, but he can't - because he is a hundred and eleven today! A big round of applause for the old fellow! A hundred and eleven! (Sniff quickly whispers; Nanny peers at note again) Er – no – he's not a hundred and eleven - he's ill. Sorry.

QUEEN: I think that's more than enough. (Pushes her aside) We are all here – (looks at audience) even the peasants – now start the coronation!

KING: Yes my dear.

SNIFF: No my dear. I mean – no – your worshipfulness.

DRIBBLE: There's still one more guest to arrive!

SNOW WHITE: Who is it? Somebody nice?

SNIFF: I think it might be!

DRIBBLE: It's the son of the King of the Fair Islands. According to this he's called Prince … er …

SNIFF: Prince Alarming!

SNOW WHITE: Prince Alarming?!

DRIBBLE: Let me see that. No – it's Prince Charm-bracelet!

SNIFF: Prince Charm-bracelet?!

SNOW WHITE: (Disappointed) Oh no. Not Prince Charles!

NANNY GOTÉ: Give it to me …(squints) er … Prince Farming …. Prince Barmy ….. Prince Smarmy …

FANFARE

PRINCE: ENTERS DR. All turn to look at him.

PRINCE: Actually, the name's Charming …. Prince Charming. (He makes straight for Snow White but the QUEEN pushes in the way)

QUEEN: Charming. What a lovely name. I am ….

PRINCE: (ignores Queen and pushes past) And you must be Princess Snow White. (gives flowers)

SNOW WHITE: Ah – did you have a pleasant journey?

PRINCE: Yes – but not as pleasant as arriving.

QUEEN: Enough! (splits them and takes the flowers) IF we are all here …. (to Sniff & Dribble) IF there is nobody else waiting to rush in? Mmmm? (sarcastic) No long lost aunt from Transylvania?

VOICE: No – I'm here already, thanks! (Waves & grins)(Maybe Front of House member?)

QUEEN: (sarcastic) Wonderful! On with the ceremony perhaps?

KING: Certainly, if you would just like to take a seat on your throne, my dear, then…

TOUR GUIDE: (ENTERS) STOP! Excuse me, madam – you can't sit on that. That's a valuHable hantiKEW. (puts rope across & sign on it) That chair dates back to the reign of King Tinkle the Incontinent. Look – you see that stain. (Queen nods). Yes! And when they said it was the reign of King Tinkle they didn't just mean …

KING: An antique, eh – do you think it's worth anything?

GUIDE: Do I LOOK like TV HOST? And to be honest, sir. We at the National Trust for Pimplevania don't judge things by their cost – we look at their part in our country's long and flowing history.

QUEEN: (angry) And you – would you like to be part in our country's long and flowing river?!

GUIDE: Ooer. Right – anyone up for a guided tour? If you like I can show you what life was like in the olden days in the kitchens!

QUEEN: And if you don't shut up straight away I will personally show you what life was like in the olden days in the dungeons!

GUIDE: Oooer. (Shuffles into background)

KING: So – now then – ahhhh – what happens next?

QUEEN: I've never been to one of these before – but I do believe you PUT THE CROWN ON MY HEAD!

KING: Quite so …. right then. (Everyone kneels, fanfare, crown is placed, big cheer.) There we are then – now if you would all like to get up, we will …

QUEEN: No! Stay down there! I have decided I do like it after all! (To KING) YOU! Come with me – there are a few changes I want to make around here. (sees Snow White with Prince) And you! (to Snow White) Come! (they exit L) (Prince exits Right)

(CHORUS EXIT)

SNIFF: That was a moving ceremony.

DRIBBLE: Yes – lovely – very moving!

NANNY GOTÉ: Good, then come and help move furniture for the ball.

SNIFF: Ooh no – can't do that sort of thing.

DRIBBLE: No – not now we're official spies!

NANNY GOTÉ: You two – spies?! What sort of spies? MI-5 spies? MI-6 spies? MI-7 spies?!

SNIFF: Even more secret than that!

DRIBBLE: So secret it hasn't even got a number! It's just called M.I. – N!

NANNY GOTÉ: M-I-N? So – you're a couple of min-spies? How festive.

SNIFF: (Proudly) That's right.

DRIBBLE: We're min-spies!

NANNY GOTÉ: Good grief (to aud) See you lot later. Byee! **(exits R)**

SNIFF and DRIBBLE stay on, dancing.

PRINCE: (enters L) Excuse me, gentlemen; have you seen the princess?

SNIFF: I think she's in the tower spinning straw into gold.

PRINCE: Really?

DRIBBLE: No – that's in Rumplestiltskin! That's a fairy story. This is real life! Prune! Come on!

(SNIFF & DRIBBLE exit)

PRINCE: (To audience) Wow! This is an odd Kingdom – but princess Snow White is really rather nice. And to think I didn't want to come here today! If I'd gone on my gap year, building orphanages in Peru, I would never have met the most beautiful girl in the whole WORLD! I must go and find her! (Exits R)

QUEEN: (MUSIC. Enters slowly L) Foolish boy. To imagine that scraggy little creature, Snow White, is more beautiful than me! Ha –ha-ha! (Looks worried) But – perhaps ……. I'll just check. (Moves L to Magic Mirror. Stage dims.) Mirror – awake!

MIRROR MUSIC. light on

MIRROR: Go away – I'm busy.

QUEEN: What?! How dare you speak to me like that!

MIRROR: Oops! A thousand apologies, oh great one – I had no idea – forgive me.

QUEEN: Very well –but here's something you can reflect on: I do have a HAMMER!

MIRROR: It will never happen again, your Georgeousness. Please tell your unworthy, humble servant what I may do. Is it the usual? "Mirror-mirror-on-the-wall-who's-the-fairest-blah-blah-blah".

QUEEN: Watch it – or would you rather be hanging in local name Rugby Club toilets!

MIRROR: Point taken.

QUEEN: (dramatically) Mirror, mirror, on the wall; who is the fairest of them all?

MIRROR: You, oh Queen, most fair of face;

none can match your charm and grace.

So elegant, with slender figure:

although your bottom's getting bigger.

QUEEN: What?! What did you say?!

MIRROR: Erk! Nothing – I mean … You, oh Queen, with radiant hair;
flowing locks beyond compare;
The fairest here, without a doubt;
A shame you're such a crabby trout.

QUEEN: WHAT?!

MIRROR: Aargh! Err – oooh … Of all the Queens, you are the top;
may your beauty never stop.
Your complexion is as clear as glass;
but you're a royal pain in the …

QUEEN: Enough! Get back to those dark depths of misery and despair from which I
summoned you!

MIRROR: Too late, TV SHOW has finished! Ta ta! (Blackout in mirror)

QUEEN: I knew I was the most beautiful in all the land. And always will be. Ha! If people
knew what I REALLY look like! Thank goodness for Nivea, regular exercise, a healthy
diet - and magic spells.

(looks at aud)

At least I haven't any competition down there! It would take more than magic to make you
lot beautiful. Just count yourselves lucky. There have been a few women who have
tried to match my beauty, but – shall we say – there are none ALIVE who succeeded!
(Exits L laughing)

Return to palace scene. Prince & Snow White enter R

SNOW WHITE: No, I don't really know the new Queen at all. I think she was princess of a
distant land and, well, Father seems very fond of her. I'm sure she'll be alright, when we
get to know her.

PRINCE: I'm sure you're right. And how about you – do you have someone special?

SNOW WHITE: Special?

PRINCE: You know – some rich and ugly prince that your father has arranged for you to
marry?

SNOW WHITE: No – nothing like that. In fact – nobody at all. How about you?

PRINCE: What – marry a rich, ugly prince?

SNOW WHITE: No – a rich, ugly princess!

PRINCE: No. My home is a beautiful island, but there are no princesses. My father the
King said that I would need to cross the sea to find a beautiful princess. So …. I got into
my ship …

SNOW WHITE: I love ships. I watch them from the beach – but …. I've never been in one.

PRINCE: Well …..

(Music starts)

SNOW WHITE: Are you going to sing?

PRINCE: Yes – would you like to join me?

SNOW WHITE: Love to!

DUET – Somewhere, over the sea (La Mer) (also in Finding Nemo)

SNOW WHITE: I must go and get ready.

PRINCE: Shall I see you at the ball?

SNOW WHITE: If you keep your eyes open! (Snow white exits R. Prince exits L)

NANNY MUSIC. NANNY GOTÉ Enters R. In very wide crinoline.

NANNY GOTÉ: Hello, it's me, Nanny Goté again! Do you like this – it's my best ball
gown. Do you like it? My last boyfriend said I was the belle of the ball. Here – I can
prove I'm the belle of the ball. (Swings dress side to side. Sound of bell tolling) Clever,
eh? (Aside to audience, in male voice) You don't want to know how I do that!

SPY MUSIC SNIFF DRIBBLE ENTER THROUGH AUDITORIUM. Dribble carrying a hand-
held scanner

SNIFF: Right then – security check. (starts to scan. Odd buzzing sounds) Some of this lot look a bit shifty.

DRIBBLE: Yeah – use the scanner on them!

BUSINESS: loud buzzing from people in front row & band. The spies pull out odd things ending with a large bra. Shriek & run onto stage.

NANNY GOTÉ: What are you two doing?!

SNIFF: I've got to do a security check on you. (Up onto stage) Put your hands up!

NANNY GOTÉ: You what?

SNIFF: It's a metal detector – to see if you have any knives or swords hidden in all of – well, whatever all that is. Now -put your hands up.

NANNY GOTÉ: You won't tickle, will you?

SNIFF: Of course not – now just stand sti …. (she slaps him round the head) What was that for?!

NANNY GOTÉ: You were going to tickle.

SNIFF: No I wasn't! Now just stand still and we'll try again.

NANNY GOTÉ: And you won't tickle?

SNIFF: I won't tickle! Put your hands up - that's it. I'll just (slap) Ow! I was nowhere near you!

NANNY GOTÉ: It looked like you were going to tickle.

SNIFF: (angrily) Well I wasn't going to tickle! Here – Dribble – you do it!

DRIBBLE: Me – but I … (it is pushed in his hand & he is pushed into place) Ooer – (approaches from distance – machine makes loud beep. Nanny hits Sniff.)

SNIFF: Ow! What did you do that for?!

NANNY GOTÉ: That thing – it beeped at me! It gave me a fright!

SNIFF: It's supposed to beep! It means there's something metal in there. Here - let me have a look. (Goes to inspect clothing – hand up skirt or down front - gets slapped again.)

NANNY GOTÉ: Hands off – cheeky.

DRIBBLE: But somebody needs to find out what you've got made of metal in there!

NANNY GOTÉ: Oh, I see. (Flirty) Why didn't you lovely boys say so? I'll just have to take my clothes off! (Despite their screams & protests she starts. Drum accompaniment. She takes off her skirt to show hoops, & under hoops enormous, brightly coloured bloomers. Next is her top, to show a huge corset.)

I need a bit of help here, chaps. Just undo the laces at the back will you. Come on now!

(They struggle to do so, circling & ducking as the ropes are untied. As it comes loose, a huge twang and they are thrown forward)

Ah – that's better.

(Has a big scratch to sound of sandpaper)

DRIBBLE: (Runs detector over corset – huge buzzing) I think we've found the problem.

SNIFF: Now put it all back on again before somebody sees us!

NANNY GOTÉ: Easier said than done, boys. (Puts her hands up) All together now.

(They put the corset round her front, circle ropes once; she holds onto edge of stage. They walk back with long bungee. Dramatic struggling **Title music from Zulu**.)

SNIFF: It's no good – I can't take the strain!

DRIBBLE: We're going to die! We're going to die!

KING: (Enters L) My word – what ARE you fellows playing at?

SNIFF: Quick – grab hold! (King holds their belts)

DRIBBLE: Whatever you do – don't – let – GO!

KING: Don't what?

DRIBBLE: Let go!

KING: Certainly.

(Lets go. Huge twang. S & D fly across stage and off into wings. Enormous long sequence of crashes, screams, breaking glass and cat wails, etc. Finally they reappear other side of stage, draped in foliage, sheets, flags, loo-seat, etc.)

NANNY GOTÉ: Don't just stand there!

KING: Who, me?

NANNY GOTÉ: Yes you – quickly – tie a knot - I can't hold my breath forever!

KING: Oh I say. This is quite fun, actually. Now – that should do the trick!

NANNY GOTÉ: Thank you very much. Cor -feels a bit tight though. (Turns round to show King with hand tied to her back) See you all at the ball! (MUSIC. Exits R, taking KING with her, calling for help)

QUEEN MUSIC

QUEEN: (Enters L) Where is everyone? I need to see people grovelling at my feet!

CHORUS & PAGES ENTER

QUEEN: (to spies) You two – why are you shaking like that?!

SNIFF: It's too horrible to talk about.

QUEEN: Now – servants and slaves and such like. I have a decree! Listen! I have been looking at the way the money is spent in this is palace and I DO NOT LIKE IT! (Aside) Not enough is spent on ME! So – to save money I intend to sack half of you! You have until nightfall to decide who is going, then pack your bags and be out! But – before then – it is my coronation day and I insist that you are all happy! Start the music!

Low music: ABBA: Dancing Queen?

KING enters with Nanny & Prince.

KING: My word that was exciting! Have we started the dancing? Are we all here? Where's Snow White?

QUEEN: Never mind her. (Pushes past him to flirt with Prince) Who wants to have the first dance with ME? How about you?! Excuse me – are you LISTENING to me?

PRINCE: I – I'm sorry your majesty – but I have just seen the most wonderful sight! Look!

KING: My word – it's Snow White!

Music changes to Snow White's song.

Snow White glides up from the audience and onto the stage in a spectacular gown. Cheers from people.

PRINCE: Snow White – please, allow me the honour of the first dance.

SNOW WHITE: Well – as you asked so nicely, how can I refuse?

KING: My dear – look at you – my little Snow White has grown up to be the most beautiful young woman in my whole kingdom!

PRINCE: There can surely be no other in ANY kingdom who can equal you in beauty! Flash of lightening & thunder, stage darkens, all cower.

QUEEN strides to mirror leaving stage frozen in darkness.

QUEEN: Mirror! MIRROR!!!

MUSIC. Lights.

MIRROR: Who is it? You again? Crikey. Seems like only ten minutes ago that …

QUEEN: BE SILENT! Listen to my question very, very carefully, and be sure to answer me truly. Mirror, mirror, on the wall – who is the fairest of them all?

MIRROR: Is that the time, crikey – I'm supposed to be … **THUNDER**

QUEEN: Mirror!

MAGIC MIRROR: All right! (Coughs nervously, twice)

You, oh QUEEN: are fair, it's true,

But now there's one, more fair than you.

QUEEN: I KNEW IT! TELL ME HER NAME!

MIRROR: Oooh – now that's a hard one; bit tricky, err …… it's on the tip of my tongue …

QUEEN: (Icily) Answer now – or you will be thrown from the highest tower in this castle and smashed into a thousand little …

MIRROR: Snow White! It's Snow White!

QUEEN: As I guessed.

MIRROR: You're not going to do anything nasty to her are you?

QUEEN: Me? Nasty? Nasty does not come even close to what I will do to that girl!
HALF TABS / FRONT TABS close behind Queen

SCENE TWO
NANNY GOTÉ ENTERS R sees the queen then tries to exit.
QUEEN: Oh – Nanny GOAT. Now – tell me – what is it exactly that you DO here, mmm?
NANNY GOTÉ: Nanny Go-TAY! And what I do here is – I look after the little children.
QUEEN: Pardon me? Little children? Do I SEE any 'little children' here? I don't THINK so! You show me these children or you – are SACKED! Come on now. Just one teeny-weeny child and you can keep your job. Come on!
NANNY GOTÉ: (To aud) Oh my – oh my. What can I do? I don't have anywhere else to go! I'll be homeless – I'll have to go and live in a paper bag, or in a hole full of worms, or - in NAME IF PLACE! Oh my! Where can I find some children? (to aud) Hello. Are there any children out there?
QUEEN: Who ARE you talking to?
NANNY GOTÉ: To the children!
QUEEN: There ARE no children! Out you go! (starts to push her off)
NANNY GOTÉ: There ARE children! Quick, children. Shout!
QUEEN: I can hear NOTHING!
NANNY GOTÉ: Louder!
QUEEN: I still hear nothing!
NANNY GOTÉ: Shout louder! There – did you hear that?
QUEEN: Alright! I might hear something. You can keep your job – as long as there are 'children' here.
QUEEN: (to Nanny) For goodness sake go away: go and do something useful. (Nanny exits muttering)
KING enters, sees Queen and also tries to sneak out but gets caught.
QUEEN: (to KING:) And you ... I see you. Come here!
KING: Who – me?
QUEEN: Yes. I have a little job for you.
KING: A little job – what sort of little job?
QUEEN: An opera house. I command you to build me an opera house.
KING: An opera house?!
QUEEN: Yes. I have a superb voice. I should have been an opera singer. I just need the appropriate place to show my talent. Well – what are you waiting for? Start it NOW!
KING: Yes dear – an opera house – right away dear. (exits in a hurry)
QUEEN: I was born to be an opera star .... a diva! A prima donna!
SONG: I WANT TO BE A PRIMA DONNA or similar! (may have to change last few lines)
QUEEN: Now to my special place – a secret chamber, buried deep beneath this castle; a dark and private place known only to me. The Hidden Dungeon of Doom.
Sharp crack of thunder, flash of lights and blackout as tabs open onto:

SCENE THREE: THE HIDDEN DUNGEON OF DOOM

Black Set. Maybe one flat each side: dark stone & slime; manacles & rats.
Centre stage is another flat. Hanging from his wrists is a prisoner: Dangling Dan - with very long white hair & beard. His feet (false) do not touch the ground. (Actor's lower legs are through back of flat & he is kneeling, secured by a safety harness)
DAN starts singing from The Sound of Music. "Climb every mountain," etc.
QUEEN: BE QUIET!
DAN: I do requests. Go on, which one do you want? "You are sixteen going on seventeen"

etc.

QUEEN: Enough!

DAN: "High on a hill stood a lonely goatherd. Yodel-odel-odel- yodel - eyeetee!"

QUEEN: I'm warning you - !

DAN: This one's everyone's favourite. "Edelweiss, Edelweiss, every morning "etc.

QUEEN: SILENCE! I can make things very unpleasant for you!

DAN: Oh yeah – like what, hang me up by my arms – in the dark – no food – no water -
with bugs the size of rabbits! Hah! "Raindrops on roses and whiskers on kittens" etc

QUEEN: Right – that's it – just you wait! I'll show you what REAL suffering is! (stamps off
L)

SNIFF: (enters R with Dribble) This is the place – you can stay down here. Nobody will
ever know!

DRIBBLE: But why me? Why can't you be the one?

SNIFF: Don't start all that again. Half the staff are sacked. That means YOU! Now
where's the sleeping bag?

DRIBBLE: Sleeping bag. Oops. Forgot the sleeping bag.

SNIFF: Clot. Run and get it! **(Dribble hurries off R)**

QUEEN: (Returns L with large feather duster, laughing. Sees Sniff.) What are you doing
down here? How did you find this secret place? It is known to none but me!

SNIFF: We – I – er – umm. Right! Yes! I'm checking the security! I'm looking for BUGS!

QUEEN: BUGS?! What is it with you people and bugs? There are NO bugs down here!

(a bug puppet comes through one of the flats)

There are NO bugs down here!

What? Where?

(it has gone) There's nothing there!

DAN: "Doh a deer, a female deer."

QUEEN: ENOUGH! (to Sniff) You!

SNIFF: Me?!

QUEEN: Yes, you, Snot, or whatever you're called. Go and fetch Snow White. Bring the
Princess here AT ONCE! (points left)

SNIFF: Certainly your Queenliness. (Sniff exits L backwards, bowing)

DAN: "How d'you solve a problem like Maria? How do you ..."

QUEEN: I warned you! (tickles him under the arms)

DRIBBLE: (enters R carrying sleeping bag) Here it is, I ..... oo er. (tries to sneak out but is
seen)

QUEEN: Spy! That was fast. Did you do as I asked and fetch her?

DRIBBLE: Er – I've got the bag!

QUEEN: The BAG! How DARE you speak of the Princess like that! (smiling) Though I do
like your honesty.

Snow White enters L

QUEEN: Ah – there you are my dear.

SNOW WHITE: What is this place? I've never been down here before.

DAN: "Ray – a drop of golden sun."

SNOW WHITE: My goodness – who are you?

DAN: I am Dan. Formerly of the royal kitchens. Breakfasts. Dan the Breakfast Man.
Pleased to meet you (shakes hands; replaces hand in manacles)

SNOW WHITE: Oh my. But why are you down here?

DAN: Ask her.

QUEEN: Pah! I can't remember every single person I hang up in chains!

DAN: It all started when SHE came here – her and her new ideas for breakfast. Toast and
porridge weren't good enough for HER. No – she wanted ... Rice Krispies! I poured
them in the bowl, put the milk on – then, off through the castle to her room, with the
Rice Krispies going 'snap, crackle & pop' – but, by the time I got there ...

QUEEN: They were SOGGY!

DAN: So I went back, I got another bowl, put the milk on and RAN down the corridor, with the Rice Krispies going 'snap, crackle & pop' – but, by the time I got there ...

QUEEN: They were still SOGGY!

DAN: (increasingly hysterical) So I went back, got another bowl, put the milk on and RACED as fast as I could down the corridor, with the Rice Krispies going 'snap, crackle & pop ; snap, crackle & pop' – but, by the time I got there ...

SNOW WHITE: They were still soggy?

DAN: YES! And on the way back to the kitchen (sobs) the Rice Krispies were laughing at me. Laughing! (in a laughing hysterical tone) 'snap, crackle – pop , snap, crackle – pop!' MOCKING: ME!

But I showed them – I got my little hammer – I took the first little grain of Rice Krispie out of the packet – and I smashed it to pieces! Then the next – and the next – until every Krispie had stopped laughing at me. Ha ha ha!

Then – I put all their little, flattened bodies back in the box, rowed out into the middle of the lake, tied a rock to it – and threw it in! (there is moment of disbelieving silence)

SNOW WHITE: Ah – so – exactly what crime did they charge you with?

DAN: (sobs) They said I was .... a cereal killer!

SNOW WHITE: Oh dear. So they put you in this horrible place. (looks round) I bet there are creepy crawlies down here.

DAN: There are bugs!

QUEEN: There are NO BUGS! (Another bug puppet appears through another flat) THERE ARE NO BUGS!! (business with aud) Enough! This is my secret place and I say ...

NANNY GOTÉ: (MUSIC. Enters L holding end of washing line) Cooe, everybody! Coee!

QUEEN: No! This is my Hidden Dungeon of Doom! What do YOU want down here?

NANNY GOTÉ: Me? This is where I hang my bloomers to dry after I've washed them! Look. (shows first pair on line)

QUEEN: Dry your bloomers! You can't do that down here!

DAN: No!! Don't say that! It's the only pleasure I have! I look forward to this day all year!

SNOW WHITE: All year?!! You only wash them once a YEAR?!

NANNY GOTÉ: It's not as bad as it sounds. I've got LOADS of them! Here (to aud) you can do something useful. You can count my bloomers for me! Will you? Great. Here goes! One ... etc

She pulls line across stage. Others continue counting when she goes into R wings.

She reappears L at other end of line. She says the number of bloomers.

NANNY GOTÉ:Great. Thanks! (exits R)

QUEEN: Grrr! This is MY Hidden Dungeon of Doom. NO MORE INTERRUPTIONS!!

GUIDE enters with tourists including the KING

GUIDE: And this is the Hidden Dungeon of Doom. Built two hundred years ago by King Zit the Very Spotty.... Notice the architecture, which is a good example of early Lego. Excuse us. (pushes QUEEN: aside) And this is Dangling Dan.

DAN: Pleased to meet you. (slips hand out of manacles and shakes hands)

KING: How do you do.

QUEEN: I don't believe this! What are YOU doing down here?!

KING: This tour is MOST fascinating my dear. Did you know that this Hidden Dungeon of Doom is the largest dungeon in the country – it's in the Pimplevania Book of Records!

QUEEN: That's it - out! OUT! (Snow White is the only one turning to leave.) No – not you! Come here my dear. I have a little job for you. I want you to deliver some fruit to a little, old lady who lives in a cottage in the forest.

GUIDE: Oooh – not the Dark Forest. (mutterings from tourists) You don't want to go in THERE alone! Remember what happened to that what's-her-name!

TOURIST 1: Red Riding Hood! I heard about that.

TOURIST 2: Oh yes – that business with the wolf. Nasty!

QUEEN: (nervously) Nonsense. That was just a story! And anyway – she won't be alone. I'll send someone with her!

Spy! I want you to go with Princess Snow White.

DRIBBLE: Eh? (looks round) What? Go into the dark Forest? Woah! No way!

QUEEN: If I say you will go into the Dark Forest then you will ..

DAN: "Climb every mountain"

QUEEN: .. climb every mountain. No!

DAN: **SONG**: Ford every stream. **(all but the QUEEN: join him for the rest of the chorus)**

QUEEN: Aaargh! (In rage she grabs Dan's legs and ties them in a knot) There! Now – the rest of you – out, OUT ,OUT!

GUIDE: Come on now, party. This way to see the torture chamber. Who wants to try the rack?

KING: Bagsy me first!

GUIDE: Right! Walk on! (they exit in excitement) To the rack!

QUEEN: Well - don't break it! (Turns menacingly on Dribble) I think I might be using it very soon. Now, Spy, you will escort Snow White into the forest. The basket's over here. (she takes SW across stage to basket, Left)

SNIFF: (enters R next to Dribble) I can't find her. Oh, there she is! Dribble! You're here! She mustn't see there are two of us! (Grabs sleeping bag and jams it over Dribble)

QUEEN: Off you go then, my dear. Go and get a warm cloak. Be careful – I wouldn't want anything 'nasty' to happen to you.

SNOW WHITE: I'll be careful. I'll get my cloak, then we can set off. (SW exits L)

SNIFF: We will? (Dribble makes frantic nodding and grunting) Oh, right. Super! (Turns back to Dribble) Where am I going? Is it somewhere nice? (Dribble nods madly) Good.

QUEEN: (Walking across and poking Dribble in the sleeping bag) What on Earth is this thing?

SNIFF: Er – it's a bug trap! The bugs crawl up these – er – feet things and get trapped.

QUEEN: A bug trap? But – there are no bugs in here! (repeat business with bugs) Enough! (Looks around) Spy! Before you go: I need to talk to you - in private.

QUEEN AND SNIFF EXIT

Dribble remains in sleeping bag

DRIBBLE: (PRE-RECORDED; ECHOING) Hello? (Pause to listen?) HelloOO?! Anyone there?

(Prince enters R)

DRIBBLE: (PRE-RECORDED; ECHOING): HellOOoo!!

PRINCE: Hello?? (looks around)

DAN : Wasn't me, mate. (nods at Dribble)

PRINCE: (Walks to Dribble) Hello?

DRIBBLE: Hello?

PRINCE: Hello?

DRIBBLE: Hello?

PRINCE: I say – (pokes sleeping bag) - is there somebody in there?

DRIBBLE: In here? (squirms) I can't SEE anybody – but it is rather dark.

PRINCE: (Grabs top of bag) Come out of there! (Pulls it off) Oh – it's you. You're that spy – Dribble – aren't you! Perhaps you know where to find Princess Snow White.

DRIBBLE: Snow White? Ooh now … hard to say really.

PRINCE: (To audience) Can you tell me where Snow White has gone? (Business) The forest?! How odd! Why would she go there?

DAN: Excuse me...

PRINCE: Yes?

DAN: If you have a moment. I seem to be a bit … (indicates knotted legs) … do you think …?

PRINCE: Come on. (They un-knot legs but one is now longer than the other) Oops! (Prince pulls other leg but that is now longer)
DRIBBLE: Here – let me ... (repeat)
(Repeat with legs until they reach ground. All look down.)
DRIBBLE: I - er – I've got some – er – washing in the machine. (starts to shuffle off L)
PRINCE: Yeah – I – er – I'll just go and find – er – Snow White. (shuffle R)
(Both dash off)
DAN: Oh well. (Looks around & hums)
SONG: SOMETHING FROM SOUND OF MUSIC. As many bugs as possible appear through the flat around him and **sing** the song vigorously! (all cast)

SCENE FOUR: THE DARK FOREST
Forest: Dappled green lighting & mist. Spooky music.
Snow White wanders about picking flowers & singing. Goblins appear briefly & vanish un-noticed.
SNOW WHITE: Ooh: this place is a bit spooky! I wish Sniff and Dribble would hurry up. I don't like being on my own. What am I saying – (to aud) - I've got you with me! I won't feel so scared with you here. Let's just think about nice things, like chocolate, and teddy bears, and Prince Charming! There, I feel braver already. But – just one more thing – if you see ANYTHING scary, will you shout out and tell me? You will? Thanks!
Business with goblins. MUSIC
SNOW WHITE: (eventually sees Goblins) My, you are funny people? Are you pixies? No? Elves? Brownies? I know – goblins! Yes! Do you live out here in the forest?
SNIFF & DRIBBLE ENTER R. The goblins get alarmed & run off .
SNOW WHITE: Don't go! This is Sniff and Dribble; they're not frightening! (Runs to wings to call them back)
SNIFF: (draws Dribble to front) This is awful! What are we going to do?
DRIBBLE: I don't know! We can't just leave her here – but we can't take her back!
SNIFF: I know! What if she leaves a trail of bread crumbs!
DRIBBLE: That's Hansel and Gretel! This is real life, not a fairy story!!
SNOW WHITE: (joins them) Which way is it now?
SNIFF: Hard to say really.
DRIBBLE: Don't rightly know.
SNOW WHITE: There's a path here. Let's try THIS way! Come on! (Exits L)
SNIFF: Where did she go?
DRIBBLE: Dunno. Ooh – it IS a bit spooky. (They huddle & walk R. As they return a goblin follows them. When they reach L and turn back a second goblin joins, etc.) **MUSIC**
OR if time is short go straight to here *
SNIFF: (Sees goblins in row beside him) Ooer – Dribble!
DRIBBLE: What?
SNIFF: Just – look – behind me!
DRIBBLE: (He does but by now they have all run behind him) I don't see anything!
SNIFF: (looks nervously behind him) Nothing! Perhaps I imagined it. (turns back to face Dribble & sees even more goblins behind Dribble) Waah!
DRIBBLE: Now what?
SNIFF: Gob – gob – goblins!
DRIBBLE: Where?
SNIFF: Behind you!
DRIBBLE: Behind me? (Sniff nods madly. They turn to see nothing. All the goblins are upstage of them in a line) Nothing!
SNIFF: Where have they gone? (The stalk off in opposite directions. The goblins fill the gap between them. Eventually the spies stop & slowly turn back. Double take.)
* They see the goblins who wave at them

DRIBBLE: Now what?

SNIFF: (Thinks) Run away screaming?

DRIBBLE: Quick or slow?

SNIFF: I think …… quick. Waaah! (they exit L & R, wailing)

All exit.

NANNY GOTÉ: (Enters grumpily, carrying laundry basket) Hello again! That Queen has sent me out of the castle to dry my washing. Now – what can I tie the line to?

SNIFF & DRIBBLE run on in terror

NANNY GOTÉ: Sniff. Dribble. What on earth are you two doing out here?!

SNIFF: Er .. bird watching.

DRIBBLE: Hunting.

NANNY GOTÉ: Bird watching AND hunting? Well – which is it?

SNIFF: Both – we watch the cute little birdies -

DRIBBLE: - then we shoot them!

NANNY GOTÉ: Hmmm. I know you two – you're up to something! Come on now – what is it?

SNIFF: (upset) It's not our fault!

DRIBBLE: It's not our idea!

NANNY GOTÉ: What isn't?

SNIFF: It's that new Queen! She hates Snow White!

DRIBBLE: She wants us to leave her out here, in the forest!

NANNY GOTÉ: WHAT?! That's terrible! You can't do that!

SNOW WHITE: WHITE: (enters L) Can't do what? Mmm? What can't they do?

NANNY GOTÉ: Er – can't eat worms!

SNIFF: Can't take our pants off over our heads.

DRIBBLE: Can't leave you in the forest to get lost. Oops! (Sniff hits him)

SNOW WHITE: Leave me in the forest?! Why would you do such a horrid thing?

SNIFF: It's not our fault!

DRIBBLE: It's not our idea!

NANNY GOTÉ: It's the new Queen. It seems she wants you - out of the way.

SNOW WHITE: Out of the way? Me? But why?

SNIFF: No idea. Perhaps it's like in Cinderella?

NANNY GOTÉ: Don't be silly. This is real life – not a fairy story.

DRIBBLE: Told you!

NANNY GOTÉ: But whatever her reason, you can't go back to the castle! You must run away and hide!

MUSIC STARTS

SNOW WHITE: Run away? But where?

Sniff & Dribble exit R

NANNY GOTÉ: Just find somewhere safe – stay out of sight. We'll go back to the castle - tell the King. He'll know what to do. Come on. You'll be alright. We'll come and find you in the morning! (Exits R)

SNOW WHITE: Somewhere safe – but where? (Owl hoots) (Looks around in panic) Oh my – I can hear something coming! (wolf howls) Oh my! What can it be? (Wolf howls louder) Oh dear. Which way?

Behind gauze OR on projection dwarf's cottage becomes visible.

Snow White turns, sees it & slowly walks toward it. Distant sound of dwarfs singing 'Hi ho'.

CURTAIN

INTERVAL

ACT TWO

SCENE FIVE: THE DWARFS' COTTAGE

A cluttered, detailed interior of carved wood. There is a low ceiling with large beams.

Stage Left is a stable door; upstage of it a small window with curtains inside, flowers outside.

Stage Right is a sink with a handle-operated pump.

In the rear Left corner is a stone well, about a meter high. Hanging above is a bucket on a windlass.

Full length upstage is a platform. Along it are the dwarf bed-ends with their names on. This is reached by rough steps. Furniture is a low wooden table, centre, + dirty mugs and bowls, and a few little stools.

SNOW WHITE: (Opens top of door & looks in) Helloo? HelloOOo! Anybody home?

(Opens bottom of door & tiptoes in)

Nobody home.

(Looks around) What a funny little house. Such tiny furniture. It must be the home of little children! But very dirty little children. And look! Tiny little beds. But so many! One – two – three – four – five – my, what a big family – six and SEVEN!

(she climbs up and gets onto a bed)

This is very comfy. (stretches & yawns) Perhaps I'll just take a bit of a rest.

Lights dim slightly. From offstage can be heard the dwarfs: "Hi ho".

This gradually builds until they all march in through the door carrying picks & spades.

WALT DISNEY OWN THE RIGHT TO THE NAMES: **DOC, SNEEZY, GRUMPY, DOPEY, SLEEPY, BASHFUL, HAPPY** SO YOU CAN EITHER RISK IT, OR USE THESE. OR YOU CAN USE YOUR OWN

(use 'replace' option in Word)

DOC - BOSS,   SNEEZY - POLLEN, GRUMPY – GRUMBLE-GUTS,   DOPEY - YOKEL,

SLEEPY – OKEY-DOKEY,   BASHFUL - SMILER,   HAPPY - CHUCKLES

BOSS: (Bossy) Right, lads. First things first. Who's going to cook dinner? (dwarfs try to run off or hide) STOP! Get back here now. (Yokel is standing on the table) Yokel! Yokel – what are you doing up there?

YOKEL: Who. Me? I'm hiding.

BOSS: Just you get down! That's better. (Pollen sneezes) Bless you. Now, you all know the routine! If there's a job to do - get the sausages!

GRUMBLE-GUTS: Ding Dang Diddly! I'm not doing all that business again.

BOSS: OK. Then you can do the cooking!

GRUMBLE-GUTS: Ding Dang Diddley! Get the sausages. (Yokel shouts & runs for the door) YOKEL! Where are you going?

YOKEL: Get the sausages?

BOSS: (Shakes head & points to cupboard under sink)

A string of large sausages is found. The dwarfs stand in a line.

BOSS: Are we ready? (they mostly are except for one) Okey-Dokey! Wake him up. (they do) Right. You all know the rules. The only one left without a sausage at the end of the song does the cooking! Ready – steady – begin!

(They start to pass the string of sausages up & down the line as they chant:)

Magic sausages of fate

Before you sizzle on the plate

Before you're stuck upon our fork

Tell us who will do the work!

BOSS: It's Chuckles! Chuckles does the cooking!

CHUCKLES: Jolly super!

BOSS: There, that's settled – next – who does the cleaning?!

Repeat of panic. Boss blocks the door) (Yokel is standing still with his hand up)

Yokel – do you know what cleaning is? (Yokel shakes head and grins)

It means "washing the floor and dusting". (Yokel thinks about this then suddenly runs for

the door screaming)
Get back in here! RIGHT! Get the sausages!!
GRUMBLE-GUTS: Ding Dang Diddly! (Boss pushes broom at him questioningly) Alright! Get the sausages!
Repeat of sausage ritual
BOSS: It's Smiler! Smiler does the cleaning!
SMILER: (Goes all shy) Oooer!
BOSS: Just one more thing! (they all yell & flee except for Yokel who is 5 seconds behind them)
Hey! It might be a NICE thing! (they all laugh and return smiling)
GRUMBLE-GUTS: Ding Dang Diddly! What could be this NICE thing! Pah!
CHUCKLES: Go on then, Boss. Tell us – what is this nice thing? (they huddle excitedly around Boss)
BOSS: The nice thing – is - - - - WASHING THE DISHES! (total panic as before) STOPPPPP!!!! GET THE SAUSAGES!!!
GRUMBLE-GUTS: STOP! LOOK!
BOSS: What is it?
GRUMBLE-GUTS: Look – somebody has been in here and ...TIDIED UP! (all amazed)
BOSS: You know what this means, chaps?
It means – (dramatic) – there is somebody else here!
MUSIC. Silent frightened huddling. Suddenly Pollen sneezes & they all jump.
GRUMBLE-GUTS: Let me at him! (makes fists) Who does he think he is, coming in here - washing our dishes?!
BOSS: It might not be a person! It might be - A MONSTER! (frantic huddling)
SMILER: A m-m-m-m-monster?!
BOSS: Yes – a great big, hairy monster!
YOKEL: That does dishes!
BOSS: Yes – a great big, hairy, dish-washing monster.
In the silence Snow White makes a sound.
SMILER: It's .... Still here! (general horror – they all cower & turn)
GRUMBLE-GUTS: Ding Dang Diddly! We're all going to be .... eaten!
CHUCKLES: It might NOT be a big, hairy, monster. Well – not a BIG one, perhaps?
BOSS: Somebody – has to go .... and have a LOOK! (others dive their heads under the table, bottoms out, legs shaking) Come out – you cowards! We'll use - the sausages!
Repeat of sausage chant – but quietly.   Yokel loses.
BOSS: Here – you need something to defend yourself. (hands him the sausages) Off you go!

Yokel stalks to the beds while the others huddle.
Half way Pollen sneezes & Yokel jumps & runs back. They make him go back.
At almost the last minute another sneeze. Repeat action. Eventually Yokel is almost at the bed.
SNOW WHITE: (Sits up and smiles) Hello!
(MUSIC STOPS)
Yokel screams & races back. Others scream. All hide under table again.
SNOW WHITE: (walks to them) Hello!
BOSS: THERE'S NOBODY HERE!
SNOW WHITE: But I can see your – (indicates bottoms) - your – you're all hiding!
GRUMBLE-GUTS: Go away – you MONSTER!
SNOW WHITE: I'm not a monster!
BOSS: You're not a monster?
SNOW WHITE: No – I'm not a monster.

GRUMBLE-GUTS: Then what are you?!

SNOW WHITE: I'm a princess!

DWARFS: A princess?! (they gradually crawl out and look; not Okey-Dokey) Wow! Etc

GRUMBLE-GUTS: I say she's a monster! A tidying-up monster!

SNOW WHITE: No – I'm not a monster. But I DO wash dishes!

GRUMBLE-GUTS: I knew it! She'll be trouble! Sheeeee'll be trouble!

SNOW WHITE: I am Princess Snow White. And who are you gentlemen?

BOSS: I (coughs nervously and glances around) I am called …. Gimli.

CHUCKLES: Balin

SMILER: Dwalin

POLLEN: Thorin Oakenshield

SNOW WHITE: (stopping the next dwarf) But – why do the names on the beds say different names? (they look shifty) Boss – is that you? Chuckles – that must be you.

GRUMBLE-GUTS: Pah! You'll never guess MY name!

SNOW WHITE: Let me see – are you Grumble-Guts? (Sneeze) And Pollen. (much blushing) Smiler. And that fellow under there might be Okey-Dokey? And you …

YOKEL: Me? I'm Boss. No I'm not – I'm Grumble-Guts. No – I'm - er …..

SNOW WHITE: Might you possibly be called – Yokel?

YOKEL: Am I? (others all nod) Oh - right!

SNOW WHITE: And what do you all do out here in the forest?

BOSS: We're miners. We dig up diamonds. And what do you do?

SNOW WHITE: Me? I'm a princess. I – er – well I – I open things.

YOKEL: Like cardboard boxes?

SNOW WHITE: No – like hospitals and bridges and things like that.

GRUMBLE-GUTS: That's not hard work. What ELSE do you do?

SNOW WHITE: I wave. (demonstrates)

CHUCKLES: That's super.

GRUMBLE-GUTS: (sarcastic) THAT must be really tiring!

BOSS: What do you do for fun?

SNOW WHITE: What do I do for fun? Well, I sing! And I dance!

DWARFS: That's what we do for fun! We play music – and dance!

MUSIC –1920's trad jaz? with pretend instruments. Gradually all join in.

GRUMBLE-GUTS: That's all well and good. But answer me this. What – exactly – are you doing out here in the forest. There's nothing to open, and there's no-one to wave at but us! (Yokel waves at her)

SNOW WHITE: It's the new Queen - she wants to get rid of me! I can't go back home.

BOSS: Then you must stay here.

GRUMBLE-GUTS: What?! Ding Dang Diddly!

SNOW WHITE: I can clean! (looks round at them) And I can cook!

GRUMBLE-GUTS: I'm warning you – sheee'll be trouble!

BOSS: Don't be so silly. What possible trouble could she be?

GRUMBLE-GUTS: You wait and see. Just you all wait and see!

BOSS: And – we can look after you, if there's any trouble. We might not be the tallest people in the land, but that don't mean we're easy pickings!

SONG: LES MIS: LITTLE PEOPLE

CURTAIN
SCENE SIX: THE DUNGEON
BLACK TAB CURTAINS OR FLATS USED EARLIER

QUEEN: (Enters L singing) I want to be a prima donna etc … Good morning, Magic Mirror. And how are we this morning?

MIRROR: **(MUSIC. Lights on)** Could be worse I suppose. My frame's a bit warped and my glass could do with a clean but I suppose …

QUEEN: Do shut-up. I don't REALLY care how you are. I was just being polite.
MIRROR: That's a first.
QUEEN: Watch it. Time for THE QUESTION. Are you ready? Mirror, mirror …
MIRROR: (sarcastic) … on the wall, whose the fairest of them …
QUEEN: You really don't know how to treat ROYALTY, do you!
Just cut the sarcasm and tell me who is the most beautiful woman in this whole castle!
MIRROR: That's an easy one.
In this castle, without a doubt
You're the one whose face stands out.
(pause while she smirks)
You know this mirror never lies,
But is it really a surprise?
With a ton of makeup, and a gallon of lotion,
Not to mention that magic potion!
QUEEN: What do you mean?!
MIRROR Well – get real. You DO use magic to look like that.
QUEEN: What if I do?
MIRROR Hah! If they knew what you REALLY look like!
QUEEN: ENOUGH!
MIRROR (aside) Talk about mutton dressed as lamb!
QUEEN: What?!
MIRROR Er … I said: what a silly mirror I am.   **(Lights off)**
PRINCE: (enters R) I still can't find Snow White. She should have been back from her
    walk ages ago!
QUEEN: Hmm. And why are you worried about that slip of a thing? Mmm?
PRINCE: I – er – well – umm (embarrassed)
QUEEN: And don't tell me it's all about 'love' and that slop.
PRINCE: What's wrong with love?
QUEEN: Just listen to me. Love changes everything!
SONG: QUEEN & PRINCE LOVE CHANGES EVERYTHING
PRINCE: I feel very sorry for you. I'm going to find Snow White! **(exits L)**
SNIFF: (enters R with Dribble) No – they said the Queen was up in her room! This is as
    far away from there as you can get! We'll hide here until the King gets back.
DRIBBLE: But …(He has seen the Queen)
SNIFF: Don't worry!
DRIBBLE: But …
SNIFF: She'll never find us here!
QUEEN: Who'll never find you here?
SNIFF: The Queen … she'll …. ah …. Ooer!
QUEEN: Did you do as I ask? Did you get rid of that girl?
SNIFF: How do you mean?
QUEEN: I mean – can you guarantee that Snow White will not be coming back?!
DRIBBLE: It's really unlikely that she'll be back any time soon!
QUEEN: 'Really unlikely' - what sort of an answer is that?! Have you done as I asked or
    not?
SNIFF: Er …. What was the question again?
QUEEN: Hah! Imbeciles! If brains were made of gunpowder you wouldn't have enough to
    blow your nose!
SNIFF: (To Dribble) Is that good?
DRIBBLE: Not too sure on that one.
QUEEN: Mirror! MIRROR!
MIRROR: **(MUSIC. lights on)** I thought you'd finished for the day.
I said before – I can't tell you who's going to win … (something topical, maybe on TV?)

QUEEN: Tell me true – am I not the fairest in all the land?

MIRROR: You, oh QUEEN:, are fair, that's true.

But in all the land – is one more fair than you.

QUEEN: WHAT?! But a minute ago you said that I was the …

MIRROR: The fairest in the CASTLE. That's true enough, but Snow White is OUTSIDE the castle!

QUEEN: Snow White?! She is still alive?! Why has she not been eaten by wolves?

SNIFF: I'm sure that was Red Riding Hood.

QUEEN: Or been crushed by a giant?!

DRIBBLE: Jack and the Beanstalk?

QUEEN: Or been sized by a troll?!

DRIBBLE: Harry Potter!

SNIFF: Don't be silly – Harry Potter's just a story! Twerp!

QUEEN: Why is she still alive?!!

MIRROR: Dwarfs.

QUEEN: What?

MIRROR: She's moved in with those dwarfs that live in the forest. **(lights fade)**

SNIFF: That's nice of them.

DRIBBLE: Yeah – dwarfs are like that.

QUEEN: You two! (They look behind them to see who she means, then look back at her & jump)

Yes, you two – go now, travel into the forest, find the home of these dwarfs, see if Snow White is there, then …

SNIFF: Hang on. (is trying to write this down) What came after 'Go now'?

QUEEN: Morons!

DRIBBLE: Is that the same as 'imbeciles', or a bit worse?

QUEEN: I shall have to do it myself! Now GET OUT! You have five seconds to be out of here or I will turn you both into toads!

They flee. Stage darkens. **Spooky music.**

QUEEN: (produces apple)

When earthly plotting fails to win,

It's time to let dark powers begin.

So now I'll use my evil magic,

And Snow White's fate will be quite tragic

This simple fruit can do no harm,

Until I work my magic charm.

A single bite will cause her death

And she will take her final ..

MIRROR: **(Lights on)** Hold on! Hang about! Just a minute!

QUEEN: What is it now?

MIRROR: You know the rules – you can only have one magic spell working at a time.

QUEEN: So?

MIRROR: Think about it: you already have one spell running - the one that makes you look beautiful! If you start messing about with magic apples – then the first spell will stop working and you'll go back to what you used to look like!

QUEEN: You're right. (thinks) But - only until the deed is done. If I cover myself, nobody will see me. (She pulls up the hood of her black cloak) There ... (inspiration) AND it will be the perfect disguise! Snow White will never recognise me! She'll take the poisoned apple from my own hand! Ha-ha!

MIRROR: Fair enough. **(Lights off)**

QUEEN: This simple fruit can do no harm,

Until I work my magic charm.

A single bite will cause her death,

And she will take her final breath!

The music reaches a peak. There is a sudden blackout and a pyro flash.
The QUEEN slips behind the flat and a duplicate QUEEN takes her place.
QUEEN: manic laughter from wings.
Duplicate QUEEN: pulls back her hood to show an ugly old woman. Exits L laughing.
BLACKOUT   BLACK TABS OPEN

SCENE SEVEN
THE DWARFS COTTAGE – THE NEXT MORNING

Same scenery as before but a cloth & flowers on the table. The dwarfs are getting
ready for work.
BOSS: A most splendiferous breakfast. (others all agree; Pollen sneezes.)
SNOW WHITE: I'm so pleased you enjoyed it.
CHUCKLES: Indeed – most wonderful!
The dwarfs go into a huddle. They open to show them all holding the sausages,
except for Smiler.
SMILER: (Pushed forward) Do you – do you want some help – (pushed again) – with the
dishes?
SNOW WHITE: Why how kind of you. No – I'll be fine. You boys run along to work.
GRUMBLE-GUTS: Work? We can't go to work! What if that Queen comes searching for
you?!
BOSS: Somebody must stay and look after you!
SNOW WHITE: That's very thoughtful of you – but nobody knows that I'm here! You go –
I'll be perfectly OK.
BOSS: I'm not sure …
GRUMBLE-GUTS: He's right. (frightening others) Why – that wicked woman could be
walking up the path to this cottage at this very moment! (points at door; they all turn and
look)
MUSIC. They all look scared. There is a sudden, loud knock at the closed door. They
all jump.
GRUMBLE-GUTS: I knew it – it's the QUEEN! (Panic. They form a circle around Snow
White ready to fight)
BOSS: Yokel – go and see who's at the door!
YOKEL: OK. …… Which door?
DWARFS: (loud hissing whisper) THAT door!!
Yokel tiptoes toward the door with the others tightly bunched following him.
There is another knock and they all jump. Start to walk again and door flies open.
NANNY GOTÉ bursts in.
NANNY GOTÉ: Hello! Anybody home?! (she is wearing a green boiler suit, or similar)
DWARFS: (Scatter in terror) It's the QUEEN! Etc.
SNOW WHITE: No – it's not the Queen It's my old Nanny!
NANNY GOTÉ: Snow White! I knew I'd find you! Thank goodness you're safe! Listen. I've
left Sniff and Dribble trying to find the King; nobody knows where he is. Are you sure
you're alright?
SNOW WHITE: Of course I am – but, what are you wearing?
NANNY GOTÉ: This? I wear this when I do my other job?
SNOW WHITE: OTHER job?
NANNY GOTÉ: I am in charge of recycling for the whole of Pimplevania. Been doing it for
years. I used to recycle all of your disposable nappies!
SNOW WHITE: Yuck! What on earth did they make THOSE into?!
NANNY GOTÉ: They made them into the Daily Mail (or other local newspaper),. Yes, they
did. Said that it was easy to turn nappies into the Daily Mail (or other local newspaper),
because it's hard to tell the difference. (aud) They're both full of…

SNOW WHITE: Nanny! Children's show!

NANNY GOTÉ: Sorry! (turns) Right then, my good fellows. I want all your old stuff so we can recycle it!

GRUMBLE-GUTS: You're not having any of MY old stuff!

BOSS: What sort of stuff?

NANNY GOTÉ: What about old newspapers?

YOKEL: Can't read.

NANNY GOTÉ: Glass bottles?

CHUCKLES: Don't use them!

NANNY GOTÉ: What? Not even beer bottles?

POLLEN: Our beer comes in barrels.

CHUCKLES: We have one barrel each – a night.

NANNY GOTÉ: A whole barrel each, every night? Get away with you!

BOSS: It's true. Here – Smiler – show her.

Smiler comes up shyly then does an enormous **(sound fx) BURP!**

NANNY GOTÉ: Fworr! (fans bad breath away) Very convincing. Well. Do you have any tin cans?

DWARFS: Nope.

NANNY GOTÉ: Cardboard?

DWARFS: Nope.

NANNY GOTÉ: But you must have something. How about scraps of old food we can make into compost?

BOSS: Ah – now there we can help you!

NANNY GOTÉ: Great. Where is it?

BOSS: Mostly in Pollen's beard. Here – use this fork to get it out. You two – hold Pollen down!

NANNY GOTÉ: That's alright thank you! Never mind about the compost. (pretends to think) I KNOW! Just the thing! To show you how helpful I am – and to help the environment – I am willing to help you by taking away any old DIAMONDS you have!

SNOW WHITE: Diamonds?!

NANNY GOTÉ: Mmm. Any old ones. You know – a bit dirty, too big to be much use, that sort of thing?

GRUMBLE-GUTS: Pah! Do you think we're completely mad, woman?

NANNY GOTÉ: (Looks at Yokel who has two sausages up his nostrils and a saucepan on his head.) Well...

(Knock at the door)

BOSS: QUIET! I heard something – outside! (all freeze in horror)

SMILER: Perhaps – it's the QUEEN! **(MUSIC)**

BOSS: Everyone HIDE! (they hide behind the table & peer over)

GUIDE: (enters briskly) And this is the next stop on our 'Lord of the Rings Film Location Tour'! This is the real-life home of Gimli and the other dwarfs who starred in Lord of the Rings.

BOSS: (To band) Quick - play the music! **(theme from Lord of Rings plays softly)**

GUIDE: In fact this very cottage was used to film Bilbo Baggins' home in Hobbiton. Mind your heads now.

TOURIST: (poking Snow White) This one's very tall for a dwarf!

SNOW WHITE: Hello.

TOURIST: Were YOU in Lord of the Rings? You look a bit familiar.

SNOW WHITE: No – I'm just a princess I'm afraid. (IF this is an NZ performance change this line to: No' I'm the person in New Zealand who wasn't in it! I'm just a princess')

TOURIST: Princess Eowyn of the mighty Middle Earth Kingdom of Rohan? (some excitement)

SNOW WHITE: No – Princess Snow White of Pimplevania.

TOURIST: Ah – (disappointment) (points at Nanny) This one looks like an orc!

NANNY GOTÉ: Watch it, buster.

GUIDE: Come along now. Time to get moving! (To SW) We're going to stage a re-enactment of the battle of Helm's Deep!

SNOW WHITE: Do you have a massive stone castle and an army of vicious orcs?

GUIDE: Not exactly … I've got a garden shed and the (LOCAL NAME) Brownies (or similar). (louder) See you later. Walk lively now. Follow me! (exits) **MUSIC**

GRUMBLE-GUTS: There – I knew she'd be trouble. They usually leave us a tip if we say we're hobbits!

BOSS: It's more important to guard the princess from that Queen!

SMILER: Don't keep talking about that Queen – she's frightening. (they all agree)

Sudden knock at door. **MUSIC**. All dive behind table again.

SNIFF: (Voice off) Hello? Anybody home?

DRIBBLE: (Voice off) See if the door's open!

The BOTTOM of the stable door opens and Sniff & Dribble peer in on hands & knees.

SNIFF: The people who live here must be very small.

SNOW WHITE: What are you two doing here?

SNIFF: Oh Snow White! Thank goodness we found you!

SNOW WHITE: Why? What's the matter?

DRIBBLE: We can't find the King anywhere: we had to leave him a note saying what had happened!

SNIFF: And the Queen knows that you're still alive! She's bound to come looking for you!

GRUMBLE-GUTS: I knew it! I said the girl would be trouble! Ding Dang Diddly!

BOSS: Shh. Let me think. Hmm.

OKEY-DOKEY: We must stay here and guard her! (others agree)

BOSS: No! We must make everything look normal. If we don't go to the mines, people will get suspicious. And these three'll be here if there's trouble.

CHUCKLES: I reckon she'll be safe here if she keeps the door locked, and doesn't let anybody else in

SNOW WHITE: Yes. I'll be perfectly safe. I certainly know what the Queen looks like- and I won't be letting her in!

BOSS: Then that's settled. But if there's any problem – send these folk to fetch us!

SNOW WHITE: I will. Goodbye now!

Dwarfs line up and exit singing Hi Ho.

SNIFF: Now what?

SNOW WHITE: Well – I've got three jobs to do: air the beds, wash the dishes and make some bread.

NANNY GOTÉ: Right. You two do the dishes, I'll make a start on the bread, and you can air the beds.

Snow White gets a blanket or two and goes outside.

Nanny gets gauze bag of flour. Sniff takes plates to sink & stares at pump.

SNIFF: How does this thing work?

NANNY GOTÉ: Easy. Just push the handle up and down and the water comes out.

Sniff lifts the handle and pushes slowly down. Lots of water squirts over him from wall.

NANNY GOTÉ: What's all the fuss. Hurry up with that water!

Sniff tries again. Water still gets him.

SNIFF: Dribble! Dribble - you come and stand here!

Sniff works handle. This time Dribble gets wet & Sniff laughs.

NANNY GOTÉ: Come on now, boys. Stop playing.

DRIBBLE: Oh Nanny! Naaaaaany!

NANNY GOTÉ: What is it?

SNIFF: We're – ah – having a bit of trouble with this pump.

DRIBBLE: Could you come and show us how it works?

NANNY GOTÉ: Pah! Can you two do nothing? Stand aside!

SNIFF: Delighted! (they move away & giggle madly)

NANNY GOTÉ: (tries handle bit it won't move) This handle's stuck. You'll have to use the well.

SNIFF: What? Let me ... (pumps handle & gets soaked)

DRIBBLE: It's working now, Nanny. Try again!

NANNY GOTÉ: (handle won't move) No – still stuck. Use the well!

DRIBBLE: Let me .... (Pumps handle and gets soaked again)

SNIFF: Look – it's loose now (cautiously moves it a tiny bit). Your turn, Nanny!

NANNY GOTÉ: Hmm. What are you two playing at? You stand over there where I can see you.

They crouch downstage of sink, hands on knees, giggling. Nanny works the pump. Water squirts from the wall over their bottoms. They look round in disbelief.

SNIFF: Let's use the well.

DRIBBLE: Good idea.

They squelch bowlegged across to the well and Sniff looks down into it while Dribble loosens the bucket directly above Sniff's head, on a traditional windlass or wheel.

SNIFF: Wow! This thing is bottomless! (pre-recorded) Helloo! (echo) Helloo .... Helloo .... Helloo ... etc

DRIBBLE: Let me see!

Dribble lets go of the bucket. It hits Sniff on the head, knocking him headfirst into the well. Dribble grabs the seat of Sniff's trousers and stops him going down.

SNIFF: (pre-recorded with echo) Aargh! Get me out! GET ME OUT!

NANNY GOTÉ: NOW what are you doing?

DRIBBLE: It's not me, it's ... (turns and lets go of Sniff, who starts to disappear, screaming, but Dribble grabs again.)

NANNY GOTÉ: You two are completely useless!

DRIBBLE: I told you. It's not me, it's .... (repeat action)

NANNY GOTÉ: Well tell him to stop playing. Pull him out of there!

Dribble tries to pull Sniff out, banging his head on the bucket. Three times. Eventually Sniff slides to floor, gibbering madly.

NANNY GOTÉ: Stop messing around and come and help me make this pastry!

DRIBBLE: What shall we do?

NANNY GOTÉ: First – hygiene. You have to put on these two jackets and these chefs' hats.

DRIBBLE: What do we have to wear these for?

NANNY GOTÉ: Have you not been to a pantomime before?

DRIBBLE: (nods) See what you mean. This is just like the jacket I had to wear in the hospital. Except that one had the arms tied round the back.

SNIFF: (has meaningful look with Nanny) Hmm. Right. What shall I do first?

NANNY GOTÉ: Get me a bowl. There's one over there. (gestures with bag of flour & hits Sniff in face)

DRIBBLE: (laughs) What shall I do?

NANNY GOTÉ: That spoon over there, please. (gesture & flour splat as before)

They get the bowl & spoon. They glare at Nanny, grab a large handful of flour each from the bowl,

and throw it at her, just as she says:

NANNY GOTÉ: Ooops. Dropped the spoon. (She ducks and the others get the flour in their faces)

SNOW WHITE: (returns) How's the cooking? (sees white faces) Oh dear.

NANNY GOTÉ: Tell you what we really need. Have they got any cream?

SNIFF: I think so. Yes – here we are! (finds can of spray cream, suitably disguised)

NANNY GOTÉ: Thanks! (takes can and makes 2 big mounds of cream on paper plates.)

Perfect!

Sniff picks up plate of cream. Goes to throw it at Nanny. Interaction with audience. At last moment Nanny moves back & Dribble takes her place, SPLAT!

Dribble wipes eyes. Sniff is laughing. Dribble plans to get him. Interaction with audience but at last moment Sniff turns, hitting plate back onto Dribble.

NANNY GOTÉ: Look at the state of you! You're getting it everywhere – let's get you down to the stream and sort you out. We won't be long, Snow White. You stay in here - and keep the door shut!

(to aud) You lot. You awake? Good. You keep an eye on her and make sure she doesn't let anyone in. Right?

Come on, you two. Out you go **(Distant rumble of thunder)**

Looks like there's a storm coming. Keep this door shut!

Exits & shuts door behind them.

Sound of distant thunder. Grows darker. Snow White sings as she cleans.

After a moment there is a big crash of thunder and the lightening at the window shows a dark shape.

In the following silence there is a gentle knocking at the door.

SNOW WHITE: Who can that be? (if anyone shouts "it's the QUEEN" say: 'No – she doesn't know I'm here'.)

Snow White goes across and slowly opens the top half of the door. Nobody there. Closes it.

SNOW WHITE: Nobody there. How strange. **(Another knock. Repeat)** How very odd. It must be the wind. I think I'd better lock the door to stop it rattling.

She crosses to the door and opens it. Loud crash of thunder; simultaneous flash from outside shows old woman in doorway.

QUEEN: Oh – did I scare you, my dear? I'm so sorry. Don't be afraid of an old woman seeking shelter from the storm.

SNOW WHITE: (alarmed) You did give me a bit of a fright!

QUEEN: Don't be alarmed. I know my days of being a beauty are long behind me, but what I always say is: it's not what you look like on the outside that matters, it's what you carry in your heart. Don't you agree, my lovely?

SNOW WHITE: (still not too sure) Why yes. Yes, indeed!

QUEEN: Do you think you could let a poor old woman come in and sit by your stove, just to warm her old bones?

SNOW WHITE: Well – I'm not really supposed to.

QUEEN: I understand, my dear. And you're quite right – you should never let a stranger into your house when you're all alone. (peers in) You are all alone, mmm?

SNOW WHITE: Yes. I mean – no. No – there are loads of people here! (they look round the empty room)

QUEEN: It doesn't matter. I'm soaked through already. A bit more ice-cold rain won't do me any harm.

I'll just go and stand under a tree, in the thunder-storm, and hope that my joints will still work when it's time to move on. Bye-bye then. (Turns away)

SNOW WHITE: No: wait.

QUEEN: Yes?

SNOW WHITE: Come on in. I'm sure it will be alright.

QUEEN: Bless you, my dear.

QUEEN enters slowly and puts wicker basket on table. While Snow White looks out of the door the Queen slowly takes the cloth off the basket and produces the large, red apple.

MAGIC MUSIC.

QUEEN: Here you are. A little gift for you – for showing such kindness to a poor old woman. (offers apple)

SNOW WHITE: How lovely. (goes to take it then stops) But I couldn't take your food.

QUEEN: Nonsense, I have a whole tree of them back home. I can't eat them all, not with these few teeth! (smiles)

SNOW WHITE: (goes to take it then stops) I shouldn't really – I just had a big breakfast. I'm not really hungry.

QUEEN: (getting impatient) Silly child. (calms herself and smiles) Well – if a smart, young lady like yourself doesn't think my apple is good enough for her .... (goes to put it away)

SNOW WHITE: Not at all. I'm sure it's a lovely apple. I'd love to eat it!

QUEEN: Here, my dear. (passes apple) I can honestly say you'll never eat another as good, ever again. (Snow White hesitates) Go on – take a bite. Just one, juicy bite ...

Snow White takes a small bite then gasps, clutches her throat and throws the apple to the floor. She clutches the table for support and staggers. She semi-collapses at the front of the stage.

QUEEN: (uses her normal 'QUEEN:' voice) So, Snow White, now I .... I will be the fairest in all the land. (Laughs in an unpleasant manner as Snow White slumps, lifeless)

MUSIC gets quieter.

DWARFS rush in, followed by Sniff, Dribble & Nanny

GRUMBLE-GUTS: (angrily) You should never have left her alone. Anything could have ..

YOKEL: LOOK!

BOSS: (Rushes to Snow White) Oh no .... she's ...... she's DEAD!

They all stare at the Queen who is backing away R.

CHUCKLES: Who are you?!

POLLEN: What have you done to Snow White?!

QUEEN: It wasn't – I mean – I've done nothing. I was passing – and I looked in and ... and saw the poor thing lying there .... I ..

Enter: KING: & Prince Charming (plus chorus when room)

KING: What's happening? I found a note. Where's princess .. oh no!

PRINCE: Snow White! (rushes across and kneels) What have you done to her?! Speak, old crone!

QUEEN: (is trying to hide her face) Nothing – I've done nothing.

KING: I know that voice! Who are you? Show yourself!

QUEEN: (backing away from him) No – you must not see me like this. You must not see me!

KING: That voice. Those clothes!

NANNY GOTÉ: It's the QUEEN!

ALL: The Queen! She's right! It's the Queen! etc.

KING: Is it you?! Show me your face?!

QUEEN: You must not see me like this! Not like this!!

As Queen backs toward the well the Prince leaps and snatches the Queen's arm from her face. She screams. Others scream: "it IS the QUEEN! etc."

QUEEN: NO! NO! I am beautiful! Beautiful! .... (She staggers back to the well.) I AM THE FAIREST IN THE LAAaaaa ...

Queen Topples backwards into well. Pre-recorded: long echoing scream fades into distance. Faint splash. MUSIC STOPS

SNIFF: (leans in to look down well then turns) Do you think we should pull her out?

DRIBBLE: (similar action) Dunno – what does anyone else think?

KING: Don't go to any trouble on my account.

BOSS: Hummph. (puts wooden lid on well. Dusts off hands)

Sad music starts

NANNY GOTÉ: My poor princess. She's still warm. As if she's only sleeping!

PRINCE: This can't be true. We only met yesterday.

SONG: 'Tell me it's not true': Blood Brothers. Prince & Full chorus.

NANNY GOTÉ: Is there nothing we can do?

BOSS: I'm afraid Snow White is beyond earthly medicine.

SNIFF: What if the Prince gives her a kiss? That works!
DRIBBLE: That was Sleeping Beauty! That's a fairy story – this is real life!
SNIFF: Well it's worth a try! (general mutters & nods of agreement)
MUSIC. Prince kneels, lifts Snow White's head and kisses her forehead.
After a second she gives a cough and gasps. Her eyes open. The Prince lifts her into his
    arms.
There is much delight.
SNOW WHITE: What happened? What are you all doing here? (stares at Prince) Did you
    kiss me?!
PRINCE: Er – well – um – sort of.
SNOW WHITE: You know that in Pimplevania the custom is - if you kiss a princess you
    have to marry her!
PRINCE: (to KING: happily,) Is this true?
KING: It is now! (helps them to their feet) And I do believe …. (turns to Nanny) … I do
    believe that it applies to Nannies too!
NANNY GOTÉ: (teasing) You'll have to find me first! (runs off: pauses) I'll be just over
    there. (Runs again. KING runs after down hall/theatre)
Snow White, Prince, Sniff, Dribble & Dwarfs stroll forward. TABS close behind them.

SCENE EIGHT

SNIFF: Happy ending then!
DRIBBLE: Yep. Just like in the fairy stories!
SNIFF: See – I told you! What shall we do now?
PRINCE: Well, I think we're going back to the palace. See you all later! (Both exit)
DRIBBLE: (look at each other's dirty, wet costumes) That's a good idea. How about getting
    changed?
SNIFF: Good idea. See you all soon. (Both exit, waving)
GRUMBLE-GUTS: And what are WE supposed to do?
SMILER: Hi Ho.
BOSS: What?
SMILER: Hi Ho
CHUCKLES: He said - Hi Ho!
YOKEL: Hi hi –hi ho – hi ho … etc
BOSS: Not yet! (slowly) This is where we get other people to help us! (slow turn to aud.
    grin)
OKEY-DOKEY: Look!
BOSS: Blimey – are you awake? What is it?
OKEY-DOKEY: There's someone coming!
BOSS: He's right! Who is it?
GUIDE: (enters down hall) Here we are: the famous (name of venue). Not the most
    beautiful theatre in the world but we call it home. At least until they knock it down and
    build old people's retirement flats here. And it looks like some of the residents have
    moved in early!
BOSS: How may we help you?
GUIDE   You want people up on the stage?
BOSS: We do.
GUIDE   Then that's what I do best. Let's get to it. How many do you want?
BOSS: Five or six!
GUIDE   Good – fifty it is then. Now – let's find some 'volunteers'.
GRUMBLE-GUTS: There'll be hundreds of em! They'll be trouble!
CHUCKLES: Nonsense. Any children out there want to come up here and help us sing Hi
    Ho?!
SMILER: Don't be shy! Just copy us ….

Hi ho - Hi ho - Hi ho - Hi ho - Hi ho - Hi ho - Hi ho – Hi
Hi ho - Hi ho It's off to work we go
With a bucket and spade and some lemonade
Hi ho - Hi ho - Hi ho – HI HO!
BOSS: Who have you got to help us today?
Ad lib chatting & introductions
 SONG
GUIDE: Thank you all!
BOSS: Come on then, fellows. One last chorus! Everybody now! **(Dwarfs exit singing Hi-ho)**
TABS open onto

SCENE NINE: THE THRONE ROOM
As before but with glitter curtains / flags

SNOW WHITE, PRINCE, KING, NANNY GOTÉ(with small crown/tiara), SNIFF, DRIBBLE
    are on stage
SNOW WHITE: Our story's run, we've no more time
PRINCE: Except to end this tale in rhyme
KING: Romance has won.
NANNY GOTÉ: We've had some fun
SNOW WHITE: And wedding bells today will chime.
SNIFF: The wicked Queen at last is beaten,
DRIBBLE: Er ..(they look at him) and all my chocolates have been eaten? Well, I'm no
    good at poetry!
SNIFF: Pimplevania another Queen has gotten. (Nanny curtsies)
DRIBBLE: Er ... (more staring) I don't know! What rhymes with 'gotten'? Is it a real word?!
SNIFF: Yes, it is a real word. Now hurry up! (chanting) Pimplevania another Queen has
    gotten.
DRIBBLE: But these ones got a fatter bot…!
NANNY GOTÉ: Oy!
PRINCE: Our tale is done, it's time to go,
SNOW WHITE: So now a song to end our show.
FINALE SONG
Principals exit.
MUSIC - WALK DOWN:
CHORUS
GUIDE and DANGLING DAN then point to MAGIC MIRROR,
KING with NANNY GOTÉ,
SNIFF: & DRIBBLE
QUEEN
DWARFS
SNOW WHITE & PRINCE
Point to Musicians
SHORT ENCORE with flags
Retreat waving.
FINAL CURTAIN

LIST OF TITLES

Click to select

1. <u>CINDERELLA</u>
2. <u>ROBIN HOOD</u>
3. <u>DICK WHITTINGTON</u>
4. <u>SLEEPING BEAUTY</u>
5. <u>RED RIDING HOOD & THE 3 PIGS</u>
6. <u>THREE MEN IN A TUB</u>
7. <u>JACK AND THE BEANSTALK</u>
8. <u>HANSEL AND GRETEL</u>
9. <u>SNOW WHITE & 7 DWARVES</u>

CONTACT INFORMATION
and PERFORMANCE RIGHTS here:

PANTOSCRIPTS.ME.UK

MORE INFORMATION

These scripts are published here for three reasons:

First, as they are formally published, they have even stronger legal protection so if any original part of the script is 'nicked' it is easier to prove! If you are simply here to get ideas for your own writing I strongly recommend that you get back onto Amazon and download my book <u>'HOW TO WRITE OR CHOOSE THE PERFECT PANTO SCRIPT'</u>. This will make your life a lot easier, and much more legal.

Secondly, many people just like reading scripts; if you are one of these fine people then I hope you enjoy this selection

Third – and this is why you are probably here – is because you have been given the terrible chore of choosing a script that is best for your club or business or charity or family to perform. Splendid.

But before you start selecting a panto script BE WARNED: there are hundreds of very weak scripts out there. For example: several stinkers think that Abanazer's name is 'have a banana' every time he comes on the stage and, worse, believe this alone is enough humour to fill a whole show (it isn't). Others are just lame rip-offs of old TV shows.

I really recommend you read my book 'HOW TO WRITE OR CHOOSE THE PERFECT PANTO SCRIPT', noting that its title includes the words 'choose a script'. Until you read that book you will not even be aware of the problems ahead of you!

Unbelievably many scripts, even ones from well-known organisations and publishers, were written over 30 years ago and never, ever updated (honest - look out for things like 'Dixon of Dock Green' or quotes from 'Ello Ello'.) By all means just choose any old script, especially if you just want a 'cheap' one, but don't be upset when your audiences start to go down! My scripts have been written and rewritten and the versions here were all updated in 2012 (or later).

If you do want to produce one of these scripts e-mail via my website:
www.pantoscripts.me.uk
Most people who get in touch just want to ask how much it costs: as a guide I normally charge just £20 for each performance, so a family or charity just doing one performance pays just £20.

A large drama club doing two weeks including 2 matinees (no Monday or Sunday performance) would pay £240. There is no charge for anything else, including amateur film/photo rights, copying scripts, rewrites, etc.

In comparison: based on minimum prices from a well-known Drama Organisation website, it costs at least £5 for each printed copy of the script (not allowed to photocopy, adapt or print your own to fit your needs), then another £30 for video rights, then from £50 to £90 for every performance, coming to at least £700, probably a LOT more if you give everyone in the show a script and have to pay the £90 a show rate. I have been told by some clubs that they have paid well over £1,000 for use of a 'professional' script.

However, charities that have used my scripts in the past, such as 'Help The Heroes' or 'Crisis at Christmas' get to use them for nothing, while professional organisations such as Warner Hotels and well-known oil companies, supermarkets and major computer manufacturers have paid a little more.

Why are my scripts so cheap? Well, 'Pantoscripts' is just me, not an office full of staff to pay and no commission to any middle-man. And I sell loads; they are performed all over the world every year. And it is just a hobby, I like to know the scripts are being used and getting such good reviews and feedback (some reviews are on my website if you want to check). And as you may have noticed I also write comedy novels (search Chris Lane on Amazon books).

And yes, I do write to commission (i.e. if you want something specific) and I do write other things besides pantos. If you want short comedy plays for any age or children's musicals then do get in touch.

If you have any questions or thoughts please contact **me at: www.pantoscripts.me.uk**
Cheers – Chris Lane

ALSO from **Chris Lane** on Amazon
'BLOODWRATH': an Amazon Number One bestselling comic novel. Very dark with some adult language and violence. A teacher kills a burglar – and is drawn into a violent spiral of mayhem, and confusion, with terrible but comic results. **Five-star reviews.**

Printed in Great Britain
by Amazon

47084890R00158